POOR

DANCER'S

ALMANAC

POOR DANCER'S ALMANAC

MANAGING

LIFE AND

A ## WORK IN THE

Project ## PERFORMING

of Dance ## ARTS

Theater

EDITED BY DAVID R. WHITE, LISE FRIEDMAN,

Workshop, AND TIA TIBBITTS LEVINSON

Inc.

DUKE UNIVERSITY PRESS   *Durham and London 1993*

Typeset in Cheltenham by Keystone Typesetting, Inc.
Printed in the United States of America on
acid-free paper ∞
Library of Congress Cataloging-in-Publication Data
appear on the last printed page of this book.

To the memory of Robert Kovich

C O N T E N T S

CHAPTER 4 THE MARKETPLACE

CHAPTER 5 HEALTH

CHAPTER 6 COMMUNITY: THE BODY POLITIC

CHAPTER 7 MANY PLACES, MANY DREAMS

A C K N O W L E D G M E N T S

This project has been made possible by grants from the Robert Sterling Clark Foundation and the J. M. Kaplan Fund, Inc.

Poor Dancer's Almanac: Managing Life and Work in the Performing Arts has been a special project of Dance Theater Workshop's Membership Services Program.

Dance Theater Workshop wishes to offer very special thanks to Darcey Hector of the Robert Sterling Clark Foundation and Suzanne Davis of the J. M. Kaplan Fund, Inc., for their support of this project.

DTW also acknowledges, with deep appreciation, those public and private agencies that support the DTW artist sponsorship and service programs out of which *Poor Dancer's Almanac* evolved: the New York City Department of Cultural Affairs, the New York State Council on the Arts, and the National Endowment for the Arts; AT&T Foundation; Capezio Ballet Makers Dance Foundation, Inc.; the Birsh Foundation; Blum-Kovler Foundation; Booth Ferris Foundation; Mary Flagler Cary Charitable Trust; the Chase Manhattan Bank, N.A.; Citibank, N.A.; Robert Sterling Clark Foundation; Consolidated Edison; the Ford Foundation; Foundation for Contemporary Performance Arts, Inc.; Fund for the City of New York; the Herman Goldman Foundation; the Greenwall Foundation; the Harkness Foundations for Dance; JCT Foundation; Jerome Foundation; the J. M. Kaplan Fund, Inc.; Marsh & McLennan; CCTV; Andrew W. Mellon Foundation; Joyce Mertz-Gilmore Foundation; Metropolitan Life Foundation; Morgan Guaranty Trust Company; the New York Community Trust; New York Telephone Company; the New York Times Foundation, Inc.; the Pew Charitable Trust; the Shubert Foundation; United States Trust Company of New York Foundation; Lila Wallace–Reader's Digest Fund; Patsy and Jeff Tarr and the members of the Dance Theater Workshop Board of Directors, and the "Friends and Neighbors" of Dance Theater Workshop for sustaining DTW during these past years.

Poor Dancer's Almanac was originally conceived and written by Ted Striggles, Senta Driver, and Margery Simkin. The second edition of *Poor Dancer's Almanac* was coordinated and edited by Mindy N. Levine and Kathy Spahn.

Their contributions to Dance Theater Workshop and to the editorial history of this book are gratefully acknowledged.

Project Staff: David R. White, Executive Editor; Lise Friedman, Project Editor; Tia Tibbitts Levinson, Project Coordinator; Laurie Uprichard, Project Coordinator through 1990; Joan Freese, Associate Editor; Janie Geiser, Illustrator; Margaret Eginton, Ivan Sygoda, Editorial Consultants; Judith Laufer, Indexer; Wendy Blum, Pamela Calvert, Laura Schandelmeier, Editorial Assistants.

Contributing Writers: Elise Bernhardt, Eric Bogosian, Meyer Braiterman, Richard Bull, Kim Chan, Ellie Covan, Merce Cunningham, Timothy J. DeBaets, Vicky Dummer, Karen Finley, Lise Friedman, Gay Men's Health Crisis, Greg Geilmann, David Gere, Marian A. Godfrey, Lillian Goldthwaite, Guillermo Goméz-Peña, Joe Goode, Mara Greenberg, Larry Greene, William G. Hamilton, John Haworth, Ellen Jacobs, John Job, Scott Johnson, Bill T. Jones, Deborah Jowitt, Demetrius A. Klein, Phyllis Lamhut, Michael Lange, Liz Lerman, A. Leroy, Mindy N. Levine, Tia Tibbitts Levinson, Elise Long, Jonathan Lorch, John Malashock, Victoria Marks, Timothy J. McClimon, DJ McDonald, Jeff McMahon, Tim Miller, Timothy Ney, Tere O'Connor, Stuart Pimsler, Jennifer Poulos, Dana Reitz, Louise Robinson, Iris Rose, Ann Rosenthal, Chiori Santiago, Peter Schumann, Michael Schwartz, Laura Shapiro, Stephanie Skura, Andrea Snyder, William Sommer, Ted Striggles, Ivan Sygoda, Lisa Gaido Tylke, Sharon Varosh, Lee Wenger, David R. White, Paul Zaloom, Elizabeth Zimmer.

Special thanks to Sally Sommer, Project Editor–1989, for getting the wheels in motion. Thanks also to Cathy Ellich, Geoff Freeman, Brian Jucha, Clare Maxwell, Ann Rosenthal, Emily Stork, Judy Trupin, and the rest of the DTW staff for their contributions of time and expertise. And, above all, thanks to the individual artists who so eloquently examined and distilled their experiences. Such honesty and insight are hard earned, the inevitable cost of struggling to lead a creative life in the United States at century's end.

DTW also wishes to thank Joanne Ferguson, Lawrence J. Malley, and Rachel Toor of Duke University Press.

F O R E W O R D *Merce Cunningham*

I find it difficult to make an introduction to a survival manual for performing artists. Being involved with the maintenance of a performing company of any form is sweat and harassment enough without having to explain its existence.

Telling Robert Rauschenberg once that keeping a dance company going was like working with a combination gymnasium, kindergarten, sanatorium, and emergency ward—he added "bankruptcy." To sustain the daily momentum, on any level, means lasting one minute longer and constant preparation for imminent disaster. I feel fortunate at the moment to be working with people who go a long way toward alleviating some of the problems—by taking them on themselves.

I didn't want a "company." I wanted dancers to work with me. In the early pieces (*The Seasons, Dromenon, Pool of Darkness, Amores,* for example), I tried working with dancers who were trained in other techniques, ballet or modern, and who had performing experience. Most were capable dancers, but their styles and ways of moving were not to my liking. So I began to attempt to give classes using what ideas I had at the time, as well as habits of movement from my previous training (my experience with the Graham technique and, to a lesser extent, the classical ballet, through my infrequent attendance in classes at the School of American Ballet), to work out the exercises and phrases for the classes.

Occasional performances took place, perhaps one or two a year, with a constant hassle to keep a studio. There were not enough funds to have a permanent studio, so I worked alone in my small, basically unheated loft on East 17th Street during the day, and rented a studio by the hour to give a class in the late afternoons. Not many students came; the first class had one. I gave the class anyway.

One had few choices in the dance world then for earning any kind of living as a dancer. I think there were two ballet companies early on, the Ballet Russe de Monte Carlo and, later, Ballet Theatre. I was not a classical ballet dancer, nor, though I envied their chances to dance, did I want to be one. The second choice was to get into a Broadway musical, which, assuming the show was a hit, would give me a weekly salary. Several opportunities came along, one in *Oklahoma,* which I didn't accept. But some time later, when my financial circumstances were really at rock bottom, I was offered a job in Agnes de Mille's *One Touch of Venus,* which I did accept. One week of rehearsal and then one week of performing in the show during its Boston tryout was it. The salary was welcome, but I knew a show atmosphere was not. I went back to my unheated loft.

So other than an outside job—being a waiter, some kind of bookstore position—what's left but teaching? I continued that, eventually getting a few teaching residencies outside New York.

In the meantime, I made solos for myself, presenting these in solo programs at the Hunter Playhouse each year—three in all, I think—and working a good deal of the rest of the time to pay off bills.

Eventually, still renting studios by the hour, there were four dancers to work with: Carolyn Brown, Viola Farber, Marianne Preger Simon, and Remy Charlip. We worked together whenever possible, and I made dances for them. One was a short work called *Rag-Time Parade,* to the music of Erik Satie, which had six dancers, including the four named above, and was presented in the Great Hall of Cooper Union on that uncomfortable stage, and, as Marianne Preger Simon remembers, was "such a hit it had to be repeated."

We were all at Black Mountain during the summer of 1953, a group of six in residence. Class and rehearsal every day, in the dining hall after the morning tables were cleared and the space swept. It was simple, hardly the ideal space, but we were fed and housed and could work together. I made four or five dances during the six-week stay, and at the end of the session we gave two performances that also included three pieces previously worked on. Now it is said that that's when my company was formed, as though by magic out of unformed clay. But it was a company, and we did continue.

Back in New York that fall we worked furiously, passed out notices, and borrowed funds to give a week of the dances at the DeLys Theater on Christopher Street. No critics from the newspapers came.

Indifference is almost harder than opposition. So back to teaching and, whenever possible, to work with the dancers on new pieces. That is where my interest basically lay, the teaching being an opportunity to see on others what I was working on. At the same time, I wanted to give exercises and phrases that would help my students develop as dancers.

If one is interested in and fascinated by movement, of any kind, but basically human movement—how it is motivated, how it proceeds, and how someone goes from one motion to another—to see the dazzling variety in that can remain absorbing, as it still does for me today.

I N T R O D U C T I O N *David R. White & Lise Friedman*

Culture is the sum of stories lived and told, each individual and original in its making, each rooted in a community of family and circumstance. The contemporary performing artist is a primary teller of these tales—hers, his, and others'. No matter the medium, no matter the literal or abstracted approach through dance, theater, performance art, or music, the role carries both relationships and obligations not only to the world at large but also to the world next door.

This book is about living and working as an independent artist within those relationships and obligations. It is about knowledge and tools, street smarts and calculated risks. It is about the fundamental struggle to balance personal survival and creative challenge—and the essential recognition of the degree to which the one influences and conditions the other. As director-choreographer Stephanie Skura wryly observes about her work, "Mere survival is wild success." Above all, it is about keeping track of personal and social values within a sometimes unforgiving professional arena where resources are scarce and cynicism often rife. Choreographer and teacher DJ McDonald underscores the issue, for himself and for us, when he asks, "How useful can dancing be when everywhere we look we are reminded of the notion that it is of so little use to care for one another?"

Poor Dancer's Almanac is a book of just such distinctive and engaged voices, reporting on their individual experiences from their personal artistic frontiers, providing their instincts, anxieties, and collective wisdom as examples from which to learn. They are artists, managers, writers, producers, and arts administrators who have seen their task evolve beyond the making and nurturing of work to the building of community and cultural activism within the larger society.

This is a book of hard information that responds to tough, pragmatic questions that occupy the zone between the creative process and the quality of life. But it is the voices, and the hearts that animate them, that compel all of us to consider why we come to ask the questions in the first place.

"The territory of art is the territory of change," Eric Bogosian reminds us, and indeed a good deal has changed for independent artists in the United States since the first version of this book was published in 1976. It was compiled by dancer-lawyer Ted Striggles, dancer-choreographer Senta Driver, and dance company manager Margery Simkin as a one-hundred-page nuts-and-bolts resource directory assembled for a special series of "Economic Survival Workshops" that Striggles conducted at New York City's Dance Theater Workshop (DTW). The goal of both the seminar and the directory was to enable independent artists and managers to take control of their personal and professional lives through inventive and subversive self-reliance, if not with adequate finances. Its setting, in the latter part of the 1970s, proved a time of dramatic growth for the working artist population that would also see the optimistic expansion of support systems—from the National Endowment for the Arts and local, state, and regional arts agencies to artist alliances and alternative performance spaces (themselves the invention of artists) across the United States. All things seemed possible in the welcoming public embrace of culture.

In 1983, DTW dramatically expanded and updated the *Almanac,* under executive editor David R. White and project editor Mindy Levine, to include extended chapters on conceptual issues directly affecting artists and their aspirations, from a history of real estate and loft space in New York City to an understanding of budgeting and management, to comprehensive explanations of the national and international marketplaces. Numerous writers from the field were enlisted, and a strong emphasis was placed throughout on problem solving and being objective about one's particular creative needs. As before, extensive listings of practical resources were included, tied to each chapter. More than two years were necessary to prepare the manuscript, in part because of the uncertain impact on the dance field of the Reagan administration's concerted efforts in the early 1980s first to abolish (unsuccessful) and then to substantially cut (successful) the budget of the National Endowment for the Arts. The realization began to dawn across the arts community of an incipient conservative agenda to limit, if not control, the terms of cultural expression in the United States by undermining the accepted public rationale, in Congress and elsewhere, for federal funding of the arts. As went social services, issues of choice, and civil rights, so would go the arts.

In the early 1990s, those fears appear to have been uncannily well founded and the agenda well advanced. Artists find themselves disenfranchised, as a combination of politically motivated censorship debates, racism, homophobia, and draconian cuts in public subsidy of the arts at all levels of government has underscored a faltering public confidence in the role and responsibility of the artist in the larger community. And, from an ominous but still unnamed storm cloud in 1983, AIDS has swelled into a full-fledged epidemic that has ripped a swath of premature death and immeasurable loss across a decade's creative landscape. Through it all, artists do what they have always done—envision and create with whatever is at hand—but, increasingly, they have been called on to defend themselves publicly, to organize, and to advocate, for the presumed right of self-expression, for the affirmation of individual and cultural identity, for the sake of simple survival.

In 1992, in *Poor Dancer's Almanac,* DTW returns to the intimate terrain of the independent artist, to a community of imagination and service and sacrifice that is clearly under fire and irrevocably transformed. This latest edition of the *Almanac* is dramatically different as well, beginning with a broader focus on all independent contemporary performing artists. Dance is still an essential part of this book, and indeed an important source of thinking on numerous topics that directly affect artists working in theater, performance art, and music. But the subject now is a community drawn together by shared ideas, structural approaches to working, and profound questions of relationship to the outside world and to the culture(s) of the United States, rather than merely and somewhat simplistically defined by categories of artistic discipline. It is now also a national community of cooperative effort but distinctive local and regional living/working environments, each with its own signature mix of artists, disciplines, cultures, and resources. While New York is inevitably one major laboratory for the book's research, a significant effort has been made to include writers, experiences, and concrete resources from other active centers around the country. Inevitably, this is an enormously difficult editorial task—every chapter could itself be a book, and many could be substantially rewritten and detailed depending on their particular location in the cultural geography of the United States. *Poor Dancer's Almanac,* at the very least, opens a window on the alternatives.

Artists live at the center of this book, in their own words and unexpurgated interpretations of the circumstances that shape their lives and work, in a way that wasn't possible in earlier editions of the *Almanac.* One artist in particular, Janie Geiser, has used her illustrative gifts to provide a visual throughline for the eloquent essays and anecdotes assembled here. Because of their presence, this is a book to be read for pleasure and insight from cover to cover. But it is also a coherent reference tool that can be consulted on a chapter-by-chapter basis, with specific resources for each subject detailed in special appendixes. The organization of the book begins with the personal needs and situation of the individual artist and moves outward through stages and cusps of life and career into issues of the community at large. By example and inspiration, case study and steadfastness, the artists and others who have contributed their perspectives are our guides through the labyrinth—from health care in the age of AIDS to touring and residency strategies in an economically strapped marketplace. They offer a bracing reality fix on lives spent in pursuit of the requirements of imagination.

In the 1983 edition of *Poor Dancer's Almanac,* DTW borrowed a dedication from a grass-roots organizing manual, even then long out of print, that appeared during the 1970 National Student Strike. Even though it is now twenty-odd years behind us, its admonition to its readers during a time of social turmoil still rings true. So once again, we echo the words of another era to underscore the real message of the combined sensibilities that together form *Poor Dancer's Almanac:*

> [We] wrote this book so that you, the reader, might go on writing it in practice. . . . Mine it for methods; adapt them to your own situation; improve on them; invent something new and write your own book.*

*From *The Organizer's Manual* by the O.M. Collective. Copyright 1971 by Bantam Books, Inc. By permission of Bantam Books, Inc. All rights reserved.

B E G I N N I N G S

They are able who think they are able.—Virgil

No Mistakes
Eric Bogosian

I get stuck. I'm sitting, thinking about my work, gripped with paralysis. I can't think of the next step, and even if I could, I don't want to make it. I think, "It doesn't make any difference, so why bother?" or, "I've lost my purity. My motives are bad."

I am afraid that I make my work only to make an impression (as if there were another reason). I am afraid that my work is self-indulgent, self-centered (what else could it be?). I am afraid that my work is too pastel or, on the other hand, too harsh. I am afraid that I am "pandering" to my audience. Or disappointing them.

I get stuck. I get depressed. I call up my friend Z., and he says, "It comes with the territory." And I remember that the territory of art is the territory of change. Perhaps the "outer world," the world of people who appreciate (but don't make) art, thinks art is about "accomplishment," but in the long run it's not. An artist spends a very small amount of time basking in "accomplishment," instead spending most of the time banging his or her head against the world, living life, crafting the work, and exposing it to an audience.

I live this life because it is the fullest life possible for me. I live it because I don't know what will come next. To orient my art-life around kudos, earnings, or applause is to restrict my art-life, to make it smaller.

I go through the above mediation, and I feel better. But I am still stuck.

What is especially exciting about art is that each turn in the path brings a new, unexpected vista. The art-life is not a stairway upward to greater and greater fame, or finer and finer craft, or more money. Those things may come with it, but like life, art-life does not reach a plateau and then even out. Just when you think you've got it licked, a new set of problems shows up. In fact, each art piece can create the next problem and, thus, the next art piece.

This is how I see my work and my life around my work. I look before me and I see a yawning chasm of indecision and wrong moves, but I look behind me and I see that there really are no mistakes. It all unfolded in the most obvious manner, leading to the here and now. My biggest mistake is when I try to fight the pattern as it unfolds.

I got to New York in 1976, after graduating from college with a degree in theater. I went to work at the Kitchen, where I answered phones and wrote publicity releases. I had given up the idea of being a theater professional; I simply wanted to live in New York and be around the arts. I didn't have a very deep knowledge of either dance or performance art, but within a year I was running the dance program at the Kitchen, and I was, for lack of a better term, a "performance artist."

I started making performance in 1977 after seeing about a dozen pieces. It seemed to me that performance art was a kind of naive theater, full of potential because there were no rules. I had been *trained* in the theater. I knew right from wrong, I knew upstage from downstage, I knew what the "method" was. But I knew too much. A kind of artistic constipation gripped me.

On the other hand, here was a community of artists living in and around SoHo who made work for the simple joy of it. Hard as it is to believe, in 1977 people made work with little thought of it as any kind of "stepping-stone" or "springboard" in a "career." The mass media were scorned. *New York Times* reviews were rare, and there were no specials on PBS or HBO.

In this context, the challenge before me was how to engage an audience ready for anything. Like most novices, I imitated the masters. And like most novices, not understanding the foundations of the masters' work, I created square wheels and three-legged chairs and a lot of incoherence.

Richard Foreman was my hero. (Still is.) He made work (*Rhoda in Potatoland*) that was small-scale theater, flat and aggressive, full of nasty stuff (nudity and black, vile characters). He wasn't afraid of sex or violence. The actors spoke in monotone and shouted at the audience. Loud bells and buzzers rang out at odd intervals. The little bleachers in the theater could hold no more than forty people.

It was hard stuff. Hard to take, hard to understand, hard to sit through. But it stuck, it was honest, it was funny. It was an experience unique to theater. It was not an imitation of life, it was a representation of the inside of Richard Foreman's head! I wanted to make something like that.

For obvious reasons, my work turned out to be very unlike Richard Foreman's. I fumbled around with tape recorders, bits of dramatic monologue, and slide projections. I built complex sets, and I gathered up small companies of actors. I choreographed, and I lit the shows according to my own taste.

People came. People were amused. But I didn't make any special impression. Or, should I say, the work didn't. The work didn't work. And I got stuck.

I thought about what I was doing. I looked at the kind of places my work was seen in and realized I wasn't excited. During the day I was making "art" in Artists Space, and at night I was hanging out at the Mudd Club or Tier Three. If I wanted excitement, I went out and saw a band like the Contortions or the Screamers. Clubs were a turn-on.

So I started making club work. I made up a character named Ricky Paul, an obnoxious club entertainer with a small musical combo (led by Joe Hannan) called the Nips. It was a cheesy bit, not unlike the numerous lousy club comedian acts being done anywhere else. But Ricky had a motive. I would try to probe the bias of the audience and, in pure punk style, piss them off.

I usually succeeded and was often greeted with hoots, spit, and flying beer bottles while I harangued. One typical night was in Berlin, where I goose-stepped around the stage and accused the angry crowd of being a bunch of children who should be home in bed. Energy was key. I would throw myself around and exhaust myself while telling bad jokes or singing off key. It was fun. I got to take the performance to the edge.

But again I was stuck. Because the audience thought Ricky was *me*. I thought of Ricky as a wonderful concoction who really meant no harm and a real catalyst for a hot performance. But after a woman started beating me as I walked offstage one night, I rethought my approach.

I liked playing nastiness. I liked probing the audience by saying what they didn't want to hear. But I wanted them to know that it was a *performance.*

Around this time I was hanging with visual artists: Michael Zwack, Robert Longo, Cindy Sherman, Jack Goldstein. We talked about ways of making work, and from these artists (and others) an aesthetic was created. It was a representational, expressionist aesthetic that left a lot up to the viewer. The artist would show, and the viewer would think about what was seen. The artist would take something and put it up against the next, and the viewer would try to make a connection.

So I did this with my solo work. I took one character and butted him up against the next. No explanation, no pause, just slam them together. Popping characters one next to the other became my modus operandi for the next ten years.

When I started, it was all deadly serious. I played rapists and men with guns and misfits. But, as accident would have it, at one performance in Minneapolis I was billed as a "comedian." I was outraged. Nonetheless, I went on.

The audience laughed. They laughed because they recognized the people I was playing. They laughed because they were nervous about the edge. They laughed because it was funny.

So humor entered my work. To this day I don't know how to control it, but I get onstage and people laugh. I note what makes them laugh and what doesn't, and I keep some of it and some of it I throw away.

I have made other detours along the way. Experiments with making my work. I have made ensemble pieces that were so deadly serious the audience had to stifle their yawns. I made pieces so violent we had to warn people to stay away if they thought they couldn't take it. I have written screenplays for

Hollywood producers, and I have written a play that was made into a film (*Talk Radio*).

Each of these experiments has led to new work, each has taught me new things about myself. (I have learned what I like to do and what I'm not very good at.) I figure the only way to find out is to try.

The solos have led me to a new chasm. Because, no matter how interesting something is, eventually it becomes too familiar, and it becomes too easy to use tried and true devices in the work. "Time to rotate the crops," as Bob Carroll used to say.

So I sit here, today, stuck. What do I do now, and how do I do it? I know the answer is in what has come before. It is in me, in what I need.

Maybe I'll live in India for a year.

No Einstein or Mozart on Mercer Street
A. Leroy

In 1969, I entered Harvard University with the intention of majoring in mathematics, my best subject in high school. I soon realized that the pond I was swimming in had gotten appreciably bigger—most of my fellow freshmen were stronger in math than I was. Clearly, I was no Einstein. Faced with the prospect of working very hard for the next four to six years, with my highest possible achievement being to teach college math, I decided to switch concentrations to a field where accomplishment was less conventionally defined. I had always enjoyed music and had played both piano and, since seeing the Beatles on "Ed Sullivan," drums. I wasn't exactly sure which direction I could take in music. I knew I was no Mozart. But it occurred to me that a composer could make up his own rules, cut his own path. Maybe I had a peculiar talent that could be cultivated. Without any specific plans, I began to take music courses.

The summer of my sophomore year I offered, on impulse, to give a friend of mine a lift to the University of California at Long Beach, where she was going to study dance. This was my first exposure to modern dance and modern dancers. Having always been rather bookish, I found it invigorating to meet people who defined themselves by what they could do, not by what they knew. After attending a few classes and seeing a few concerts, I concluded that there was still much left to be explored in the relationship of dance to music. Such is the presumption of youth. I spent the next two years at the Harvard Summer School of Dance, composing and performing.

After graduation, I figured the place to go was New York. It was sufficiently big, busy, and diverse for me to fit in. Also, it seemed to be the center of modern dance in the United States. I was a little anxious that I wasn't ready, but once I realized they wouldn't be giving music exams at the tollbooth of the George Washington Bridge, I decided to give it a try. I rented a loft on the Lower East Side, worked a part-time day job, and practiced piano, snare drum, and marimba six to ten hours a day. I didn't know a soul and felt isolated, but I went to a lot of dance concerts and studied and wrote music. Finally, after two and a half years, all my practicing got to my neighbors, and I had to move. I found an unfinished basement on Mercer Street in SoHo, and that is when my life changed. In 1976, there were more artists than stockbrokers living in SoHo. Many of them were doing construction work for a living. Power Boothe, a painter, set designer, and filmmaker, put in my plumbing. John Malpede, a performance artist, did my carpentry. I was later to collaborate with both of them. SoHo was a friendly and vibrant neighborhood, and it was easy to meet people with shared interests. Sometimes I wonder if I would ever have gotten a start in the performing arts in New York if I hadn't moved to Mercer Street. Out of such a mixture of determination and happenstance began my life as a composer.

■ If familiarity always bred contempt, artists wouldn't make it through their first week. Each morning we wake up with the same biochemicals floating around in the same brain, engaging in pretty much the same activities as yesterday, and somehow hope that all this sameness will result in something new before it's time to go back to sleep—a new idea, or a tightened bolt and a fresh polish on one from last week. With no one else monitoring our daily progress, we can't afford contempt for our familiar routines, a situation we share with hunter-gatherers, researchers, and free-lancers of every stripe. For composers, choreographers, painters, writers, and the like, familiarity most often breeds a self-involvement that might be called narcissism by people unfamiliar with the requirements of self-motivated work.—Scott Johnson, composer ■

The Financial Realities of Performance Art
Iris Rose

I honestly cannot tell you how to make a living as a performance artist since I have not yet figured that one out myself. However, I do know that it involves balancing four basic elements: bookings, touring, funding, and the day job. Each performer must find her/his own unique combination of these elements and create a balance that she/he can live with. Some performers succeed in eliminating the necessity for a day job; others come to accept it as inevitable and find one that allows them to continue to perform. Some never apply for funding; some exist on it almost exclusively. You will have to find out what you can live with because each approach has its drawbacks.

1. Bookings. I began my career in Los Angeles in 1981. I had recently quit the punk band that had been my life for the previous three years and had created a "performance piece" inspired by my explorations with an experimental theater collective from 1976 to 1978. Because I was uncertain where my work belonged, I wanted to present it in as many kinds of spaces as possible. It was undoubtedly a piece of theater, but I was disillusioned with the theater and its audience and was seeking a new audience to which I could present my work. *People Like Us* (1981) was presented in a park, a backyard, a nightclub, and a gallery. The park and backyard performances were arranged through friends, but for the nightclub and gallery bookings I had simply walked in off the street and said, "I have this performance I want to do." The gallery audience was the most receptive, so I decided I was a performance artist.

I present this rather lengthy personal anecdote simply to illustrate that there is no one way to get started performing. Obviously, each performer's work is different and has its own particular needs, and the performance scene is always changing. When I moved to New York in 1982, for instance, I found that, although the galleries' interest in performance had waned, there was a flourishing scene in the nightclubs of the East Village. I did a public performance in my own loft, then I got a booking at the Pyramid Club through a friend and one at the White Columns gallery—by walking in off the street and being persistent. One general rule: *Bookings lead to more bookings.* Perform wherever you can. There are places that book by the audition process (rare), and those that require some documentation and a good concept. Mostly, you will find out what's available to newcomers by asking other performers. The more people you know who are in a similar situation, the more pertinent information you will receive.

The established performance spaces generally book one to one-and-a-half years in advance, so you have to get used to projecting into the future. I always have an outline in my head of my plans for the next two years. There are numerous exceptions to this rule, but for the most part it pays to plan ahead.

2. *Touring.* Performance spaces prefer new work. Work is usually rebooked at the same, or another, space only if it is extremely successful the first time around. This means that in order to perform a piece more than a few times you must take it out of town.

To be honest, this is the portion of the four-part equation with which I have the least experience. I have found it very time consuming and difficult to deal with bookings and publicity long distance, though I did manage to set up three short tours in California. Consequently, my out-of-town bookings have been, for the most part, limited to places to which I was invited, usually because someone from another city had seen my work in New York and wanted to present it at her/his own space. Without such eyewitness observers, good press is essential. The more press you receive, the easier it is to book out of town.

Some performers travel constantly. Tom Murrin, the Alien Comic, averages fifty shows a year. Paul Zaloom tours New York State by car, performing for Rotary Club banquets as well as in alternative spaces. Frequent shows eliminate the need for a day job but require constant booking, flexible production values, and a small cast (preferably solo performers). During my time with Watchface, a seven-member performance collective, we often discussed touring more, but found the prospect of funding and organizing a tour for seven people formidable. And leaving day jobs for extended periods created obstacles for various members. It can be something of a Catch-22—you can't make any money without touring, but you can't tour unless you quit your day job, but you can't quit your day job until you're making some money. Which brings us to funding, the magic key that can provide an exit from this vicious circle.

3. *Funding.* The most important thing you need in applying for grants is *documentation.* Get videotapes of everything you do, the best quality you can afford. Think of this as an investment because the better the documentation, the better your chances of raising money from it. Of course, the quality of the performance documented counts for a great deal, but I know for certain that I was turned down for a grant in the past because of a bad video of a good performance. I once sat on a panel to choose the performances for the next year's season at Franklin Furnace. This was an invaluable experience, as it allowed me some insight into the circumstances under which funding decisions are made. A group of people sit in one room for hours on end—in the case of big organizations like the NEA, days on end, sending out for food and endlessly watching videotapes and listening to proposals. These people are operating at diminished capacity owing to sensory deprivation. Now imagine

your precious videotape making its appearance in the midst of this ordeal. If our panel was at all representative, this is how most tapes are received: The panelists carefully study the first minute or so and form an idea about its quality, watch a few more minutes to corroborate their first impression, then fast forward on scan to see if there's anything different farther on. As a consequence of this experience, I now edit together a compilation tape of thirty-second to two-minute clips of only the very heart of the best of what I have on tape.

Funding for individuals falls into two categories: project grants and fellowships. Project grants require a well-written, well-thought-out proposal in addition to documentation. They also require a budget. Since the award covers a specific project only, it will not contribute to your ability to support yourself, unless you write a large artist's fee into the budget. Most grants are not large enough to allow for this and will only encourage you to spend more and more on your performances, which will then make them harder and harder to travel. Which, in turn, encourages you to write another grant for tour expenses, etc. Grants do, however, make it easier to pay for publicity (mailings, posters, etc.) and documentation, two particularly expensive items, and, of course, to dream larger dreams on stage.

Fellowships are basically prizes for work you have already done, to encourage you to keep working. They are based solely on documentation and past work. It helps a lot if the panel members are already familiar with your work. By this I don't mean to imply that it's all who you know. It's more who knows you, though I'm certain that fellowships are given all the time based on the obvious creative potential implied in the documentation (once again pointing up its importance). A fellowship is usually not enough to live on by itself, but in combination with bookings and touring it can provide the necessary financial cushion to allow you to quit your day job. A small piece of advice: It's taxable, so set some aside for the IRS.

4. The day job. The more flexible your day job, the more available you will be to accept opportunities that arise. Some energetic folks manage to work forty hours a week and still rehearse every night. I can't. In New York I have supported my performance habit by working as a bookkeeper and a cleaning lady (sorry for this prefeminist designation, but "housekeeper" does not describe what I do), both fairly flexible, part-time, no-benefits kind of jobs. Health insurance is a perennial problem for artists of all kinds. [See the articles on health insurance in chapter 5.] Other performers I know wait tables, do child care, haircutting, construction, and shiatsu massage. Still others have office jobs and make a lot of personal phone calls from their desks. My advice: Learn a skill that pays a lot per hour that you can do free-lance.

When to quit your job is a personal decision. For some, the moment is obvious; for others, it's an act of faith. For me, it hasn't happened yet. When I got a big fellowship from the NEA, I had a nine-month-old baby and used the money as a transition into part-time motherhood and part-time employment. I managed to keep working on performance through it all, so it certainly was not wasted. Right now I'm in graduate school, attempting to change my day job from cleaning lady to college professor. Since I have a small child, I'm not particularly interested in touring much at this time, but I will continue creating and presenting my work in whatever way I can for as long as I can. That's the whole point—if you really want to do it, find a way to do it. Your way won't be the same as anyone else's way.

■ Having a sense of humor certainly helps. Life is too hard otherwise. Rehearsals can be fun. They might be hard work, but there needs to be a sense of ease in the atmosphere. When you think of the amount of time spent rehearsing, compared to the amount spent performing, you realize that rehearsing is what you are living your life doing.

I ask an enormous amount from the dancers I work with—in time, energy, and creativity—but I respect them enormously and am aware and appreciative of what they are giving. This is probably true for any choreographer who continues to have a career and a company.—Stephanie Skura, choreographer ■

■ Some lessons to be learned from someone who is still trying to learn them:
—Don't trample over the "little" going for the "big."
—Think narrowcast, not broadcast: that's your network.
—Give your work time to evolve, even when it seems that you have to get everything perfect instantly. Trust your rhythm and your integrity.
—Don't believe in the system; it serves you, don't end up serving it. We make systems to make things less chaotic, so make up your own and cut out the chaos.
—You can go home again. Keep a professional connection to someplace be-

sides New York City, maybe your hometown. It is worth the investment. New York is great for getting work out of you, but you need somewhere else to take it. Making New York your exclusive artistic focus is hard on your ego and on the hungry audience outside its borders.

—Check in regularly to assess where you are going. Don't follow a five-year plan that you made when you were nineteen. You can reinvent your career and redefine your goals and connections to your field at any time. Keep things dynamic; aiming toward a fixed goal from a long way down the field is okay, but it's the zigs and zags along the way that make the play.

—Get new information, new input occasionally. It doesn't always have to be from "your field"; some of the best insights come from people who aren't "soaking" in it.

—Take a break—have dinner with friends, take time to pursue something seemingly unrelated to your work. Lie on the floor and wander around your mind. This is research.

—Reach out from your formal creative work into less defined areas. Do some lapidary work on the edges.

—Work with kids, with old people, with the mentally and physically challenged. You just might get the immediate feedback you aren't getting from the audience–art community matrix.

—Keep redefining your awareness of community, of audience. Don't keep yelling in an empty theater.

—Remind yourself why you do what you do. Is it giving you pleasure and freedom? Is it growing with you? Are you still creating something? Who is it for? What will it do?—Jeff McMahon, choreographer ∎

T H E   S H O W

The butcher, the baker, the grocer, the clerk

Are all secretly unhappy men because—

The butcher, the baker, the grocer, the clerk

Get paid for what they do but no applause.

They'd gladly bid their dreary jobs goodbye

For anything theatrical and why—

There's no business like show business.

—Irving Berlin

■ The problem is space. You've got to have a space in which to perform, a space you have at least some control over. I once had an office in an abandoned bowling alley. The bowling lanes stretched out behind me, useful for rehearsal. The place gave a straight and narrow look to my choreography; it was my "linear" period. Audiences were spare but appreciative; concerts were followed by bowling parties. It was a time of growth and discovery. —Richard Bull, choreographer ■

From Studio to Stage
Greg Geilmann

Production is the vehicle by which your work is presented to an audience. How you bring the event to the public's attention, where you present it, and how you choose to light and costume the artists will influence that experience. A work costumed in bright unitards will be viewed differently than the same work performed in gray sweatpants; a work presented in a homey loft is not the same if performed on a sand dune or in a proscenium theater with plush velvet seats; a concert plagued by technical foul-ups will not allow the audience to perceive the performance adequately. Production creates a context and a frame for the work—a frame that is as much a part of the performance as the work's content.

Self-Producing versus Being Produced

First things first. Who is putting your work onstage? If you are lucky enough to find someone to produce your work, she/he will assume—in part or in whole—the responsibility and financial burden of bringing your work before the public. If your answer to the above question is yourself, don't despair. Most performing artists self-produce in the beginning of their careers; many continue to do so throughout. In fact, self-producing has its advantages. By doing all the work yourself—and making all the decisions—you will gain invaluable experience, so that when your guardian producer shows up, you will be fully aware of what you need to put on a successful show.

It may seem like splitting hairs, but it is important to understand the difference between producing and production. For our purposes, we will refer to "producing" as the business management of the engagement, covering all the areas in front of the curtain, and to "production" as covering everything that happens behind the curtain. If your work is small in scale, it is possible for one *very* busy person to act as producer and production stage manager.

Producing

Finding performing space

It is important to look for performing space far ahead of your projected concert. Spaces are booked months, sometimes even a year or more, in advance. Most spaces accept applications only at a certain time of the year (often late winter/spring for the following year). When looking at space, remember to examine it in relation to the work you plan to present as well as the audience you hope to draw.

Do you create a work for a specific space, or do you create the work and then find the appropriate performance space? Keep in mind that the longevity of your work will depend to a great extent on its ability to be staged in varying spaces. If you create a work in an unusual space, you may be limiting where it can be performed in the future without significant restaging. Once you have determined the type of space you want, you will need to look at what is available in your area.

Wherever you end up, it is important to note the advantages and disadvantages of the space before you make the agreement and to avoid the surprises and dilemmas that can make the whole experience miserable. Listed below are some factors you should consider:

Cost. What is the fee for renting the space? (Be wary of hidden costs.) Which things are billed additionally? What are the staffing needs—front of house, box office, ushers, technical crew? Are they included in the cost and spelled out in the contract? Will you be required to use the space's technical personnel, or can you bring in your own staff?

Rehearsal time. Make sure you will have adequate access for spacing and technical rehearsal time. Do not assume that this will be thrown in with the deal. If you need extra time, will it be available? At what cost? Will other groups be booked into the space during the week of your performance? Is the space used for other purposes during the day?

Floor. Try out the floor. Move around on it, jump on it. Is it resilient and free of flaws? Is it necessary to bring in a portable floor covering? While this will correct minor surface flaws and add a little resiliency, will the expense be worth it?

Sound and lighting equipment. If you have imagined dramatic lighting effects or even simple blackouts, can the space accommodate them? Is the lighting equipment provided in-house, or must it be rented from an outside supplier? Is sound equipment provided with the space? Is it suitable in format (i.e., reel-to-reel, half track, quarter track, full track, cassette, mono, or stereo) and quality? Sound equipment can be expensive to rent. Will the available electrical power support your lighting and technical needs?

Facilities. Is the house size appropriate to your work? Don't make the mistake of booking yourself into a five-hundred-seat house if you can at best draw one hundred people a night. Is the performing area the right size for your work? Is the space a box with no exits? Do you need exits, entrances, and hidden crossovers? How many? Will the appearance of the space detract from the work? Will the flowered curtains match the costumes, and does the radiator hiss in the wintertime? Will the work look silly in a space that is either too formal or too informal? Is heat or air conditioning provided? Is it part of the basic cost or an extra charge?

Lobbies are not absolute necessities, but they are a convenience for dealing with early arrivals while you continue to rehearse or warm up onstage. And they provide a change of scene and a place to stretch at intermission. Where will the box office be set up? Are there facilities for a box office?

Are there adequate dressing and toilet facilities? It can be terribly uncomfortable to be crammed into a small closet waiting to go on and downright miserable performing with a full bladder.

Is the space clean and in working order? It can be aggravating to spend rehearsal or tech time picking up garbage or fixing equipment.

Audience considerations. Will the audience be provided with chairs, or will they be asked to sit on the floor? Will they have to take off their shoes? Is there a reasonable amount of space for seating? Are the sightlines good? Will the audience have enough distance to view the work as a whole? If the seating is more than two rows deep, you may want to consider using risers or platforms for those in back. Do you need to rent chairs or risers?

Location and accessibility. Finally, is the space accessible by public transportation? Is the area well known to the projected audience? A space might be perfect, but if it's in an unfamiliar neighborhood, the audience may be reluctant to venture there. Will the audience be expected to climb stairs, or is there an elevator? Is parking available for the audience as well as for unloading and loading your equipment and props?

Existing versus created spaces

Of course, you will want to explore the "legitimate" theater spaces in your community, such as high school or college or civic auditoriums, but do not overlook other sites that could accommodate your production. Many churches have social halls in addition to their chapels. Community centers usually have a large multipurpose room for town meetings, as do fraternal organizations such as the Elks and Eagles clubs. Many public libraries housed in relatively new buildings have small auditoriums. There is a multitude of abandoned movie and vaudeville houses in the downtown areas of many cities.

You may also consider vacant retail spaces in the commercial core of your city. Keep in mind that if you are putting a space to an alternate use, a warehouse or loft, for example, you will be required to meet the life-safety regulations within the city building codes. Fire codes are one aspect of life-safety. Limits on maximum number of occupants, evacuation plans, and emergency lighting may also be part of your city's occupancy codes. The best loft in town may not have adequate stairwells to meet current emergency evacuation requirements. Are there public toilets? Is there enough electrical service to handle the stage lighting you plan to use? Can you make the necessary technical improvements, such as altering the lighting positions or hanging sets, in the space? Will the lease or rental agreement require you to return the space to an "as was" condition at the end of the rental period or lease?

If you decide you really want to convert a space for your use, you should look to the local chamber of commerce for assistance. Chambers of commerce across the country are eager to support activities that will bring people to their city centers. A chamber could help in securing a vacant space for little or no rent and assist with the city licensing of the space for your occupancy. It is not unreasonable to imagine creating a permanent home for yourself and other artists. Many small community theater companies found their beginnings in raw and vacant buildings. Beware: While it may be very rewarding to create a Phoenix, starting from ground zero requires a core of dedicated and untiring volunteers and, realistically, may take your energies away from creating work.

Another word of warning: Don't fall in love with a particular location until you have done the homework to see if it passes all the legal requirements to hold a public gathering. If the structure you are considering does not have valid or current city permits, it is possible that you or the property owner will be required to file and obtain all the legal permits needed to conduct business on the premises. Many cities require a CO, or certificate of occupancy, stating the type of business you can conduct and that you have fulfilled all the legal requirements of the city building codes. Is the heating system operable? Are the public rest rooms in working order?

Contracts and agreements

When you find a space, you will probably be required to pay a deposit. In addition, you will most likely sign a contract or letter of agreement. If the rental facility does not provide a written agreement, write one yourself stating what your obligations and responsibilities, financial and otherwise, will be. It should specify the time of payment and the responsibilities and obligations of the person operating the space. Do not make assumptions about things that are not included in the document. And make sure to specify in writing the facilities, equipment, and services that are essential to your performance. The times you will be allowed in the space (including spacing, technical, and dress-rehearsal time) should be specified in the agreement, as should the availability and cost of extra time, should you need it, prior to your performances. Contracts, though stipulating a set of agreed-on conditions between two parties, are ultimately a matter of honor. In an unresolved dispute, legal action on the fine points in a contract is a matter of last resort. [See "Legal Issues" in chapter 3.]

You may find out—and this is the best time to find out—that many items are excluded from the agreement and available only at an additional charge. This may affect such fundamentals as chairs, drapery, lighting equipment, sound equipment, overnight storage (for props, costumes, etc.), insurance (personal and property), the use of a piano, heat, air conditioning, programs, box office personnel, the house reservation service, technical help, and house management. Again, don't assume. Ask.

If you do not understand the proposed agreement, ask to keep it overnight. Have a lawyer or a friend who understands such things read it and explain it to you. Don't be afraid to suggest your own substitutions or amendments.

Finally, it can never hurt to ask around. Talk to others who have used the space. You may find out useful information not only about the space but also about the person or persons who constitute the second party to this agreement and who are thus responsible for delivering the "goods."

Business license, insurance, and fire codes

You may be required to obtain a business license allowing you to conduct business in your city. (If you are being presented, you will not need to obtain a business license.) And by all means do not overlook insurance. Have a professional assess your needs. Public liability, property damage, and loss should be covered. Some areas of insurance may already be provided by the theater if you are renting an existing space or being presented by an organization. If you are creating a new performance space, it is highly unlikely that your landlord will provide insurance, and it is most likely that your rental agreement or lease will require you to show proof of insurance. The Fire Department and the Department of Consumer Affairs also have jurisdiction over performing spaces. Many cities require a permit of assembly, issued by the Building Department, indicating the maximum number of people allowed in the space. For information or specific questions, contact the individual departments of your city government.

Box office and front of house

Ticket printing
Having tickets printed can be an unnecessary expense—especially if you are using an unreserved seating policy. If you want to use tickets, you can buy a standard numbered roll in a stationery store. Or you can use the program to identify audience members who have paid admission. If you have a rubber stamp with your logo and organization address, you can add a personal touch by stamping cards as admission tickets.

Reservation services
You could sit by your phone each day waiting for reservations to come in—an utter waste of time. Another possibility is to use an answering machine. In either case, your phone will be tied up, and somebody (probably you) has to transcribe messages, keep lists, etc. There are, however, organizations and companies that will provide a reservation service for you, often at a reasonable cost. Remember to make arrangements with them before printing their reservation number on your flyer.

Box office procedures
You should have a tally sheet that provides an accounting for your box office receipts—including number of tickets sold, Theatre Development Fund (TDF) vouchers received for redemption in New York, and press and complimentary tickets given out. A very useful publication on general box office procedure is *How to Run a Small Box Office* by Kirsten Beck, published by Alliance of Resident Theatres/New York.

Programs
This is primarily a do-it-yourself item, but it helps to have access to a good word processor. Get a sample program from another artist to use as a guide, and start assembling the information as early as possible. If you are including

bios, have your performers write their own, but let them know that you will be editing for length and consistency. Check and double-check the spelling of names. (Get the performers to put in writing the way they want their names to appear; do not rely on your memory.)

Remember to include composers, lighting designers, costumers, videographers, and photographers along with all other collaborator credits. Check with all your corporate, foundation, and government funders for the proper acknowledgment. (Some of them require an exact wording, which they will supply.)

It's not a bad idea to include a notice of upcoming performances and a funding pitch—yes, there are audience members out there looking for an opportunity to give some money away! Make sure you include the dates (month, day, year) of the present performances somewhere on your program for archival purposes. A program can be used as proof of your performance for tax purposes, among other things.

Finally, have at least two people proof the copy for typos and content. Ask them to check if you've left out anything important. The cheapest printing will be offset printing. Ask various theaters and dance companies for referrals since quality, price, and scheduling vary widely.

Production

Designing your production

Each component of production—lighting, sound, scenery, and costumes—is important to the design of your show. Under ideal circumstances, it is best to bring the design team together in the beginning, when the concept for the production is being developed. Realistically, however, this probably will not be possible.

Whether you meet with the designers during the conceptual stages (sound design may happen very early—prior to the choreographing, for example) or much later (lighting design may not happen until you are in the performance space), there must be a balance between objective and subjective information exchanged between you and the designers. Whenever possible, it is good to engage designers whose work you know and trust and who likewise are familiar with your work.

Productions can be designed in as little as two weeks. However, it is not unusual for a production to take four to eight weeks or more to design from beginning to end. A lot depends on the complexity of the project and the ability of your design team to commit time to the process. Free-lance designers may be working on more than one show at a time. It is important that they communicate their availability.

Equipping your production

There are three major elements that should guide you in making decisions about equipment: the needs of the production; what is provided by the venue presenting your work; and what your budget will support if you need to rent equipment. There is always the chance that you can borrow equipment, especially if you are working in a community that has a good track record of cooperation among arts organizations.

Lighting equipment

One of the most important elements of any theatrical production is stage lighting. With the possible exception of a danceable floor for dance productions, good lighting is the least expendable production element. Your lighting designer will ultimately be the one who will decide how much, where, and what is needed. There are no steadfast rules and formulas. If you want a best-guess estimate of the numbers of lighting instruments required for your production, you should consider the average instrumentation for various venues. A small black box or small theater-in-the-round might be equipped with fifty to one hundred instruments, depending on how small the room is and how complex the production. A small proscenium theater space of forty feet wide by twenty-five feet deep might be equipped with as few as fifty lights, or it might be fully equipped with 150 to 200 instruments, with the larger quantity attributed to a dance production requiring sidelights in all the wings; a large proscenium dance production could easily require even more.

It is fairly obvious that the more instruments you have in your production, the more dimmers, cable, and electrical power you will need. What is not so obvious is the kind of lighting control board you will want. Control boards for lighting systems change almost monthly. What was state of the art last year may be obsolete this year. There are small preset boards that require manual operation. It can be time consuming to set lighting cues or run rehearsals on these boards. There are memory-assisted preset boards that are a step up from the manual type. These boards may be adequate for very simple productions, but they do not have the capacity of a memory board.

As with all elements of production, it is important for anyone working on the artistic end of the show to have a solid understanding of stage lighting. Whether you are a director, choreographer, or stage manager, if you have not had basic training in stage lighting, make it a priority before you launch into a new production. If a lighting course at a local college or university is not possible, you may want to read a textbook on stage lighting: *Lighting Design Handbook* by Lee Watson, and *Stage Lighting* by Richard Pilbrow are recommended publications (see Directory). A basic understanding of lighting will be invaluable in your creative process and will help you realize the maximum potential of your work.

Sound

Unless your performance will be presented with entirely live music or done in complete silence, it is most likely that you will be using recorded sound. If this is the case, it is imperative that you have acceptable "source" material. It is difficult, expensive, and not always possible to "clean up" a poor recording. With the advent of the compact disc, many of the drawbacks of vinyl recordings can now be avoided. If your budget allows, recordings should be done by a qualified sound technician on equipment other than a home stereo.

The most frequently used tape format for performance is the reel-to-reel type. If you need your tape to start and stop precisely or to be edited (rearranged), then you need reel-to-reel tape and playback equipment. In most cases, cassettes are not appropriate for use in performance because they are hard to cue up and are unpredictable.

Not all reel-to-reel decks are compatible (in other words, you may not be able to play a tape made on one deck on another). There are quarter-track and full-track, stereo and mono decks. Most of the less expensive home stereo equipment is quarter-track stereo. Many theaters have half-track decks. Ideally, you should have several performance tapes in different modes. On tour, a mono tape (which can be played on several different systems) is useful because it anticipates widely varying sound equipment in theaters. Always have a backup cassette tape for rehearsal and emergencies.

Note: Be sure you have addressed any royalties required when using recorded music or sound. Performance royalties must be carefully considered. The recording industry is becoming less patient with people who use copyrighted material without permission or payment of performance royalties. If a certain recording is an integral element of your production, be sure you can obtain the rights to use it. [See "Legal Issues" in chapter 3.]

A good theater sound technician can advise you on the equipment you will need for your performances. Chances are the theater you are planning to use has the equipment already in place. And before you rent, don't forget to check with your friends. They may have a lot of the components you need.

Curtains and draperies

Stage draperies are generally required for proscenium productions. If you have selected a black box or theater-in-the-round, your need for stage draperies will be limited. Most proscenium theater spaces are equipped with basic stage curtains, including a main curtain, black legs and borders, and a black backdrop. If the theater hosts musical or dance events, a cyclorama or sky drop is also available. When using a cyclorama—especially for dance productions—you will want to consider a scrim, generally black, as well.

Whether you use stage draperies is generally decided by the set or lighting designer and the director. If your production does not have a set designer, you and the lighting designer—and possibly your stage manager—will make these decisions. Theaters generally have some draperies already.

Flooring

If you are producing a dance performance, you will need to pay special attention to the floor of the performance space. The floor construction determines the resiliency, or "spring," of the floor. Theaters and performance spaces constructed today usually give specific attention to the floor construction, especially if they are going to be presenting dance in the proposed space. The accepted options are, in general order of preference, a five-layer basket-weave sprung floor, a three-layer basket-weave sprung floor, a floor over sleepers on resilient pads, and a floor over sleepers on springs. Five-layer basket weave has the most spring.

If you are planning to perform in a theater built before 1960 or in a space that was not built for dance or theater productions, it is likely that the floor has been constructed without either basket weaves or sleepers. Gymnasiums are the exceptions and have usually been constructed with sleepers on resilient pads. The floors of these spaces should be physically tested by you or by a performer who knows what is acceptable for dance.

The three-layer basket-weave floor called the D'anser can be rented in a portable version that is assembled in sections, the same as portable basketball floors in large arenas. This portable version can also be permanently installed in performance spaces.

An alternative to the D'anser is the L'Air Pneumatic Suspension Floor System, a sectioned, cushioned floor. The L'Air can be used as a portable floor or installed permanently in a performance space.

The second consideration for floors is the surface, or finish. The surface finish determines the slickness of the floor, not the spring. Generally, a ballet production prefers a floor that is not slick, whereas a modern dance production does not want to perform on a floor that is sticky or been abused by too much rosin. The solution for all this is a portable rolled floor. It is available from several manufacturers in a variety of formats and must be used on an already smooth, sturdy surface. The trade name most commonly used today is Marley, even though authentic Marley flooring is no longer manufactured. Marley-style flooring is available from all dance-flooring companies.

Costumes and scenery

Unless you have particularly demanding needs, you should find an independent seamstress to construct your costumes and a free-lance carpenter to build your scenery. Remember, though, that theatrical scenery does have its peculiar needs. It should be light, portable, and flame retardant. Take into account, too, the complexity of the design. A simple backdrop is not as important to the performer as is a stage set with multiple levels or structures that she/he must negotiate onstage.

Do not overlook the possibilities in your own backyard. Community colleges with theater departments often welcome the opportunity to provide students with practical experience in designing and building sets, props, and costumes. If you are being presented, it is possible that the presenter has a staff or an arrangement with shops that build sets and costumes.

It seems sets and costumes are always late or barely make their scheduled debut at the theater or studio. Perhaps it is because they typically are constructed in remote locations, or maybe it is just the nature of the beast when creating a custom-crafted product. Remember that the performers must have adequate time in a costume to guarantee that they can move the way the direction or choreography dictates. It is frustrating for the performers to discover that their new costumes impede movements set in early rehearsals or that the set takes more space onstage than you had planned. It is best to discover problems very early in the process by having sets and costumes delivered well before final rehearsals.

Staffing your production

The purpose of defining staff responsibilities goes beyond who is expected to do what. It should help you define what needs to be done and serve as a checklist when structuring your staff. If you already have a good working relationship with a core of production people, you have a good start in staffing your production. If you are looking for staff, the best approach is to seek recommendations from other artists who have been successful with their productions. Many production associates free-lance for more than one artist.

The number of personnel working with you will be determined by the complexity of your production. How you staff the positions required to run your show may vary from engagement to engagement. It is not unusual when touring, for example, to travel with only one technical person and to supplement your staff with the house crew of the theater where you are performing.

The responsibilities of your crew will depend on the complexity of your production. It is a good idea to have one person—a technical director or production stage manager—who is ultimately in charge of and responsible for the production work. In the theater, a setup and run-of-show crew will need to be considered. Again, the size of both crews is dictated by the nature of your production. Often using the house crew is more cost effective than bringing in outside personnel, especially if you are using equipment owned and provided by the theater. The house crew will have the knowledge of the gear and how it works best in that particular performance space. As always, you should know in advance what the costs are.

Union and nonunion crews
Most small performance spaces are not staffed with and do not require union crews, but there are a few that do, especially when a smaller performance space is operated by the management of a larger one. It is wise to know the situation in advance of selecting the venue.

It is the union locals, not the headquarter internationals, that establish prevailing local union requirements; these vary widely from city to city. A strict union crew will generally not "cross department lines," meaning, in general, that an electrician will not help hang drapes and a carpenter will not focus stage lighting. It is helpful to find out how strong the "lines" are when considering a union crew. Generally, if you have established a good rapport, a union crew will assist you in every way possible.

A good crew is a good crew, union or not. A lot depends on the attitude and personalities of many individuals—whether crew or your staff. The working relationship with any crew depends on the working environment that is established in the beginning. Trust and respect are two-way streets.

Volunteer personnel
It is possible, especially at the onset of your career, that you will use a non-paid crew. Because they are not employees, you do not have much recourse when they fail to fulfill a commitment. You can replace them immediately or threaten to do so. Those are the only options. Replacing someone in the final days or hours of a production is not an easy task. If a crew member appears to be undependable, deal with her/him before the final rehearsals. Not all volunteer crews are undependable; most are terrific, especially if they are your friends and care about your work.

Logging the technical requirements
It is a good idea to keep an accurate record of all the details of the production, including the technical requirements. An accurate record will make it easier to tour the production in the future. Many presenters ask for a document that states the requirements for your production before agreeing to present it. The tech requirements should include the number of crew members and the time

allowances needed to set up and run the production as well as the facility requirements to accommodate it. Since the presenter generally pays the expenses of mounting the production in her/his theater, she/he will want to know exactly what that cost is, including all rehearsal time required as well as every piece of equipment needed. It is much easier to identify your technical requirements while you are in production than to try to do it later.

Keeping your production on schedule

A comprehensive and realistic timeline will keep everyone involved on track and prepared when their deadlines arrive. As with budgeting, it is a good idea to put your production schedule down on paper.

For small-scale productions, this may involve jotting notes at a production meeting. For larger productions, consider a block schedule or an overall master plan of what needs to be accomplished from beginning to end. A weekly schedule will supplement the overall plan, detailing each day, hour by hour, and should be distributed to everyone involved—artists, theater management, and technical crew.

In order to prepare a block schedule, the time needs of all components must be addressed: studio rehearsal, costuming, lighting, scenery, and props (including design and construction of each); musical composition and scoring; technical time in the theater prior to onstage rehearsals; work-light rehearsal onstage needed for the director to mark, space, and make necessary adjustments from the studio; lighting and technical rehearsals; and, finally, the dress rehearsal.

The block schedule should also integrate the press, marketing, and front-of-house timelines. It's very difficult to provide photographs to the press if your costumes are not completed until hours before the dress rehearsal. When is the performance date announced? When are the marketing materials designed, produced, and distributed? When and where do the tickets go on sale?

The budget timeline should also be included in the master schedule. The settlement of expenses and income is usually at the top of the list, and it is not uncommon that some settlements are required before or on the night of the first performance. Those expenses could include design fees, guest artist fees, settlement of crew costs in the theater, theater rental, and box office expenses. Certain expenses may come due before you move into the theater. They could include costume and scenery construction and equipment rental from sources outside the theater. All this depends on the agreements made during the planning of your production.

Follow-up activities should also be included in the block schedule. What needs to be returned following the final performance? Are there final reports required by granting and funding agencies?

The failure to create schedules and follow them is probably the biggest downfall of young artists and arts managers with limited experience. Don't be overoptimistic about time. Be realistic. Include a cushion of time each week to fix unanticipated problems or complete activities. Don't get hung up on a problem you are having difficulty solving. Readdressing it after a break will often give you a better perspective.

Do not fall into either of two common thought traps: (1) The work cannot be rushed; we must take as much time as it takes. (2) We allowed plenty of time for this and do not need to be conscious of the clock. Both are dangerous philosophies once your timeline and budget have been determined.

If you are having difficulty estimating adequate time, ask the advice of other artists, choreographers, and directors who have had experience with producing. There is a big difference in the time requirements for mounting a new work and remounting an existing work. Creating a new work is a meticulous and demanding process, and it requires the most time. If you are remounting a work you have previously created and are happy with, you should be able to do so without lengthy stage time.

Beware of mounting a work of another artist. Depending on the work and the artist, this process could be as time demanding as a new work. If the artist is the least bit difficult, a small problem could easily turn into an international incident.

There is always the possibility that the time requirements will change as the production evolves. This is acceptable. The entire concept of the work might change during the creative process, thus changing the plans you made during preproduction. The key to managing the evolution effectively is to take control of the situation by integrating the new requirements into the timeline and making the necessary changes in the schedule.

[*Much of this information was drawn from the second edition of the* Poor Dancer's Almanac. *The contributing editors were Dave Feldman, Don Firestone, Mindy N. Levine, Tia Tibbitts Levinson, Victoria Marks, Phil Sandström, and William C. Yehle.*—Eds.]

Video
Michael Schwartz

Of all the arts, dance has been the most profoundly affected by the widespread use of video technology. Choreographers, dancers, critics, historians, and producers now have a tool that can preserve the ephemeral material of rehearsal and performance—for repeated, detailed viewings. Video has affected not only the preservation and teaching of established repertory but also the work process itself. Instant replay allows the dancer and choreographer to rework and edit a dance as it evolves. And the finished work, preserved in an objective medium, can be further redefined as an artwork of a different kind, frequently seen in performances and in television programs like "Alive from Off-Center," "Great Performances," and "New Television." Edited into promotional tapes, video documentation has become an essential part of the business of all performance—a tool required by funders and presenters to determine who receives funding and who is presented.

Producing a History of Dance

In the best of all possible worlds, archival recordings would consist of fixed-camera recordings of a dance, in its entirety, from the front, back, and overhead. A three-angle recording facilitates reconstruction by providing dancers with more accurate information and clearer spatial references. Whenever appropriate, recordings of individuals or small groups would be made to clarify their relationships to the whole dance as well as to provide a more detailed view. Similarly, there would be close-ups of the upper body, head, hands, and feet to allow careful scrutiny of details.

In this same ideal world, periodic recordings would be made during rehearsals to capture the choreographic process. Interviews with, or observations of, the choreographer, dancers, and musicians would provide a fuller context for the creation of the dance. All video documentation would be done on broadcast-quality BetaCam and edited on one-inch videotape to ensure the highest-quality images.

Documenting dances in such detail is a luxury and probably will not happen at the beginning of one's career because of the high cost of equipment and personnel. However, by following certain guidelines, high-quality documents can be achieved with a single recording using a single camera. Recordings at this level of production can serve as archival/reconstruction tapes and, in edited versions, as promotional tapes.

For single-camera, one-time-only archival recordings, every figure on stage must be framed as a full figure. If there is a solo, then the frame should include the figure only, from head to toe, following it as it moves in literal space. If there is a duet or trio, then only those figures and the space they occupy are included in the frame, etc. The feet of the performer most downstage must be placed as close to the bottom of the frame as possible in order to establish the proper relationship to gravity and give a sense of more weight. The framing should be as tight as possible. Thus every movement of the dancer in literal space will require a corresponding movement of the frame. This creates a subtle underscoring of all movement, which adds vitality to the customarily cool medium of video.

How to Select a Videographer

When a new work is ready to be performed, it is important to have a professional, high-quality recording of the dance. Anticipate spending around $500 (in 1991). There are a number of questions you should ask a videographer before you hire her/him for a shoot:

1. What equipment will be used? Does the camera have chips or tubes, and how many? Which tape format will the master be on? Does she/he have other formats on which to duplicate distribution copies?

At a minimum, your work should be recorded with a three-chip high-end industrial or broadcast-quality camera onto three-quarter-inch broadcast-mastering-quality videotape.

High-end industrial- and broadcast-quality cameras have three chips (or three tubes): one for red, one for green, and one for blue. A camera with only one chip will have to share all color and luminance information. Since most recordings are done in performance, low-light capabilities are important. Cameras with chips will handle low-light levels and contrasts better than tubes. The lower the footcandle and lux rating for a camera, the less light required to record good video. A camera rated at twenty-five lux (2.5 footcandles) will work well in low light.

Presently, three-quarter-inch tape, the industry standard, will yield very good first- and second-generation tapes (an edited master and its copies) and can be readily copied onto VHS or some other format. In the not-too-distant future, high-end industrial Sony Hi8 or Panasonic S-VHS recorders (three-chip cameras, industrial quality) may become the mastering format of choice. They offer the benefits of component video, small-tape formats for easier storage, and can be copied onto VHS for distribution if necessary. We are at a transition point in 1992, where the half-inch industrial (as opposed to consumer) S-VHS and Hi8 systems are challenging the three-quarter-inch systems. The important factor in using a half-inch system is that it should be an industrial, not a consumer, product.

2. What is the training and background of the cameraperson? Does she/he have experience shooting dance? In performance? Will she/he view the performance beforehand?

Shooting dance is highly specialized. A person with a background in athletics or dance will have a distinct advantage when recording dance: She/he will understand the movement kinesthetically and respond with the camera instantaneously. Whatever the background, the videographer should have an understanding of the idiosyncrasies of choreography and dancing. It is crucial that the choreography to be recorded is viewed before shooting so the cameraperson will know the work, be able to anticipate entrances and exits, know the light levels and changes in levels, and have a "feel" for the dance. Shooting in performance is preferred because dancers seem to have the best energy when they are performing for a large group of people, and the responses of the audience help enliven the video. A cameraperson who knows the physical characteristics and problems of a space and has an on-going relationship with the technical crews and house management will be able to accomplish the complicated task of performance recording with few mishaps.

3. What postproduction will be done? Is the facility a full-service one?

After you've had your performance recorded, you are going to want titles, copies, promotion-tape editing, labeled cassette covers, etc. A facility needs to have a variety of formats to ensure that distribution copies are made on the required format. People who know your work will help you perform tasks quickly and economically.

4. How many crews are trained to do performance documentation?

During busy performance seasons, archivists are in great demand. Make sure that the company you're using is not farming out the work to people inexperienced in the field of dance documentation. If you need a multicamera shoot, it's important for seamless editing that all the camerapeople achieve a cohesive style. Conceptualizing, directing, and editing dance is highly spe-cialized. Don't be shy about checking references or looking at samples of work. The tape of your performance is the only record you will have with which to reconstruct the work, solicit grants, and book engagements.

Video as an Aid to Choreography

Video equipment is invaluable as a choreographic sketching tool. If you are dancing in your own work or making a solo, video allows you to view yourself in your work. Because of video's tendency to diminish energy and flatten depth, it emphasizes dead spots in the choreography. You can play the work in fast-forward scan and watch the movement at five-times speed to get a better sense of the structure and architecture of the work. Watching it in reverse or slow motion may give you new movement ideas. Some choreogra-phers who have access to an editing system or a second VCR cut and paste movement sequences as a way of developing new material.

To Buy or Not to Buy?

Buying equipment is generally an agonizing process because of the speed with which technology changes. If you are in a position to purchase equipment, it helps to be as informed as possible about what exists now and what is coming out. Do your research. Talk to video professionals and friends who have equipment, and get their recommendations. Go to two or three retail outlets that are low key and have patient, sympathetic salespeople (they do exist). You don't have to buy there, but you can get good information. If a salesperson has been especially helpful, you may want to spend the extra money in that store to ensure good rapport and support services.

Always look for the simplest designs and spend the most you can afford for the features you decide you need. Equipment with lots of frills presents more opportunities for things to break. A good low-end industrial-quality camera will probably do better than a high-end consumer model, but those distinctions are becoming more and more blurred.

VHS is the format to buy. The largest installed base of video decks is VHS. Your tapes will have a greater chance of being compatible with sponsors', grant makers', and friends' equipment.

The History of Dance—the Future

Fifty to one hundred years from now, the view of dance in the late twentieth century will be informed by what resides in five major repositories: the Library of Congress, the Harvard Theatre Collection, the Dance Collection of the Performing Arts Library at Lincoln Center, the San Francisco Performing Arts Library and Museum, and the Schomburg Center. Government and private funding will be crucial for the development, storage, maintenance, and access of performance history via video.

In the brief amount of time that cameras have been pointed toward dancing, pioneers in the field—Merce Cunningham, Twyla Tharp, and the creative staff of "Dance in America" among them—have established some important guidelines from which future experimentation can proceed.

We are at the first stage of a generation of dancers who have had the tools of video at their disposal from the onset of their careers. They don't have to develop a system of notation to record their experiments—dancing in front of the camera provides them with the basic information, so more of their time can be spent investigating the movement.

Hitting the Road
Paul Zaloom

As a performing artist, you may want to wander beyond your home borders and take your show on the road. If you are a soloist, you may eventually be able to make a living touring. If you have a company, you may generate income, break even, or lose money on the road, but the increased regional and national visibility can help in many other ways (grants, commissions, festivals, international touring, etc.).

Getting started. In order to interest presenters in booking you, you first need to build a strong local and regional base for your work. In addition to your home season of performances, your visibility can be raised by appearances at benefits, special events, and group shows. By having a mailing list sign-up sheet at all your gigs, you can build a core of local support; presenters, funders, and other arts advocates can be added to this list. Contact your local and regional arts agencies, as they can provide you with information on touring subsidy programs, arts-in-education possibilities, and lists of presenters. If they like your work, your regional arts administrators will want to spread the word about you to other presenters and funders across the country.

Finding work. When you are starting out, looking for touring dates can be pretty daunting. Don't get discouraged. Every phone call and contact spreads your name and interest in touring. Some gigs take years to get; patience and persistence do pay off.

Once you have secured lists of presenters, you can launch "cold" or unsolicited mailings of promotional materials to targeted venues. These mailings should always be followed up by phone calls no more than two weeks after mailing. You can also participate in regional and national booking conventions, but they require a substantial investment of time and money and often yield few results until you are in demand. Again, don't hesitate to contact your local and state arts councils for information and advice. That is what they are there for.

Negotiating the fee. The practice of selling oneself is abhorrent to many artists, but it is vital to learn if you want to quit your day job. In order to determine what your fee should be, you can ask comparable artists or companies what they ask for and accept. The fee should reflect your expenses, both at home and on the road. Decide if you will ask for a flat fee—out of which you cover travel, hotel, and other expenses—or if you will ask for a fee plus expenses. I prefer the latter, as expenses are often hard to estimate accurately during negotiations.

A presenter will usually initiate negotiations by asking you your fee. Less often, she/he will make an offer to you based on her/his expectations and budget. You have previously determined the lowest figure you can live with, but ask for a higher "ideal" fee that can be either accepted or negotiated. Workshops, lecture/demonstrations, master classes, and other outreach activities can sweeten the deal by helping the presenter fulfill her/his funding obligations. You should try to contact other presenters in the area and try to "block book" a tour in one region. Offer your original presenter a discount if she/he can help you get other gigs on your tour. The presenters can all share savings on travel and other expenses, thus making your show more attractive to book.

Servicing the gig. As you talk with presenters, it is extremely important to keep detailed and dated notes of your conversations, especially those involving fee offers and counteroffers. You should also keep written track of when and which materials were sent, when contracts were issued and returned, and what the payment schedule will be. Ask friendly artists and agencies for contracts that can serve as models for your own. Some presenters insist that you sign their contract, but you should do so only if their contract covers all the points in your verbal agreement. This can often be achieved by both of you signing both contracts.

Attach a copy of your tech requirements as a rider to the contract to make explicit your needs. [See the discussion and sample contract in "Legal Issues" in chapter 3.] If you deal with the technical aspects of a show early in the process, you will avoid nasty surprises when you arrive. Your tech rider and notes of conversations can disprove claims of ignorance of your needs.

Out the door. You will want to be as professional as you can be before, during, and after the gig. Word of flaky or irresponsible artists spreads fast among presenters and can kill your touring career. So have a great trip, knock them dead, and don't forget to turn off the stove.

Dixon Place
Ellie Covan

In the summer of 1985 I was in Paris, and it was there, at 15 rue du Cherche Midi, that my life was changed. Dixon Place began as a "salon" in *my* living room. It sounds romantic, and it was. Except that it wasn't exactly my living room that was invaded every Tuesday night. I kind of borrowed a living room, and it all happened so fast I just didn't get a chance to tell the owner. He wasn't there, and I didn't know where he was. As a matter of fact, I didn't even know him. It all began because my lack of funds and friends led me to spend endless days in this amazing sixteenth-century apartment building—I was not supposed to be there—reading Gertrude Stein and Henry Miller (better late than never), which led me to write some pretty lousy fiction that I was very pleased with. Consequently, I was easily coerced into reading this lousy fiction aloud once a week to a very attentive audience of artist types who spoke almost no English but were appreciative and made me feel really special. Dixon Place in Paris was essentially an accident, which is not incredible. Dixon Place in New York was not an accident, which is incredible.

When I think about it, the transition of my living room into a performance space seems bizarre. But the really incredible thing is that it still exists. The original idea was that Dixon Place in New York would be a short-term project—something new, something fun, something like an experiment. I can honestly say that I was an antisocial person before starting Dixon Place, and having so many people over to my house was something new for me.

I was shocked to discover the interest and need for Dixon Place in the New York community. The transition from "salon" to "laboratory" was not gradual. Having a salon sounded great in theory, but pretentious, trendy, and potentially disastrous. But the lab—now that fascinated me. As an artist I was more interested in the process than the product. If I was moved by the work of other artists, I wanted to know them personally. Besides, there wasn't another venue in New York presenting works-in-progress.

Since Dixon Place began with fiction readings in Paris, I decided to continue that tradition, though presently the fiction series runs biweekly and has a curator other than myself. And, unlike the rest of the programming at Dixon Place, the fiction series is not works-in-progress but completed and most often published writing.

Now we're up to the part of the story where I'm presenting informal performance on a regular basis. It's hard work, fun, and sometimes really exciting. I find the performances almost always inspiring. I had wondered if I would become bitter or jealous watching other people perform. That didn't happen. I love watching the performers—sometimes it's a vicarious experience, and other times I get totally caught up along with the rest of the audience in what's happening.

The fact that I feel trusted is perhaps the most satisfying part of the job, that artists feel safe enough to open themselves up, to take risks, to fail, to succeed, to invite their families, to take off their clothes—whatever! Whatever it takes to find that moment they were hoping to find—and to do all that *at my house!* I am truly lucky!

Promoting Your Performance
Ellen Jacobs and Mindy N. Levine

Once your performance has been scheduled, it is essential to get the word out—to the media, the critics, and the public. Effective and economic promotion of your work can be achieved by an interweaving of publicity (i.e., free media coverage), advertising, and direct mail.

The Press Release

The press release is a basic, and critical, fact sheet containing vital information about your performances that goes out to the print press and broadcast media. It serves to notify critics, television and radio stations (which often make free public service announcements—see below—of cultural events), and magazines and newspapers (which generally use releases when preparing free listings of cultural events).

There is no one way to write a press release. Everyone works with a slightly different set of rules. But certain truths are unalterable. A release should be tailored to news style: The name and phone number of the person to contact for press information and tickets should be in the corner at the top of the page. A release date (the date the editor can print the information) follows directly underneath. Most artists and companies use the phrase "For Immediate Release." A headline then announces the event.

The first paragraph, or "lead," should include the *who* (the name of your company and/or the presenting organization), *what* (type of concert), *where*, *when* (dates and times of performances), ticket price, and anything special (a premiere, for instance)—all in one grammatically correct sentence. After that, you are on your own to describe the concert (keep the descriptions terse and vivid), the history of the company, and biographical material on the artistic director. The release, which generally should not exceed two pages, might also include some information about recent and upcoming tours, awards, and grants. If the release exceeds one page, type "more" at the bottom of the first page and identify and number the second page at the top. The end of the release is marked with "30" or "end" or "###."

The final draft should be neatly typed and offset on your company letterhead. Double-spacing is usually used for the sake of clarity, but use your own judgment—single-spacing may be more appropriate if there is a great deal of copy. Presentation counts: A sloppily prepared release may raise questions about your professionalism.

Publications have varying deadlines, so it is important to make a schedule of mailing deadlines. For example, most monthlies schedule two months ahead; critics, thirty days; weeklies, twenty days; and dailies, fourteen days. Releases should be sent to cultural and/or arts editors, listings editors, and critics. Press lists (contacts and addresses) can often be obtained from your local arts service organization or purchased from a local theater.

Listings

Free listings provide a major source of publicity for companies and independent artists working on a limited budget. You simply submit the relevant information to the appropriate listings editor before deadline (usually two to four weeks before publication for weeklies, six to eight weeks for monthlies). Often editors will adapt the information in your press release for inclusion, but it is better to prepare a special, condensed version of the release. Check local and national newspapers and magazines to see if they have arts listings.

The Public Service Announcement (PSA)

A PSA is a brief announcement of an event aired by radio or television free of charge. Stations are swamped with requests and give preference to free events of general interest to the community. If you try to obtain such coverage, you should send a notice, similar in format to a press release, that can be read over the air as is. It should be no longer than sixty seconds (thirty seconds or less is preferable), with the time indicated on the notice. It is best to submit at least two separate PSA spots—a short one consisting of the most basic information and a second, longer one that includes a more detailed description of your program.

Advertising

Your concert opens in a few weeks, and you're anxious to make sure everyone knows about it. You've sent out press releases to magazines, newspapers, radio and television stations, and critics; you've printed posters or flyers that you're getting ready to put up around town. There's still one thing left to do, and it's a big one: newspaper display ads. Ads are seen by everyone—by those who already know about your concert and by those who don't. For those who have already heard in one way or another, ads will be a timely reminder, appearing close to the actual performance dates. For those who haven't heard, ads will be their sole announcement.

Not all artists consider ads indispensable. Some are tempted to save the money and rely instead on the free listings published in newspapers, reasoning that for first concerts a large audience, apart from friends and personal contacts, can't be expected. However, if your work is to be ongoing and, you hope, widely viewed, you have to work to create public awareness of your artistic identity over a period of time and throughout several concert seasons. Consistent advertising from the start, no matter how minimal, is necessary to establish at least the existence of your work in the public eye. It's good to use advertising with this long-range effect in mind as well as for its immediate payoff. (Small ads are easily repaid by the relatively few ticket sales they may generate.) Check with your local arts service organization for suggestions of where to advertise.

When to advertise

If you advertise in a weekly publication, there's always the question of which issue to use in relation to when your performances begin. If only one ad is being placed, artists usually go with the issue that comes out during the week of their performances, although some will argue that the issue of the week prior to performance gives more adequate advance notice. The ideal, of course, is to run the ad twice, both the week prior to and the week of performance. If you are clear about what size ad you want, then your budget will determine how many ads to place.

Size of ads and mechanical requirements

By looking through an issue of the publication in which you are planning to advertise, you will get an idea of various sizes of ads and how effective they are on the page, in terms of size and design. Ask for a line-rate card from the publications that interest you. Ads are measured and priced according to the *column width* and *depth in inches.* The width of a column varies from paper to paper. Call various papers, and ask for whatever mechanical specifications you need.

Preparing the ad

The need to become familiar with all the technical specifications for constructing the artwork for an ad may be avoided by hiring an experienced graphic designer. If a flyer has already been designed, there are usually elements from it that can be incorporated into the ad, and a strong graphic identity can be maintained for a given concert series. However, you can't count on simply reducing a flyer to ad size and expect it to work. This usually results in too-small type as well as a lot of needless information.

There are various techniques you can use to help an ad stand out on a page full of similar performance ads. For instance, you could have the ad photostated in reverse, giving you white type on a black background (the majority of print ads are black on white). Or you could use a grid background or assorted line patterns to create texture. You can use illustrations, drawings, photographs, and bold type.

In addition to the particular graphic elements or special design you are using, an ad should always include the title of the event, the name of the artist or group performing, the performance dates and times, any special credits that might have drawing power (e.g., the composer, if there is an original score), the name and address of the performing space, ticket price, and telephone reservation number.

If you want to eliminate the cost of a graphic designer, you could create an ad with press-type (available at art-supply stores) and have it reduced at a stat (photostat) store to the proper size for the paper, according to the column-width sizes. Or you could do it on a computer attached to a laser printer. If you use a photograph in the ad, it has to be "screened." A screen (or velox) transforms a photo or tonal illustration into a series of black-and-white dots varying in size. This process simulates the original tonality of the photo or illustration for printed reproductions. It is essential to check a publication's halftone screen requirements as veloxes are available in a wide range of screens.

If you have no particular graphic look in mind for your ad and don't want to pay a designer or do it yourself, you can go to the papers directly and have them typeset your copy into the size ad you specify.

A word should be mentioned about commercial advertising agencies, which will design and place your ads. In general, it costs no more to insert ads through agencies (you pay the open-line rate), but an agency's graphic design and artwork charges can be very expensive. They are geared to create the overall planning of an advertising design and marketing campaign.

Direct Mail

Direct mail is a highly economical way to reach your potential audience. With limited funds at your disposal, direct mail enables you to target your efforts toward a select group of the most likely prospects. It is also an investment in your career. Even if a mailer does not induce someone to attend your concert, it still increases your visibility to that potential audience.

When planning a direct mail campaign, two considerations surface at the onset: time and money. Because producing even a simple one-color flyer or postcard requires the involvement of many individuals and organizations—graphic designer, printer, mail house, and the thoroughly unpredictable postal service—it is imperative to create a well-padded timetable. Of course, you must also determine at the onset how much money will be available, as this will dictate how many pieces you can mail and how elaborate the mailing piece can be.

Who should receive the mail

If you decide to use direct mail to reach your audience, how do you determine to whom you will mail?

If you have never performed before, you'll probably be assembling the names of your friends and the friends of people in your company. Unless you have several thousand friends who are guaranteed to show up, you'll also probably need to mail to outside mailing lists as well.

If you have performed before, you will have some data already. Questionnaires distributed at performances are an extremely valuable tool for extracting all kinds of information about your audience, including their age, income bracket, reading habits (this is helpful if you plan to supplement your direct mail campaign with print advertising), and what else they do with their leisure time (helpful in determining which outside lists to use). It is never too early to begin to accumulate data about how your audience is changing and how they are responding to your growth.

Most important is the building of your own mailing list. It is never—repeat *never*—too early to start building your own list. At each performance, there should be a mailing list sign-up sheet for names and addresses.

Maintaining your mailing list

The only useful mailing list is a well-kept one. If you keep sending mail to someone who has died or moved out of town, not only will you fail to make a sale, but you are also wasting money.

The most primitive system is keeping names and addresses on 3- by 5-inch index cards. The cards should be kept in zip-code order to facilitate third-class bulk mailings—a special mailing procedure available to nonprofit organizations, which reduces postal rates considerably but requires special preparation. Flyers are hand addressed, using the information on the card. This system is fine when your list is small and allows room for you to make notes on individuals.

As your list grows, you will probably need to use a more sophisticated system, a home computer or a mailing house, to maintain your list and print out labels. A word about mailing houses: It pays to shop around. You will be amazed at how widely prices differ for the same services. To find a mailing house, sit down with the Yellow Pages (under "Letter Shop Services"), or, better yet, call around to local theaters to find out which mailing houses they use.

Computers are not cheap, but they are extremely useful for artists doing their own publicity. If you have computer skills (or have a willing friend who has the skills), the computer allows you to store all kinds of information about individuals: which events they see, how much they spend on your performances in a year, whether they contribute, and how much. If you do not have easy access to or expertise with a computer, try a computer service bureau. A service bureau takes over an aspect of your operations. It performs a service—for example, maintaining mailing lists—for a fee. Or you can rent time on a computer through your local copy shop. Many of them now have "computer labs" for customers to come in and use. Some even provide tutoring for beginners.

There are two kinds of labels you can obtain from mailing houses and computer systems:

Pressure sensitive. These labels can be peeled off a backing sheet and affixed to the mailing piece. You must use this type if you plan to do the mailing yourself.

Cheshire. These labels must be printed out on large-scale paper, within specific dimensions, and the labels must be affixed by a special machine. You will need to contract the services of a mail house.

You can get printouts of your mailing list from mailing houses and computer systems—useful as an in-house reference tool. Remember that your list should be "cleaned" periodically. This can be accomplished by including "address correction requested" on the mailing piece, just below your return address. There is a cost for retrieving this information; check with the post office.

Using outside mailing lists

If you are a new or small company, or a larger one and wish to expand on your existing audience, you may need to rent lists from (or exchange lists with) other organizations. You will want to select groups doing work similar to your own or those with whom you share some affinity. If you work with pedestrian movement, it would probably be foolish to use the list of the American Ballet Theatre. But if you happen to be renting the space from a theater that produces experimental plays, you might want to use their lists since they have a group of people already accustomed to attending events at that location. You should also ask when they last cleaned their list.

Never use huge quantities of a list you haven't used before, just because it looks good; you might stick to mailing within your own and neighboring zip-code areas. If you are doing an advance-ticket-sales mailing, you will want to code the response panel on your mailing piece with a number or letter, so that, as the responses come in, you can determine which lists are doing well and which are not. Keep in mind that a 1 percent return is considered perfectly acceptable. That means that if ten people respond to a mailing based on a list of one thousand names, it is probably a list worth using.

Most arts organizations are cooperative about list exchanges, as it is mutually beneficial. The exchange is for one-time use only, and all lists should be "seeded" to ensure this. This means placing a name on the list at your address, so that you know each time your list is used. You may find that some arts organizations withhold certain segments of their lists (contributors, in most cases). Good sources for lists include performing arts companies as well as theaters and art galleries if these seem appropriate to the event you are trying to sell.

Creating the mailing piece
Everything you send out in the mail represents you; it is image building. The mailing piece should be simple, attractive, and visually arresting. There is a lot of mail cluttering mailboxes these days. If your mail goes out without pertinent information, such as the performance time (don't smirk, it happens), or with misspelled words, it stands as a reflection of your work in the mind of a potential audience member. If you are selling tickets to a specific event, you must tell people what the event is, where and when it is happening (date and time), how to get tickets (a phone number to make reservations or mail-ordering information), and how much tickets cost.

In addition to these basics, it is important to consider whether to offer a special incentive—$2.00 off with this flyer, special discounts for low-attendance performances (Saturday matinees, possibly), a two-for-the-price-of-one offer, or student and senior citizen discounts, to name just a few. It is important to realize that accompanying benefits and services are perceived as part of the total event "package." Anything you can do to make that package more attractive is desirable. Are there parking garages or restaurants in the neighborhood willing to offer a discount in exchange for free publicity? It never hurts to ask.

Also, if you have performed before and your work has been reviewed favorably, a few quotes from recognizable sources carry more weight than the most glorious things you can think of to say about yourself.

To the uninitiated, the graphic-arts process can seem baffling and complex, for it makes use of many technical processes and draws on the skills of numerous craftsmen—designers, typesetters, and printers. It can be simplified and better understood if it is conceived as a six-step procedure: (1) developing a design concept; (2) obtaining printing estimates; (3) preproduction—typesetting; (4) preproduction—artwork; (5) building mechanicals; and (6) printing the "job."

Before you contact a designer (or sit down to create your own piece), you must have a clear conception of what you wish your graphics to accomplish. A graphic designer can be of enormous help. She/he can make creative decisions about the most effective way to arrange material for maximum legibility and clarity and can oversee your job from concept to finished piece. But a designer cannot tell you what you should say or how much money you can, and should, spend. Initiate the design and printing process by asking the following questions:

What information must be communicated? Consider content, tone, and length of copy and then type a rough draft.

What artwork or photographs are available or can be obtained? Make a selection of several photographs, both vertical and horizontal, that are sharply focused and have good contrast.

How much money is available? Be realistic. Printing one thousand copies of a mailer can cost as little as $300 for an offset, handwritten flyer or thousands of dollars for a four-color process brochure.

When must pieces be delivered? It is imperative that you start your project well in advance. Mishaps can and do occur, so allow sufficient lead time. The Dance Theater Workshop (DTW) publicity calendar, included in the DTW membership kit, provides a day-by-day ten-week timetable of how you should proceed.

Consult with other artists or your local arts service organization for suggestions concerning talented, low-cost designers. When you meet with the graphic designer, communicate as explicitly as possible how you conceive your piece, review budgeting constraints, and establish a firm time schedule working backward from the time you want finished pieces in your hands. Ascertain the designer's fee and what services it includes. Designers generally charge a flat rate for design concept and follow-through work, but then bill separately for the preparation of the mechanical and the cost of photostats and typesetting. The designer will then prepare two or three rough sketches (or "comps") of possible design solutions.

If you cannot afford to hire a designer, consider contacting a nearby university or art school. Inexperienced designers will often work for a negligible fee in order to build a portfolio of printed material. Remember, however, that, although these individuals may possess an excellent design sense, they frequently lack experience dealing with typesetters and printers and therefore may fail to make the most economical and expedient design choices.

If you decide to handle the job yourself, keep things simple. In dealing with printers and typesetters, don't be afraid to ask questions. Try to work with craftspeople who care about your piece, even if it is a relatively small job.

Whether or not you are working with a designer, you should be aware of the following elements of the design process:

Size. It is advisable to choose standard paper sizes. Odd-size designs can lead to paper wastage and significantly increase the cost of your project. Discuss size considerations with your printer. Certain presses have size limitations or are particularly suited for handling specific jobs. Remember that postal regulations for third-class mailing pieces include size restrictions. Check with the post office.

Folding. A piece allows for the isolation and organization of material in different quadrants. Cut a piece of paper to the size of your mailing piece and experiment with various folding methods. Many artists find that a nonfolding postcard efficiently meets their design and information requirements.

Type size and weight. A sample type book, showing various type styles and sizes, can be obtained free of cost from a local typesetter. Do not use type that is smaller than ten points (one point equals 0.0138 inches), except for photo credits, disclaimers, and coupons, because it will be too hard to read. If you plan to use reverses (white type on a dark background), do not use type that is smaller than twelve points. Similarly, avoid thin type faces as they are very difficult to read when reversed. You can have your type generated at a typesetting store or create it yourself on a computer attached to a laser printer. Many print shops will do simple typesetting for a fee.

Artwork. If you do not have photographs or illustrations that are appropriate for your piece, they can be obtained from several sources. Dover Publications prints a series of books containing line art on numerous subjects. Volumes in the series range from art nouveau decorative borders to bold geometric shapes, from floral patterns to astrological symbols, and can be purchased at most art stores and even many general interest bookstores.

Postal regulations. Be certain that your piece conforms with postal regulations. Regulations for third-class bulk-mailing pieces concern size, weight, folding, and placements of indicia, logo, and address.

Using color. Color can bring clarity, flexibility, and complexity to a design. But the mere introduction of color does not automatically make a piece successful or "classy," and it can be expensive, with each additional new color yielding a corresponding (but not strictly proportional) increase in price. Properly used, one or two colors can offer a full range of design possibilities.

Choosing paper. A choice of paper should be made as early as possible in the design process. The primary characteristics to be concerned with when choosing a paper are its weight (brochures are usually printed on sixty-, seventy-, or eighty-pound paper stock), opacity, and finish (coated paper is generally preferred when printing photographs, but it is not always necessary and is much more expensive). Your aesthetic preferences, the requirements of the job, and economic factors will influence your choice.

Building the mechanical

A mechanical is the master from which a printing plate is made in order to print your piece. It contains all design elements—type and photostats of art— pasted in position on a piece of illustration board. Photographs, which are treated separately by the printer, are not pasted onto the mechanical unless veloxes have been made. Veloxes are pasted down.

When the mechanical is finished, make sure that there are no stray marks or glue. Cut a sheet of tracing paper and attach it to the upper edge of the mechanical with masking tape. This protects your mechanical and provides a place to write special instructions to the printer concerning ink color, tint percentages, and reversals of type. Also indicate the number to be printed and the number to be folded. Attach a folded dummy so that there is no misunderstanding as to how the piece should be printed and folded. For added protection, a heavy sheet of paper should be attached over the tracing paper.

Proofing mechanicals

Before a mechanical is delivered to the printer, it must be carefully checked and rechecked. If a piece prints on both sides, there will be two mechanicals. If it folds, some elements will appear right-side-up and some will appear upside-down. In reviewing a mechanical, be certain that (1) all type and art are in the proper place, (2) there is no dust or dirt on the surface, (3) there are no typographical errors in the copy, and (4) artwork is properly labeled.

Obtaining printing estimates

Don't wait until you're ready to go to press before you begin to think about printing. Liaison with the printer is the responsibility of the graphic designer. If you are handling the job yourself, sit down with several printers for estimates on your job (get suggestions of good, inexpensive printers from your colleagues). When the printer quotes a price for your job, as for a written estimate. This will facilitate comparisons between various quotations and help avoid misunderstanding at a later date. Don't assume that a price is absolute. If the printer you most want to work with has not given you the lowest bid, call and ask if a price adjustment is possible.

Estimate the quantity you require carefully. The principle cost of a printing job is the "make-ready"—that is, setting up the press for printing—and remains constant, no matter how many copies you print. Therefore, the larger the run, the lower the cost per piece. It is safer and more economical to print slightly more than you need than to be forced to go back to press a second time because you underestimated quantity.

Printing the job

Printing methods are all based on the differentiation of the printing image from the nonprinting area. The image is either raised (letterpress printing), recessed (gravure, also known as intaglio or engraved), or differentiated through chemical treatment (offset). Today over 75 percent of all printing is done by offset. Offset presses come in many varieties. The type of press you use will be a function of the length of the run, the number of pages, and the number of colors in the job. Many copy shops also have offsetting equipment. Shop around. Prices, quality, and service vary widely. Find out how long the job will take to print and deliver. A good rule of thumb is to expect the entire job to take two weeks (although it could take considerably less time).

Getting the mail out

Nowhere are there more horror stories than in the area of bulk mailings since postal regulations are complex and unbending and it is possible to do everything wrong. Assume nothing. Take nothing for granted. Nonprofit organizations are eligible for a postal permit to mail third class at a subsidized rate (as this book goes to press, this federal subsidy is in severe jeopardy). Applications are available at your main post office. If you go in person, bring your federal income tax exemption, your certificate of incorporation, and your statement of purpose. There is a one-time application fee ($60.00 in 1992) plus an annual fee (also $60.00 in 1992). If you are not incorporated as a not-for-profit organization, you may still be able to take advantage of not-for-profit third-class rates under the umbrella of another organization. Check with your local arts service organizations.

The post office requirements cover everything from size and shape to the minimum number of pieces you can mail and the way the piece must be folded. And, after all that, be prepared to allow three to four weeks for delivery, although some pieces may arrive in a matter of days. The holiday season is especially treacherous for bulk mailers. Take the time to familiarize yourself with the regulations and to develop a working relationship with your local post office officials. It is always a good idea to show them a copy of what you are going to be sending out prior to the actual mailing.

Each piece must have a zip code, all pieces must be identical (no personal notes, nothing underlined), the mailings must be sorted and bundled according to postal regulations, and all pieces must be addressed to locations within the United States. When you write a personal word or message inside the flyer, it becomes first-class mail. Also, if you are sending out fewer than two hundred pieces, they will have to go first class with the appropriate postage placed over the bulk rate permit information. Oversized pieces require additional postage. Check with the post office for measurements and exact pricing.

Postal regulations

Your mailing piece, whether it is a postcard or folded self-mailer, should be no larger than 9 by 12 inches and no smaller than 3½ by 5 inches, weigh less than 2.8 ounces, and be thinner than ¼ inch. Mailers smaller than letter size should leave at least 3½ inches from the top and 3½ inches from the right of clear space for address information. Mailers larger than letter size must leave 3 inches from the top and 4½ inches from the right of clear space. The address, logo, and indicia (the third-class bulk mail permit number) must be parallel to the flyer's length, with the logo and return address in the upper-left-hand corner and the indicia in the upper-right-hand corner. The closed fold must be on top. Also, all margins must be indented ¼ inch, and there must be 1 inch of clear space between the logo/return address and any other copy or graphics. Flyers should be machine cut and machine folded.

Remember, direct mail is one component of a multifaceted publicity and promotion campaign. Use it to interact with and reinforce your other efforts.

The Inequities of the Fame Game
Ellen Jacobs

It took Martha Graham ninety years to wake up on a Sunday morning to a wall-to-wall photograph of herself splayed across the top half of page 1 of the "Arts and Leisure" section of the *New York Times*. It took rap star Vanilla Ice only twenty-two years to conquer the same space. Is Vanilla Ice more precocious than Martha Graham had been? The absurdity of such a question suggests the paradoxical, capricious, contradictory, highly complex, and sometimes absurd thinking that governs media logic.

The job of the print and electronic press is to deliver news and commentary to its audience. Money is news; war is news; death is news; sex is news; longevity is news. Art qualifies only when it incorporates one, or preferably more than one, of the above. Probably breaking the world record among dance artists, Martha Graham made "real" news (the front page of the *New York Times*) twice. She appeared on page 1, which is reserved for "serious," nonarty issues, first in 1970, when she stopped dancing at age seventy-six, and two decades later, when she died at age ninety-six.

Though she created a new art form and changed the face of American culture, Martha Graham also had the right friends: Liza Minnelli, Halston, Woody Allen, Gregory Peck, and, most recently, Madonna, to give her the artsy glamor that legitimized her to the general public. Of course, she in turn gave her friends the respectability of being associated with a priestess. Through her friendships, Graham's revolution was given new meaning—and visibility. She could now be the subject of pieces in *People, Life,* and *House and Garden,* among other slick magazines.

The reason the review photo of *Miss Saigon* made the front page of the *New York Times* when it opened was not because the show had made an artistic breakthrough but because it had the highest advance box office in the history of Broadway. Its unprecedented ticket sales were due in no small measure to the racial and casting news the show had made even before the Broadway contracts were signed. On April 21, 1991, the front-page coverline for the *New York Times* story about the premiere of the New York City Ballet's new production of *Sleeping Beauty* read: "Arts and Leisure/Section 2: City Ballet embraces a $2.8 million *Sleeping Beauty* with a little help from Broadway."

As high-minded and noble as we may wish the media to be, newspapers, magazines, television, and radio are ultimately commercial ventures. One explanation of their increasing coverage of film, television, and pop music has to do with their cynical appraisal of the American mind, the assumption that Mr. and Mrs. Typical American have the literacy and cultural instincts of a twelve-year-old. This obviously makes the battle for arts coverage, particularly for the more experimental arts, an even greater challenge to the wit and imagination of the artist and/or publicist. Broadway, ballet, classical music, opera, and painting are more likely to claim space than a debut at the Kitchen, simply because of the vast sums of money invested in their productions and the size of the audiences they attract.

Art multiplies its sex appeal when surrounded by a whiff of sexual scandal. Think of the coverage that *Vanity Fair* accorded the Peter Martins/Heather Watts duo. Disaster, too, has news glamor. The threat of financial collapse attracts the kind of interest that translates into column inches—the economic troubles suffered by the Dance Theatre of Harlem probably received more editorial coverage than the opening of its New York season. A battle between heads of multimillion-dollar companies also has news appeal—Baryshnikov and Jane Hermann at ABT, Gerald Arpino and Anthony Bliss at the Joffrey. A new work or a good season are not reason enough for media celebration.

With the economic wealth of the eighties came a new set of assumptions by artists. There was more money to spend. For newspapers, this was translated into great fortunes resulting from increased advertising revenue. Since the number of editorial pages in newspapers correlates with advertising revenue, the papers could afford to be more generous with arts coverage. Even young dance artists performing in Off-Off-Off-Broadway spaces became recipients of the largess of editors and publishers. Gail Conrad's 1983 sci-fi tap dance, *Mission,* was the subject of a Sunday "Arts and Leisure" story, as was Marleen Penninson's *The Routine* at LaMama Annex. Some of the hardest nuts to crack for dance, glossy magazines and television, were suddenly running dance pieces.

One of the by-products of the proliferation of media coverage has been younger artists' willingness to buy into an unfortunate equation: Fame is quality, media visibility is success. The size and placement of an article is not necessarily a measure of talent or a promise of immortality. Now that dance has achieved a certain amount of media exposure, dance artists have become more impatient and assume coverage almost as a birthright. Consequently, they often misunderstand the concerns of the media and its responsibility. While individual critics and dance writers may be sympathetic to a young dancer's troubles, her/his editors cannot afford to be. The job of an editor would be at risk if she/he were to run photos, stories, or reviews in order to help ticket sales or so that an artist could include them in a grant or foundation application. Newspaper publishers and broadcast corporate heads feel no responsibility for an artist's financial survival. An editor's job is to second-guess what the public is interested in, not to respond to a public that the artist wishes she/he could have.

In trying to secure the interest of an editor, a publicist can feel as helpless and hapless as an artist trying to seduce the Muse. But while there is an inevitable play between the tangible and the intangible in determining the visibility accorded an artist—the quality of the photographs, the good looks, charm, and wit of the artist, the amount of other news or arts copy scheduled for that day, a sudden "hole" on a page, a friendship, a particular interest by an editor or writer—talent is not a negligible consideration.

A glowing review of a past concert helps justify an advance story for the next. As the target of a campaign for a Sunday feature in the *Times* on Ralph Lemon's Joyce season in May 1991, Gene Lambinus, the dance page editor, was sent a letter. Attached was Anna Kisselgoff's review of Lemon's piece for the Lyon Opera Ballet, in which she declared that the work changed Lemon's status from a young downtown choreographer to one of international stature. "Oh well, with that kind of recommendation," Mr. Lambinus said. "Is Mr. Lemon in town right now?" Unfortunately, space considerations won out, but Lemon did get a story in the daily.

Critics delight in forecasting new directions and identifying new talent. While it may be flattering suddenly to find oneself the darling of a critic or, even better, of a coterie of them, being thrust into the glare of adoration can blind one to realities. The sky is crowded with stars shot from critics' canons. It is also scarred with the remains of those artists who did not fulfill their initial promise. Whose fault is it? The critics' for their premature enthusiasm, or the artists' for not living up to the critics' expectations?

Just as every artist may want to have the talent of Picasso and the glitz that surrounds Michael Jackson, every critic wishes to be a seer. Part of her/his passion for the arts comes from an identification with an artist's talent. What if the next season does not match the one that had previously won accolades? A sense of betrayal on the part of both parties is inevitable. A bad review or one in which the critic's yawn is visible between words is not merely disappointing. For most artists it is tantamount to a declaration of war. Of course, the critic can be dead wrong. While an angry phone call or letter may help exhaust some of the outrage, soothe the pain, and sweeten the bitterness, a terrific performance is the best revenge.

The tremors of the dance boom began to be felt in the sixties. The sexual revolution that took place during that decade helped loosen America's chastity belt and weakened the puritanical hold on our conscience that had made dance so threatening. The subsequent rise in the nation's economy over the next two decades certainly played a significant role in promoting the health of the art form. If it also gave rise to false expectations and misguided notions of success, the tough times presently being suffered may help redefine inspiration and commitment.

That Merce Cunningham worked in virtual obscurity until fairly recently did not stop him from choreographing some of the greatest dances of our century, nor did it stop Paul Taylor from creating masterpiece after masterpiece, or Alvin Ailey from breaking down racial barriers and creating a glorious company en route. Think of the loss to American culture if it had.

Regarding Dancers and Publicity

Deborah Jowitt

[*This article first appeared in the* Village Voice *on November 22, 1983. Following it, the author revisits the subject for a look at publicity in the nineties.* —Eds.]

Match the Artist to the Publicity (A New Game)

There's a game that goes with this job, and it's getting harder to play. It's called Separate (If Necessary) the Artist from His/Her Publicity Campaign. Madison Avenue expertise has been summoned in aid of those able to pay for it. And why not? Humble advertising doesn't make one a better artist (and it may prove one a ninny in the marketplace).

Accuracy and good taste needn't, however, be ruled out entirely. The season Ruth Mayer and William Carter are presenting this month at the Joyce is being touted by an expertly engineered ad masquerading as a questionnaire for potential audience members. It's more than a bit arch, but the sell is gentle until just before the ticket order form, when cultural snobbism is brought into play: "Answer only if you've elected to act with flair." It lacks the outrageousness of the publicity designed for Paul Taylor's work a couple of seasons ago, which claimed, as I remember, that you'd understand sex and a number of other things better after you'd seen these dances.

The Taylor ads with their mystery-of-life allusions were more like perfume ads than dance ads; all you could do was throw up your hands at the foolishness of them. The recent publicity generated on behalf of the City Center season of Senta Driver's Harry was a paragon of taste compared to the Taylor publicity, but it saddened me. Here's how it went: "You already know two remarkable choreographers who emerged from the Paul Taylor ensemble early in the '70s: Twyla Tharp and Laura Dean. Come to the City Center Space in October, and meet the third." Setting Driver's name in conjunction with prominent others is fair, I guess. But I also guess only the high financial stakes involved could have enabled Driver herself to stomach this. Tharp danced with Taylor's company for two years, Dean for about seven months: His influence on them could not be said to be profound. Driver, on the other hand, worked with Taylor for six years, and very faint traces of inherited characteristics are discernible. A choreographer of some repute since her debut in 1975, she's hardly a newcomer to anything. Except to the big time.

So does this kind of thing sell tickets? Probably. Does it mislead audiences? Possibly. Has this theory been proven correct: Get people to the theater by whatever means you can; once there, they'll love it? I doubt it. I've seen audiences beguiled by inappropriate publicity. They can be tigers.

As full of pitfalls as the high-powered hype is, the little games aimed at critics can prove even more tricky to play wisely. Some are so glittery you don't even have to try to mount your defenses; your hackles just rise. The boldest attempt was the Hamburg Ballet's UPS presentation to critics of small tape recorders with cassettes bearing personal invitations to attend *A Midsummer Night's Dream* delivered by a solemn male voice against a swelling of Mendelssohn's overture. More useful, gracious, but possibly self-defeating were the gifts to the entire opening-night-gala audience for the Bat-Dor: The occasion was a benefit for the Dance Library of Israel, and spectators were provided with fold-out cardboard binoculars with which to scrutinize the dancing.

Downtown choreographers fighting for recognition go for the serious press release. One choreographer once questioned me closely about how I thought she ought to design these; the purpose of her questions seemed to be whether she could use language more effectively to make me see exactly what she wished me to see in her dances. In this game, the two players have different aims. The choreographer's is as above, or at least to convince the writer of his/her probing approach to art. The critic's is to be aided by however much of the publicity makes sense without allowing his/her viewing to be thoroughly shaped by it.

An Update (1991)

Rereading an article I wrote on dance publicity in 1983 for the *Village Voice* was startling. Much has changed. Since I wrote the piece, we have lost William Carter to AIDS, and Senta Driver has announced that her company's sixteenth-anniversary season was also its last.

Yet not all the changes are saddening. The 1980s notion that outrageous and exuberant hype never hurts, and might even kick a choreographer into the big time, seems to have retired with Reagan, the show-biz president. It's rare now that elaborate publicity campaigns are mounted by choreographers as relatively untried as Carter and Ruth Mayer were in 1983 (both better known as dancers with the American Ballet Theatre). I was even surprised that in 1991 the Matsuyama Ballet from Tokyo would send American critics two books on Japanese culture in order to prepare them for the company's visit. American choreographers appear to know that such a gesture can seem pretentious and even undermine the work—which might well fail to deliver the promised cultural complexity.

As I scan the press releases that flood my desk, I'm grateful for those that offer facts without telling me how the work is supposed to strike me. This, for example, is useful: "The work explores an imaginary community at work and at play as it evolves within a landscape of cardboard boxes." So is this: "The piece explores a front-back geometry, continually flipping the space patterns around a central reference point." Facts count.

Good, clear writing is, of course, appreciated. So is clever writing. But if the writing is *too* colorful, it calls attention to itself more than to the choreographer or event it seeks to promote. Breezily labeling Bebe Miller's company a "Band of Gypsies," as one press release recently did, sounds snappy. Harmless fun. But what does it mean? Are we to expect fiery folk with gold earrings and wild dancing to fiddle music, or something like *A Chorus Line*? Do either of these represent the Bebe Miller we know? If not, what purpose do they serve?

It's standard practice for releases to offer quotes from reviews. Only then do phrases like "wry and poignant," "tensely charged," and "haunting text and desperate physicality" mean anything (if then)—although I tolerate them better when they've been coined by press agents than when they've been made up by choreographers. It's significant that the exceptionally skilled publicist Ellen Jacobs used only one such term ("shimmering lyricism") in a two-and-a-half-page release about Trisha Brown. As for telling anyone that a dance is "an exploration of space and direction as man seeks his purpose in the world around him and his legacy from the world beyond," forget it. A dance may *be* profound, but few can live up to such a lofty pronouncement, and experience has shown many artists that disappointment can be a dangerous response to provoke. In any viewer.

Sample Press Release

Ellen Jacobs & Co.
1841 Broadway, NY NY 10023
212-245-5100, fax 212-397-1102

For Immediate Release
Drums & Bugles Herald New York Premiere of
Trisha Brown's *Foray Forêt;* Company Plays City Center
March 5–10
Season Features 25 Years of Choreography

They'll literally bring out the band when Trisha Brown returns to town to celebrate her Company's 20th anniversary with a week of performances at

City Center, March 5–10. Featuring the New York premiere of *Foray Forêt* and the first New York performance of *Homemade* since its premiere in 1966, the season will present a panoramic look at one of the country's foremost experimental artists.

Softer and starker in quality and slower in speed, *Foray Forêt* suggests a shift in direction for Ms. Brown, whose most recent dances were marked by a shimmering lyricism. The music for *Foray Forêt* will be provided by the prize-winning Cadets of Bergen County, who will perform the music while marching outside the theater at City Center. (At the 1990 Lyon Biennale de la Danse, where the dance had its world premiere in September, the music was provided by a local high school marching band.) Ms. Brown's long-time collaborator, Robert Rauschenberg, designed the visual presentation for the work. A bicontinental and multi-institutional commission, funding for the dance was provided by the Lyon Biennale de la Danse and the Centre National de la Danse Contemporaine in France, and the Wexner Center for the Visual Arts (Columbus, OH), The Walker Art Center (Minneapolis), Jacobs Pillow (Lee, MA), and Cal Performances/Berkeley in the United States.

Making visible the changes in her work over the past 25 years, Ms. Brown will perform selected solos marking artistic landmarks in her career. *Homemade,* for instance, a section of a three part work, was created in 1966 and reflects her experiments with technology during the period. Robert Whitman filmed Trisha Brown dancing. With a projector strapped to her back, Ms. Brown then performs the same dance on stage while the projector projects Whitman's film onto a screen. Ms. Brown will also perform *Accumulation,* a solo created in 1971, to the Grateful Dead's "Uncle John's Band," as well as *Accumulation* with *Talking plus Watermotor,* this time with a signer. Although this version of the dance was first performed in 1977, Ms. Brown spontaneously added the signer at the inauguration of the Wexner Center in 1989.

In addition to the solos, and the revival of *LineUp* (1977), the City Center season will celebrate Ms. Brown's adventurous collaborations with visual artists and composers: There will be *Newark* (1987), with visual presentation by Donald Judd and sound orchestration by Peter Zummo, and *Son of Gone Fishin'* (1981), with score by Robert Ashley. *Lateral Pass* (1985) uses a visual presentation by Nancy Graves and a score by Peter Zummo.

In addition to *Foray Forêt,* the choreographer's most recent work with Robert Rauschenberg, the season will offer performances of two previous Brown/Rauschenberg collaborations: *Set and Reset* (1983) performed to an original score by Laurie Anderson; and *Astral Convertible* (1989) danced to a score by Richard Landry. The Third Entr'Acte from *Carmen,* which Ms. Brown choreographed for Lina Wertmuller's 1986 staging of the opera, will be seen on the Saturday night program.

After its City Center engagement, the company will embark on a month-long domestic tour with dates that include: the Walker Art Center in Minneapolis (April 11); the Northrop Auditorium in Minneapolis (April 12); Helena Civic Center in Helena, MT (April 20); the University of Montana in Missoula (April 23); Alberta Bair Theatre in Billings, MT (April 27); Loretto Heights Theater in Denver (May 3 & 4); and the Wells Theatre in Norfolk, VA (May 10).

The Brown Company will present the premiere of *Astral Convertible II* at the National Gallery in Washington, May 14–18. This new version of the dance was commissioned by the National Gallery.

In December 1990, the Brown Company received its first Challenge Grant from the National Endowment for the Arts. The $200,000 grant will be used to develop long term residencies at presenting sites throughout the United States where Ms. Brown can choreograph in a theater setting.

The opening night curtain at City Center (March 5) is at 7:30PM; all other evening performances are at 8PM. There is a 2PM matinee on Saturday, March 9; the season's final performance is at 3PM on Sunday, March 10.

Tickets for the Brown Company's City Center engagement range between $15 and $35, and can be purchased by telephone by calling Ticketron 212-246-0102. The City Center box office phone number is 212-581-7907. City Center is located at 191 West 55th Street. (See attached for night-by-night programming.)

# # #

APPENDIX THE SHOW

Addresses and phone numbers of the following resources may be found in the alphabetized Directory at the end of the book.

Production

Locating space

Alliance of Resident Theatres/New York (A.R.T./NY). (Reference file of spaces geared primarily to theater. Includes larger proscenium theaters. The Real Estate Project assists members in locating theater and office space.)

Dance Theater Workshop (File of spaces available for rehearsal and performance. Includes a range of spaces from lofts to small proscenium houses, updated periodically.)

New York State Council on the Arts Presenting Organizations Program (Maintains a list of sponsors funded for presentations in New York State.)

Technical Assistance Project (TAP)/Performing Arts Resources (Maintains an international file of performing spaces, primarily the larger, proscenium type. Resources may be useful in preparing an out-of-town tour. It also has a seminar series.)

Publications

A Guide to Los Angeles Area Performing Venues.

Space Chase. A survey of new and lesser-known performance opportunities in New York.

Spaces for the Arts. Lists spaces for dance rehearsals and performance rentals.

Space for Dance. A resource guide for planning and building a performance space for dance. Covers many aspects of theatrical production.

A Space to Create and Showcase Primer.

Will It Make a Theatre. A joint project of NEA Dance and Design Arts Programs. Covers design or adaptation of spaces for dance, from traditional proscenium to alternative spaces.

Production staff (personnel referrals)

Dance Theater Workshop (Maintains a resume file on technical services. Consultations and referrals.)

Technical Assistance Project (TAP)/Performing Arts Resources, Management Assistance Project (Interviews and maintains files on all categories of theater professionals.)

For referrals in other cities, call your local arts service organization.

Publication

Sterns Performing Arts Directory (formerly the *Dance Magazine Annual Performing Arts Directory*). Annual resource directory.

Royalties

American Society of Composers, Authors, & Publishers (ASCAP)
Broadcast Musicians, Inc. (BMI)

Staging equipment and services

Costumes and dancewear in New York City

Capezio Dance Theatre Shops (Complete selection of dancewear. Substantial discounts available at Dance Factory Outlet.)

Capezio East (Dancewear, shoes, etc.)

Danskin (Dancewear, shoes, etc.)

Freed of London Ltd. (Dancewear, shoes, etc.)

Rivoli Shoe Repair (For fastening of taps and rubberizing shoe soles; discounts for dancers and companies.)

S&S Hosiery (Gives discounts, but merchandise is already low priced.)

Costume rentals

Look in the Yellow Pages under "Costumes—Masquerade & Theatrical."

Costume Collection (Rents costumes to not-for-profit organizations. Rates vary depending on house size and number of performances. The collection is extensive and available for viewing by appointment.)

Creative Costume, Inc.

Eaves & Brooks Costume Company

Materials

Shopping districts in New York City frequented for costume materials include:

Artificial flowers, feathers, ribbons, beads, trimmings—36th, 37th, 38th Streets between Fifth and Sixth Avenues.

Fabrics, fastenings, and tailor's supplies—38th, 39th, 40th Streets between Seventh and Eighth Avenues.

Bargain Fabrics—Broadway between Prince and Canal Streets; First Avenue between 10th and 11th Streets; and Orchard Street below Delancey Street.

Costume designers

Dance Theater Workshop (DTW) (File of free-lance costume designers and seamstresses.)

Technical Assistance Project (TAP)/Performing Arts Resources, Management Assistance Project

For referrals in other cities, call your local arts service organization.

Dyeing

Eagle Lace Dying
Master Dyeing Company

Period costumes

Brooklyn Museum Costumes and Textile Department
Costume Institute of the Metropolitan Museum of Art
Design Laboratory—Fashion Institute of Technology
Library for the Performing Arts at Lincoln Center, Dance and Theatre Collection

Draperies, cycs, and scrims in New York City

Alcone Company, Inc. (Fabric, draperies, track; theatrical supply house.)

J. C. Hansen (Rental. For the most part, very inexpensive.)

Mutual Hardware (Sales.)

Novelty Scenic (Manufacturer of soft goods. Sales and rentals.)

Rose Brand Textile Fabric

Syracuse Scenery & Stage Lighting Co., Inc. (Manufacturer of stage draperies. Full-line theatrical supply house, makeup to hardware.)

I. Weiss & Sons (Sales. Drapery rigging and hardware. Also provides cleaning and flame-proofing services.)

Contact your local arts service organization for more information about draperies, cycs, and scrims.

Cleaning and flameproofing

Spartan Flame Retardants (Do-it-yourself flameproof materials. They service by Federal Express, UPS.)

I. Weiss & Sons

Floors

American Harlequin Corp. (Temporary flooring.)

H. Barnett Associates, Inc. (Rents and sells dance floors. Delivers.)

Brett Theatrical (Sales and rental: Harlequin and Lonstage. Write for samples.)

Excellent Floors (Ceramic tiles, vinyl composition.)

Gerritts International (Sells Vario, a vinyl floor similar to the old Marley. They primarily sell but will rent one small floor—31½ feet by 49½ feet, Black/White.)

Pinay Flooring Products (Sells Halstead flooring, Tajima Flooring Hi-end vinyl tile. Write for samples.)

Rosco Labs (Sells Roscofloor. Write for samples.)

Stagestep, Inc. (Sales and rental: Bravo, Quietstep, Timestep, Dancestep II. Write for samples.)

Haywood-Berk Floor Company

Kenneth Snopes Engineering and Design (Makes a portable sprung floor for permanent situations.)

Technical Assistance Project (TAP) (Has a file containing information on various floors and a study of floor-building techniques, domestic and international.)

Theatre Machine

Hardware

Longacre Hardware

Mutual Hardware Corp. (Catalog available.)

Silver and Sons Hardware Corp. (Broadway favorite.)

Lighting equipment in New York City

Altmann Stage Lighting and Rentals
Big Apple Lights
14th St. Stage Lighting
Production Arts Lighting
Times Square Lighting
Universe Stage Lighting

In other cities, call your local performing arts service organization for referrals.

Publications

Lighting Design Handbook

Lighting Dimensions Directory. Published once a year; emphasizes lighting and special effects resources.

Stage Lighting

Makeup

Look in the Business Yellow Pages under "Theatrical Makeup."

Alcone Co., Inc. (Theatrical makeup, stage blood, latex; theatrical supply house; catalog.)

Bob Kelly Cosmetics, Inc.

Make-Up Center, Ltd. (Carries a variety of theatrical cosmetics and offers lessons for beginners.)

Playbill Cosmetics/Ideal Wig Co. (Makeup pencils in 55 shades and makeup remover pads.)

Props

Centre Firearms Company (Firearms rental requiring large deposit and letter of intent.)

Eclectic Encore Studio (Furniture and prop rentals. Printing services, such as period newspapers, tickets, etc.)

Props for Today (Wide variety of props, furniture, decorative items.)

Publications

Chicago Prop Finders Handbook

Set building

Look in Business Yellow Pages under "Scenery Studios."

Acadia Scenic, Inc. (Full-service scene shop.)

Thomas Bramlett & Associates, Inc. (Nonunion.)

Field Studios, Inc. (Nonunion.)

Messmore and Damon (Union shop. Full-service scene shop. Has a variety of painted drops and used sets, two-folds, and scenery at low prices.)

Theatre Machine Scenic Shop (Union shop.)

Sound equipment in New York City

Audio Force
GSD Productions, Inc. (They deliver.)
ProMix Inc. (They deliver.)
Tapestry Sound
Theatre Technology/Best Audio East

Recording studios in New York City

Angel Sound
Harmonic Ranch
Harvestworks Inc. Studio PASS
Synergy Productions
Tapestry Recording
Theatre Technology/Best Audio East
Unique Recording Studio
WK Studios

For sound resources in other cities, contact your local arts service organization.

Touring cases

Fiber Built Cases, Inc.
Fibrecase and Novelty Company, Inc.
John R. Gerardo Luggage
Oxford Fibre Sample Case Corp.
Progressive Fibre Products, Inc.

Discount tickets

Bryant Park Music and Dance Tickets Booth (Sells half-price, day-of-performance tickets to music and dance events in the five boroughs of New York.)

Theatre Development Fund (TDF Voucher Program) (Offers voucher program for music, dance, and Off-Off-Broadway events to students, teachers, unions, and performing arts professionals. Box office redemption is $5.00 per voucher.)

In other cities, check for reservation and voucher programs with your local arts service organization.

Reservation/box office services

Dance Theater Workshop (Takes reservations and provides concert information. Available to members at a modest per-performance-week fee.)

Ticket Central (Provides reservation service, voucher charge service, or hard ticket service to not-for-profit organizations.)

Special constituencies

Hands On (Consultants who assist performing arts companies in making their productions accessible to deaf audiences. Special expertise in sign-interpreted performances and audience development.)

Hospital Audiences, Inc. (HAI) (Provides equipment and "describers" to translate your performing arts production for blind audiences.)

Special Constituencies Office of the National Endowment for the Arts (The Endowment advocacy effort to encourage quality arts programming for older Americans and disabled institutionalized populations. Provides information and referrals.)

Publications

How to Run a Small Box Office

Little Red Book and *Producers Guide.* Details of Theater Development Fund (TDF) programs and how to tie into TDF programs, respectively. Newsletter about theater and TDF also available.

National production resources on a more local level

There are unsuspected resources right in your own backyard. The following are sources you might want to pursue.

State and city film commissions (Many states and certain cities have film commissions that promote producing motion pictures in their area. Many of them maintain a local directory of personnel and services for the film industry. These local listings contain free-lance technicians and designers as well as businesses such as scenic studios and lighting rental houses.)

College and university theater departments (Many theater departments welcome outside opportunities for their students to acquire practical experience in the design and construction of theatrical productions. Some schools offer college credit for projects students take on. The technical director of the scene shop may want to build your set for a very reasonable fee in order to provide students with additional work. The same could hold true for the costume department. And there are always young lighting designers looking for experience.)

Local telephone directory Yellow Pages (Don't overlook the good old Yellow Pages of your local phone directory. They actually are a good source of what is available in your own city. Don't be afraid to ask businesses for recommendations for designers and technicians. Many businesses employ individuals who also free-lance as designers and technicians. Each Yellow Pages directory may list businesses under different headings. Take the time to cross-reference all the possibilities.)

Headings to consider include:

Costumes—Masquerade & Theatrical
Dancewear
Display Designers
Halls, Auditoriums, Theaters
Scenery (Scenic) Studios and Shops
Stage Equipment and Supplies
Theatrical Agencies
Theatrical Consultants
Theatrical Costumes
Theatrical Equipment and Supplies
Theatrical Makeup

Publications

Doing It Right in LA: Self-Producing for the Performing Artist. A workbook-style manual addressing the needs of independent performers and producers in the Los Angeles area. (Some information is useful for artists in other locales.)

The New York Theatrical Sourcebook. A 550-page resource book listing over 2,000 companies offering a full range of production services to the theatrical industries. The book includes an appendix listing support services, health and safety organizations, and New York theaters, from Broadway to small performing spaces.

Sterns Performing Arts Directory (formerly the *Dance Magazine Performing Arts Directory*). A 500-page directory that includes a substantial resource section listing designers, consultants, ad agencies, service organizations, ticket services, dancewear, costumes, equipment, and much more.

Theatre Crafts Directory. Published twice a year, TCD offers up-to-date listings covering every production need, from consulting to transportation and storage. Good source of information on converting a building for performing space. Explanations of building codes, fire laws, etc.

Theatre Crafts Magazine. A directory of manufacturers and dealers.

Unions

Actors' Equity Association (Equity, AEA) (For actors, singers, and dancers in live dramatic and musical theater.)

American Federation of Musicians (AF of M) (For professional instrumental musicians.)

American Federation of Television and Radio Artists (AFTRA) (For performers on phonograph recordings and live and taped television and radio.)

American Guild of Musical Artists (AGMA) (For dance, music, and opera—musical theater artists as well as concert, operatic, and instrumental artists.)

American Guild of Variety Artists (AGVA) (For performers in live variety entertainment.)

Association of Theatrical Press Agents and Managers (ATPAM) (For press agents and company managers in the dance, theatrical, and entertainment fields.)

International Alliance of Theatre Stage Employees (IATSE) (For theatrical stage employees.)

Screen Actors Guild (SAG) (For all performers—including dancers—in film.)

Society of Stage Directors and Choreographers (SSD&C) (For stage directors and choreographers on Broadway, Off-Broadway, and in regional theater.)

United Scenic Artists (USA) (For scenic designers, lighting designers, and costume designers in theater, opera, movies, television, and dance.)

Video

Audio, film, and visual services and equipment:

Adwar Video (Sales, service, and rental of most brands of video equipment.)

Association of Independent Video and Filmmakers (AIVF) (Reference and information center.)

Audio Visual Workshop (Sales and rental of video equipment.)

Bay Area Video Coalition (BAVC) (Nonprofit video arts center that helps dancers and dance companies with the creation of videotapes—promo reels, PSAs, broadcast programs, etc.—and training in the use of video equipment.)

Character Generators (Video documentation)

CTL Electronics (Sales, service, and rental of video equipment)

Dance Brew, Inc. (Nonprofit organization that provides a full range of videotaping services, from on-location shoots to studio shoots, to video resumes and television commercials. Editing, demo tapes, script writing, lighting, titling, and music videos.)

Film Video Arts (A NYSCA-funded project. Lends out video, film, and sound equipment to not-for-profit organizations at significantly reduced rates.)

Independent Feature Project (five regional offices—see Directory) (Associations of independent filmmakers and distributions that encourage creativity and diversity in films produced outside the established system. Provides referrals for videographers.)

MPCS Video Industries, Inc. (Sales, service, and rental of video equipment.)

Reliance Audio Visual

Video D (Dance, performance, and concert music documentation.)

Dance archival and notation services in New York City

Arts Interactive Multimedia (AIM) (Nonprofit organization concerned with long-term storage of, preservation of, and access to dance video.)

Dance Notation Bureau (Has correspondence courses in beginning and intermediate Labanotation.)

Laban Institute of Movement Studies

Contact your local arts service organization for notators in your area, or call the Dance Notation Bureau.

Major archive collections

Harvard Theatre Collection
Library for the Performing Arts at Lincoln Center, Dance Collection
Library of Congress
San Francisco Performing Arts Library and Museum
Schomberg Center

Producing

Producing organizations in New York City

Brooklyn Academy of Music (BAM)
Brooklyn Dance Consortium
Creative Time
Dance Theater Workshop's Bessie Schonberg Theater
Dancing in the Streets
Danspace Project, St. Mark's Church in-the-Bowery
Dixon Place
Emanu-El Midtown YW-YMHA
Evolving Arts Dancespace
Extrapolating Studio
The Field
Gowanus Arts Exchange
Home for Contemporary Theatre and Arts
The Kitchen
The Knitting Factory
Lincoln Center Out-of-Doors
Movement Research
NADA (formerly Theatre Club Funambules)
National Black Theatre
One Night Stand
Performance Mix
Performance Space 122 (P.S. 122)
Triplex Performing Arts Center at Borough of Manhattan Community College

Places where you can self-produce in New York City

Cooper Square Theatre
Cubiculo
Merce Cunningham Dance Studio

Dance Theater Workshop
Eden's Expressway
Ethnic Folk Arts Center
Extrapolating Studio
Joyce Theater
Marymount Manhattan College
Kathryn Bach Miller Theatre at Columbia University
Mulberry Street Theater
Ohio Theater
The Open Eye NEW STAGINGS
Pace Downtown Theater
Performance Space 122 (P.S. 122)
Symphony Space
Taller Latinoamericano
Theatre of the Riverside Church
Washington Square Church

Producing organizations across the country (National Performance Network Primary Sponsors)

African American Museum of Fine Arts (San Diego, CA)
Alverno College: Alverno Presents (Milwaukee, WI)
Asociación de Músicos Latino Americanos (Philadelphia, PA)
Black Arts Alliance (Austin, TX)
Carver Community Cultural Center (San Antonio, TX)
Centro Cultural de la Raza (San Diego, CA)
El Centro Su Teatro (Boulder/Denver, CO)
Colorado Dance Festival (Boulder, CO)
Contemporary Arts Center (New Orleans, LA)
Contemporary Dance Theater, Inc. (Cincinnati, OH)
Dance Center of Columbia College (Chicago, IL)
Dance Place (Washington, DC)
Dancer's Collective of Atlanta, Inc. (Atlanta, GA)
Dance Theater Workshop (New York, NY)
Dance Umbrella (Cambridge, MA)
Dance Umbrella, Inc. (Austin, TX)
DiverseWorks (Houston, TX)
Durham Arts Council, Inc. (Durham, NC)
Euliprons, Inc. (Boulder/Denver, CO)
Florida Dance Association (Miami, FL)
Flynn Theatre for the Performing Arts, Ltd. (Burlington, VT)
Guadalupe Cultural Arts Center (San Antonio, TX)
Helena Presents (Helena, MT)
Highways Performance Space
Inquilinos Boricuas en Acción (Boston, MA)
Institute of the Arts at Duke University (Durham, NC)
Jomandi Productions (Atlanta, GA)
Junebug Productions, Inc. (New Orleans, LA)

The Kitchen (New York, NY)
Kuumba House (Houston, TX)
Life on the Water (San Francisco, CA)
Los Angeles Contemporary Exhibitions (LACE) (Los Angeles, CA)
Miami-Dade Community College, Wolfson Campus (Miami, FL)
Minnesota Dance Alliance (Minneapolis/St. Paul, MN)
El Museo del Barrio (New York, NY)
Museum of Contemporary Art (MOCA) (Los Angeles, CA)
On the Boards (Seattle, WA)
Painted Bride Arts Center (Philadelphia, PA)
Performance Space 122 (New York, NY)
Pittsburgh Dance Council, Inc. (Pittsburgh, PA)
PREGONES Theater (New York, NY)
Present Music (Milwaukee, WI)
Randolph Street Gallery (Chicago, IL)
St. Joseph's Historic Foundation, Inc. (Durham, NC)
Several Dancers Core (Decatur, GA)
Sushi Performance and Visual Art (San Diego, CA)
Theater Artaud (San Francisco, CA)
Third World Performance Space (Columbus, OH)
Walker Arts Center (Minneapolis, MN)
Wexner Center for the Arts (Columbus, OH)
Women & Their Work (Austin, TX)

NPN U.S./Canada Performance Initiative Primary Sponsors:

Agora de la Danse/in collaboration with Festival de Theatre des Ameriques (Montreal, Quebec)
Dancers' Studio West (Calgary, Alberta)
Danceworks/in collaboration with The Music Gallery (Toronto, Ontario)
Firehall Arts Centre/in association with Vancouver East Cultural Centre (Vancouver, British Columbia)
Brian Webb Dance Company (Edmonton, Alberta)

TAKING CARE

OF BUSINESS

Drive thy business, let not that drive thee.—Benjamin
Franklin, *Poor Richard's Almanack*

What Is Management?
Ivan Sygoda

A camel is a horse designed by a committee. —La Rochefoucauld

As our society becomes increasingly complex, many independent artists find that the fulfillment of their artistic goals requires interaction with potentially intimidating components of the body politic—lawyers, bankers, presenters, critics, agents, corporate executives, and government agencies. The artist who wishes to concentrate on her/his work may become overwhelmed by the seemingly irrelevant tasks that must be accomplished in order to keep doing that work. One must be not only an artist but also a recording engineer, electrician, seamstress, accountant, paymaster, grant writer, secretary, and maybe even spouse and parent, all in one twenty-five-hour day.

Most artists reach a point in their development where they question the way they have been organizing their lives. Growth brings new responsibilities—to other people, who must be paid or supplied with materials; to organizations, which might require information or accounting. Artists find that, like it or not, their personal and artistic existences have been tangled into a legal and fiscal Gordian knot.

The very real problems caused by these complications have nurtured a myth among artists: that there is a character on a white steed, called a Manager, who will charge in, slice the Gordian knot, and make it all go away. It is the considered opinion of the contributors to this book that, in the unlikely event that such a character rides into your life, you should marry the individual and leave the rest of us to cope with reality in more practical ways.

Although management may be embodied in one or more persons, it is first and foremost an attitude and a process by which you structure your relationships with the outside world. Some artists who take great pride in their handiwork are reluctant to let an outsider put strange hands on important aspects of it, such as the way it is presented to the public. Other equally talented artists can be quite blasé, even careless, about the same processes. It isn't easy to walk the line between fear of losing control on one side and abdication of responsibility on the other. In short, engaging management services can be stressful, but it can also empower the artist and amplify what she/he can accomplish.

Rather than giving rise to panic or daydreaming, an artist's inevitable stock-taking should be the occasion for positive reassessment of goals and priorities. The way management services enter an artist's life should result from rational planning.

Nonetheless, compromises will often be necessary in an area where compromise is anathema. It is the artist's responsibility to minimize these compromises and to safeguard the integrity of her/his art. This is emphasized, not because managers or consultants are evil or unthinking, but because money, technology, bureaucracy, and ignorance are eating away at the power of all of us to control our own lives and the way we relate to each other.

Most likely, the independent artist is already familiar with the farming out of certain artistic tasks—costume design and execution, for instance. Reflecting on this experience can be instructive. She/he certainly knows when the costume should be completed and can assess the quality of the work even if details of fabrication forever remain a mystery. People are professionals or they are not, and expertise costs money. Thus, many artists have made economic sacrifices in order to hire a professional costume designer. Most likely it made a difference.

The artist's experience in this area parallels what might be expected when management tasks are delegated. Rethink the above example, substituting "accountant," "publicist," "tour manager," "grant writer," "graphic artist," "booker," "letter writer," or "box office manager" for "costume designer." Every artist who does this exercise will have a different reaction as each substitution is made, and that is precisely the point. Some are comfortable doing accounting and bookkeeping tasks. Yet the same artists may not feel capable of writing a coherent sentence.

Sooner or later, these decisions have consequences. Financial chaos can go on for years, or it can lead promptly to law courts and bankruptcy proceedings. Poorly written press releases sent to outdated addresses can result in a performance not being listed or covered by critics. This in turn can lead to poor attendance and increased financial losses. Inadequate or poorly conceived funding requests can close doors that might otherwise have been open.

Artists are professionals. They set standards for themselves and work hard to live up to these standards. Similarly, the arts and entertainment business has been around for a long time, and professionals exist whose specialties involve accomplishing every one of the tasks we have been discussing.

The attitude of the artist toward these fellow professionals can have a considerable impact on the nature of the relationship that eventually develops and on the quality of the work that gets accomplished. The artist-manager relationship can be enriched or complicated by a construct of expectations and needs peculiar to the arts. The matter is important enough to warrant a digression.

The artist is thrown into the difficult position of needing outside expertise from nonartists while at the same time possibly resenting that need. It doesn't help matters that such needs are relatively expensive to fulfill. Management professionals in our society usually make a better living than working artists. This fact of life can foster resentment. There is a temptation to ascribe dark motives to the individual when the root problem is the place our society accords its creative artists.

Second, the creative artist is usually in a remarkably intense relationship with her/his own work. The artist may become suspicious or distrustful when, as is most often the case, the manager or consultant seems not to share the same intensity. The person involved may well "love dance" or be "committed to the arts" or some such abstraction, but it is rare indeed when time and tribulation reveal a level of commitment to the artist's work akin to the artist's own. The artist-manager relationship has been compared to marriage in its intensity, in its difficulty, and in the possibility of its being incredibly rewarding for both partners. But trouble can brew when the artist insists that such a relationship spring full blown from the contract or letter of agreement instead of helping build it step by careful step.

If the artist assumes that managers utter magic incantations in plush offices to make things happen, then the artist will be disappointed. Most of what a manager needs to do is routine in nature and very time consuming. The rules of accounting, for instance, are public knowledge for all who care to learn them. The professional accountant has taken the time to learn the rules, and experience has added knowledge of shortcuts and ways to save effort and avoid false moves. This time and experience is what costs money and explains why the hourly or daily rate for professional assistance seems so high.

The artist's time and experience are worth money, too. If the artist could create a new work with the energy that otherwise goes into balancing ledgers and writing checks, then the hiring of an accountant can be an economical investment in the artist's own work.

This evaluation process should be done in all areas of possible management activity. Every artist needs to keep track of her/his finances, but not every artist needs an accountant as a first priority, or a press agent, or a tour manager.

Since management can cost more than the artist would like to pay, certain alternatives must be examined. Why pay for it if you can get it for free?

Management Options

Volunteers and interns

We seem to have weathered the "me" decades, and one can hope that the nineties will produce enlightened amateurs ready and willing to provide needed services to the artist. The problem is locating them. The artist's own associates are the first people to turn to. They are likely, alas, to be under-employed and also, happily, to be familiar with the work and the artist's way of doing things. (On the other hand, they may be unable or unwilling to question the artist's way of doing things.) If the artist knows what needs to be done in certain areas and is willing to assume the job of training and supervising (and to accept ultimate responsibility for the outcome), much can be accomplished at a fraction of the cost of professional management.

Interns are another source of free or low-cost assistance. As part of their performing arts or arts administration programs, many colleges and universities have developed structures to give their students experience in areas of management that will be needed in future careers. Depending on the institution involved, such interns may be available for defined periods or on a part-time basis throughout the academic year. Certain institutions require that their interns be placed with not-for-profit organizations, and many require time-card records and written evaluations of the interns' progress and performance.

As is the case with volunteers already known to the artist, interns will most likely need to be instructed in the responsibilities they are to assume and will require supervision. The intern cannot be expected to reinvent the wheel and to rediscover the procedures, rules, and tricks of the trade that come with experience. Furthermore, if the intern's sojourn is to be a limited one, considerable time and effort devoted to training will have to be amortized over an unsatisfactorily short time. Another disadvantage of rotating interns and volunteers is that the already busy artist's mind becomes the only locus of institutional memory—what processes were set up with whom and what follow-up is required or advisable? The artist should weigh these considerations against her/his own priorities and decide which course of action makes sense.

Consultants

Another approach to the general problem of accomplishing management tasks involves enlarging the skills that artists and helpers already possess. There are people out there who know a lot of the things you need to learn. Trouble is, there are very few individuals who know *all* the things you need to learn. You have to acquire your knowledge piecemeal.

It is important to remember two points. One, the performing arts industry has a product to sell. The management tasks at issue pertain to many industries and businesses. You can learn a great deal from people who are not otherwise candidates for management consultancies specific to your situation. Look first in your own backyard. If Uncle Louie runs a small factory, perhaps he will volunteer his bookkeeper to explain basic accounting procedures. Similarly, if a family friend is a salesperson, perhaps she/he will share wisdom about selling a product or service to strangers by phone, an essential part of the booking process.

Two, the performing arts are also unlike any other business, and not-for-profit enterprises do not have the same priorities as assembly lines and department stores. A particularly salient example of the difference involves the area of marketing. Something like clothing or appliances can be redesigned and repackaged to suit market trends, but few artists of integrity would consciously change their work in the interests of popularity. What this means is that knowledge and advice must be filtered through the artist's special needs and goals and unique sensibility. And common sense. A number of organizations specialize in providing free or low-cost consultancies in performing arts management. [See the Appendix.]

Professional management

Finally, the independent artist's needs and situation may dictate that professional management be hired. Such tasks may be accomplished either "in-house" or "outside," and the choice, as usual, involves questions of finance as well as of temperament. Some large companies do all their management in-house. These are complex operations that need to be monitored and coordinated by the company's corporate hierarchy. At the opposite end of the quantitative scale, many small or emerging artists and companies have in-house arrangements out of sheer necessity, as described above.

A less expensive option is to have management tasks performed outside by a person or an agency that specializes in performing-arts management and has other artist clients. A trade-off may be involved, however. Management tasks, as stated earlier, are labor intensive and time consuming. In a cooperative or multiclient arrangement, the artist can command only a reasonable proportion of the manager's total time. This has varying degrees of consequence, depending on the job involved. A payroll is done when the checks are distributed. A grant application is complete when put in the mailbox or, as is more usual these hectic days, picked up by Federal Express. But in areas like public relations, booking, and fund-raising, the job is never done. All good managers go home (usually late) with guilt. That is why temperament is such an important part of the artist-manager relationship. If, having engaged a professional manager, the artist cannot resolve to trust that manager, especially in out-of-house or time-sharing arrangements where the artist may not be able to monitor progress and results as closely as desired, then the relationship will be a difficult one. An artist used to near-absolute control in the rehearsal studio may feel queasy when put on hold, figuratively and literally, by a manager. Patience is required on both sides.

It must be stated again: Managers have no magic formulas to solve the problems that have plagued artists for centuries. Efficient fiscal administration will not make money appear that simply is not there. Professional public relations cannot guarantee the big review or that that review will be good. Professional booking representation can take years to bear fruit, or, perhaps worse, it can result in a flurry of bookings and then nothing.

At no point can the artist wash her/his hands of responsibility for anything that affects the work because it is the artist's work, not the manager's (Diaghilev notwithstanding). It is the artist who reads into the soul of things, who knows when to say yes and when to say no.

The Structure of Your Operations
Ted Striggles and Mara Greenberg

Omnia Gallia in partes tres divisa est. With these words, Julius Caesar began his great treatise on arts administration. As you will doubtless remember, Caesar divided all "long-haired Gauls" (i.e., "artists") into the following three personae: (1) barbaric, grasping, selfish, fierce, uncouth, self-centered; (2) orderly, businesslike, practical, responsible; (3) overcivilized, complicated, Byzantine, convoluted. Caesar was right. In order to manage your business affairs effectively, you must acknowledge and come to terms with these three aspects of your character. This task requires neither advanced training in psychology nor familiarity with Caesar's collected works. If you've ever spent a day rushing from rehearsal to a restaurant job to a meeting with a potential funding source, hectically changing from faded sweat pants and a T-shirt, to jeans and a work shirt, to a vintage jacket and tie, then you are already acquainted with this idea. Performing artists literally and figuratively spend a great deal of their time changing clothes, adopting first one persona, then another, in order to get through the average day.

How did this convoluted process evolve? In the beginning—or rather in your beginning—you were a completely private, selfish person. Somebody provided more or less adequately for your housing, diapers, and food. That private persona still gets hungry and remains an expensive burden on her/his provider. With maturity, that provider is you. You have had to create a second, business persona to care for the basic economic needs of your private self.

Your business persona earns money as an employee or free-lance operative, maintains a checking and/or savings account, leases an apartment or working space, pays telephone and utility bills, fills out tax returns, and otherwise carries out the normal business activities that concern much of this book. For many creative people, that is enough. Unfortunately, a surprising number of performing artists dream that by creating a "third" persona (usually a "corporation") they will solve all their financial problems and probably help with a few of their creative, emotional, and spiritual difficulties as well. Wrong. The truth is that many performing artists plunge into the world of abstract entities unnecessarily.

The sole proprietorship

Let's assume that your second, business persona has been functioning for a while; you may be working regularly as a salaried employee or doing work on a free-lance basis, or both. Every year when you fill out your federal tax returns you show money earned as an employee in one place and the free-lance money earned (and expenses deducted from those earnings) in another place. That "other place" (usually Schedule C of your federal 1040 tax form) is where your financial activities as a "sole proprietor" are reflected. That term "sole proprietor" means exactly that; you are the proprietor of a business that you run by yourself.

Many large enterprises employing hundreds of people function effectively as sole proprietorships. It is important to note, however, that the introduction into this discussion of individuals who work for you as "employees" does not necessarily change the nature of a sole proprietorship. The concept of "employment" requires a side trip and is dealt with later in this article. At this juncture, it is sufficient to note that, in the arts, abstract entities such as corporations generally function through regular, salaried employees, while sole proprietorships most often pay flat fees to individuals ("independent contractors") who have provided occasional services to them.

The sole proprietorship is a basic unit of most performing artists' business operations. Money typically comes in and goes out of your own pocket or personal checking account. Of course, you need to keep separate records of business versus nonbusiness expenses and perhaps maintain separate bank accounts, but there remains behind those record-keeping devices the same old free-lance second persona with which this chapter began. If you create a piece, enter into a contract, shortchange a booking agent, or bribe a public official, there is only you to own the rights, receive the fees, defend the lawsuit, or go to jail.

As a sole proprietor, you can achieve many of the results that most people think require sophisticated third-persona organizations. You can, for example, obtain the right to operate your sole proprietorship under an "assumed name" (e.g., your stage name or the trade name of your performing troupe) by listing the name with, and obtaining a certificate from, the county clerk's office in the county in which you are doing business. Through such a filing, you can obtain permission for "doing business as" ("d/b/a") the White House Dance Ensemble or whatever name you have chosen. Once filed, a certified copy of that certificate can be used to open bank accounts under the assumed name. This local permission to use your trade name (and protection from its use by others) frequently can be augmented by a state or federal trademark (usually a "servicemark") that can provide statewide or national protection for you in the use of the name. To the extent that your yearning for a third persona is nothing more than the desire to use and protect a business name, it can thus be fulfilled easily and without substantial complications.

The Third Persona

We live in an era of complicated, Byzantine, and convoluted arrangements. The material that follows is designed to introduce you to those arrangements. It presents the most commonly encountered abstract entities (third personae) through which artists sometimes do business. Its purpose is to familiarize you with the concepts involved so that you can anticipate problems and, when they occur, have a sensible conversation with an expert about solutions.

The partnership

Informal partnerships. Assume that you are a performance artist whose freelance, sole proprietorship persona has just completed a collaborative concert with another performance artist with whom you shared expenses and split the box office. You probably created a partnership. It required no written agreement or formal organization, and you needn't have known about the partnership concept or even intended to create one. The partnership had a limited purpose and duration, and it was terminated when you split the box office and went your separate ways.

At their simplest, partnerships like the one just described come and go with no perceived impact. Suppose for a moment, however, that the collaborative concert did not go according to plan. Suppose the other artist thoughtlessly filled her blank pistol with real bullets and unintentionally, though fatally, shot a certain unsympathetic *New York Times* critic at the dramatic high point of her part of the program during her solo section of her piece performed to her music as recorded by her. Could the critic's widow sue you as a "partner"? Possibly so. Now suppose instead that a high-rolling producer saw the concert and took the other performance artist's work (but not yours) to Broadway, where it ran for years. Would you, as a "partner" or "collaborator," have a right to half the Broadway box office receipts or at least half the portion given the other artist for the right to use her pieces from your collaborative effort? How about half the other artist's share of the show's sale for a feature film? Possibly so. Finally, suppose that the producer wants to take the whole show to Las Vegas to be performed in a "Nudie Cuties" review and you approve while the other artist does not. As a partner, can the other artist forbid the producer to take her pieces to Las Vegas? Can she stop your pieces from going? Possibly so.

The actual results of these hypothetical disputes would depend on an analysis of the specific details of the creative and business relationships between you and the other artist. Generally, if you both intended to create and produce together the whole show and all its parts, you were partners and will hang together when the lynching party shows up. If you were not partners, then your contributions and responsibilities can be more easily separated from one another.

Informal partnerships such as the one just described pop up quite frequently. Sometimes they result from conscious choices by independent artists; sometimes they develop out of what begins as a free-lance engagement by one individual or the other; occasionally they grow out of an employer-employee relationship. The "third persona" created by such partnerships is transient and becomes significant only in unusual situations such as those just described. But such unusual situations can and do occur. It is therefore advisable to come to clear understandings (preferably written) with your collaborators on each of your areas of responsibility and authority. [See "Legal Issues" later on in this chapter for a more detailed discussion of this process.]

Formal partnerships. Longer-lasting partnerships, particularly those in which the prospective partners have taken the sensible step of writing down the terms of their relationship, are subject to various state and federal requirements governing partnership operations and record keeping. Such partnerships can be very complex. Wall Street law firms, for example, are usually organized as partnerships and, as you might expect, have gigantic malpractice and general liability insurance policies to protect themselves against the possibility of lawsuits. Despite this drawback, many individuals still decide to form partnerships because they offer tax advantages, allowing the partners to avoid what is known as "double taxation." After paying taxes on their profits, big corporations distribute what's left as dividends to shareholders, who in turn must pay taxes on those dividends. Most partnerships are structured so that profits are taxed only once; their earnings "pass through" the partnership entity to the individual partners, who are taxed on what they receive.

Limited partnerships. A hybrid partnership that maintains some of the advantages and avoids some of the disadvantages of a partnership is called a "limited partnership"; it is best known to performing artists as the means by which Broadway shows are typically financed. A limited partnership has one or more general partners—individuals or entities that look and are treated much like ordinary partners in an ordinary partnership. These "general" partners are in charge of the limited partnership's affairs and run the risk of lawsuits etc. for wrongdoing by one another or by the partnership as a whole. A limited partnership also has "limited" partners. These are individuals or entities who typically invest money in the partnership but do not otherwise play a part in the partnership's affairs. If things go badly, these limited partners can lose their investments, but nothing more—and they can usually "write off" those losses for tax purposes. Also, these limited partners cannot ordinarily be sued for the acts of the general partners. On the other hand, if things go well and the partnership makes money, the limited partners get their share of profits directly, without "double taxation."

The unincorporated association

Suppose for the moment that you have joined with other people to conduct an activity that has a common purpose—perhaps the annual march on the state capitol to demand increased arts funding. Your relationship is too complex and ongoing to be described adequately as a bunch of sole proprietors acting independently of one another. You don't want to form a partnership, and you haven't formally organized into a corporation. You may have formed an unincorporated association. As a practical matter, this type of organization is rarely created as a conscious choice for producing arts performances. This is partly because of problems with its structure and legal impact and partly out of habit—most managers, lawyers, accountants, etc. are unfamiliar, and therefore uncomfortable, with unincorporated associations.

At first glance, operating as an unincorporated association seems tempting. Such organizations appear to be flexible and convenient. Their creation and operation don't much depend on compliance with complicated statutes or regulations. It doesn't cost anything to create them. Ordinarily, no government agency has to approve or consent to the creation of unincorporated associations, and you can establish any reasonable rules or regulations for the conduct of their internal affairs. These rules of organization and operation may be embodied in written articles of association, bylaws, or other documents, but they don't have to be. If they are written, the rules can usually be amended or repealed without government approval whenever the welfare of the group requires it. Indeed, unincorporated associations often operate with no written documents to govern their operations at all. In theory, unincorporated entities can even secure recognition of tax-exempt status under the U.S. Internal Revenue Code. By doing so, such entities can—in theory—become eligible for various types of government and foundation grants and can assure individuals who donate money to them that their contributions will be tax deductible. As a practical matter, however, such recognition is more difficult for an unincorporated entity to obtain than for a corporation.

In order to obtain tax-exempt status, such associations must operate under written articles and rules. This requirement limits the flexibility and ease of organizing that are the main virtues of the unincorporated association mechanism. Moreover, banks, vendors, and landlords are often skittish about dealing with such entities; they are accustomed to dealing with other, more familiar entities. Finally, and most important, the members of unincorporated associations do not have the benefits of "limited legal liability" described below. Each member risks being held personally liable for obligations incurred by the group or, in some circumstances, by its other members. If your pistol-packing former collaborator wants to revive her piece for the governor during the march on the capitol, watch out.

All in all, most knowledgeable advisers to performing artists conclude that unincorporated associations in the real world tend to have most of the disadvantages of other forms of organizations with few of their advantages. If you've gone that far, they almost universally counsel that you take the next step and look into creating a corporation. Even if you don't take that next step, you may look so much like a corporation that you'll be treated as one "de facto" by the state and carry a corporation's tax and other burdens without getting its benefits.

The For-profit corporation

Corporations are "legal fictions." To create one in most states, you need only think it up, then draw up and submit a document to the appropriate authorities for their approval and pay some fees to the state in which the corporation is being created. Once created, a corporation has a life that is separate from that of its creators and that can survive their departure from it. To care for a corporation, you need to feed it a balanced diet of paperwork generated by required procedures and digested by the various federal, state, and local regulatory and taxing agencies that oversee its operations. A properly created, well-fed corporation can be immortal; it can in turn feed and fatten generations of lawyers, accountants, bookkeepers, and bureaucrats. It is also a terrible bother. Still, it does provide important benefits that may make the trouble worthwhile.

Limitations on liability. Along with immortality, a chief attribute of corporations is their capacity to provide their human operators with limited liability. This is generated by a corporation's capacity to exist and to act as a legal entity apart from its members or stockholders. As a "legal person," the corporation generally is afforded the same rights and is subject to the same obligations as a "natural person." Thus, when a corporation acts, it is usually the corporation—rather than its incorporators, members, employees, shareholders, directors, or officers—that bears responsibility for, and enjoys the benefits of, the action it has taken. The shareholders have "limited liability" and usually risk only the loss of their investment when business goes badly. Assuming that the various rules have been followed, the individuals who control the corporation or who are its members or shareholders will not ordinarily be liable for corporate obligations—they generally can't be held liable for the corporation's debts, broken contracts, etc. Only the corporation itself is liable. Since corporations can properly incur debts, it's not unusual for a corporation to owe money without giving its creditors any recourse to the shareholders for repayment of the debt.

There are nevertheless special circumstances in which courts disregard the corporate entity and hold the individuals affiliated with the corporation (members, employees, shareholders, directors, officers, etc.) liable for the corporation's obligations. This is usually called "piercing the corporate veil." Obviously, such liability for individuals may result from certain conscious wrongdoing by the individuals, but it may also arise from their mere failure to make clear to people with whom they are dealing that they are acting on behalf of a corporation and not for themselves as individuals. Similarly, if corporate funds are mixed with funds of individuals associated with the corporation, or if the corporation fails to fulfill certain formal requirements for authorizing or approving corporate actions, or if the corporation violates certain laws or even its own charter in some circumstances, or if the corporation fails to maintain accurate records of its actions and to file required periodic reports—then the responsible individuals may risk personal liability for the corporation's debts or wrongdoing. For some kinds of wrongdoing (e.g., failing to pay the government tax withholdings from salaries), there are special statutes that empower the government to reach right through the corporation to various officers, directors, or shareholders.

Financing operations. Another important aspect of corporations is the flexibility they provide for arranging financing for their operations. In its simplest form, a corporation sells stock to profit-oriented individuals who, by the voting power of that stock, control the corporation. The corporation uses the money obtained from the stock sale to establish its business and begin operations. If business is good, the corporation makes profits that are paid out as dividends to the stockholders. If business is bad and the corporation fails, the stockholders' losses are limited to their investment so long as the corporation was honestly and carefully operated.

Of course, there are variations on this traditional corporate structure—usually dictated by tax considerations. A highly paid sports or entertainment figure, for example, typically sets up a "loan out" corporation, keeps virtually all the shares of stock for her/himself, and then causes the corporation to enter into contracts with the outside world to provide her/his services. If your earnings have reached a level at which such an arrangement sounds inviting, see your accountant and lawyer tomorrow, and send a large contribution to Dance Theater Workshop today to support the next edition of this book.

The S corporation. For "closely held" corporations that have relatively few shareholders and a straightforward organizational structure, there exists under the Internal Revenue Code a special classification for tax purposes that permits profits from operations to pass directly to the shareholder or shareholders without the "double taxation" described above. Although there are some limitations on their operations, a great many family or individually owned businesses are operated through these "S" corporations. (They used to be called "Subchapter S" corporations.) If run properly, "S" corporations can couple the limited liability feature of corporations with most of the tax benefits of partnerships.

The nonprofit, tax-exempt corporation

It is important to keep in mind that the fundamental urge of the traditional for-profit corporation is still that of the basic sole proprietorship—and to conduct its business with limited risks to those whose money and energy give life to the entity.

The corporations most frequently found in dance, theater, and the other performing arts appear in many external ways to be similar to traditional for-profit corporations—but with a critical difference. Their stated purpose is to serve the public and the art form rather than to serve the profit motives of investors. Although such "nonprofit" ("not-for-profit" in some states) organizations may well come into existence because artists (usually a creative artist or a group of performers) want a vehicle for their artistry, still, once it is created, the nonprofit structure must serve the public benefit rather than the interests of private individuals. Indeed, although the organization's directors may well be friends of the artists' and agree to serve on the board of directors because of that connection, their responsibility under the law is to the public, not to the artists who persuaded them to serve.

Nonprofit. A fundamental characteristic of a nonprofit organization is that the entity does not contemplate making a "profit" from the performance of its functions. Any surplus of income over expenditures (normally considered "profits") must be used only for the special "nonprofit" purposes for which the organization was formed. Individuals may not take those surpluses from the organization's activities for themselves (e.g., as dividends, extra salary, or bonuses). Nobody can "own" any stock or other interest in the enterprise that she/he could later sell for personal advantage. Individuals connected with nonprofit organizations can receive only reasonable salaries for their services, sell goods to the organization at fair prices, and be reimbursed for money properly spent by them on the organization's behalf. Most states have a specific category of nonprofit corporations that serve "charitable, educational, religious, scientific, literary, or cultural" purposes, into which performing troupes fit.

Tax exempt. Even though an entity has been organized under state law on a nonprofit basis, it is not automatically tax exempt. In order to qualify for exemption from federal income taxes (the most important exemption), the entity must fit into one or more of several categories of exempt organizations listed in Section 501(c)(3) of the Internal Revenue Code. Arts groups normally qualify for federal tax-exempt status as groups organized or operated for "educational" or "charitable" purposes, provided that the members of the group do not obtain any improper private benefit from its operations. In order to ensure that a nonprofit organization qualifies for exemption from federal income tax, its sponsors must file an application (IRS Form 1023) with, and obtain a favorable ruling letter from, the Internal Revenue Service. The receipt of such a favorable IRS determination is essential if those who are potential contributors to the organization are to be assured that their contributions will be tax deductible under Section 501(c)(3) of the Internal Revenue Code. Moreover, IRS acknowledgment of tax-exempt status makes it possible for the organization to receive grants from a variety of government, foundation, and other sources that can award funds only to tax-exempt entities.

Once obtained, nonprofit status is retained and protected through the satisfaction of state requirements, and tax-exempt status is similarly protected through the satisfaction of state and federal requirements. Tax-exempt status can also free the organization from some local sales taxes, real-estate taxes, and other governmental levies, although these must generally be applied for separately from the application for federal tax exemption. In New York, for example, exemption from state taxes requires filings with the Department of Taxation and Finance.

Once an organization has been granted federal and state tax-exempt status, it should also contact the finance administration in the municipality in which it is located to ascertain the procedure for obtaining exemption from local taxes. An organization based in New York City should write the New York City

Department of Finance, Office of Legal Affairs. [See the Appendix.] Once the required information has been submitted, the organization will be notified in writing as to whether it qualifies, from which local taxes (such as commercial rent tax) it is exempt, and what ongoing filings thereafter will be required.

It is possible to receive many of the benefits of tax-exempt status (e.g., eligibility for tax-exempt contributions, government grants, and certain postal discounts) without setting up your own nonprofit, tax-exempt entity. This can be done by working under the "umbrella" of an existing nonprofit, tax-exempt corporation. In New York City, Dance Theater Workshop, the Cultural Council Foundation, and the Foundation for Independent Artists (administered by Pentacle) provides this service to many individual artists and smaller companies in New York State whose activities are consistent with the umbrella organization's purposes. Churches, schools, and other already existing tax-exempt entities might also serve as umbrellas that can sponsor your artistry on a short-term basis. Umbrella organizations such as these, however, remain answerable to state and federal authorities for the projects they undertake to sponsor.

How to incorporate. In most states, a "for-profit" corporation can be created in a few days. The process of establishing a "nonprofit" corporation under most states' laws often takes several months. This aspect of the legal system is not for amateurs. Professional assistance is usually expensive, but free or low-cost help can be obtained in New York from Volunteer Lawyers for the Arts (VLA) as well as from the Community Action for Legal Services and the Council of New York Law Associates. If you live outside New York, contact your local arts council or VLA in New York City for information on low-cost legal services in your area. [See the Appendix.]

There are four basic steps to incorporating as a nonprofit (not-for-profit) corporation in New York State: (1) select a corporate name, then clear and reserve it with the secretary of state's office; (2) prepare a certificate of incorporation; (3) obtain approvals and consents from the necessary state officials, both administrative and judicial; and (4) file the executed certificate and documents with the secretary of state.

The Employer-Employee Relationship

Independent contractors versus employees

You may already have entered into arrangements with individuals to whom you pay money for services they provide to you. Some of these individuals are clearly not your employees by any normal definition—your plumber, your lawyer, your occasional hit man. For those individuals, your free-lance persona is just paying money to their free-lance personae for services rendered to you. Other individuals have a relationship to you that is certainly employer-employee by every definition—your secretary, the hourly workers in your sweatshop, the year-round crew on your yacht.

Sooner or later, individuals who provide you with regular or ongoing services become your employees for purposes of accountability for federal, state, and local "withholding" tax, Social Security taxes, disability insurance, unemployment insurance, and workers compensation insurance. The rules that govern the particular point at which an individual becomes your employee under each of these systems differ somewhat from one system to another. Those differences are discussed in "Government Financial Services" in chapter 3. Generally, it just isn't worth the difficulties (and the very real potential for personal liability) inherent in trying to make clever distinctions between the several systems. Instead, lawyers almost universally advise their arts clients to take care in structuring each relationship so that it is clearly and for all purposes an "arms-length" independent contractor, nonemployee relationship (e.g., your hit man) or clearly an employer-employee relationship (e.g., the crew on your yacht). Of course, whole law firms still agonize over the point at which too frequent use of an independent hit man may create an employer-employee relationship under state disability insurance laws.

Relationships in the performing arts are not so simple as those that result from the use of the occasional hit man or the engagement of the normal year-round yacht staff. Individuals who dance, act, compose, choreograph, design, build, or record for your concert have a relationship to you that is somewhere in the middle.

Performing arts troupes, whether incorporated or not, face essentially the same federal, state, and local requirements concerning individuals who provide them with services as do other businesses. An "employer-employee relationship" is generally one in which the employee is subject to the supervision and control of the employer, both as to what is to be done and as to how and when it is to be accomplished. It doesn't matter that the work is part-time or irregular.

One nearly comprehensible federal publication describes the relationship as follows:

> Generally the relationship of employer and employee exists when the person for whom services are performed has the right to control and direct the individual who performs the services, not only as to the result to be accomplished by the work but also as to the details and means by which that result is to be accomplished. . . . In this connection, it is not necessary that the employer actually direct or control the manner in

which the services are performed; it is sufficient if he has the right to do so. The right to discharge is also an important factor indicating that the person possessing that right is an employer. Other factors characteristic of an employer, but not necessarily present in every case, are the furnishing of tools and the furnishing of a place to work to the individual who performs the services. In general, if an individual is subject to the control or direction of another merely as to the results to be accomplished by the work and not as to the means and methods for accomplishing the result, he is not an employee.

In most circumstances, a performing troupe's lawyer and accountant are not its employees; they follow an independent trade or business. Similarly, the composer, lighting designer, and costume designer for a particular performance also follow an independent trade and are probably not employees. On the other hand, the stage manager, dancers, actors, stage crew, and musicians engaged for the performance should generally be treated as employees.

Naturally, the particulars of the relationship must be considered in determining whether any of these individuals is an employee. That determination hinges on the nature of the relationship and not on the type of entity (sole proprietorship, partnership, corporation, etc.) that is paying for their services. Remaining unincorporated does not ensure that you do not have to fulfill the obligations of an employer—especially if the costume designer doubles as a dresser, or the lighting designer comes every night to call the show, or the composer is also one of the musicians.

In more innocent times, Judy Garland and Mickey Rooney could gather the kids together and put on a show in the old barn. Nobody worried about violations of fire codes, zoning regulations, or child labor laws or about the need to withhold federal and state tax payments and to provide Social Security, unemployment, workers compensation, and disability insurance coverage. Virtually all performing groups begin their activities with similarly innocent intentions.

In the real world, however, such innocence is impossible outside the movies. The performing arts universe has become the victim of a "big bang" effect or, more accurately, a "big band" effect. Years ago, swing bands with substantial budgets used to pay their musicians with "fees" as "independent contractors," thereby avoiding all the costs of employment described in the budget chapter of this book. Eventually the practice was uncovered, and various government entities conducted audits and investigations that brought down the house (of cards) on the leaders of those big bands. Bands that had incorporated to protect their leaders from personal liability also learned how ineffective that technique was in covering up attempts to cheat workers; the bands' leaders often found themselves personally liable for the unpaid taxes and insurance premiums.

So long as these investigations were confined to big-budget scams that were intended to cheat employees, they served a useful purpose. In recent years, however, state and federal authorities have extended these investigations to the activities of small performing troupes and arts centers. The result in several states has been to bankrupt some small performing groups and, in some cases, their leaders. Even personal bankruptcy, however, will not protect against some unpaid tax obligations, so for some real life Judy Garlands the pursuit continues beyond their financial graves.

This problem is currently sweeping over the performing arts field with devastating effect. And there are no tidy solutions to it. Some performing groups are surrendering to the problem by establishing full-blown payroll systems and treating everybody as employees—with the attendant costs and administrative headaches. Other groups are seeking the administrative protection of umbrella organizations that already have established payroll systems and treating the umbrella organization as the employer of everyone connected with the troupes' performances. So long as it is understood (and preferably written down) that the author, choreographer, composer, designers, etc. continue to own their artistry and are merely "licensing" that artistry to the umbrella organization for the purpose of sponsoring the rehearsals and performances, this solution works, but it is quite expensive. Indeed, there are a growing number of nonprofit umbrella organizations that have been established precisely to meet this need (e.g., Pentacle's Foundation for Independent Artists in New York City and Dance Bay Area in San Francisco).

Still other troupes are taking the dangerous, but theoretically possible, route of treating their participating artists and crew as independent contractors for income tax and Social Security withholding purposes and paying them flat fees that are then reported as fees to federal and state income tax authorities at the end of the year on Form 1099. For the purpose of state workers compensation, disability, and unemployment insurance statutes, however, those troupes treat their artists as employees and pay the premiums for those insurance policies. This solution is dicey, but provides the artists and crew with important insurance coverage. (Unemployment insurance payments to laid-off artists probably represent the greatest single source of funding for the arts in the nation.) This solution is relatively inexpensive, relatively easy to administer, helps ensure that the participating artists' copyright interests in their artistry are not lost to their "employer" as "work-for-hire" under federal copyright laws, and helps the artists establish, for various useful tax purposes, that they are indeed independent, free-standing individuals following their own trade or business. But it's tough to persuade the IRS of the fine distinctions among definitions of "employment," and a miss may well result in personal liability of the troupe's leaders for some unpaid taxes when a performer fails to file a return or for withholding and Social Security payments that should have been paid even if the performer did pay her/his taxes.

The joint venture

Finally, there are a few troupes that use the whaling ship approach to performances. They pay the bills for the performances and then split up what's left from ticket sales and other sources of income in proportions that reflect their contributions to the enterprise. In theory, they form a short-term joint venture that dissolves when the activity is complete, leaving each participant with her/his artistic contribution to the enterprise intact. In their view, there is no "employer" at all, and nobody has the right to direct or control the manner in which anybody does anything. Although embarrassingly close to an accurate description of some performing groups, this strategy is not recommended for proposal to unionized stage crews. It will also be tough to sell to officials from the various state departments of labor, who will be determined to find an employer somewhere.

Filing Requirements

The filing requirements for employers are detailed and must be made to federal, state, and often local authorities. The following description summarizes many of these requirements. Tables 1 and 2 at the end of this article summarize the requirements as well as certain further filings that apply to not-for-profit corporations.

Unemployment insurance. [See also "Government Financial Services" in this chapter.] State unemployment insurance systems protect employees who are laid off from their jobs through no fault of their own and who are "ready, willing, and able" to work. The program is usually administered by the state's department of labor, with a small annual federal tax added on. Typically, an unincorporated entity or a corporation becomes liable for this payroll-based tax when it has either paid "cash remuneration" to employees of an amount set by state law in any calendar quarter or employed a certain number of individuals for a period set by law. Once liable, the organization should register with the state's department of labor and make premium payments (usually quarterly). In New York, in 1991, for example, each employer's premium was based on its history of layoffs and claims. The premium is based on a percentage of the first $7,000 of each employee's salary, and the maximum is 5.4 percent of that first $7,000. These payments, by law, may not be deducted

Table I   One-time reports required from not-for-profit corporations.

Form	Required from
Form 1203 Application for Recognition of Exemption	All organizations seeking IRS tax-exempt status
Form SS-4 Application for Employer Identification Number (EIN)	All organizations, whether or not they have employees
New York State/NYCF-l with Attorney General as a charitable corporation	All not-for-profit registration organizations
ST-119.2 (12-86) New York State and Local Sales & Use Tax Application for an exempt organization certificate	All organizations seeking exemption from state and local sales taxes
IA 100N (12-89) Report of Not-for-Profit Organization to Determine Liability under the New York State Unemployment Insurance Law	All organizations
State of New York Registration Statement— Charitable Organization	All charitable organizations except those not intending to solicit and not actually receiving contributions in excess of $25,000 during the fiscal year (unless paid fundraisers are used)
Workers Compensation Insurance Policy	All corporations that have employees
New York State Disability Insurance	Organizations with one or more employees for 30 days in a calendar year

Date due	Submit to
As soon after formation as possible	If principal place of business is Manhattan: Internal Revenue Service EP/EO Division P.O. Box 1680, GPO Brooklyn, NY 11202
As soon after formation as possible	With a copy of Form 1023 to: Internal Revenue Service Ctr. Holtsville, NY 00501
As soon after formation as possible	NYS Dept. of Labor Registration Section Charities Bureau 120 Broadway New York, NY 10271
As soon after formation as possible	Sales-Tax-Exempt Organizations Taxpayer Assistance Bureau Dept. of Taxation & Finance W. A. Harriman Campus Albany, NY 12227-0125
As soon as possible after formation, but immediately after either $1,000 in remuneration has been paid in any quarter or 4 or more persons have been employed on at least 1 day in each of 20 weeks during the current or preceding calendar year	NYS Dept. of Labor Unemployment Ins. Division W. A. Harriman Campus Albany, NY 12240
30 days after receiving $25,000 in contributions	Charities Registration 162 Washington Ave. Albany, NY 12231
Before issuing first payroll	Annual policy may be obtained through an insurance agent such as: Marsh & McLennan, 1166 Ave. of the Americas, New York, NY 10036-2774
Before issuing first payroll	Annual policy, with payments made quarterly, semiannually, or annually. May be obtained through an insurance agent: Marsh & McLennan, 1166 Ave. of the Americas, New York, NY 10036-2774

Table 2 Periodic reports required from not-for-profit corporations.

Form	Required from
IRS W-4 Employee's Withholding Allowance Certificate	Each employee at start of employment
IRS Form 8109 Federal Tax Deposit	All employers. Preinscribed copies of Form 8109 are sent to employer after application for EIN and should accompany deposits of taxes withheld.
IRS Form 941 Employer's Quarterly Federal Return	All employers subject to income tax withholding or FICA
IRS W-2 Wage and Tax Statement	All employers
IRS W-3 Transmittal of Income and Tax Statements	All employers
IRS 1099-MISC Statement for Recipients of Misc. Income and Nonemployees Compensation	Employers of persons (nonemployees) who receive $600 or more in fees, rent, or $10 or more in royalties.
IRS 1096 Annual Summary and Transmittal Form of U.S. Information Returns	All employers
WRS-21 New York State Wage Reporting System	All corporations that have employees that reside or are employed in New York State
New York State Form IT-2101 or IT-2103-(PNS)*: Semimonthly returns	Employers withholding more than $7,500 but less than $35,000 in either semiannual period
Monthly returns	Employers withholding more than $800 but less than $7,500 in either semiannual period
New York State Form IT-2103 Annual Reconciliation Return for IT-2102s (Send copy 1 of IRS W-2s with form.)	

Date due	Submit to
Before each employee's first paycheck	Retained by employer, except those W-4s that claim exempt status or show 10 or more withholding allowances. Copies of those forms should be sent to the IRS each quarter with Form 941.
Monthly, by the 15th day of the following month if undeposited taxes are less than $3,000. If at the end of any period undeposited taxes exceed $3,000, deposits must be made within 3 banking days. (Deposits can be made less frequently if the amount is less than $500.)	A qualified depository for Federal taxes. Make check or money order payable to that depository.
Within 1 month after end of quarter, i.e., 4/30, 7/31, 10/31, and 1/31	IRS office for your area
January 31	Each employee
Must send copy A of all W-2s with W-S by February 28.	IRS office for your area
January 31	Same "nonemployees"
IRS copies of 1099-MISC, with 1096, by February	IRS office for your area
Reports due 1 month after close of the quarter, i.e., 4/30, 7/31, 10/31, and 1/31. (No fees are required.)	NYS Dept. of Taxation and Finance WRS Report Processing Unit W. A. Harriman Campus Albany, NY 12227
Twice monthly, within 3 banking days after the 15th day and last day of the month (except return and payment for tax withheld for second December period, due 1/31).	NYC Income Tax Bureau Processing Unit P.O. Box 1970 Albany, NY 12201
Monthly, by the 15th of the following month (except return and payment for tax withheld during December, due 1/31).	
Must send copy 1 of IRS W-2s with IT-2103 by February 28th.	NYS Income Tax Withholding Tax Unit W. A. Harriman Campus Albany, NY 12227

(Table 2 continued)

Form	Required from
Form IA-5 NYS Dept. of Labor Unemployment, Insurance Division, Employer's report of contributions	All corporations that have become liable under New York law
IRS Form 990	All IRC Section 501 (c) (3) organizations after they have received $25,000 in contribu- tions in 1 year, filed annually thereafter
NYS/NYCF-2A, or IRS 990 and Schedule A with certification. Annual Report of Charitable Organization to Attorney General, State of New York	All not-for-profit organizations instead of NYS/NYCF-2A may send IRS 990 and Schedule A with a formal certification that they are "true, correct, and complete" (model of certification is included with instructions to NYCF-2A
Form 497 New York State Annual Financial Report Charitable Organization*	All organizations that solicit or receive contributions in excess of $25,000 annually or pay anyone for fund-raising functions. All organizations registered with the Depart- ment of State under the provisions of Article 7-A of the Executive Law, regardless of the amount of contributions solicited or received.

* Report Categories and Fees

Organizations whose contributions did not exceed $25,000 and who did not engage the services of
a professional fund-raiser or commercial co-venturer during the fiscal year completed:
—Form 497, place an "X" in the box specified on page one and sign the Certification by
Charitable Organization on page two
—No fee required
Organizations receiving $75,000 or less in "Total Revenue" (on form 990, line 12):
—Copy of completed Form 990* with attachments
—Form 497 (neither an independent public accountant's review or opinion is required)
—$10 fee required
Organizations receiving over $75,000 but not more than $150,000 in "Total Revenue" (on Form 990,
line 12):
—Copy of completed form 990* with attachments

from the individual employee's salary. The payments to the qualified laid-off
employee are based on the individual's average weekly earnings during the
previous year or during a designated "high quarter" of the year, depending on
the state. In some states (including New York), nonprofit organizations may
elect a "benefits reimbursement" procedure that frees them from paying the
premium but makes them liable on a dollar-for-dollar basis for all benefits

Date due	Submit to
Quarterly, by end of month following close of quarter, i.e., 1/31, 4/30, 7/31, and 10/31	NYS Unemployment Insurance P.O. Box 1589 Albany, NY 12201-1589
15th day of 5th month after close of fiscal year. (A penalty of $10/day is charged for late filing.)	Internal Revenue Center Holtsville, NY 00501
6 months after close of taxable year. Filing fee of $25 to $1,500 required, depending on corporation's net worth (fair market value of assets less liabilities).	Charities Bureau NYS Dept. of Labor 120 Broadway New York, NY 10271
15th day of 5th month after close of organization's fiscal year (same as IRS). An extension of up to 180 days may be requested in writing to the NYS secretary of state prior to the date the report is due. Extension may be requested on company letterhead or by submitting a copy of IRS Form 2758 ("Application for Extension of Time to File").	Charities Registration 162 Washington Ave. Albany, NY 12231

—Form 497 (independent public accountant's review required; independent public accountant's opinion not required, but may be furnished in place of a review)
    —$10 fee required
Organizations receiving over $150,000 in "Total Revenue" (on Form 990, line 12)
    —Copy of completed Form 990* with attachments, including Schedule A
    —Form 497 (independent public accountant's opinion is required)
    —Noted to financial statements
    —$25 fee required
Organizations wishing to submit combined financial statements should contact the office of charities registration at the above address prior to initially doing so. A fee of $25 plus $10 for each organization included is required; total fee shall not exceed $500.
Forms submitted to the Internal Revenue Service should be filed with the IRS Center for the region in which the organization's principal place of business is located. Address for New York organizations is: Internal Revenue Service Center, Holtsville, NY 00501

paid to laid-off employees that are charged to the nonprofit's account. This benefits reimbursement election is generally not sensible for performing arts groups since the benefits paid out to laid-off employees usually far exceed the premiums that would be due under the regular system. For further information, both employees and employers should request appropriate pamphlets from their state department of labor. [See the Appendix.]

Workers compensation insurance and disability insurance. Workers compensation insurance provides medical and other benefits to those employees who cannot work because of job-related injuries, while disability insurance provides benefits to employees who cannot work because of non-job-related injuries or illness. Both forms of insurance are required of most employers, and, with the exception of a small portion of disability, the premiums cannot by law be deducted from an employee's earnings. They are expenses that must be borne by the employer. Premiums for workers compensation are usually paid annually either to a state-run insurance entity or to a private insurer. They are based on an estimate of the organization's yearly payroll, the number of people covered, and the type of work they do. Disability payments are made on a quarterly, semiannual, or annual basis, depending on the insurance carrier.

Withholding of income and Social Security taxes. By law, employers are required to withhold certain federal, state, and local taxes from their employees' paychecks. The amount withheld is determined by referring to published tax charts and is dependent on the employee's filing status and number of exemptions. (This information is obtained from the employee on her/his W-4 form.) These monies must be paid over to the federal, state, and local taxing authorities. Failure to do so is serious since this money actually belongs to the employee. It is deposited with the government, but it can be reclaimed by the employee at the end of the year if her/his actual taxable income (after all deductions are calculated) falls below the estimated taxable income that was represented by the amounts withheld. In addition to these "withholdings," employers (including nonprofit organizations) must pay over a separate amount for each employee into the federal Social Security fund. This employer's contribution is roughly equal to the amount that was withheld from the employee's salary for Social Security (FICA) taxes. The failure to turn over withheld funds to the government when they are due will result in interest and penalty payments that can eventually dwarf the basic amounts that are not paid in.

Unemployment Insurance
Ivan Sygoda

In certain times and in certain states, unemployment insurance has been the single most important funding source for performing artists. People used to joke that the lines at the Upper West Side and Greenwich Village unemployment offices in New York City could sometimes be mistaken for audition line-ups, there were so many dancers and actors waiting to sign for their weekly checks.

Somewhere along the line, probably near the beginning of the eighties, after the demise of the original Dance Touring Program, which kept some dance troupes reasonably active, many dance artists lost their grip on this resource. A number of factors were involved. Arts organizations were so strapped for funds that the payroll-based taxes/fringe benefits line item became a burden. [See "Budgeting" in chapter 3.] Performers, equally strapped for funds, appreciated getting all that was coming to them on the spot, packaged as a fee, instead of coping with the various deductions and withholding taxes. To the degree that this arrangement suited both employer and employee, it became the norm, especially for experimental artists and those working on a project or pickup basis. This artistic activity was sort of underground as far as the mainstream world was concerned, and most of the time nobody noticed. Once in a while, usually because a performer who had worked on a fee basis mistakenly reported it as salary when applying for unemployment, the auditors would descend and wreak a little havoc. Thanks to the efforts of pro bono lawyers with a passion for the performing arts, the damage was sustainable, and people went about their business.

Of late, at least in New York, one detects a new vigilance on the part of Department of Labor officials and auditors. In a word, they intend to apply the letter of the law to performing arts groups, and the letter of the law says that if someone works under your control, she/he is your employee and you are her/his employer. [See "The Structure of Your Operations" in chapter 3.] Similar rumblings have been heard in California, the other state with a large performing arts industry.

As arts budgets grow, so does the cost of compliance with these regulations. And so does the cost (back payments, interest, penalties) of getting caught with your pants down, to put it bluntly. You can reason all you want that your artistic colleagues are indeed equal collaborators and not slaves who serve at your beck and call. You're absolutely right, but your protests are useless unless the law is changed. You're a ninety-nine-pound choreographer, and the Department of Labor is the proverbial five-hundred-pound gorilla. We suggest that you educate yourself about local regulations, learn how unemployment and the other government financial services work and what expenses are involved, resolve to factor these into your plans and budgets, and see if you can't convince yourself that the protections offered by these programs indeed constitute a valuable service to you and to the people with whom you work.

Unemployment insurance is part of a three-pronged system that also includes workers compensation and disability insurance. Workers compensation insures you against being unable to work at your job(s) because of a job-related injury or illness. Dancers and aerialists will immediately perceive the potential benefits. Disability insures you against being unable to work because of a non-job-related injury. The applicability of this to AIDS is still a work-in-progress. Unemployment insurance pays you a certain amount each week in taxable benefits if you are "laid off," perhaps because the company you perform with has no work for a while. The formula for calculating the weekly rate for which a worker is eligible, the cap or maximum weekly payment, and the number of weeks one can collect unemployment vary from state to state and with prevailing economic conditions.

From the point of view of the employee, the existence of these protection programs is a function of salaried employment. It doesn't matter if what is involved is one steady job, a patchwork of part-time jobs, or a succession of gigs. It doesn't matter if some are in the arts and some are not (except that the unemployment office can insist that you seek and accept any sort of work your record shows you are capable of doing).

Unlike welfare (see below), unemployment insurance is an insurance policy, not charity. As the *New York State Handbook for Employers* states:

> New York State's Unemployment Insurance Program is financed by employers through payroll taxes. It is exactly what the name implies—insurance—and when unemployment strikes, benefits are paid for in advance by a tax on industry—and paid only to job seekers who are unemployed through no fault of their own and who are ready, willing, and able to work.

Note that it is the employer who pays the premium on the policy. It is illegal in New York for an employer to deduct any part of the premium from the employee's salary (although a small portion of the disability premium may be deducted).

It is an administrative problem that neither the employer nor the employee can pick and choose among these and other legally mandated programs such as Social Security. Until the laws are changed, which is rather unlikely, for all intents and purposes it's all or nothing at all. An employer may prefer to pay the worker a fee, or even to pay her/him "off the books," to avoid the paperwork and expense entailed by compliance. An employee may well prefer not to have withholding taxes and Social Security payments deducted. To paraphrase an immortal couplet:

> Yours is not to reason why,
> But to live, pay taxes, die.

Employer and employee alike should understand the system so that both can deal with it efficiently and with as much flexibility as the law allows. Also, remember that, in cases where the work is being accomplished under the aegis of a not-for-profit corporation, the artistic director is an employee of the corporation just like everyone else and consequently eligible for the same benefits.

Contact your local unemployment insurance office for details as they pertain to your state. You will find it in the telephone book under "State Department of Labor."

Food Stamps and Welfare
Mindy N. Levine

Food Stamps

Administered locally by city and county governments, this federal program provides individuals with stamps that can be used to purchase food. The amount of stamps to which an applicant is entitled is determined by a formula based on the applicant's net income and assets. If one is eligible, one receives an identification card. It can be taken to a local bank or check cashing outlet to obtain stamps. Applicants need not be disabled, blind, or even unemployed to qualify for food stamps. The basis for establishing eligibility and determining allotment of stamps is strictly economic. It is much more likely that artists will qualify for food stamp assistance than for any of the other relief programs. A pamphlet explaining food stamps can be obtained from local offices of the Food Stamp Program. For information and referrals, contact your local office.

Welfare and Supplemental Security Income (SSI)

Welfare (public assistance) programs are funded through local, state, and federal taxes. In New York City, for example, the New York State Department of Social Services administers those programs that are most likely to be of help to impoverished performing artists, including Aid to Families with Dependent Children (FADC) and Home Relief. If you qualify, you can receive money, food stamps, Medicaid, and a variety of counseling and support services. Eligibility and assistance amounts are based on need, which is determined following an analysis of information provided by the applicant and, occasionally, an independent investigation or mandatory medical examination. Substantial efforts are currently under way to limit abuses in these programs, and prosecutions are ongoing.

Pamphlets that describe these programs are available at local welfare offices, listed in your telephone book under "Social Services Department, Income Maintenance Centers."

Supplemental Security Income (SSI) is a federal relief program for the aged, blind, or disabled. It is administered by the U.S. Social Security Administration, although it is funded out of general taxes rather than Social Security contributions. More information about SSI can be obtained at any local office of the Social Security Administration (dial 800/772-1213 for the central office).

Taxes and Record Keeping
Meyer Braiterman

Government services are funded through local, state, and federal taxes, which almost all individuals are required to pay. The requirements of the tax system necessitate that you keep careful track of all money you receive, so that it can be reported as income on your tax return, and all money you spend, so you can deduct business-related expenses and thus lessen your tax obligation. While the tax system may seem to impose burdensome requirements on the way you operate your affairs, it in fact encourages you to develop record-keeping habits that are absolutely essential for the rational management of your financial life. If you do not know how much money is coming in and how much is going out, you will never be able to determine logically if you can really afford to buy a season subscription to the New York City Ballet or register for an intensive five-week workshop. Also, your personal tax returns provide an important record of your business affairs should you later decide to form a company and develop more sophisticated budgeting and accounting procedures. [See "Budgeting" in chapter 3.]

The easiest way to keep track of money coming in is to deposit all money you receive into a bank account and record its source in your checkbook. Note that, for most self-employed people, a separate bank account is not warranted as many items (rent, phone, utilities, travel, etc.) have a combination of personal and business allocations. For undeposited funds, keep a ledger or a journal or record them in your appointment calendar. Artists sometimes receive cash payments "off the books" and do not report this income in order to reduce their tax burden. The IRS may not catch up with you, but the practice is illegal. Also, getting paid off the books means that you forgo such benefits as unemployment insurance, Social Security, workers compensation, and disability, to which you are legally entitled as an employee.

To keep track of money going out, pay as many expenses as possible by check. However, save all bills and receipts because IRS auditors will accept only canceled checks as proof of payment of a bill. (One exception is doctor's bills.) Keep an accurate journal or diary of all daily expenditures. Many artists assume that they have no deductible expenses, but a subscription to *Dance Magazine,* transportation to and from rehearsals, and a postrehearsal meal with the choreographer at which you discuss the work could all be business expenses that you can deduct.

For artists unfamiliar with record keeping and tax preparation, an essential handbook is *The Artist's Tax Guide and Financial Planner,* available through Volunteer Lawyers for the Arts. [See the Appendix for ordering information.]

Retirement Plans
Meyer Braiterman

Social Security is a federal "insurance" program administered by the Social Security Administration (SSA) of the U.S. Department of Health and Human Resources. All employees are covered by it. Under this program, some of the premium is withheld out of each employee's salary, and the rest is paid separately by the employer. Independent self-employed or free-lance artists pay the premium annually when they file their tax returns. The Social Security program has many components (e.g., survivors and disability benefits), and the SSA administers a number of independently funded programs (e.g., Medicare and Supplemental Security Income). The heart of the system, however, is its retirement plan. This is the basic retirement plan for nine out of ten of the country's workers. To trigger minimum retirement benefits, you must have been covered by (i.e., paid premiums into) the system for ten years (actually forty "quarters") of your working life. The years need not have been consecutive or have been achieved with a single employer or in one type of self-employed work. Your retirement benefit rate will depend on your overall contributions and the number of years you were covered. For an estimate of what your benefits will be, call 800/772-1213 to obtain the "Request for Earnings and Benefit Estimate Statement." You will also receive a list of each year's Social Security earnings as well as the summary benefits available. This list may not be correct if an employer did not report your payments or kept the money; now is the time to get this corrected. There are clearly written pamphlets on Social Security available at any office of the Social Security Administration.

Many employees are covered by additional plans through their jobs or by plans they set up for themselves. The virtues of such plans are that they encourage regular saving for retirement and they make it possible to defer the payment of taxes on the money put away until retirement.

The best-known personal retirement program is the IRA (individual retirement account—or annuity). If you or your spouse is an active participant in any other pension or retirement plan, you may contribute up to $2,000 a year ($2,250 if a joint plan) of your combined earned income only if the earnings are below $25,000 if single or $40,000 if you file as married. A lesser contribution can be made for singles with incomes under $35,000 and marrieds with incomes up to $50,000. Of course, if you do not participate in any other plan, you may make the full allowable contribution of $2,000, $2,250 if a joint plan.

A regular tax-deferred account is being touted, allowing contributions to be made with taxable income as "non-deductible IRA contributions." If you put the money into an annuity, even though it is not an IRA, it will be tax deferred but will not be subject to cumbersome IRA laws. There is no limit on such contributions.

If you are self-employed, you may prefer to use an HR-10 Plan, also known as a Keogh. There are many ways to set this up, and the limits of contributions are much higher than an IRA. You can have a Keogh even if you participate in another plan (but you can't have an IRA if you have a Keogh, based on the limits indicated above). Some simple plans allow contributions of 15 percent of your self-employed income, while others (i.e., defined-benefit plans, which can be costly) can allow as much as 60 percent or more of self-employed income. Before setting up a Keogh, be sure to review it with a knowledgeable professional so you will understand any hidden costs, such as annual filing.

Those who are employed by a nonprofit corporation can elect to use a TSA (tax sheltered annuity—or account) that IRS Code 403(b) allows. (A warning: Accountants tend to confuse this with 401[k], which is a similar but very different retirement and savings plan.) If your employer cooperates, you can set aside from 16.666 percent to 20 percent of your pay in this plan. Your employer enters into a "salary reduction agreement" with you, reduces your pay by however much you designate (within legal limits), and contributes that exact amount into the plan for your account. This has many advantages over an IRA in addition to the higher contribution limit (an absolute of $9,000 a year in 1991). One big advantage is that you can borrow your own money out of the plan for very little interest if you need it before age 59½. You do have to pay the loan off within five years (thirty, if used to mortgage your own home). Although the law allows loans, most instruments for TSAs do not. Shop among annuities and then be careful of the conditions for loans stated in the contract.

Warnings here about all retirement plans: Look for the cost of the instrument(s) (where you put the money—which bank, insurance company, or brokerage firm) you are using to be sure your savings aren't eaten up by fees. Some fees are taken off the amount when it is contributed, some are taken out annually, and others are taken only if you take money out of the plan at later dates. Also, any withdrawal before age 59½ from any tax-deductible retirement plan or tax-deferred annuity will incur an IRS penalty of 10 percent. (There are various exceptions with each plan.) Before age 70½ you must start withdrawals based on your life expectancy.

Whatever you do, be sure to review your plans with an accountant or other financial adviser who knows the law. Some do not.

Although a single year's earnings may warrant the tax deduction gained by using a retirement plan, if you may need the money later, it is not a good idea to tie it up long term. It can be costly to get the money out prematurely.

Legal Issues
Timothy J. DeBaets

[*This chapter was written with dance companies in mind, yet many points apply in general to all performing arts companies.*—Eds.]

In theory, *any* agreement between two people can be considered a legal issue. In practice, people enter into agreements all the time without recourse to the judicial system or without feeling the need to seek legal advice. But in the dance world there are many complex issues—from contracts, to copyright, to cable television—that make having the ready assistance of a lawyer indispensable. No better advice on legal issues can be given to a choreographer or dance company manager than to find free ("pro bono") or low-cost legal assistance.

Finding a lawyer is not easy. Perhaps there is a trustworthy lawyer in your family or among your friends or fans who can help. Or you can take specific arts-related problems to Volunteer Lawyers for the Arts (VLA). VLA has staff lawyers who can provide preliminary help and orientation, and, for impoverished artists, VLA can provide volunteer lawyers to give legal advice on a problem-by-problem basis. VLA also runs the Art Law Line to answer artists' questions over the telephone. If there is no VLA-type organization where you live, start your search for legal counsel by contacting other volunteer service organizations, or contact VLA. [See the Appendix for VLA and other legal resources.]

Unfortunately, VLA-type organizations are forbidden to help individuals who can "afford" to pay for a lawyer. So if you are making a decent living, you may not qualify for volunteer legal help. Still, the economy of the dance world is such that most dancers, choreographers, and dance companies qualify easily for VLA help.

Once you find a lawyer, try to get her/him excited about your work and involved in ongoing projects. Sometimes single-problem representations can grow into longer-term advisory relationships. Remember, lawyers who accept volunteer projects from VLA or directly from artists would not do so if they did not have a special interest in the arts. Make the most of this. Consider putting the lawyer on the board of directors or board of advisers to your organization. Mention the lawyer's name as your legal adviser in programs. Invite the lawyer to company parties and rehearsals.

Then educate yourself. The best clients, the ones who get the best service and loyalty, are those who learn to think for themselves. You won't be able to do without the lawyers, but you can learn to spot legal problems before they become crises, and you can learn to use your legal adviser efficiently. Here follows a first step in that education process.

Contracts

Two basic facts about contracts should be remembered at all times: (1) Virtually any agreement between two parties can be interpreted as a contract; and (2) contracts need not be in writing to be considered legally binding. For example, a choreographer says she will pay her dancers one hundred dollars per week for five weeks of rehearsal prior to a concert. The dancers rehearse, but the choreographer refuses to pay. She has "breached" (broken) her contract with the dancers. The fact that the contract was oral does not make it less binding on her. A binding agreement has been broken, and contract law provides that the dancers are entitled to sue. If they win, they'll get a "judgment" for the amount owed to them by the choreographer.

Of course, the oral agreement contained in the example should have been in writing. The existence of an oral contract is harder to prove than a written one. Moreover, the "terms" of an oral contract are easier to dispute since memories differ. At a minimum, the "handshake" oral agreement on which you usually rely should be clear and should cover the most important issues (money, duties, etc.). But virtually everything of significance should be put in writing and signed by both (or all) sides whenever possible. Ideally, there should be signed written agreements between the dancers and the company, between the company and the landlord who is renting out the theater or rehearsal space, and between the company and any composer, designer, or other artist whose artistry is being used in the performance. The existence of a contract does not ensure that everything will go according to plan. It does help clarify rights and responsibilities and avoid misunderstandings.

Now a third basic fact: Everything is negotiable. Whether you develop your own standard written form contract for bookings and other "must-be-written" situations or just wait until you are presented with a form contract by the other party, virtually all the terms are negotiable. Never be intimidated by somebody else's written contract when it is presented to you. Until you accept it (usually by signing), it's just a proposal. Read it in its entirety, especially the small print. Give it to your lawyer, ask questions about everything, and if there is something you do not like, see if it can be changed. Take the contract seriously. Usually parties enter into agreements and accomplish their business without need to refer to the contract. But, when disputes arise, everyone will be unhappy and will then examine the contract very carefully.

Representative contract

What follows is a discussion of a contract between a dance company and a sponsoring theater. Its aim is to demystify the language and general format of contracts and to provide specific information about a type of contract commonly encountered in the dance world. It suggests issues and potential problems that you should consider when you negotiate a contract—everything from compensation to technical considerations. An actual contract used by a New York City–based company can be found at the end of this article. In reviewing the attached contract, remember that it is meant simply as a model to be referred to while reading this discussion and must be modified to reflect the particulars of your situation.

In negotiating a contract, it is a good idea to consult with fellow choreographers and dancers who are experienced with contracts and may be able to warn you about issues you should consider and problems you can avoid. (Numbers in parentheses refer to sections of the sample contract.)

Preamble. (1) Most contracts begin by reciting the names and addresses of the contracting parties. (This format need not be adhered to. Many people prefer using the letter format [a sample of which can also be found at the end of this article]: One party writes to another outlining the terms of the agreement, and the latter countersigns the final page of the letter.) The preamble in a formal contract usually states what the parties plan to do together. In this case, the "Company" will present its works and the "Sponsor" will be responsible for all details related to the production. At this point you may wish to recite the dates of performance, although that could be stated later in a separate paragraph. You may even want to agree here about the times of performances and the times when the performing space will be available for rehearsal.

Compensation. (2) Next come the hard facts of compensation. While information about precise amounts cannot be provided here, certain warnings about fee structure can be made. If you are to receive not a flat fee but rather a percentage of ticket sales, be sure to state with specificity the deductions (if any) that the sponsor may make before paying your fee.

If you are to receive a flat fee, ask to be paid in installments, with one substantial payment (perhaps as much as 50 percent) to be received prior to the engagement, before your departure if you must travel (so you can cover expenses). It is reasonable to demand that the remaining payment then be made before the last performance or during the intermission of the last performance. This way you have not delivered all your services and have some leverage should the sponsor renege on her/his commitments.

Also consider whether payments will be made to the company in the event that the performance(s) cannot be completed as scheduled. There should be some provision for at least minimal payment to the company even if the producing entity is unable to present your company for justified reasons. If you have received an advance, stipulate that you are entitled to keep it.

Credits. (3, 4) The contract should specify the requisite credits for the company and its dancers. There is a saying among entertainment lawyers that you can foul up the money due your client and she/he may stay with you. But if you foul up the artistic credits, you will definitely lose the client. List in the contract all credits you want acknowledged, announcements to the public, and any additional information that should be in the program. You may even wish to be so specific as to designate the type size for credits of artistic principals.

Promotion. (3, 4, 5) Responsibilities for promotion should be spelled out. If the sponsor is to provide publicity, do you want approval of all releases?

Technical considerations. (5) Every technical need and condition must be stated explicitly in the contract, with nothing assumed or taken for granted. The technical requirements for production must be understood and complied with if the company is to render its full artistry. For instance, it would seem obvious that a good dance floor should be provided, but state this requirement explicitly; otherwise, you unexpectedly may end up dancing on concrete. It is helpful to prepare a rider—a separate piece of paper that spells out your technical needs. It should be attached to the contract and made part of it by specific reference. Even if your technical requirements are minimal and can be stated in the body of the contract, as the company grows and changes, the technical requirements will enlarge and become varied. Including a technical rider provides an efficient method of modifying a form contract to suit the particular situation. Other details, such as transportation, should be spelled out. If your company is going to be in residence, the contract should describe the housing facilities required.

Warranties and representations. (6) The form agreement appended to this article contains a list of warranties and representations to be made by the sponsor. These are assurances that the sponsor has the authority to enter into the agreement and will carry out its terms as stated. These should be included in your own form agreement. The wording may seem legalistic and obvious, but these clauses are of importance in the unfortunate event that a dispute arises.

Indemnity clause. (7) The sponsor should indemnify your company against any lawsuits that might arise from the performances. An indemnity clause requires the sponsor to pay any claim, judgment, settlement, or costs—including attorneys' fees—arising from a threatened or actual lawsuit. If an audience member is injured by falling in the aisle, it is probably the fault of the theater owner or the sponsor, not the dance company. However, an enterprising lawyer representing the injured party may well sue your company as well as the theater owner and sponsor. The indemnity clause should require the producer to assume your defense in case of a lawsuit and pay all costs and attorneys' fees. This is important because if it's difficult to find an attorney to represent you free of charge for something as attractive as a cable television project, it will be virtually impossible to find free legal assistance for a personal injury lawsuit.

Reservation of rights. (8) It makes good sense to prohibit the sponsor from taping or filming your work in any fashion, except for archival purposes, and then only if you are given a copy of the work. By all means, do not give the sponsor any right to sell your work to any media, whether it be cable, public, or even a local television station, without negotiating a separate agreement. Describing such an agreement is beyond the realm of this article. Suffice it to say that it is essential to maintain control over audiovisual records of your work. If you've granted rights to someone else, you may be prevented from negotiating a deal at a later date. Should a cable or public television company be interested in your work, they will probably insist on exclusive rights to its use.

Copyright and permission. (9) You should guarantee to the sponsor that you have obtained appropriate permissions to perform the works that you intend to present. If the only choreography you plan to use is that of an artistic principal of your company, there is little problem. However, if you intend to present someone else's choreography, you must obtain permission to use that choreography. Copyright law (see below) provides that a choreographer has the right to control all public performances of her/his work. For instance, you may consider yourself capable of presenting the definitive version of Michel Fokine's *The Dying Swan,* superior to that done by Pavlova and the many illustrious dancers who have performed that work. However, you are committing a copyright violation if you do not obtain permission from the Fokine estate, no matter how superior your artistic achievement. The same laws apply concerning the use of music (see below).

Indemnifying the sponsor with respect to copyright matters within your control is appropriate. Just remember that the cost of a lawsuit can be substantial and the embarrassment keen if you have not obtained the needed rights. Presentation of copyrighted work without permission of the copyright owners can jeopardize state or federal funding since these grants often include the requirements that such permissions be obtained.

Exclusivity. (10) Agreeing not to perform for thirty to ninety days before and after the engagement within a fifty-mile radius is a reasonable concession to the sponsor. Sponsors sometimes seek to present advertising within such a radius for another engagement. Be careful not to violate such limitations when planning a tour. This is the type of provision in form agreements that is often overlooked and inadvertently violated. Such a breach of contract may give the sponsor just cause, or an excuse, to cancel the engagement.

Complimentary tickets. (11) Surprisingly, the question of complimentary tickets is often a sore point between dancers and sponsors. Negotiate this, and put it in the contract, but realize that you will probably have to pay for house seats. Dance events rarely generate a pot of gold. Some sponsors may be stingy with comps. Try to make provisions so that the company and its dancers can have agents, friends, well-wishers, and representatives from arts organizations in attendance.

Excuse from performance. (12) It is a good idea to release yourself from the contract should you be unable to present the concert (as a result of injury to the leading dancer, for example). Also consider negotiating to retain some portion of the fee in the event of a legitimate cancellation to cover up-front expenses.

You must keep in mind that the contract is not illusory. You cannot fail to show up just because it does not suit your purposes. There must be a serious reason for failing to perform, or you may have breached the contract and be liable for damages suffered by the sponsor. Admittedly, there is usually so little money involved in dance events that there are very few lawsuits. In one case, however, the Nederlander organization did sue Natalia Makarova and her husband for $800,000 concerning the New York City presentation of "Makarova and Company" in 1980. The suit alleged that she had represented herself as being capable of dancing a full schedule with her company, although she knew that certain physical injuries would limit the number of her performances.

Arbitration. (14) If the sponsor will agree, you should add a provision that the contract will be governed according to the laws of the state in which your company is located. In addition, require that all disputes be submitted to arbitration according to the rules of the American Arbitration Association at its office nearest your headquarters. Arbitration is fair to the sponsor, although the sponsor may insist that the law of her/his state apply.

Emendations. (19) Finally, it is standard to add a clause requiring that the contract cannot be amended or revised except by a written agreement signed by both parties.

Signatures. The end of the contract will contain signature lines for the parties. If the letter format is used, the writer will provide the recipient of the letter with a copy to be countersigned, usually on the last page under the phrase "Agreed to and Accepted by," and returned to the writer. Thus, although the parties will not have signed the same document, each will have in its possession a copy signed by the other party and enforceable against it.

Copyright

The Copyright Act

Copyright is a matter of law, but it is also one of respect. If you are a choreographer creating your own work, you want people to respect your work and not use it without your permission. Nor do you want it used in an adulterated fashion. Conversely, if you are going to use someone else's choreography, you should obtain the permission of that choreographer.

Copyright has been the subject of great confusion in the dance world. This is because choreography was omitted from copyright protection until passage of the new Copyright Act, which took effect January 1, 1978. Before that, for all practical purposes it was not possible to copyright choreography. Under the current law, copyright comes into existence when the work is first created. However, the work cannot receive copyright registration until it is embodied in a "tangible expression," that is, a copy, so as to give some permanence to the existence of the work. This, unfortunately, does not coincide with the way in which choreography is usually created, that is, set on dancers who perform from memory without notation or score or audiovisual record to assist them.

Creating a record. The problem then is one of recording. Although copyright technically exists as soon as the work is created, for practical purposes without a record you cannot prevent others from using the work. Remember that if you wish to sue someone because they have "stolen" your work, you must be able to prove this in a court of law. Is one piece of choreography like another? No judge or jury will ever be able to tell unless they have some evidence by which to make a comparison. You should reduce your choreography to notation, using either your own idiosyncratic notation or the services of a notator; it is becoming increasingly popular to make a videotape record of choreography. Any of these ways may be used to register your work with the copyright office at the Library of Congress, Washington, DC. There is no requirement that you register your work, but until you register, you cannot sue for copyright infringement.

Once you have reduced your work to notation or videotape, the work should be affixed with the appropriate copyright notation. This consists of the word "copyright," the abbreviation "copr.," or the universal copyright symbol, which is the small letter "c" in a circle "©." This could be followed by the name of the copyright holder and the year in which the work was first created. A typical copyright notice may read, "© Donna Dancer 1991." It is recommended that the phrase "All Rights Reserved" be added to this notice. Since the United States has recently become a signatory to the Berne Convention, it is not necessary to use a copyright notation. All recorded copies of the work (videotape, film, notation) should contain the appropriate copyright notice.

Rights. The Copyright Act protects five important rights: (1) the right to perform the work publicly; (2) the right to reproduce or make a copy of the work; (3) the right to prepare a derivative work, such as an adaptation of the choreography in a motion picture; (4) the right to sell or otherwise distribute copies of the work to the public; and (5) the right to display a copy of the work to the public by means such as a film or some other medium.

These rights are self-explanatory, except, perhaps that concerning derivative works. It allows the choreographer to control adaptations of her/his own work. Conversely, it prevents choreographers from making derivative works from copyrighted material. This is particularly relevant to the dance world since dance works are commonly based on creative works in other fields. If the underlying creative work is protected by copyright, the choreographer will be committing an "infringement" if permission of the copyright holder is not obtained. Thus, a choreographic version of *Bonfire of the Vanities* requires the permission of the book's author, Tom Wolfe. No such permission is needed if the underlying creative work is in the "public domain"—not subject to copyright law because of age or special circumstances. Thus, Shakespeare's *Othello* may be used without permission as the basis for a dance work. Be careful to check, or you may find that you have created a work you cannot perform.

Duration. Under the old Copyright Act, it was necessary to renew one's copyright periodically. This requirement has been changed. Copyright now exists for the life of the copyright creator plus fifty years.

Publication. A key aspect of the copyright law is the matter of *publication.* This term is defined as the distribution of copies of the work to the public by sale or other transfer of ownership or by rental, lease, or lending. Offering to do the same may also constitute publication. Live performance of a choreographic work is not considered publication and does not put it in the public domain (though many artists include the copyright notation in their concert programs). It is thus not necessary, and indeed not possible, to register choreography with the Copyright Office if it is not recorded and is presented only in live performances. Without recording, there is no "tangible expression" to which statutory copyright protection can attach. This also permits a work in progress, such as a Broadway show in previews, to be presented and changed without endangering subsequent copyright protection if the work is recorded.

Registration. Copyright registration requires that you deposit a copy of the work with the Copyright Office. If the work has been published, the Copyright Office wants two copies of the "entire copyrightable contents." The Copyright Office will keep the copies in its archives. Remember that the version deposited must be used in the event you find it necessary to sue for copyright infringement. If you have both written notation and film or video, the written notation must be deposited. Written copies are preferred for their longevity. Also, it is generally held that they give better detail in case of infringement.

A special document, Form PA, must be submitted to the Copyright Office for registration of a choreographic work. If the instructions for completing this nine-section form do not answer all your questions, do not hesitate to call the Copyright Office. Volunteer Lawyers for the Arts can also be of assistance. On

Agreement— Part I

This agreement is made between _____ (hereinafter called "Sponsor"), whose address and phone number are _____, and Dance, Inc. (hereinafter called "Company"), whose address and phone number are _____.

Whereas, the Sponsor wishes to engage the Company, the details of which are set forth below, therefore, in consideration of the mutual promises and agreements of the parties hereto, it is agreed as follows:

1. The Company agrees to present: _____.

2. The Sponsor agrees to pay the Company, not later than the day of the first public appearance by the Company, without any deduction or offset whatsoever, the sum of _____ Dollars ($_____), in cash or by check payable to Dance, Inc. The time of payment is of the essence of this agreement. The Sponsor's failure for any reason whatsoever to comply with any covenant or obligation herein contained, including, without limitation, the failure to make timely payment, shall be cause for the Company, at its sole option, to refuse to perform and/or to suspend its engagement, free of any claim by or obligation to the Sponsor, and without prejudice to any monies theretofore paid pursuant to the terms thereof.

3. The Company will supply and furnish for said engagement the services of such dancers, technicians, managerial personnel, costumes, and properties as the Artistic Director, Donna Dancer, in her sole discretion, shall designate, to include choice of program and choreography. The Company will provide as well the following:

   a) The exact program copy for all performances, which shall not be altered or edited without the express consent of the Company. All programs shall state the following:
   1) Cast and program subject to change.
   2) The taking of photographs or use of any sound recording device during performance is strictly forbidden.
   3) Dance, Inc., is an activity of _____, a nonprofit, tax-exempt organization. For further information, contact:
   Administrator
   Dance, Inc.
   (Street)
   (City, State, Zip)
   (Phone)
   b) Publicity materials, to include presskit and publicity photographs, which the Sponsor shall use to publicize the engagement and for which the Sponsor shall pay only postage or other shipping costs.

4. Each engagement shall be billed and advertised under the title: Dance, Inc.

5. The Sponsor shall provide at its own expense the following:
   a) A theater, or other performing space, that is acceptable to the Company in its sole judgement, and such other adequate spaces as residency activities shall require, each of which shall be well heated or cooled as is necessary, clean, in good order, cleared of other equipment prior to the arrival of the Company, licensed, with suitable dressing rooms, and having an acceptable surface for dancing. An acceptable surface does not include floors that are concrete, cement, or any like hard surface, nor wood or linoleum over concrete, cement, or the like. (See Technical Requirements also.)
   b) Front-of-the-house staff including box office personnel, ticket takers, doorkeepers, ushers, janitors, porters, wardrobe managers, and such other personnel as may be necessary for the efficient operation of all residency activities. (See Technical Requirements also.)
   c) All publicity pertaining to residency activities (the materials listed in 3 a) & b) excepted) which the Sponsor agrees to give the widest possible local distribution (or national/international, if applicable), and all local mailing, posting, or other distribution services.
   d) All tickets, programs, posters, and other promotional material necessary for residency activities, including the cost of printing.
   e) Any local transportation that residency activities require, including transportation of the company's personnel and equipment to and from the nearest transportation center of arrival and departure for the engagement, e.g., airport, railway station, bus station.
   f) Essential suitable and appropriate technical equipment to operate the theater or performing space, sufficient time reserved in the theater or performing space, and adequately skilled technical and stage personnel for taking in and out, setting up, hanging, rehearsing, striking, and working all residency activities. (See Technical Requirements also.)

6. The Sponsor warrants and represents:
   a) That it has the full power and authority to enter into this agreement and fully perform in accordance with the terms thereof;
   b) That it has obtained legal permission to use the theater, or other performing space on the dates of the engagement, permitting presentation of the Company, and has obtained liability insurance from an approved company to cover said engagement;
   c) That fulfillment of its obligations hereunder will not violate any applicable law, statute, regulation, or ordinance, or any applicable regulations or requirement of any union having jurisdiction;
   d) That the Company shall have the exclusive use and right to perform in the theater or performing space during the engagement;
   e) That it has obtained approval and cooperation of all unions having jurisdiction over the facility where the engagement will take place, with respect to all services, equipment, and materials to be supplied by the Company and Sponsor;
   f) That only upon the Company's receipt of the Sponsor's full description of the theater or performance space can the Company's program be determined and can the Company's full technical requirements be provided to the Sponsor;

Sample Contract: Company and Sponsor

Note: This is a sample agreement, provided here to introduce you to the language and format of contracts. Your own contract must be reflective of your personal needs and situation and should be drawn up in consultation with a lawyer.

g) That the Company will be notified of any changes in the facilities described and/or any unforeseen technical difficulties in presenting the Company;

h) That the Company's needs will be adequately and fully communicated to each and every responsible member of the Sponsor's staff;

i) That the specific arrangements regarding facilities, attendance, announcements, and so forth, pertaining to the Company's open rehearsals and additional services will be made with the same care as described above regarding arrangements for performances. Said arrangements shall be mutually agreed upon by the Sponsor and the Company;

j) That it will not discriminate against any performer concerning compensation for a performance on the basis of race, color, or creed. The Sponsor agrees that the Company shall not be required to appear in any theater or place of performance where discrimination is practiced against any patron as to admissions or seating arrangements.

7. The Sponsor agrees to indemnify the Company against all claims of all personal injuries or property damage arising in any manner in connection with the Company's engagement except to the extent that any such claim may be occasioned by the negligent acts of the Company or its employees or agents.

8. The Sponsor agrees that it shall prevent any broadcasting, photographing, or reproducing of any engagement activities by radio, television, or any other device unless the express prior consent of the Company has been obtained. The Sponsor also agrees that there shall be no joint or assisting artists appearing in connection with any residency activity and no conflicting or interfering activities permitted unless the prior written consent of the Company has been obtained.

9. The Company agrees to defend and indemnify the Sponsor against all claims, demands, and expenses that the Sponsor may incur by reason of infringement or violation of any copyright or other artistic proprietary right by any of its activities.

10. The Company agrees that it will not accept any other engagement for a period of thirty (30) days prior to or following and within a radius of fifty (50) miles from the location of the engagement described above without the express prior consent of the Sponsor.

11. The Sponsor agrees to provide the Company with _____ complimentary tickets for each performance. The Sponsor shall be the only party authorized to issue such complimentary tickets.

12. Neither the Company nor the Sponsor shall be liable for failure to appear, present, or perform in the event that such failure is caused by the physical disability of the Company, or acts or regulations of public authorities, labor difficulties, civil tumult, strike, epidemic, interruption or delay of transportation service, blackout, intergalactic implosion, fire, accident,

act of God, force majeure, or any other cause beyond the control of the Company or Sponsor. The Company will use its best efforts to provide replacements of the same substantial artistic quality should any member of the Company be unable to perform as scheduled and shall be the sole judge of the artistic quality of such replacements.

13. This agreement shall be interpreted in accordance with and in all respects governed by the laws of the State of New York.

14. The parties agree to submit all disputes to arbitration at a hearing to be held before a single arbitrator in New York City pursuant to the then-applicable rules of the American Arbitration Association. The decision of the arbitrator shall be final and binding. The parties hereby consent to the jurisdiction of all state and federal courts in the State of New York for purposes of enforcement of the decision of the arbitrator.

15. The Company shall at all times retain sole artistic control over all residency activities and performances.

16. The Sponsor agrees to obtain and pay a) for any and all local work permits, union fees, taxes, and other local licenses that may be required for the Company to carry out the residency activities covered by this agreement, and b) for any musicians or other personnel not necessary for residency activities that are imposed by local unions or other organizations.

17. If at any time the Company or its representative determines in its sole discretion that the financial credit of the Sponsor has been impaired, then the Company or its representative may cancel the agreement unless the fee is paid on demand in advance of the residency.

18. Neither the Sponsor nor the Company shall have any right to assign or transfer this contract without the written consent of the other party.

19. This agreement incorporates all agreements between the parties, and there shall be no variation or modifications of it except in writing signed by the parties to this agreement.

20. Funding for this residency is available at _____% of the Company fee from the National Endowment for the Arts.

Dance, Inc.

By _____

Date_____

(Sponsor)_____

By_____

Date_____

Note: Both Part I and Technical Requirements/Part II constitute the entire Agreement.

Dear _____:

This is to memorialize our agreement with respect to music that I have composed for your dance work entitled _____. The music was composed during the latter part of _____ and will be first performed by you during your tour of the United States in _____.

You have agreed to pay me, and I have agreed to accept, a flat license fee of _____ for the commission of this work. You will pay _____ upon execution of this agreement, and the remaining amount within _____. We have agreed that there shall be no royalty fee for the first _____ performances. Thereafter, you will pay me the sum of _____ per performance.

I agree that within four months from _____, if requested by you, I will provide modifications of the music to suit the purpose of your dance. Thereafter, any further modification would require additional financial consideration to be negotiated between us in good faith.

Your license to use my music shall be confined to live dance performances only in connection with _____ (title of work). Your use of the music for such purposes shall be exclusive to you for ___ years from _____. The music shall continue to be exclusive to you so long as during any one calendar year either you or the company for whom you have set this dance work performs it and thus use my music for a total of at least ___ performances. In the event that fewer than ___ performances take place, use of the music for live dance performances shall be nonexclusive to you, but you may otherwise continue use of it perpetually in accordance with the terms of this agreement.

You, of course, have the right to transfer your choreography to another company or performer of your choice. I hereby agree that you may grant the right to perform my music with your choreography for live performances only, so long as I receive from you _____ percent (___) of whatever license fee you receive from the company. In addition, the company will be required to pay me _____ per performance. You agree that you will notify me of any pending transfer to another company so that I may contact the company to insure that my per-performance royalty is paid directly to me. I understand that the ___ (percentage of your license fee which I am to receive will be received directly from you.

It is understood that you will separately copyright the choreography and I will separately copyright the music. You hereby grant me permission to copyright the music under the name _____. I will otherwise retain all rights in said music and will have no rights in your choreography. The licensing of any other right in my music, such as for use in any and all media, is expressly reserved by me and cannot be licensed or negotiated on my behalf. This also applies to any company or individual to whom you may transfer the choreography along with my music. You hereby agree to notify such transferee that it has no right to any use of my music other than for live dance performances. Any such other use of my music shall be subject to further negotiation.

I hereby give you the right to tape or film ___ including use of my music strictly for your own archival purposes, such as for rehearsals, or for purposes of promoting performances of the work.

You agree to provide me with an accounting describing all uses of my music, to be accompanied by a check for any sums due, on a quarterly basis. The first such statement shall be due _____, and every quarter thereafter.

You hereby agree to note in any program or other announcement to accompany live performance of the dance work that the music is subject to my copyright. You will also require any company or individual to whom you may transfer this work to include such copyright notice in any program or other announcement of a performance issued by such company or individual.

Payment of any fees to me, and any notices made pursuant to this agreement, shall be sent to the following address: _____. A copy of any such notice shall be sent to my attorney, _____. Any notice that I shall give you will be sent to the above-mentioned address.

You agree that you, any company you are associated with, and any company or individual to whom you might transfer this dance work will give me appropriate credit as the composer of the music in all playbills or other announcements of the dance to accompany any performance of it. I will supply you with appropriate biographical information for inclusion in such programs. I hereby give you permission to use my name in conjunction with the dance work as composer of the music in any other performance announcement, such as newspaper advertisements. In the event that my music is given in live performance apart from your dance work, or recorded in any form, I agree that you shall receive credit in any program or other announcement or on the container of the audio device as having commissioned the music.

In the event that there is dispute between the two of us, we both hereby agree to submit any such dispute to arbitration pursuant to the rules of the American Arbitration Association at a hearing to be held in New York City before a single arbitrator. The laws of the State of New York shall govern this agreement. Any award issued by the arbitrator shall be final and binding upon all parties. We both hereby submit to the jurisdiction of all state and federal courts in New York for the purpose of enforcing the award.

If you are in agreement with the above, would you please sign the enclosed copy of this letter and return it to me.

Very truly yours,

_____

Agreed to and Accepted by:

_____

Sample Contract: Composer and Choreographer

Note: This is a sample agreement, provided here to introduce you to the language and format of contracts. Your own contract must be reflective of your personal needs and situation and should be drawn up in consultation with a lawyer.

submission of the form and a fee and acceptance by the Copyright Office, the choreographer will receive a certificate containing the registration number of the work and a date indicating when registration became effective. To request forms, contact the Copyright Office. [See the Appendix.]

Music

The same principle of respect that applies to choreography applies to musical scores used as accompaniment to a work. Music is fully protectable under the copyright law, just as is choreography. You simply cannot use music (assuming that it is not in the public domain) without the permission of the composer. That such abuse is widespread is no defense, nor is ignorance of law.

A written agreement with the composer is essential. (See the copy of the letter of agreement appended to this article prepared on behalf of a composer.) The agreement should carefully describe your use of the music. Most likely, you will be limited to live stage performances requiring a royalty fee determined on either a per-performance or a sliding-scale basis. The agreement should also spell out whether you as a choreographer have the right to set your choreography on another company without first consulting the composer. All too frequently choreographers unfamiliar with copyright law license their choreography to a third party without consulting the composer, without written permission, and even without paying compensation to the composer. Again, this is as much a matter of respect as of law.

If your work is a collaboration with a composer, you must make an arrangement with her/him if you are going to use the music for any reason other than those expressly stated in your original written agreement. This is particularly relevant should you be approached by a cable television company or other media entity wishing to tape or film your work. Presumably, the producer will be sophisticated enough to require you to obtain the music rights. Please contact the composer immediately.

The question of music, of course, is not a problem if the music is in the public domain. Tchaikovsky's *Nutcracker Suite* is in the public domain, and you may do your own version of the *Nutcracker* as long as you do not infringe existing copyrighted versions set to that music. However, do not make unwarranted assumptions about what is or is not in the public domain. Be careful, and check with the Library of Congress to determine if there is any copyright protection for the music.

You can use recorded music for performances, assuming you have the rights to use the music, without having to secure permission of the record producer. Record producers were not entitled to copyright "sound recording" until the copyright law was amended in 1972. The copyright symbol for sound recordings is the letter "p" in a circle "℗." Record producers now have copyright protection that prevents the re-recording of their records. In addition, sound recordings are protected by the state record piracy law. However, Congress did not grant the right to control public performances of the record to owners of sound recording copyrights. Thus, if you have the right to use the underlying music, you may use the record without permission.

The foregoing highlights two legal areas—contracts and copyrights—that dancers frequently encounter. There are, of course, others. Legal issues can and often do become exceedingly complex. Develop a sense of when a matter seems "legal," and consult someone with expertise in the field.

Budgeting
Ivan Sygoda

Financial Planning: The Individual

As self-supporting individuals, we all know the experience of having to make choices and decisions based on monetary restrictions. Almost all of us know what it feels like to open our checkbook at the end of the month and realize we can't both pay the rent and buy that new CD player. Making such choices is a form of budgeting. Simply put, financial planning is an individual's attempt to live within her/his means.

To be a good money manager, you must be in control of your money. There are a number of bad fiscal habits that are distressingly easy to acquire, such as not balancing your checkbook as you go along. The ubiquity of automated teller machines makes it even easier to lose track of one's balance. If you misplace or forget about one withdrawal receipt, you can be driving blind for the rest of the month. Artists living on the edge are often tempted to wriggle out of a financial squeeze by writing checks against deposits that haven't quite cleared yet. This game can become both embarrassing and expensive. The same landlord who is so slow to fix the sink runs a four-minute mile to deposit your check. Credit cards are another velvet trap. Our society makes it very easy to buy now and pay later—at 18 percent interest.

On the other hand, advance planning and accurate record keeping are essential habits to acquire.

If you spend a few moments at the beginning of every month estimating your anticipated expenses and income, then there is a better chance that money will be there when you need it. If you develop and maintain a system for tracking your expenses, you will acquire a better sense of what those expenses add up to and have a much easier time of it on April 15.

Financial Planning: The Organization

Financial planning for an artistic entity or organization, whether it be a solo artist, an unincorporated association, or a not-for-profit tax-exempt corporation, involves the same principles and concepts as it does for an individual. The entity will not survive if it doesn't operate within its means. If theater rental has to be paid, costumes designed and executed, and ads placed in the newspaper, then you must know in advance whether contributions and projected box office receipts will also cover the performers' fees. It can ruin the thrill of a rave review to discover the morning after you close that there are surprise bills yet to be paid but no more money in the till. Banks don't accept reviews as collateral.

Maintaining control of your organization's finances is integral to maintaining control of your artistic destiny. Poor planning can derail your enterprise. If you don't husband the available resources, your work will suffer because it won't look as good as it can. If you ignore financial realities, your organization could have to close its doors.

All the above applies whether or not you are your own bookkeeper or accountant. The artist is captain of the ship and bears ultimate responsibility for its course and for the fate of the mission. Money management is taking place all the while, whether or not the artist is paying attention. If your artistic goals are precious to you—and one assumes that they are—then you must also take charge of the financial planning without which those goals are unlikely to be met.

Budget: Definition and Purpose

Given that a budget is necessary to active financial planning, a complete understanding of its ramifications is essential. The dictionary defines the term in the following ways: an *estimate,* often itemized, of expected income and expenses; a *plan of operations* based on such an estimate; an *itemized allotment* of funds for a given period.

In practice, a budget is really a process that moves through the three definitions, as the diagram given in this article illustrates. It begins with an estimate, an educated guess about what a particular project might cost or how large a grant you might receive from a funding agency or donor. From this estimate of anticipated expenses and/or income, a plan of operations is drafted. Artistic decisions are made and plans for the project formulated with a realistic idea of the monies available and the costs involved. Often, several plans will be drafted to allow for variations in the initial estimates. Once the plan and any alternative plans have been formulated, the budget provides a method by which the actual receiving and spending of monies can take place, an itemized allotment of funds over a given period of time. As time passes and more information becomes available, the estimates are revised. The project plans are altered, if necessary, to reflect the revisions, and allotments of money are changed accordingly. The process is cyclical, ongoing, and constantly subject to revision.

Beyond dictionary definitions, a metaphor may help elucidate the process. A budget is like an architect's blueprint: It is a convenient model of the architect's vision, an informational tool to help the architect's collaborators realize the vision, and a plan for actually doing it.

Just as a blueprint reduces a three-dimensional structure to a piece of paper, a budget simplifies an intricate and dynamic entity to numbers and notations. Examination of a budget should tell you how many performers a company plans to employ, the length of the engagement, the relative allocation of funds to administrative and artistic expenses, whether your government grant will arrive before rehearsals begin, and if you will have sufficient funds to pay all the payroll taxes and fringe benefits required by law.

No architect would bulldoze land, pour concrete, order steel struts, or hire workers without a blueprint in hand. So, too, you should not rent a theater, invest in costumes, hire performers, or commission designers without first budgeting expenses and income. Furthermore, once developed, a budget is not meant just to be filed away. While you don't actually have to clutch your budget to your bosom, you should refer to it periodically, refining it so that it accurately reflects the actual income and expenses in your day-to-day operations.

Two more points, and then we'll scrutinize the details.

1. Unless you're a one-person band, your budget is a tool to get your collaborators (your designers, your techies, your board, your staff, even your funders) on your wavelength and to keep them there.

2. Don't forget that it's *your* budget, a useful and revealing way of translating *your* work into a form that will further it. And if it's not *your* budget, incarnating your hopes and dreams, then it's going to be someone else's budget attempting to do the same. You'd better trust that person a lot.

How to Prepare a Budget

Once you have some understanding of what a budget is and the purpose it serves, it's fairly easy to begin to prepare one. Budgets are divided into two major categories: (1) income (or receipts), monies coming into your account; and (2) expenses (or disbursements), monies going out of your account. The same final results (or bottom line) can be obtained by either increasing income, decreasing expenses, or doing both in some combination. There is no rule that states that the budgeting process must begin with either the income or the expense side of the project. Your choice should be guided by such factors as which items in your particular project appear fixed and which appear variable or dependent on another item. For instance, the cost of airline tickets, hotel rooms, printing of flyers, newspaper ads, and space rental are less flexible than how much you pay your lighting designer or yourself. There will be many gray areas since the terms *fixed* and *variable* are relative, not absolute. Indeed, the very purpose of a budget is to indicate which expenses or income might be altered if the project must take place under changed circumstances.

Don't get sidetracked by the mechanics of actually sitting down to begin the process. All you need is a sharp pencil and a piece of paper. And an eraser. You might find it convenient to get a pad of ledger paper at the office supply store. These are available in different sizes and with different numbers of columns, useful for separating out the different phases of a project or the different projects that constitute your year. Ledger paper also has faint rules running down each column so that hundreds-digits are under hundreds-digits and so forth. Invest in a calculator, preferably a printing one.

Now that computers have become cheaper, many artists have access to them. If this is your case, then you should consider learning how to use a spreadsheet program to do your budgeting. The beauty of a computer spreadsheet program is that it automatically recalculates subtotals and grand totals whenever you change a number anywhere.

Be it lead or silicon, the procedure is the same. Let's assume that you choose to begin with the income side of the project, which often makes sense because the income side of the project tends to be fixed relative to the expense side. You must first clarify what types of monies you will be receiving. Income is usually broken down into two subdivisions, which are defined by their source: earned income and contributed income. *Earned income* generally refers to money paid to you for a specific service or commodity. Examples include performance and residency fees, box office income, commissions and royalties, class or workshop fees, proceeds from concession sales, and space or equipment you rent to others. *Contributed income,* also called "unearned income" (even though you can sweat just as hard for it), refers to money received as gifts from individuals or as grants from federal, state, city, private foundation, or corporate sources.

Suppose now that you have been offered a fee to perform and teach at a university in the Midwest. Can you accomplish the project for the amount of money proffered? You must turn to the expense side and estimate what the related costs will be.

Expenses are usually more confusing to deal with than income because they are so numerous and variable. It's a good idea to classify expenses into broad categories based on the nature of the expense. Although each artistic entity is unique, several basic categories are fairly universal, and a listing of them follows. If you anticipate receiving a government grant of any sort for your project, it would be a good idea to preview that government agency's budget forms and final report forms since sooner or later you'll have to categorize things this way. Most important, however, is that the budget categories you use make sense to you and are appropriate for your own enterprise. Following is a rundown of the expense categories.

Personnel. Included within this category are all those who work for you and whose time or activities you control (see the "Special Note" about employees vs. independent contractors at the end of "Outside Professional Services"). It is often useful to subdivide this category by the nature of the work performed, that is, administrative salaries, artistic salaries, technical salaries, etc. Let circumstances dictate whether further subdivisions make sense, such as core company members versus guest artists versus spear carriers or other supernumeraries. In these as in any other budget areas where subtotals are the result of multiplying a certain rate by an amount of time, make sure that you clearly note the rate and time used for the calculation. It won't be easy for you or a colleague to work on budget revisions a month later when all there is to work with is "Crew: $1,000."

Payroll-based taxes and/or fringe benefits. These are a combination of state programs, such as unemployment insurance, workers compensation, and disability insurance, and federal Social Security (FICA). The employer contribution for each is calculated as a percentage of the gross salaries you pay. Together, these add up to about 25 percent, higher in states like New York. If you offer other fringe benefits such as Blue Cross/Blue Shield or major medical, these must also be factored in. Since the cost is expressed as a percentage, it is easy to allocate these items among various projects. For instance, if your budget assumes that 30 percent of salaries are for rehearsals and 70 percent for performing, then 30 percent of the fringe is for rehearsal and 70 percent for performing.

Outside professional services. These are the fees you pay to individuals and firms who are not employees of you or your organization but who work as free-lance independent contractors, performing a particular, finite task for an agreed-on fee. They do not work for you on an ongoing basis, although they may work for you more than once. In the examples that follow, those toward the top of the list are more likely to be considered independent contractors by state employment offices than are those toward the end:

—fees to actual incorporated businesses (where the person performing the service for you is someone else's salaried employee, not yours);

—fees to lawyers, accountants, and other professionals who are in business for themselves and who are not arts professionals; fees to graphic, set, and costume designers and videographers, photographers, and sound-recording engineers (all professionals who have a fair investment of their own in equipment and supplies and who work for many different artists, sometimes at the same time);

—musicians and other performers who are coming in just to perform some preexisting set piece live (as when you rehearse to a recorded piece of music all month and the pianist first appears at dress rehearsal to play the Chopin prelude;

—commissions to composers and choreographers and fees to free-lance theater directors (but be aware that working side by side and week after week with the composer who is making a score that suits your particular needs is an activity that looks mighty like employment to labor department auditors);

—fees to free-lance technical directors and stage managers (this gets especially dicey if they also go out on tour with you); fees to your technical crew and to temporary or part-time office clerical helpers.

(This is the end of this incomplete list: Proceed with caution.)

Special note: personnel employees versus independent contractors; salaries versus fees. Because the arts are so labor intensive, it is usual to begin with personnel expenses, the preponderant part of most arts budgets. We immediately fall into a thicket. What is at issue is the distinction between employees and independent contractors. The issue and the distinction have become thorny of late and need to be discussed.

In a nutshell, employees are supposed to be salaried, which means that, in addition to the taxes withheld from their paychecks, contributions must be made to various insurance programs. This is in distinction to the *fees* paid to so-called independent contractors. In the latter case, it is the contractee who does whatever needs to be done regarding taxes and insurance. [See the discussion in "The Structure of Your Operations."] For many historical and moral reasons, government has assumed an activist stance regarding the conditions under which people work (they shouldn't be exploited) and how and when they pay their taxes (they shouldn't not pay them). Since the Great Depression, a host of federal and state social, insurance, and welfare programs have attached themselves to wages—unemployment insurance, workers compensation, disability, Social Security. Government insists that working people have access to these programs and that this access be paid for in the ways laid down by law. What this amounts to is that the employer (you!) must pay amounts that are calculated as percentages of employee wages. The rates vary from state to state and from industry to industry. In New York State, for example, and in the performing arts, the employer's expenses for these items amount to about 28 percent. In other words, if you budget $100 to pay a performer to appear in your performance, you must also budget an additional $28.00 for payroll-based taxes and fringe benefits.

Because work in the arts can be so irregular, and because so much happens on a project basis, artists tell themselves that the rules of employment apply only to "regular, ongoing" working relationships. No such thing. The rhythm of the work has nothing to do with it. Nor does the amount of money involved. If you tell somebody where and when to rehearse and where and when to perform, even if it's just a week of rehearsal and a single performance, then the government says that somebody is your employee. Even if you pay that person only $50.00, the government still wants its cut.

If you don't do it right and you get caught, the results can be disastrous. Your state department of labor can audit your books and decide you owe not only for the current year but also for previous years—back payments, interest, and penalties—and for everybody. If you don't have the dough, they can go after your board members.

Since unemployment insurance is the province of the states, you must check the regulations and practices that pertain where you live and work and then keep abreast of any changes. Sources of information include the relevant offices in your state bureaucracy, your local Volunteer Lawyers for the Arts, and staff members of one of the larger cultural organizations in your vicinity.

Budget conservatively in this area. Assume that all the performers and technicians who work under your direction must be salaried and that you must budget for payroll-based taxes and fringe benefits accordingly. The situation is a bit more ambiguous as regards commissions and design fees for composers, choreographers, lighting, set, and costume designers, and such. They may well insist on receiving fees from you because (1) it is more convenient for them and (2) it is what they are used to. Just remember, however, if you run afoul of these regulations, it is you who will have to ante up, not them. At the very least, have proper contracts with each, and demand invoices on letterhead so as to emphasize the degree to which they are in business for themselves and are being paid to accomplish a task. In agreeing to a fee for their services, you and they may well base it on the number of weeks you estimate it will take them to do their job, but don't package it that way.

Space, facility, and real-estate rental. Studio rental, theater rents, and office rents all belong in this category.

Travel and transportation. Two major expense items fall into this category. They are the actual cost of travel and the amounts spent for food and lodging while away from home. Travel these days usually means airfare, and you should budget conservatively. As for lodging and food, companies handle these items in different ways. Some pay touring personnel a per diem (Latin for "per day"), which is meant to cover normal costs of lodging and meals. Each person is then free to make her/his own choices about singles and doubles and whether to survive on squirrel food and pocket the difference. Other companies arrange and pay for housing directly and then pay a food per diem. You should be aware that the Internal Revenue Service issues regulations concerning the per diem reimbursements that a wage earner can treat as nontaxable. In theory, employers are supposed to treat per diem amounts above these limits as taxable income and do the paperwork accordingly. Local transportation should also be included in this category.

Advertising, promotion, and public relations. This includes the cost of newspaper, radio, and television ads, printing and postage for promotional mailings, and any expenses related to booking your work.

Remaining expenses. An expense not covered by the above categories must by definition be a remaining expense. This category may be subdivided into "Remaining Production Expenses" and "Remaining Operating/Overhead Expenses." If any such category is a large and consistent one for you, you can always elevate it to its own division in your budget. Items that don't seem to fit anywhere else can always be grouped under a "Miscellaneous" category. Finally, it would be prudent to include a "Contingency" category, often calculated as a percentage of total costs, to cover emergencies, unforeseen price increases, and so forth.

One of the greatest potential pitfalls in financial planning is the omission of expenses from your budget. Given the infinite variety of working artists, no book such as this one can include every possible item. If you're relatively new at this, here are three suggestions: (1) Close your eyes and mentally walk yourself through your whole project. Who does what and where and in what order? What resources and materials do they need to do it? This is the process that will make you remember, say, costume cleaning or musical instrument rental. Then walk through your project backward, so to speak, identifying each goal you have in mind and reviewing the operations entailed in achieving that goal. Oops, ticket printing. (2) Go through your own checkbook and tax returns. If you're like many artists, your personal life and your professional life are intertwined, and you have paid for many items yourself that should be included in your project budget. (3) Examine the sample budget provided and any other budgets you can get your hands on. You don't have to reinvent the wheel. By outlining each and every conceivable cost that might be applicable to your artistic endeavor, your chances of omitting any substantial expenses are greatly reduced. We've already given some tips on estimating what certain expenses might amount to. The key word is "ask." Ask your travel agent. Call Amtrak. Most of the hotel chains have 800 numbers. Somebody wants to sell you everything you will need to buy; she/he would be glad to tell you its estimated price. Use the phone book, that most underutilized of arts resources. Ask your fellow artists.

Be conservative in your estimates. Inflation alone might add 5 percent or more to your budget between now and a year from now. The airfare promotion you counted on might end. Indeed, the airline might go out of business. The cheap hotel you scoped out might be unavailable because no one told you it was homecoming weekend. We could lose the nonprofit postal subsidy, which would wreak havoc on your promotion budget. The place where you rehearse for $10.00 an hour might be sold to a developer.

When you've added up projected income and expenses, the next step is to compare them. The difference between your total estimated costs and the total anticipated income will give you an educated idea as to whether your project is financially feasible. It would be fun if income proved greater than expenses. Most likely, income will have to be increased and/or expenses lowered for the project to work. This is precisely the most creative and most difficult part of the budgeting process because this is where you exercise artistic control.

Balance Sheet
Dance, Inc.
June 30, 19XX

Assets:
Cash (in bank) $100
Total Assets $100

Liabilities & Fund Balance:
Accounts Payable $2,000
Loans Payable $500
Total Liabilities $2,500
Fund Balance ....($2,400)

Total Liabilities and Fund Balance $100

Dealing with the gap between income and expenses is the beginning of your plan of operations. Start with the income side again since it is preferable to increase revenue than to cut expenses. How much more money do you need? Can earned income be increased by renegotiating the fee for your services? It never hurts to try, but expect the people and organizations who buy your services to be as financially strapped as you are. Are there any untapped sources of contributed income? Is this the time to press your board or friends for contributions? Will the proverbial bake sale bring in enough revenue to justify the people costs in time and energy? You have to husband your human capital just as you have to control your financial capital. Perhaps your experience teaching movement or voice to the physically challenged could result in workshop fees around the performance that is the nucleus of your endeavor. If you can't raise contributed income, you can always try earning it. Any work you can find during a week when your performers are already on salary is a godsend, providing it doesn't interfere with your preparations.

When you have exhausted every possibility of increasing earned and contributed income and there is still a budget gap, you will have no choice but to reevaluate project costs. It's easiest to reexamine fixed costs first, although there will be different definitions of which costs are fixed and which are variable and to what degree. You may be able to do little about airfares, but you might have the option of taking a train or bus instead. Research will almost always unearth cheaper lodgings. Will you pay yourself? More worrisome are the choices that impinge on your artistry. Which is more important: the extra week of rehearsal or the costumes you had in mind? Live music or new scenery? These are the choices that only you can or should make. Stay centered on the work and its artistic values. This will help orient your choices.

When this process gets discouraging, which it will, try to remember the old adage about two planks and a passion. If your work has good bones, it will stand proud, if slightly naked. We all know artists who have gotten mired in too many sets, costumes, collaborators, concepts, and other finery. It's amazing what audiences don't miss if they like what they see and hear.

Using the Budget as a Plan of Operations

When you have finished the process of translating your artistic goals and ambitions into budget categories and real numbers, you are ready to begin your plan of operations, which is the process of implementing your goals in the light of fiscal realities. Up until now, we have been looking at your budget as a whole. Implementation, however, takes place over time, and so you must deal with cash flow, the timeline according to which income will become available to you and according to which bills must be paid. Receiving $10,000

Company Budget, July 1, 19XX—June 30, 19XX.

Last Year Total Organization	Income	Total Organization
	A. EARNED INCOME	
	Performance & Residency Fees	10,900
	Box Office Receipts	2,000
	Commissions/Royalties	2,000
	Concessions/Sales/Parking	
	Publications/Rentals-Gross	
	Tuition/Class & Workshop Fees	15,000
	Gross from Fund-Raising Events	
	OTHER EARNED INCOME	
	(itemize)	
	Total Earned Income	**29,900**
	UNEARNED INCOME	
	B. NONGOVERNMENT	
	Corporate/Business Contributions	
	Foundation Grants	
	Memberships	
	Private/Individual Contributions	2,050
	Total Nongovernment	**2,050**
	C. GOVERNMENT	
	Federal/NEA	
	State/NYSCA	5,000
	County	
	Municipal	
	Total Government	**5,000**
	D. OTHER UNEARNED INCOME	
	Interest and Other Unearned	
	Income (itemize)	
	Total Unearned Income	**7,050**
	(Add B)	
	Total Cash Income	**36,950**
	(Add A, B, C, & D)	

Expenses

	E. PERSONNEL	
	Administrative	8,000
	Artistic	
	Choreographer/Art. Dir.	1,800
	Dancers (4-6)	7,000

Breakdown of Total Organization Operation Revenue for Year 19XX

General Overhead	Local Production	Tour #1	Tour #2	Other Company Projects
		6,600	4,300	
	2,000			
	2,000			
15,000				
15,000	**4,000**	**6,600**	**4,300**	
	2,050			
0	**2,050**	**0**	**0**	
	5,000			
0	**5,000**	**0**	**0**	
	7,050	**0**	**0**	
15,000	**11,050**	**6,600**	**4,300**	
6,000	1,000	500	500	
	1,000	400	400	
0	4,500	1,000	1,500	

(Company Budget, July 1, 19XX—June 30, 19XX., continued)

Last Year Total Organization	Expenses	Total Organization
	Composer/Musical Dir.	
	Musicians	
	Other Artistic Per.	
	Technical	
	Lighting Designer	900
	Stage Manager	
	Total Personnel	**17,600**
	Payroll-Based Taxes (fringe)	
	(@ 20%-25% of total personnel)	3,700
	Personnel & Fringe	**21,300**
	F. OUTSIDE PROFESSIONAL SERVICES	
	Administrative	
	Management Fees	
	Booking Commissions	300
	Artistic	
	Choreographer	
	Composer	
	Dancers	
	Musicians	
	Technical	
	Lighting Designer	
	Stage Mgr. & Crew	
	Other Fees	
	Costume Designer	250
	Set Designer	
	Photo & Video	350
	Sound Recording Services	150
	Graphic Design	250
	Legal & Accounting Fees	750
	Total OPS	**2,050**
	G. SPACE/FACILITY/REAL ESTATE	
	Rehearsal Studio	1,200
	Theater/Performance Space	1,000
	Office Rent	
	Total Space	**2,200**
	H. TRAVEL & TRANSPORTATION	
	Travel-Touring	2,750
	Food & Lodging/Per Diem	500
	Local Transportation	200
	Total Travel & Transportation	**3,450**
	I. ADVERTISING/PROMOTION/PR	
	Posters/Flyers	500
	Ads	500

Breakdown of Total Organization Operation Expenses for Year 19XX

General Overhead	Local Production	Tour #1	Tour #2	Other Company Projects
0	300	250	250	
6,000	6,800	2,150	2,650	
1,200	1,500	450	450	
7,200	8,300	2,600	3,200	
		300		
	250			
	350			
	150			
	250			
750	1,000	300	0	
700	200	150	150	
	1,000			
700	1,200	150	150	
		2,500	250	
		500		
100	100			
100	100	3,000	250	
	500			

(Company Budget, July 1, 19XX—June 30, 19XX, continued)

Last Year Total Organization	Expenses	Total Organization
	Printing/Copying	300
	Mailing/Postage	400
	General Promotion	600
	Video/Photo	300
	Total Adv. & Promo	**2,600**
	J. REMAINING OPERATING EXPENSES	
	Equipment Purchase (noncapital)	
	Equipment Rental	150
	Office Supplies	250
	Records/Tapes/Films	100
	Telephone/Telegraph	600
	Insurance	400
	Costumes/Props	650
	Production Expenses	200
	(itemize)	
	Fund-Raising Expenses	
	Miscellaneous	
	(itemize)	1,000
	Total Remaining	
(2,400)	**Operating Expenses**	**3,350**
	Total Cash Expenses	**34,950**
	Total Cash Income	**36,950**
	Surplus (or Deficit)	2,000
	Total Income - Total Expenses	
	Accumulated Surplus (or Deficit)	**(400)**

for a five-day residency may look great on paper. But consider the circumstance where the fee won't actually be paid to you until the end of the residency, to which must be added the time it will take your bank to clear the deposit. If all your credit cards are at their limit, and if your travel agency can't extend credit, how will you pay the airfare needed to get you there in the first place? The project may prove unfeasible despite a workable budget.

A budget has to make provisions for the timing of receipts and expenditures. Go through the income side of your budget again, and make note of when the different revenues will arrive. As in the residency example above, it may be necessary either to accelerate income or to postpone expenses, or to

Breakdown of Total Organization Operating Expenses for Year 19XX

General Overhead	Local Production	Tour #1	Tour #2	Other Company Projects
150	150			
250	150			
500		50	50	
	250	25	25	
900	**1,550**	**75**	**75**	
	150			
250				
	100			
500	**25**	**50**	**25**	
400				
	600	25	25	
	100	50	50	
675	250	50	25	
1,825	**1,225**	**175**	**125**	
11,475	3,375	6,300	3,800	
15,000	11,050	6,600	4,300	
3,525	(2,325)	300	500	

do a combination of both. The organization engaging you may be able to advance you some of the fee. Be aware of two things, however. Government agencies, including state and community colleges, are rarely able to do this. Also, even when it is theoretically possible, an advance is much easier to arrange at the outset, before you sign a contract, than on an emergency basis well afterward. On the other hand, it is usually not very difficult to get a check you can cash on arrival in the host community for distribution of per diems and for lodging expenses. You should be aware of your own bank's policies regarding the clearing of deposits. You may want to arrange payment by cashier's check or by wire if this will make the money available to you sooner.

Funding agencies may be able to accelerate grant payments to you, although bureaucratic procedures make this a long shot. Some arts service organizations have "bridge loan" programs [see the Appendix], but often only against state grants. You may have to seek a regular bank loan or entreat a board member to make a short-term loan, preferably free of interest.

On the expense side, your performers might prove willing to defer part of their salary for a short and meticulously defined period of time. As with any of the human beings you depend on to help you make and show your work, it would be poor policy to spring such surprises on them, even in desperation. Any such arrangement with your collaborators should be negotiated at the beginning of the process or project. Similarly, your costume or set designer will obviously need cash to purchase materials and supplies but might be willing to defer all or part of the design fee. Equipment you were planning to buy might better be rented, even if outright purchase makes better financial sense in the long term.

To stay in control of your cash-flow situation, you should divide your project into whatever time periods are relevant and then calculate income and expenses for each period. If your project involves a research phase, that might be considered one time period, even though it may be several months long. When you are in the thick of rehearsals, you will probably need a week-by-week analysis. If you will be on tour, each stop should be analyzed. For a complicated production entailing many cash outlays during performance weeks, you might go so far as to break it down day by day. Weigh the time it takes to do all this against the pain and anxiety that results from running out of money just when you need to be concentrating on your work.

When you know how much money will be coming in and how much your project will cost and have a time frame within which to work, your plan of operations is complete.

The Budget as Part of an Organization

The third part of our budget definition refers to an itemized allotment of funds for a given period of time. So far in describing the budgeting process we have been referring to a "project." An artistic entity or organization usually has more than one project during the year or even more than one project happening or in various stages of development at any given moment. The organization's total artistic activity is the sum of these projects. In addition, floating above it all are general overhead and administrative expenses. The budgeting process has provisions for translating this total picture into numbers. The key is in the phrase "allotment of funds."

You will notice that the sample budget allows for a breakdown of income and expenses for a certain time period, often defined as the entity's fiscal year. This can be any twelve-month period you define. Some artists use the calendar year as their fiscal year, which is convenient in that it coincides with most citizens' tax year. However, many cultural organizations prefer the more common July 1–June 30 fiscal year, or even September 1–August 30, which coincides with the school year and the usual performing arts "season."

The sample budget allows you to categorize income and expenses, for example, general overhead, local production, touring, and so on. Each column has been given a specific heading and is a "project" of the organization. The total of all projects is the organization's total operating budget.

This system allows you to budget several projects simultaneously and to see, at all times, how your entire organization is doing financially. It will show you areas that tend to lose money as well as those that are potential sources of revenue. Suppose, for example, that, after preparing a budget for the local performances you will produce yourself, you project a deficit of $2,500. Looking at the organization's projects and budget grid, you might also see that a cost-effective tour to a neighboring state nets a surplus of $2,500. These two activities would "net out," as they say; the tour surplus would compensate for the local performance overrun.

Perhaps you have received a National Endowment for the Arts matching grant to help defray your administrator's salary. Where will you find the non-NEA portion of the match, and how will you justify your math? One way is to allocate the administrator's time over one or more projects. You might decide, for example, that 50 percent of the time is spent on tour-related business, 25 percent on your home season and 25 percent on general company business. By allocating the administrator's salary (and fringe) in this way, you will be able to deal more effectively with identifying the match. By the way, time sheets should routinely be kept to justify such allocations of time and effort. Government funding agencies are being more meticulous than ever about the ways in which public money is spent and accounted for.

Conclusion

Through good bookkeeping ("the profession or art of keeping a systematic record of business transactions," that thing you found daunting at the beginning of this chapter but now regard with respect if not love), financial data can be organized to supply budgets with accurate and up-to-date figures on expenses and income. Ultimately, the bookkeeping system creates an organization's financial report, which in turn kicks off the budgeting process again.

Often the best place to start your estimating process for the coming season is to look at what was done the previous year. Thus, your work as a money manager is never done.

Optimally, you will find that taking active control of your budgeting process will improve your skills as a money manager and hence as the manager of your creative projects. Until our society changes its priorities and devotes more resources to the community of working artists in its midst, money will remain a concern, and your ability to handle it effectively will play a role in your survival.

A Case Study: Budgeting Applied

You are now ready to apply the concepts of budgeting and financial planning. The following example will illustrate these processes in action. Remember, it is designed as an exercise in thinking and represents only one of many possible scenarios you might encounter. As you read through it, refer to the schematic illustration of the budgeting process to help in conceptualizing the process in practice.

Assume the following: You have just been hired as the business manager for Dance Inc. You are lucky because the company just completed its most recent year on June 30th, and the financial statement for that period has already been prepared (Step V of diagram). You realize that you are not so lucky when you look at the balance sheet that precedes the sample budget and note that you have inherited a deficit; that is, at the close of the year, the company did not have enough money to pay all its bills. Some of those unpaid bills and loans from last year have to be budgeted into this year's operations. For example, Dance Inc. owed Travel Agent Inc. $2,000 for airline tickets for the June tour. Obviously, this bill should have been paid in June, before the close of the fiscal year. To maintain credit with your travel agent, the bill must be paid soon. In addition, the president of the board loaned the company $500 during its New York City season last January. This was a short-term loan to help the company with some cash-flow problems. Somehow it was never repaid. Although you don't know how it was overlooked, this too is your responsibility. Because the checking account at the close of the fiscal year had only $100 and the total of the bills and loans outstanding is $2,500, the deficit or fund balance for the Dance Inc. company on June 30th is $2,400.

You are now at the point where you move from Step V on the diagram back to Step I. The financial statement from the previous year has provided you with information that will help in beginning your job as business manager: The company must raise $2,400 to pay off old debts.

STEP I	STEP II	STEP III
Estimates	Plan of Operations	Allotment of Funds
Income and expenses are estimated and several alternative budgets are proposed.	Cash flow is analyzed and various plans to carry out the project are arrived at.	All projects of the organization are reviewed together to get the organization's total budget.

Revisions   *Revisions*   *Revisions*

Source of Information to Begin Process

STEP IV
Bookkeeping

Systematic method of recording actual income and expenses.

STEP V
Financial Statement

Full accounting of an organization's financial history.

The above diagram illustrates the concepts and principles that are involved in the budgeting process. It is important to remember that the process, never ending and cyclical in nature, is meant to generate a plan, or "blueprint" of your organization's activities.

Schematic Diagram of the Budgeting Process

How do you begin to budget the prior year's deficit into this year's operations? As mentioned earlier, there is no correct way to handle the problem. What you need to find out is what the organization's budget will be for this year. Will there be excess revenues that can be applied to the deficit, or will additional monies have to be raised?

You meet with the artistic director and discuss the two signed residency contracts for this year. These fees have already been agreed on, and though it is possible to request additional monies from a sponsor, to help cover increased airfares, for example, you realize that these sponsors are also on tight budgets and that it might not be good public relations to try to alter a previously signed agreement. Since it is always easier to begin with what is known and relatively fixed, you begin here. The first residency date is in the fall at Midwest University in Midwest, U.S.A. The agreed-on fee for the two-and-a-half-day residency that includes teaching and a single performance is $6,600. (See the sample budget.) The contract allows for fluctuations in the number of dancers, stating that the residency will be carried out by a four- to six-member company. The second contract, also in the fall, is for three performances at the nearby Suburbia Arts Center in Bedroom Community, New York.

The fee for this engagement is $4,300. Applying the principles that apply to Step I, you are now ready to sit down with pencil, paper, and calculator. Since the contracts have been signed and you have decided not to renegotiate, the amount for the two residencies is "fixed," and you therefore begin with the income side. Because the two dates are three weeks apart, it is easier to look at each as a separate tour and to budget accordingly. Discuss the different expenses that relate directly to each tour with the artistic director. Begin with those that are essential, such as the cost of travel, food, and lodging. Make some phone calls and get estimates on the different airfares, hotels, etc. Using this information, start preparing several alternate budgets for each tour to determine what is most realistic. Discuss with the artistic director the priorities of the company: Can the company perform with a smaller cast in the Midwest and save the extra airfare and dancers' fees? Is it necessary to travel with a lighting designer/stage manager, or does the university have someone who could do the job? It doesn't take a financial wizard to see that the easiest way to save money while touring is to work with as few people as is artistically acceptable. For that very reason, the company's repertoire is flexible enough to handle fluctuations in cast size.

After playing with the figures, you arrive at what you feel to be a realistic budget for the two dates. (See expense category H.) As one would expect, the Suburbia tour (Tour #2) is economically more successful given that, even with a cast of six, the tour generates excess revenues of $500. The savings, of course, are the result of not having to cover the costs of food and lodging and of not having to travel any great distances by plane or train. The Midwest tour just about breaks even by cutting expenses and using fewer dancers. You know that if these two tours went according to plan, and if they were the only activities of the company (Step III of the diagram), the company would have a financially successful fall season and would even have some funds to help pay off the prior year's debt.

There are, however, some costs that do not relate to these specific projects but are the costs of running the overall organization. Luckily these are minimal. Since the company's office is a corner in the artistic director's home, most office expenses are minimal. Rehearsal space needs are solved by having a share in a loft for a monthly rent of $100. The major general organizational expense is your salary, which you feel cannot be allocated totally to the two fall tours and local productions. Although not much, these are the general expenses of the organization and can be looked at as another "project" of Dance Inc.'s organizational budget. Over the years, the company's touring activities have fallen off; there are no longer enough excess revenues generated from touring to allocate to general overhead of the company. For this reason, the artistic director secured a teaching job at a local university last year. From last year's financial statement, you see that this provided the basic ongoing source of revenue for the company.

At this point, we could still say that if the only projects of the organization were the two fall tours and the general overhead of the company, we would be financially successful. Unfortunately, we are looking at an entire year period for this budget. (Remember, every budget covers a particular time period.) After some discussion concerning the company's spring activities, you have the final information to complete the puzzle.

The artistic director has given you the dates and place for the company's spring home season. You also learn of the possibility of a choreographic commission with a small, local company that would coincide well with the home season by giving the artistic director a chance to premiere a work outside the Big City. A fee for this commission is still under negotiation.

As business manager, you are now faced with a difficult task. How do you arrive at a proper fee to ask for the commission, and how do you prepare a budget for the self-produced home season? What makes these tasks difficult is that there is no known quantity to start with. It is always easier to fit expenses to a set income or raise revenue to meet known expenses, but when both the income and the expense sides are vague, it is difficult to know where to begin.

From your experience, you know that local productions without outside funding are notorious for losing money. On the other hand, a choreographic

commission can be a cost-effective way of raising additional company revenue. You decide to look at the projects together, because one activity is able
to generate revenues for the other, and because the artistic director will be
creating a new work for both purposes. Perhaps arbitrarily, you begin estimating food, travel, and lodging for the artistic director's stay with the company
while the work is being staged. You are ready to begin fee negotiation now,
knowing that whatever is left after paying food, travel, and lodging can be
applied to local production costs. Although the artistic director feels that the
new work merits a fee of $3,000, within the context of the situation you accept
a contract for $2,000.

By dealing with the situation in this way, you now have a place to begin the
local production budget. After travel, food, and lodging, there will be excess
revenues of $1,000 from the choreographic commission. These can be used
toward the local production project. Since the theater has already been reserved, the cost of the space rental is also known. It is now possible to estimate what box office receipts might be, given the capacity of the space. You
also know that there is currently a grant application before the Big City Arts
Council. The company has a good history of funding, and it is reasonable
(knock on wood) to anticipate some good money. By again going through the
procedure of creating several alternative budgets and ordering artistic priorities, you arrive at the most realistic budget.

The process is now complete. Examining the sample budget, you will see
that certain projects of the organization are supporting others, so that, for
this particular period, Dance Inc. shows a net of operations for the organization of $2,000. This is the amount of money you were looking for to apply to
last year's debt. Notice, though, that, as projected, there is still an unpaid loan
to an officer of $500. This time, however, it was not an oversight. You have
spoken to the board member and presented the proposed budget. You have
highlighted areas where discrepancies between actual and proposed income
and expenses can occur. Because of your responsible approach, the board
member has agreed to continue to allow the company to use the $500 at no
interest charge.

You have a working budget to begin the year's projects. You have moved
from Step V on the diagram to repeat the cycle at Step I. The estimates are in
place, and a plan of operation is now necessary (Step II on the diagram). You
begin to look at the timing of when monies are received and when bills have to
be paid. For example, the travel agent will not issue tickets for the Midwest
tour until the prior year's bill has been paid. An obvious solution is to request
a partial advance on the residency fee to cover travel costs. If that's not
possible, perhaps a company member's credit card could be used, or maybe
the board member would loan the company money again. Step I has given the

dollar information you need; Step II requires a certain amount of creative thinking to get the project under way. As mentioned earlier, a lucrative residency does no good if you can't get there to do the performance.

Assuming that you've just made it back from the Midwest, what next? Begin the bookkeeping process. This will give you an accounting of actual expenses and income for Tour #1. You were able to cut costs at the last minute: The sponsor met you at the airport, so you saved money on a taxi; the university arranged for a discount at the hotel. You might, however, also discover that you underestimated some miscellaneous expenses and the small projected surplus of $50.00 was quickly used up. Compare your actual costs with those that you had originally projected to learn where you made mistakes in estimating.

With this information, go back to Step I, and revise your estimates if necessary. Then proceed to Step II, and see if this has an effect on your plan of operations. Will you need more cash sooner, or do you now have more cash available earlier than projected? Remember that certain funds from one project can be transferred to another in Step III, but a change in one project will create a domino effect throughout the entire organization. So apply these revisions to Step II as well.

If, after each project, you repeat the process of constantly revising and updating the proposed budget as more information is acquired, then, by the year's end, you will have directed the organization toward its financial goals. Your financial house will be in order, your budget as blueprint having guided you there. You will be in control of the organization's activities, and, by maintaining financial control, you will be able to ensure control and survival of your artistic activities.

FUNDING

Federal Funding
Andrea Snyder

The National Endowment for the Arts is the primary source of support for the performing arts that comes from the federal government. The NEA's budget is appropriated by Congress for the express purpose of funding the arts. It was established in 1965 along with the National Endowment for the Humanities, taking its lead from the New York State Council on the Arts [see "State Funding" below], established in 1961. Its first program budget was a little over $2 million. As of fiscal year 1992, the NEA budget stands at $175 million.

The chair of the NEA is appointed by the president and is advised by the National Council on the Arts, which is made up of twenty-six prominent arts professionals, who are also appointed by the president. The National Council on the Arts and the chair determine the overall policies and objectives of the NEA. They determine what portion of the total NEA budget is given to each of its programs. As currently constituted, these programs include Artists in Education, Challenge, Advancement, Dance, Design Arts, Expansion Arts, NEA Fellows, Special Constituencies, Research, International, Folk Arts, Presenting and Commissioning Literature, Media Arts, Museums, Music, Opera–Musical Theater, Locals Program, States Program, Theater, and Visual Arts.

The Grant-Making Process

Decisions as to which individuals or not-for-profit organizations receive grants are made by panels of peer professionals. Each NEA discipline program has a yearly policy panel of advisers drawn from the field. This panel determines priorities and direction for the program and helps decide how the program's money is divided up among the program's grants panels—the groups of people who actually decide on applications. Grants panels in each discipline are based on reasonable divisions within the discipline. In dance, for example, there are panels for applications in choreography, companies, and services to the field, among others. Panel members are chosen for their diverse backgrounds and experience within the discipline so as to achieve as broad a representation of geographic and artistic experience as possible. The grants panels choose among the applicants those whom they feel are of greatest merit, in accordance with stated review criteria in each discipline category, and decide on the levels of funding. Their recommendations are then carried by the program staff to the National Council on the Arts for approval and, ultimately, to the chair of the NEA. The chair may choose to overrule the panels and/or the National Council.

The NEA Dance Program

By way of example, I will outline the Dance Program at the National Endowment for the Arts. Performance artists should note that, while discussion of the Dance Program will offer insight as to the workings of a specific program, most performance art is funded in the Theater or Visual Arts Programs, each of which has its own infrastructure.

The Dance Program assists all forms of professional dance and strives to be as aesthetically, culturally, and racially far-reaching in its panel makeup and application pool as possible. Grants are generally awarded in the following categories (other funding possibilities may be available. Contact the NEA Dance Program [see Directory]):

Choreographers fellowships. These fellowships provide financial assistance for an individual's artistic growth. They are not commissions, and work done in the grant period need not culminate in a performance. Funds can be used for any project or activity that will aid a choreographer's creative development, including travel for dance-related purposes. Individual choreographers are eligible whether or not they are incorporated as a tax-exempt organization. Unlike most NEA grants, fellowships are not required to be matched by support from other nonfederal sources.

Dance company grants. This category assists professional dance companies of the highest artistic level and of national or regional significance across the spectrum of aesthetic, cultural, and racial perspectives. Grants are available to support dance companies' seasons: creative work, rehearsal time, commissions, home seasons, touring, administrative projects, the care and compensation of artists, educational/outreach activities, etc. Applicants may request assistance for new projects to continue and strengthen their existing activities.

Services to the field. This category assists exemplary projects that identify and respond to professional, artistic, and human needs facing the dance field today, including but not limited to the dissemination of information, access to affordable rehearsal and performance spaces, increasing financial and managerial stability, and addressing safety and health issues.

Eligibility criteria for application in each category are listed in the guidelines. Up-to-date guidelines and applications are available from the NEA. [See the Appendix.]

Dealing with the NEA Dance Program

The party line is this: Get information, follow advice, fill out forms, meet deadlines, cross your fingers, and wait. Feeling victimized by the system? Here is some nuts-and-bolts advice.

Step number 1 is to get the Dance Program guidelines, which are published each year by late summer for the next cycle of applications. Call the program, and give your address. Get the name of the person with whom you speak, so that if the booklet hasn't arrived within two or three weeks you can call back and say, "Remember me? I never received the guidelines. Can we try again?"

Writing for the guidelines is OK, but don't trust the mail if you are short on time. Also, never assume that the guidelines will automatically be mailed to you. Yes, there is a huge mailing list, but it is on computer, and we all know horror stories about those things. If you don't receive them, make the call.

Once you have the guidelines, read them carefully. Even if you are interested in only one category, read everything. Don't call the staff with questions until after you have done this. For every ten calls a program specialist receives, at least seven of them could have been avoided if the caller had simply read the guidelines. Bear in mind that only a handful of staff people are dealing with upwards of five hundred choreographers, three hundred dance companies, and two hundred service organizations and sponsors per year.

After you have read the guidelines, make notes on what you want to know, then make the call. This expedites the process and also personalizes the situation because the program specialist can give attention to your particular circumstance rather than reciting a boring litany of prefabricated answers.

In the Dance Program, applications are treated with enormous care by people whose jobs revolve around that category (or categories). The number of applications the program handles is staggering, but nothing is done on an assembly-line basis. Each application is read in full by the program specialist. Help yourself by including thorough and accurate information (inaccuracies and exaggerations have a way of being found out, by the panel if not by the staff) and a phone number where you can be reached in case something is missing or needs clarification. It is not advisable to call the program after the application is submitted unless you have something to add or change. Asking for the status of your application is useless. No one can tell you anything until after the panel has met and the National Council on the Arts—which meets quarterly, in November, February, May, and August—has approved the panel's recommendations. The dates listed in the guidelines indicating when you should expect notification are real.

The Application Process

Don't be intimidated by it. If you approach applying with order and logic, it will be (almost) painless. This means doing things in advance and developing certain habits that become part of your life-as-artist.

Point 1 is, keep the Dance Program up to date on your performance activities. They aren't kidding about needing six to eight weeks of advance notice in order to schedule a personal evaluation of your activity, known as a site visit. Getting seen is the bottom line: If no one on the panel or consultant roster has seen and reported on your work, you haven't got a prayer for funding. Site visits are conducted year-round. The guidelines provide clear information about site visits in each category where they are necessary for the evaluation process.

This leads to point 2, which is that grantsmanship has little to do with getting money from the Dance Program. A coherent application is important, but the primary criterion for review is the panel's judgment of the applicant's artistic quality and, when applicable, its stability as an organization. The review criteria are listed in each category in the guidelines. These are the only criteria used by the panel in deliberation. Your application should reflect nothing more or less than what you are as an independent choreographer or dance company, service organization, sponsor, special project, basket case, whatever. Don't inflate your budget dramatically, don't spend extra money on getting things to look pretty (the applications are torn apart the minute they reach the grants office anyway), try to get your project description (a summary at least) on the first page, and don't bother with letters of recommendation from other people—the panel never sees them. What the panel receives of your application in the big black books called "panel books" is the project description, budget information, and resume (unless it is nine pages long). If it is a Choreographer's Fellowship application, the book includes a list of works choreographed or other relevant information particular to the specific category. In some categories, lead panelists receive a supplementary book that contains the full application materials. The other material requested sits in a folder and is read by the program specialist who handles the category.

The third point about applications is, take the deadlines seriously. In most cases, late applications will not be considered for funding. You are encouraged to request a return receipt when mailing from the post office to verify delivery to the Endowment.

Work well enough in advance so that your actual application is in the mail before the deadline date. It spares you the agony of brinkmanship; it means you can reach somebody on the program staff if in the course of writing you have a question (in the past, some staff have been known to disappear on the actual deadline day); and it is insurance against the application getting lost or sent to the wrong program when several close deadlines bring an inundation of applications into the grants office, where everything is officially logged in and then distributed to programs.

Within six weeks after the deadline, you should receive in the mail a little card with an application number on it. If nothing comes, you should call the program, ask for the specialist in the category for which you applied, and find out if they received your materials. If the answer is no, don't panic. Ask if you can send a copy. (Always keep a copy of your application, along with the post office receipt that proves that your application was mailed by the application deadline.) Usually the answer is yes; they just haven't gotten to the review yet.

In general, for all but the Fellowship category, program specialists, in reviewing application materials, will contact applicants with questions for clarification prior to panel.

The last point about applying is, don't try to take things into your own hands. There is a balance you must find that allows for watching out for yourself (i.e., some follow-up about receipt of the application, site visit information, etc.) without gaining notoriety throughout the program as one of the people who inspires a staff member to go to lunch at 9:30 in the morning in hopes of missing your next call.

In tandem with this, it is not a good idea to try to buttonhole panelists or consultants to persuade or complain to them, particularly if it is in relation to a rejection. If requested, the staff can send you a comprehensive list of the yearly roster of consultants and panelists, but addresses are not provided, and exactly who sits on each panel is not made public until after the review meeting has occurred. Again, the fate of applications rests primarily on the artistic review.

Site Visits

Given the significance of the artistic review, getting seen is of paramount importance. This is where your cooperation with the staff is critical. Panelists and consultants are under no obligation to see anyone's work for the Dance Program if it does not ask them to go, and they are not paid for work the Dance Program does not ask them to do. You should not contact panelists or consultants yourself to request that they attend a performance of your work. You should send the full information about the concert—time, place, date, whom to contact for tickets, etc.—to the Dance Program's site-visit coordinator, who in turn will be in touch with panelists about attending the performance. One copy of this information is sufficient. If you provide a yearly schedule or something listing several months' worth of activities, it is shifted into the appropriate file from month to month. Do not send multiple invitations or material to panelists in care of the Program; it is postage wasted on your part because only one copy is maintained in the file. The purpose of providing advance performance schedule information is solely to have your work viewed by Dance Program panelists or consultants, not to report on the range of your yearly activities. Concerts given under less than ideal circumstances need not be included on your performance schedule. The guidelines include detailed information about site visits and a sample form for easy use and to copy for future requests.

The task of organizing schedules, communicating with panelists and consultants, and maintaining easy access to the reports that are filed is a massive effort that repeats itself month after month and requires the time and energy of many more people than are available both on the staff and in the field. You can aid the process by sending the information in advance, notifying the staff if details change, and not calling every other day to find out if someone is going to come. The staff will not provide you with information about which panelists might attend, nor can they tell you for sure that someone has gone, even after the performance has occurred. Often there is a lag of weeks, even months, between the time a performance happens and the time a written report is in hand. Sometimes panelists who are committed to attending a concert must, at the last minute, cancel. The staff does not always know this right away. In short, the system is a good one, but not a perfect one. The staff does everything it can to get as many applicants seen by as many panelists as possible as often as performances occur.

One last note on site visits. If a performance is canceled, let the dance program know right away. On more than one occasion, panelists have literally been in airports ready to board planes bound for a city where a performance was occurring and on calling to confirm been told casually, "Oh, that isn't happening. We lost that booking a month ago." There have been times when panelists have gone to theaters at the appointed hour to find the doors locked, and janitors have told them the dancers were here last week. One panelist flew over five hundred miles, only to sit in an auditorium and be informed that no performance would take place but would she like to hear a history of the company? Don't let these things slip. They are remembered by staff and panel alike. It is your responsibility to keep the information flow accurate.

About Rejections

Nobody wants to be told no. More people, however, get a no than a yes from the Dance Program. Sometimes it is because of the budget crunch, other times because the panel review did not go well. If you receive a rejection letter, try at first to put things into as much perspective as possible. Applying repeatedly does not increase your chances of receiving an award, except insofar as it heightens your profile with the staff and panel. Remember that the competition in every category is fierce. When you have thought all those thoughts, and if you are still wounded and/or mad and/or bewildered and/or interested, you can phone the program, ask for the specialist in your category, and request a summation of the panel review of your application. You will get a version of one of three answers. The first is, We did not have enough current information on your work for the panel to make a positive recommendation. Please keep us informed of your performance activities, and we will make you a top priority for a site visit in the coming year so that reports will be on hand when your next application is considered. The second possible response is, You received a good artistic review, and the panel is very interested in your work, but there just wasn't enough money to go around. Please keep in touch regarding your performances and apply again next year. The third answer is the hardest, and that might be, The artistic review was mixed or not good at all. Each specialist handles this as delicately as possible, attempting to give the applicant a clear understanding of the reasons behind the rejection. Conversations like this are always uncomfortable, and the only insight that can be offered is that whomever you are talking to did not make the decision, may not share the opinion of the panel, and should not be expected to alter or fight the final recommendation. The staff is there to serve every applicant, not just grantees, which includes giving honest answers to the most personal question in this funding business: "Why didn't they like my work?"

Summary

Dealing with the Dance Program need not be burdensome if you have a good understanding of four things. First is the Program's calendar. Mark up your own calendar so you will know when deadlines are occurring, when guidelines are available, and how far ahead you need to plan for site-visit requests and application submissions. Second, know what is in the guidelines. Third, deal with the person who is responsible for the category or areas of concern to you. She/he will help you with whatever is not clear from the calendar and guidelines. Fourth, the Dance Program staff is friendly and eager to assist you.

The more organized you are, the smoother the process becomes, the less time it all takes, and the more time you have for your work. That's what it's really all about anyway.

Other Programs at the NEA You May Wish to Consider

The Dance Program is not the only source of support for dance at the NEA. In order to understand what grants are available through each of the NEA's discipline programs, you should keep a copy of the NEA's overall *Guide to the National Endowment for the Arts* on hand. You may also want a copy of the NEA's most recent annual report, which lists the year's grants and panelists in each program. Each discipline also issues its own guidelines. It is worthwhile to request copies from other disciplines if you feel your work might draw on an element of these disciplines. Those programs that may be of particular interest to dancers are described briefly below. For further information, write or call the appropriate program at the NEA. [See the Appendix.]

Design arts. The Design Arts Program supports a variety of projects in architecture, landscape architecture, urban design and planning, interior design, industrial and product design, and graphic design. The program offers individual fellowships and grants to organizations.

Expansion arts. The Expansion Arts Program supports professionally directed arts organizations of high artistic quality that are deeply rooted in and reflective of the culturally diverse inner-city, rural, or tribal community.

Folk arts. The Folk Arts Program offers assistance for the presentation and documentation of traditional arts and artists.

Media arts: film/radio/television. The Media Arts Program offers assistance to individuals and nonprofit organizations involved in film, video, radio, and television.

Music. The Music Program offers fellowships to composers and to creative artists, including choreographers working with composers. The Program also offers assistance to music performing and presenting groups and to jazz artists and solo recitalists.

Opera–musical theater. The Opera–Musical Theater Program offers assistance to companies and to groups producing opera, musical theater, and experimental musical theater. The New American Organizations category supports the creation and development of new works, including the work of creative artists such as choreographers.

Presenting and commissioning. The Presenting and Commissioning Program supports artists experimenting in interdisciplinary or collaborative projects, organizations that present arts events in two or more performing arts disciplines, and organizations that provide services in these two areas. Funds are available for presenting organizations, artists communities, multidisciplinary service organizations, and artists' projects. All projects must have national or regional impact.

Theater. The Theater Program offers assistance to professional theater companies, including their work with professional choreographers, and to theater artists, including directors, designers, and solo theater artists.

Visual arts. The Visual Arts Program assists organizations and individuals working in a wide variety of visual media, including conceptual and performance art.

Advancement. The Advancement Program is designed to help organizations of artistic excellence develop specific strategies to eliminate deficiencies in organizational management practice and to take carefully planned steps toward the achievement of long-range goals. The Program consists of two phases: Phase 1, Planning/Technical Assistance; and Phase 2, Advancement Grants (generally ranging from $25,000 to $75,000), which must be matched at least three to one. Current plans call for eligibility according to the following timetable: Fiscal Year 1992: Dance, Expansion Arts, Folk Arts, Literature, Media Arts, Opera–Musical Theater, and Visual Arts; Fiscal Year 1993: Arts in Education, Design Arts, Inter-Arts, Museum, Music, and Theater.

Challenge grants. Challenge Grants are intended to provide a special opportunity for arts institutions to strengthen long-term institutional capacity and to enhance artistic quality and diversity. The Challenge program has two forms of support: Institutional Stabilization and Project Implementation. Organizations may apply for only one form of support. A Challenge Grant must be matched three to one (four to one for construction, renovation, or purchase of a facility or equipment). Institutional Support is aimed at permanently strengthening the balance sheets of arts institutions in accordance with the applicant's artistic and financial plans and priorities. The goal of Project Implementation Support is to encourage and to stimulate increased support for projects of the highest quality that can strengthen and sustain excellence in the arts, improve access to the arts, or deepen and broaden appreciation of the arts. Project Implementation Support provides one-time-only funding for major projects.

Office for Special Constituencies. The Office for Special Constituencies assists individuals and organizations in making arts activities accessible to older adults, people with disabilities, and those in institutions. You may contact the office for assistance and materials, including examples of how arts groups make their programs available to special constituencies, and model project guidelines. Copies of *The Arts and 504,* a how-to handbook for making the arts accessible to disabled people, may be obtained from the Government Printing Office. [See the Appendix.]

International activities

U.S. Information Agency Arts American Program. Under a Memorandum of Understanding signed in 1978, the discipline panels of the NEA serve as artistic advisers to the U.S. Information Agency (USIA) Arts America Program. In response to requests from U.S. embassies overseas, Arts America develops touring programs that involve a limited number of highly recommended U.S. performing artists. In addition, the USIA may be able to provide some facilitative assistance for companies and individuals who have arranged tours abroad. Send your confirmed overseas touring schedules directly to the Arts America Program. [See the Appendix.]

Fund for U.S. Artists at International Festivals and Exhibitions. The Rockefeller Foundation, the Pew Charitable Trusts, the USIA, and the NEA jointly sponsor this fund to support performing artists invited to international festivals abroad and to fund U.S. representation at major international exhibitions of visual art. Individual performers and performing arts groups who have been invited to international festivals and who need additional support to make their performances possible should contact Arts International [see the Appendix] for further information.

International exchange fellowships. Five fellowships for work and study in Japan are awarded each year to American artists in various disciplines. Outstanding practicing artists for whom the opportunity to live and work in Japan for six months would help enrich their art must apply through the appropriate discipline program. There are no requirements for teaching, public demonstrations, or artistic creation while in Japan. A similar exchange opportunity for up to ten artists each year has been established with France. Contact the discipline programs for further information.

Other Forms of Federal Support

The National Endowment for the Arts is only one of the thirty-eight federal agencies and organizations with potential support for arts organizations. Of course, it is the only federal agency whose central mandate is to nurture the arts, and it is by far the most visible. Its "sister" agency, the National Endowment for the Humanities [see the Appendix], makes grants to organizations and individuals for research, education, and public activity in the humanities. Historical, theoretical, and critical studies in the arts are eligible for assistance. For example, a scholarly dance publication on research involving the reconstruction of a dance work might be funded through the NEH. Each of the other agencies has some other central mandate. Consequently, as an essential first step, you must become familiar with the central purpose of each of the agencies you intend to approach for help.

The Economic Development Administration (EDA) is a good example of this point. EDA is not in the business of funding choreographers. They provide money for projects that create jobs on a large scale and have an ongoing economic impact on a city or town. This purpose doesn't mean that EDA is unimportant to the arts. EDA provided, for example, loans and grants for the renovation of midtown Manhattan's Theater Row because the project was presented as something that could bring jobs and economic development to the Times Square neighborhood. Stroll along Theater Row these days, and you will pass new restaurants, new bookstores, new shops—all to some extent attributable to the effect of the renovation of Theater Row on the economic life of the neighborhood.

This example may only convince you that the Economic Development Administration is not likely to be concerned with your personal economic development. It should also illustrate the importance of understanding how an individual federal agency defines itself so that you can describe yourself and what you want to do in the agency's terms. Since the other thirty-seven agencies were set up to do something other than support performing arts activity, it is incumbent on you to explain how the funding of dance or any other art form is necessary to the achievement of their goals. Thus, a consortium of performing and visual artists once described themselves as "similar to an industrial park." They were, they claimed, a group of diversified enterprises with central management.

For all that, you may not want or need to go so far afield in an attempt to gain enough support to continue your work. After all, it's never a good idea to focus more energy on obtaining funding than on doing the work you really want to do. You ought, however, to be familiar with a few federal agencies other than the NEA that are the best-known funders of dance activity.

Department of Education. [See the Appendix.] This agency recognizes the performing arts as a tool to be used in accomplishing its primary goals, including the enrichment of school curricula, the improvement of local educational practices, and the elimination of discrimination in educational settings, etc. Much of this money is granted to local school boards, which in turn purchase the services of, or regrant funds to, performing artists.

Department of the Interior. [See the Appendix.] Twenty-four of our national parks, under the Department of the Interior, sponsor artist-in-residence programs. During residency, artists offer programs for the public, training for park staff, and performances of their work.

Smithsonian Institution's Performing Arts Program. [See the Appendix.] The Smithsonian's Performing Arts division sponsors a series of dance, drama, and music performances at the Smithsonian. Most productions have some reference to traditional American forms since one of the goals of the Smithsonian is the preservation of American regional and ethnic traditions.

The Federal Council on the Arts and Humanities. [See the Appendix.] The Council continues to function, although on a much-reduced level. Its staff can offer guidance to those who choose to tackle the federal structure. Moreover, goodwilled people who care about the arts continue to work throughout the federal government. Finding them and the programs they administer, learning to speak their language, and familiarizing them with your work are well worth the effort.

These agencies bear exploration, and, with a little research, you may find others whose goals your work can appropriately address. But be realistic. Under current budget restraints, most attempts to obtain federal support from agencies other than the NEA may not be worth the effort. Almost all these agencies' budgets have been cut, and the pressure to reduce or dismantle their programs has grown. The federal bureaucracy, sprawling though it may be, still responds to priorities set by the White House. In times such as these, federal agencies fall back on the most narrow definition of their roles.

State Funding
Larry Greene

The story of public support for the arts is, in a way, the story of the New York State Council on the Arts (NYSCA). In addition to the NEA, NYSCA was a persuasive voice in the development of a host of other state arts agencies. Something must have worked: Appropriated funds for the fifty state and six territorial arts agencies in fiscal year 1990 totaled $292,304,002. NYSCA accounted for nearly $60,000,000 of this amount. But state government funding took an ominous downturn in fiscal year 1992 when a total of $211,937,069 was appropriated.

How do you get your hands on some of this money? To be honest, we're not sure. That's because the fifty-six state and territorial arts agencies probably have fifty-six different ways of funding individual artists and arts organizations. Some agencies, like NYSCA, are legislatively prohibited from directly supporting individuals. By profiling the operations of the nation's largest state arts agency, the New York State Council on the Arts, we'll introduce you to most of the issues you'll need to become familiar with regarding government funding for the arts within your state.

An Agency's Mission

The Council on the Arts has described its mission as follows:

In view of the wealth of cultural resources within New York State, the Council on the Arts is committed to ensuring that artists have the freedom to create; that arts organizations have the means to serve and present; and that audiences across the State have the opportunity to experience, first-hand, the varied and rich cultures of our people. Through its funding policies, the Council affirms its mission, according equal respect to the best of all artistic forms and traditions while recognizing the cultural diversity of this State.

It is important to know the mission of your state's agency since it serves as the organizing principle for the agency's operation and funding mechanism.

Agency Structure

NYSCA is governed by a board of twenty members, known as the council, who serve without salary. These members are citizens who are appointed by the governor and confirmed by the state Senate. Headed by a chair, chosen from among its members by the governor, the council reviews funding recommendations made to it by the staff and panels. Final approval of an award rests with the council, which meets a minimum of four times annually.

Currently, NYSCA is made up of two program divisions under which its sixteen departments operate. The departments are known as NYSCA's local assistance programs. They are Architecture, Planning and Design, Arts in Education, Capital Funding Initiative, Dance, Electronic Media and Film, Folk Arts, Individual Artists, Literature, Museum, Music, Presenting Organizations, Special Arts Services, State and Local Partnership Programs, Theater, and Visual Arts. Each department has a staff and an advisory panel.

The Advisory Panel

In making its funding decisions, NYSCA turns to its staff and to advisory panels for award recommendations. The involvement of advisory panels means that an applicant's artistic and administrative peers are part of the overall process. Panel members are chosen by the chair with the approval of the council's governing board. Nominations to the panel are made by staff, current panelists, council governing board members, and the public. Panelists must have a demonstrated expertise in their program discipline of appointment. NYSCA also strives to achieve a cultural, aesthetic, and geographic diversity among its panel membership. Panelists serve for one-year terms that are renewable for up to three years. Each year approximately eleven panelists conclude their appointments. This builds in a measure of continuity within a system of change.

The panel usually meets three times during the funding year, in two-day sessions. The names and addresses of panel members are made available to prospective and current applicants. NYSCA encourages arts groups and individuals to mail notifications of upcoming events to panelists to enhance their familiarity with the work of an artist or organization.

Eligibility

Probably at the top of the list of your questions is, Am I eligible to apply for funding? Each state agency has its own eligibility criteria. In New York State, for example, only nonprofit organizations may apply. An organization's nonprofit status is assessed by NYSCA in one of a few ways. A federal status of nonprofit operation takes the form of a 501(c)(3) designation by the Internal Revenue Service. While that certainly suffices for NYSCA's needs, so does a New York State confirmed status established by filing under the New York State Registration of Charitable Organizations. This registration is fairly uncomplicated and is explained in NYSCA's guidelines. A drawback of a Charities Registration status without an accompanying federal status is that the Internal Revenue Service does not consider financial contributions to these groups to be tax deductible. The arts community has addressed this problem through the existence of several nonprofit organizations that will (for a nominal fee) serve as a repository for these donations so that they are deductible.

The word "organization" means that individuals are ineligible to apply to NYSCA. But this restriction doesn't entirely close the door on individuals. In some instances, individual artists can receive support indirectly by having their projects sponsored by a nonprofit organization. In this case, when appropriate, the sponsor assumes full responsibility for the individual's project: filing the application and seeing it through the review process, completing supplementary forms and reports, and receiving and dispersing funds to the individual artist. Finding such a sponsor isn't easy. Therefore, NYSCA has channeled major support to the New York Foundation for the Arts [see the Appendix] to conduct a fellowship program to which artists who reside in New York State may apply.

At NYSCA, you may still not be eligible for support even if you seem to fit the bill as a nonprofit organization. The agency's program departments often include additional criteria of either a qualitative or a quantitative nature. For example, at NYSCA, a dance company must be a professional ensemble that has been evaluated in live performance a minimum of two times within a two-year period just prior to application. "Professional" is both a state of mind and a state of being. It defines a company that aims for professional standards in its artistry and in its business practices. The evaluations play a role in assessing a company's artistic accomplishments. Among the business practices examined is whether the dancers are paid for their services. This doesn't mean that a company is obligated to pay union-scale equivalents. Rather, it means that the dancers are paid something.

Funding Categories

Let's presume that you qualify as an eligible applicant to your state arts agency. What should you apply for? A review of your agency's funding categories, described in its guidelines, will begin to make this clear. More than likely, two parallel forces helped shape these categories: the priorities of the agency and the needs of the artistic field. Some of the priorities relate back to the agency's mission or to the state legislature's concerns. But most of the priorities are shaped by ongoing policy discussions at the staff, panel, and governing board levels, where the needs of the field are weighed against the financial resources of the agency. Resources and needs change, and so do funding categories. No agency can have something for everyone, and some worthwhile arts projects may fall outside an agency's ability to fund them.

Let's sharpen the focus and take a look at the ten funding categories in the three divisions of the dance program at NYSCA. Performance artists take note: As with the NEA, most performance art is funded through the Theater and Visual Arts Programs.

Institutional support. Such support is intended to meet the fuller administrative and artistic needs of a company over, generally, a two- or three-year period. Within the Dance Program, General Operating Support and Long-Range Development are Institutional Support categories. General Operating Support now accounts for a majority of the Dance Program's spending. As its name indicates, General Operating Support is meant to cover all aspects of an organization's operation, excluding those for which separate NYSCA Project Support is sought. But the category makes clear that it is not intended for first-time applicants (among the eligibility criteria, one must have been supported for the last three consecutive years by the Dance Program). Long-Range Development Support carries a similar eligibility criterion but is geared to a three-year project of administrative and artistic growth. Applications under either of these two categories preclude support under the three Project Support categories.

Project support. The Project Support categories are Professional Performances Home Base, Professional Performances Touring, and Services to the Field. The first of these categories is where most dance companies receive their initial support. The category answers a basic need: assistance for dancers' salaries related to performances by a company in its home county. Professional Performances Touring applies the same approach to performance projects taking place outside a company's home county. Services to the Field, by contrast, offers support to organizations that provide professional services to dance groups and individuals.

Incentive project support. The Dance Program's remaining five categories fall under this area. While support under these categories is also directed to a specific project, those projects are considered to be in response to special initiatives and therefore receive separate consideration from other requests that may have been submitted.

Mindful of the imbalance in the distribution and representation of dance in

New York State, NYSCA's Dance Program created two Incentive Project Support categories that seek to give dance a greater presence in upstate regions. The first of these, the New York State Touring Plan, represents an inspired blend of support for upstate touring engagements and for the creation of a marketing videotape (to secure and promote tour dates) over a three-year period. The second category, Long-Term Residency in New York State, is engineered to make possible residencies of a minimum of three weeks duration in a targeted upstate region. Creative time for the company and a greater amount of interaction with the host community are two identifying characteristics of a Long-Term Residency. Among the eligibility criteria for these two incentive categories is that a dance company must have been supported by the Dance Program during two of the last three years preceding an application.

Rehearsal Space, another Incentive Project Support category, has tried to keep the cost of rehearsal space affordable by subsidizing nonprofit organizations that offer low-cost studio spaces to dance companies and artists. The last two Incentive Project Support categories are deeply involved with the creative process. Building Ballet Repertory funds workshops that bring together capable ballet dancers with young, developing choreographic talents who have chosen to work within the classical ballet vocabulary. This process-oriented category was established to identify new ballet choreographers. Commissions help dance companies commission new or existing works by guest choreographers. Funds under this category are directed solely to the fee of the choreographer or restager.

The Application

Life can be full of pleasant surprises, but it's a mistake to think that your application to a state arts agency should be one of them. Notifying your agency of an intention to apply can be mutually beneficial, ensuring that labors are not wasted over the completion or handling of an ineligible application. As with an NEA application, read your agency's guidelines and be prepared to ask informed questions. Talk to a program staff member about your project and how you plan to apply. When submitting your application, be sure that it's signed and that you've supplied the necessary number of copies. Some agencies appreciate receiving additional background information (for example, a press kit) on new applicants. Find out if it's appropriate to include such material as an attachment. If you find government forms and applications intimidating, you may want to seek out the services of a professional who will help you complete the application. But any initial intimidation may evaporate if you're reasonably well organized. A simple and straightforward approach to the completion of the application should suffice. Dazzling narratives should be saved for your memoirs. Nor does your name have to be Archimedes when it comes to completing information about your organization's financial operation. The real menace is an organization's record keeping. If your financial records are in good order, you should have little trouble with most applications.

NYSCA's Dance Program generally advises first-time applicants to limit themselves to one or two funding categories. Residents of other states will probably encounter a similar recommendation from their own arts council.

How much money should you ask for? To a large extent, this should be based on your forecasted need, resulting from a realistic projection of income and expenses. Find out what, if any, minimum grant awards exist under the funding categories. Examine your agency's annual funding report to get a sense of its overall funding behavior.

The Review

Because NYSCA has only one deadline (March 1 for all funding categories), applications are assigned for review at one of four panel meetings held between June and January. That assignment is made either on the basis of the funding category you've applied under or on the timing of your project. Applicants are notified of their panel meeting assignment well in advance of the review. Panel meetings at NYSCA are closed to the general public, but, as an applicant, you'll get a chance to meet with NYSCA's program staff prior to the panel meeting. This meeting gives the applicant and the agency a chance to get to know each other and to have an in-depth discussion of a variety of topics: the application, the company's history and artistic aspirations, current events affecting the company's administrative and artistic endeavors, and the operations of the agency. NYSCA also permits some revisions to the application. The application and any revisions are reviewed at some length in the staff-applicant meeting so that the panel and council can examine an application that's complete and comprehensible. Thus, it's rare that an application is rejected by NYSCA during the review process because of incomplete information.

After the meeting between staff and applicant, the NYSCA staff member assigned to the applicant composes a report detailing the company's artistic and financial operation. That report is sent to members of the Dance Panel approximately two weeks in advance of the panel meeting. Accompanying the report is a staff recommendation concerning support of the application and the latest performance evaluations. At NYSCA, these performance evaluations are confidential reports known as audits. NYSCA's Dance Program uses a system of live performance evaluation to determine funding. This includes information from auditors, staff, and panel. Some states use videotapes. If yours does, be sure to have appropriate videotape support materials.

Next comes the panel meeting. During a two-day meeting at which dozens of applications are considered, the panel evaluates the merits of your application in a discussion that can range anywhere from a few minutes to much longer. Some of the factors that determine the length of the discussion are the panel's familiarity with the company in a live-performance circumstance and the complexity of the organization or application (number of requests, nature of the funding category you've applied under, etc.). Panel members speak from their own experience. They do not refer to press reactions, to videotapes, or to the responses of other colleagues or funders in their discussion. NYSCA's panels try to make up their minds as autonomously as possible. In some states, panel meetings are open to the public. At NYSCA, only those panel meetings devoted to policy-making are open. That is not to say that any discussion of your organization's application is top secret. Program staff usually invite any interested applicants to call after a decision is final to find out, in a general way, how the discussion went at panel. With the conclusion of discussion of an application, a vote is taken. The results of that vote form the panel's funding recommendation. That recommendation is reviewed by a committee of the NYSCA's governing board in a public meeting. The committee examines the recommendations of staff and panel and reviews a written summary of the panel's discussion of the application. The committee, closely guided by the panel and staff, makes a recommendation of support that is then reviewed in a meeting of the full governing board. Council committee representatives summarize their actions for the full board's approval. It is with their approval that a funding decision becomes final.

Per Capita

As you learn more about state government funding for the arts, you may hear the words "per capita." Per capita assesses how a state's arts funding shapes up relative to its population. By dividing the total annual arts dollars by the population, you arrive at your state's per capita funding of the arts. New York State operates under a per capita requirement: Each county in the state must achieve an annual per capita equivalent of no less than $0.40. So while it was true that, on average, New York State had a per capita of $3.10 in 1990–91, this amount varied county by county (to no less than the stipulated minimum per person).

Arts Funding Is Not a Perennial Flower

It's important to keep in mind that state arts agencies are appropriated funds by their legislatures on an annual basis and are affected by a variable climate of economic forces and legislative priorities. For example, a study by the National Assembly of State Arts Agencies [see the Appendix] reports that, in fiscal year 1991, the total of all appropriated funds fell for the first time in thirteen years. But while eighteen agencies had decreases, thirty-eight others reported increases in fiscal year 1991. The bottom line is that, as either an individual artist or an arts organization, you should become familiar with your state's system of appropriating arts funds. Sooner or later you're bound to be affected by it. If there's a legislative appropriations committee for the arts, find out who's on it. Also learn the names of your state government representatives. Stay informed; become involved.

Some Final Advice

While it's probably not a good idea to get carried away by big plans when you contemplate state government funding, it doesn't hurt to think expansively. For example, if you've assembled a performance project that will involve the participation of a visual artist or composer, it's possible that you may be able to pursue support for her/his participation by applying to additional program departments. Are you a performance artist? Does your agency have a program set up to review performance art? Again, this brings us back to your agency's guidelines. Request them and read them. The latter may prove challenging: Most guidelines are not strong on narrative. But you should approach them with the imagination of a prospector.

Local Funding
John Haworth

Throughout the country, there are hundreds of communities—from large urban centers to small towns in rural areas—that have local arts agencies. Some local arts agencies are public entities of their local governments, while others are private nonprofit organizations. Local arts agencies have the responsibility to further local cultural and artistic interests through funding and other programs. Generally, local arts agencies distribute arts funding (which can be from government or private funds) through competitive funding programs organized either by artistic discipline or by function (general operating support, support for arts education programs, special initiatives). Some local arts agencies serve as presenting organizations or produce arts festivals and other events. Some communities also support the arts through other public and private agencies, including but not limited to parks and recreation departments, tourism and economic development offices, and united arts fund drives.

New York City Department of Cultural Affairs

By way of example, we will outline the New York City Department of Cultural Affairs (DCA) [see the Appendix], which represents cultural communities city-owned cultural institutions, and creative artists who live and work within the boundaries of New York City's five boroughs. The agency administers the funding for cultural programs, oversees capital construction of cultural facilities, develops city policy, and addresses issues that confront the artistic community in New York. Check with your city government to find out about your local arts agency.

Funding Divisions

A variety of appropriations derived from city budget allocations, and in some instances state and federal funds, enables DCA to provide support through the following units:

—*Cultural Institutions Unit* provides basic operating support to thirty-one cultural institutions, which for the most part occupy city-owned buildings and land. Support is provided for security, maintenance, programming, administration, and energy costs at a variety of cultural institutions including theaters, museums, zoos, gardens, and historic preservations.

—*Facilities Services Unit* provides funds for capital improvements and maintenance at cultural institutions and other organizations housed in city-owned buildings. The unit is responsible for planning, monitoring design and construction of capital projects, and coordinating the same with other city agencies.

—*Program Services Unit* provides programmatic funding to nonprofit arts organizations in the form of public service contracts, which enable the arts community to provide cultural experiences throughout New York City. These contracts support diverse artistic disciplines and cultural traditions.

—*Percent for Art* implements the "Percent for Art" law (City Charter, Chapter 9, Section 234), which requires that eligible construction projects in city-owned buildings allocate 1 percent of construction costs to public artworks.

Other

The National Assembly of Local Arts Agencies (NALAA) [see the Appendix] is a membership organization that provides services and information related to the local field. Most state arts agencies also have extensive information about local arts agencies in their areas; some have coordinated statewide decentralized funding programs to provide arts funding in partnership with local arts agencies.

Foundations
Marian A. Godfrey

A foundation (as defined in *The Foundation Directory*, a source book and excellent guide to foundation fund-raising [see the Appendix]) is "a nongovernmental, not-for-profit organization with funds and a program managed by its own trustees or directors and established to maintain or aid social, education, charitable, religious, or other activities serving the common welfare primarily through the making of grants." There are approximately 30,000 foundations operating in America, of which 22,500 have assets of over one million dollars and 7,500 make grants in excess of $100,000 annually.

Probably the most significant event in foundation history with regard to funding for the arts took place in 1957, when W. McNeil Lowry, then director of educational programs at the Ford Foundation, began making grants to visual and performing arts institutions. Over the next eighteen years, the Ford Foundation granted hundreds of millions of dollars to the arts and humanities, allowing theater, music, and dance companies to flourish throughout the United States. During this period of time, Ford spent approximately $29.8 million to assist in the development of American ballet companies.

Foundations support the arts because they believe that society will benefit from cultural enrichment and think that they can thus most effectively and creatively serve special constituencies that interest them (such as children or elders). Depending on their structure, foundations also donate to particular causes because they reflect the interests of the original donor or the communities they serve.

Like corporations, foundations provide both general and special project support, depending on their individual interests and grant-making policies. Foundations interested in making grants to individuals are probably the most difficult to find. There are, however, foundations (like the Guggenheim) that provide fellowships to composers, directors, choreographers, and other creative artists. The book *Foundation Grants to Individuals,* which can be found along with an abundance of foundation research material at Foundation Center libraries and their branches [see below] throughout the country, should certainly be consulted by individuals seeking personal project grants.

Types of Foundations

In seeking foundation support, it is important that the fund-raiser understand the structure of a particular foundation and be fully aware of that foundation's interests and reasons for supporting a given project. There are five major types of foundations making grants to arts institutions. They are as follows:

Proprietary foundations. These include foundations, such as the Vincent Astor Foundation, where the actual donor (or spouse) is alive and active in the foundation's work. Many corporate foundations, which have professional staff members administering their granting procedures, also fall within this category because the corporate foundation exists as the donor.

Family foundations. This type includes foundations such as the Rockefeller Brothers Fund, where leadership has passed into the hands of family members, usually siblings, children, and grandchildren of the original donor. Many of these foundations also employ a professional staff to assist in determining policy and implementing the philanthropic interest of the donor's family.

Trusts. These include foundations such as the Emma A. Sheafer Charitable Trust, where responsibility for the foundation has passed into the hands of friends, partners, or business associates of the original donor. In many cases, these foundations are administered by banks and law firms.

Community foundations. This type includes foundations such as the New York Community Trust or the Cleveland Foundation, where funds are derived not from an individual donor but from a variety of bequests and gifts. These foundations have special legal requirements and are managed by professional staff members and boards that must have some elected community representatives. Community foundations serve particular geographic areas (there is usually only one to be found within a certain location) and respond to the special concerns and interests of their constituent communities.

Professional foundations. These include foundations such as the Ford Foundation, where control has passed entirely into the hands of professional staff members who bear no relationship to the original donor.

Applying for a Grant

There are several specific steps one must take in order to receive funding from a foundation. If successfully employed, this step-by-step process should also work in corporate fund-raising. [See "Corporations" below.] Personal contacts through board members and other individuals will provide (as in the case of corporate fund-raising) the strongest link between the arts organizations and most foundations. These personal contacts must be pursued intensely, making board development a priority in successful fund-raising. In the case of professional and corporate foundations, personal contacts should be sought between the foundation's professional staff and the arts organization's artistic and management staff.

Whether or not a company has personal contacts in the funding world, the following process will help strengthen the company's position when applying for a grant.

Identify your constituencies. From what sources will the company raise money (e.g., foundations, corporations, special events, etc.)?

Research. The need for extensive research cannot be overemphasized. Too many groups waste time applying for grants that are totally inaccessible to them. Small companies particularly should focus their initial research on foundations that operate within their home communities. Only the largest companies with national reputations receive funding from sources outside their geographic location. Touring companies, however, may be able to raise funds from sources based on their touring locations and should research these prospects. Small companies might also be well advised to start their search for funds by examining small foundations in their communities and skipping over the largest, most well-known sources until they can gain access to them.

Brief call or letter of inquiry. This call, usually made to a secretary, will allow you to confirm information about or abandon hope of working with the foundation that you have discovered in your research. This call serves primarily as your personal introduction to the foundation. It informs the foundation that you would like to, or intend to, apply for a grant, and it should be kept brief and to the point. You should ask for printed guidelines, if available, and the annual report, which will indicate what types of programs are of interest to the foundation. Many foundations request or require a letter of inquiry prior to the submission of a full proposal. Letters of inquiry should be brief (no more than one-and-a-half to two pages long); they should include a very brief introduction to your company, a description of the project for which you are seeking support, and a request for a specific amount. If you submit a full proposal, be sure to follow the foundation's guidelines by including all financial and other support material requested. In a full proposal, you should:

—introduce your company and state its purpose and artistic mission;
—cite some of your company's performing highlights and impressive statistics;
—note who is served by your company;

—briefly mention other foundation contributions;

—note the impact of the potential contribution on your company (in this section you should also directly request support, asking for an appropriate amount that has been determined by your research); and

—make a point of inviting the foundation to a performance, and indicate when you will be calling to follow up the proposal.

If the proposal addresses a special project, the objectives and components of that project should be explained in the proposal after you have acquainted them with the general goals etc. of your company. Proposals should be neat, concise, and factual, citing your organization's actual accomplishments and presenting your institution in the most professional and organized manner possible.

Follow up your inquiry or proposal with a phone call, and, if possible, arrange a meeting. Sometimes, particularly when a company has a personal contact, a meeting can be arranged prior to submitting the proposal. The knowledge gained at a meeting can help the fund-raiser to strengthen the proposal. In most cases, however, where no personal contact is involved, foundations like to see a proposal before arranging a meeting. Above all, it is important to remember that people give to people and that, whenever possible, personal contact with the funding source is an advantage. With some foundations, the ability of a staff or board member to see a performance will be key to a positive grant decision.

Attend the meeting. Again, it is important to present your company as both artistically significant and administratively well organized. You should be well prepared for the meeting and take the appropriate representatives of your company along with you (although usually no more than three people should attend). Make your presentation interesting and concise.

Follow up after the meeting. Send a note to the people with whom you met, thanking them for taking the time to meet with you.

Grant award notification. If you are fortunate enough to receive a grant, make sure to respond as soon as possible by sending a personalized thank-you note to the foundation.

Building a sense of ownership. Follow up throughout the year by inviting donors to productions. Good follow-up activities will enhance your chances for a renewal of the grant the following season. Remember, though, except in the case of long-term grants, applications are received annually. It would be a dangerous mistake for a company to assume that funding will automatically be renewed. In fact, many foundations provide no more than three-year funding to any specific project, so the company would be wise to continually search for new foundation prospects.

Corporations
Timothy J. McClimon

Before 1970, corporate grants and contributions went overwhelmingly to education, health, and social welfare. While this is still true, the seventies and eighties saw a dramatic rise in corporate support of the arts. In 1967, the Business Committee for the Arts (BCA) [see the Appendix] reported that the business community had contributed $22 million to the arts. By 1989, that figure had risen to over $700 million.

Overall, corporate contributions to nonprofit organizations totaled more than $5 billion in 1989. However, only about 12 percent of the total corporate charitable dollar goes to the arts, according to the 1990 study by BCA. Of this amount, only a small percentage—perhaps 3 percent—goes to dance and performance.

Because corporate support of dance and performance is limited and the number of arts organizations seeking support from corporations is ever increasing, it is important to understand

—why corporations support the arts;
—what determines corporate giving policies;
—what kind of corporate support is available; and
—how corporations decide which organizations to assist.

Why Corporations Support the Arts

Corporations support the arts because the arts are important to their employees, stockholders, and customers. They support the arts in order to foster creativity and to enhance the quality of life in communities in which their employees and customers live and work. They also support the arts in order to contribute to the economic vitality of communities. In short, corporations believe that a healthy arts community is good for business.

Corporations also recognize the public relations value of supporting the arts. By underwriting arts events, a corporation can link its name with a quality product as well as a public good. In this way, a corporation hopes to enhance its image in the minds of the public and to affect positively Americans' attitudes toward business in general and itself as a corporation in particular.

What Determines Corporate Giving Policy

A corporation's giving policy generally reflects its markets, products, image, and the economy. Industries dependent on large consumer markets, such as banking, telecommunications, and utilities, tend to give highly visible and generous support to the arts, and industries in need of a better corporate image, such as oil, mining, chemicals, and tobacco, are inclined to support the arts because they are recognized as a public good. In contrast, wholesale manufacturing firms often have little arts giving policy.

The state of the economy also affects a corporation's giving policy. The size of a corporation's contribution budget is often tied to profits earned in the prior year. Very few corporations fund foundations with their own assets, so the higher a corporation's profits, the more money there is to give to charitable causes.

A prospective corporate funder should be analyzed in terms of its particular industry, economic condition, and image. Your grant request should be tailored to reflect this information.

What Kind of Corporate Support Is Available

Corporate support to the arts is generally of three types: (1) general support; (2) special project support; (3) and in-kind donations.

If an arts organization requests an unrestricted gift to cover operating expenses, such as salaries, supplies, and rent, this type is called "general operating support." Grants given for general operating support are usually small, ranging from $500 to $5,000.

Support for special projects is money restricted to the specific project for which support is requested, such as a commission, a new production, or a tour. A special project tends to appeal to a corporation if the project will attract a large and diverse audience and serve as a public relations vehicle for the corporation. The grants are usually larger, ranging from $5,000 to $100,000.

In-kind support is a donation of corporate services (e.g., graphic design, computer time, or printing), furniture, space, or executive expertise (e.g., financial, computer, or marketing). Services are rarely donated to an arts organization unless a prior funding relationship or board member contact with the corporation exists. Some corporations have policies prohibiting donations of their products.

How Corporations Decide on Grants

A corporation's decision to fund an arts organization depends on many things. Besides wanting to assist high-quality organizations, a corporation's typical first requirement is that the applicant be a nonprofit, tax-exempt organization. Second, corporations usually require that organizations have been in existence for a minimum length of time (e.g., three years). Rarely do corporations provide start-up costs for arts organizations. Corporations with national giving programs (e.g., AT&T, Philip Morris, American Express) may also require "national recognition."

Corporations will often look at the professional qualifications of an arts organization's board of directors as well. A qualified board indicates to the corporation that the organization has stable and reliable management. A corporation generally will not take the risk of funding an organization with a weak board of directors.

Successful fund-raising depends heavily on personal contacts. Often corporate contributions officers are responsible for the fields of health, education, and welfare as well as the arts. Because of the enormous number of applications and the large number of persons with whom a corporate contributions officer must deal, it may be difficult to make an appointment to see her/him. However, as a representative of an arts organization, you should politely pursue an appointment and try to establish a working relationship with the contributions officer in the corporation being approached. You should be prepared to spend time introducing yourself, your board of directors, and your art to the corporate officer by way of invitations to performances, lecture demonstrations, and behind-the-scenes tours. In addition to seeing the quality of your company's performances, a corporate contributions officer will also observe the makeup of your audience and the professional management of your company.

Once the contributions officer has seen your company perform, you should submit a formal written request for support. The request for support should be no more than three pages long and should explain what type of work your company produces, what makes it unique in the performance community, and what you plan to do with the money requested. Mail the request to the contributions officer with the following:

—a letter of tax-exemption determination under section 501(c)(3) of the Internal Revenue Code;
—a list of the board of directors, their affiliations, and their qualifications;
—a project budget, a current operations budget, and past audited fiscal statements; and
—descriptive materials such as brochures, booklets, and reviews.

When raising funds from corporations, several things should be kept in mind:

—A corporation's primary responsibility is to earn a profit for its stockholders. It does not have a legal duty to contribute funds to charitable organizations.

—A dance or performance company should not assume that a corporate contributions officer understands dance or performance as an art form or is able to distinguish one company from another. (On the other hand, many contributions officers are quite knowledgeable.)

—Corporations generally do not take risks with the funds they contribute. A corporation that gives a grant to an arts organization is making an investment in the future of that organization. As with other investment decisions, a corporation will look at the organization's financial stability and management qualifications as well as its artistic credentials in making its funding decision.

—Personal relationships play an important role in corporate fund-raising. If artistic and financial qualifications are met, a corporate contributions officer will usually recommend funding for organizations headed by people she/he feels confident can excel and propel their organizations forward.

—No two corporations are alike in their giving patterns or procedures. It is wise to know as much as possible about a corporation's giving policies before asking for a grant.

—Once a corporation gives a grant to an organization, there is no guarantee that the grant will be renewed in subsequent years. A corporation's decision makers and funding priorities may change from year to year.

Support from Individuals
Mindy N. Levine

It's a mistake to think of your funding efforts as a perpetual courtship of government agencies, impersonal corporations, and seemingly austere foundations. Even if you manage to convince these agencies that your work is worthy of support, soliciting funds from individuals should be an important component of your funding efforts. Friends, fans, and relatives are the most likely sources of support, particularly in the early years of your career.

There are several ways you can encourage support from individuals. A request for funds on your promotional literature and programs reminds audiences that their contributions are essential to the survival of the arts. A fund-raising appeal in the form of a personal letter can also encourage someone who cares about your work to make a contribution. Whenever appropriate, published materials should carry a notation similar to the one that follows:

> Performing Arts Company, Inc., is a not-for-profit tax-exempt organization. Contributions in support of Performing Arts Company's work are greatly appreciated. All contributions are fully deductible to the extent allowed by law.

If you are not incorporated as a nonprofit organization but are a member of an umbrella organization, like On the Boards, in Seattle, you can arrange to have contributions made to that organization on your behalf.

Once you persuade people to contribute to your company, make them feel they are part of your organization. Place their names on your programs, and thank them publicly for their support. Invite them as special guests to your opening night, and include them in your cast parties.

Fund-raising events are also a way to generate funds. Plan an event that's fun and entertaining, and people won't mind paying a little extra, knowing that the money is going to a good cause. It could be something as simple as a cocktail reception after the show or as elaborate as a star-studded evening of entertainment.

Given the fact that most artists would rather be performing than filling out lengthy grant applications, and considering the current funding climate, tapping the support of individual contributors may be the most efficient way to secure funds.

Loans
Timothy Ney

The path to a grant is long and winding. After all the application deadlines, performance audits, fiscal evaluations, panel meetings, and budget revisions, you may be the proud recipient of the grant-award letter—your money is on its way, but. . . .

Alas, you may find that your grant requires vouchers, contract numbers, and other bureaucratic approval. The dollar bills that finally seemed just around the corner may be further delayed weeks or, in some cases, months. Once again you are faced with disgruntled landlords, disconnect notices from the utility companies, theater deposits, printers' bills, and dedicated but financially strained dancers. You're experiencing a problem in cash flow.

You need a loan. Bank interests are sky high, and a pound of flesh is out of the question. Fortunately, there are a few alternatives. [See the Appendix for a listing of revolving loan sources.]

The Foundation Center

The Foundation Center [see the Appendix] is a national nonprofit service organization established in 1956. Its mission is to collect, organize, and disseminate factual data on foundation and corporate philanthropy. Free public access to this information is offered through four Center-operated libraries and a nationwide network of Cooperating Collections. In addition, the Center's publications program features many titles on philanthropic giving and other nonprofit-sector concerns. A program of regular orientations and educational seminars has introduced thousands of grantseekers to the Center's resources.

The New York City, Washington, DC, Cleveland, and San Francisco reference libraries operated by the Foundation Center offer a wide variety of services and comprehensive collections of information regarding foundations and grants. Cooperating Collections are libraries, community foundations, and other nonprofit agencies that provide a core collection of Foundation Center publications and offer free guidance in funding research to all visitors. Because the collections vary in their hours, materials, and services, it is recommended that you call each collection in advance of a visit.

APPENDIX   TAKING CARE OF BUSINESS

Addresses and phone numbers of the following resources may be found in the alphabetized Directory at the end of the book.

Management

Arts Resource Consortium Library (Joint project of American Council for the Arts and Volunteer Lawyers for the Arts. Library staff will assist arts managers and individual artists with inquiries over the phone, by fax, and by mail. Library may be used in person on appointment basis. Information on art law and nonprofit arts management.)

Box Office Management International (BOMI) (A professional association that provides a forum for the exchange of ideas on effective box office management, promotes the advancement of management techniques, and encourages the development of high professional standards.)

Business Volunteers for the Arts/Chicago

Business Volunteers for the Arts/Florida (Provides bookkeeping, planning/budgeting, tax assistance, insurance analysis, marketing, and public relations.)

Business Volunteers for the Arts/NY (BVA/NY)—a program of Arts and Business Council (Service organization for NYC arts groups and businesses. Consultants from the business community available to assist arts groups on pro bono basis with specific management problems. Projects are usually longer term; however, volunteers may be available for specific projects related to crisis issues such as cash-flow analysis, budget development, personnel, crisis response teams, and credit-related areas.)

Center for Non-Profit Management

Classical Performing Arts Management (Represents opera singers and chamber music groups.)

Dance/USA (Membership. Information and advocacy on issues affecting the national world.)

Downtown Art Co. (Provides a wide variety of low-cost professional management/fundraising services for independent performing artists and small performing artist companies.)

Performing Arts Resources, Inc. (Serves performing arts community. Staff advice and referral services regarding critical situations and staffing issues.)

Volunteer Consulting Group, Inc. (Provides consulting services for board development, governance planning, and the recruitment of board members to enhance the managerial strength of the organization. Assistance is available when an organization is confronted with a leadership crisis.)

Professional managers

Listed below are a few not-for-profit dance management organizations. For additional references of commercial and not-for-profit managers, consult *Stern's Performing Arts Directory* (formerly known as the *Dance Magazine Annual*).

Circuit Network (Joint management organization serving artists and companies with budgets under $50,000. Offers booking representation, fund-raising and financial services, fiscal receivership, and public relations.)

Pentacle (Offers a menu of management services—fiscal and payroll administration, grant writing, press and publicity, and booking representation to selected companies and individual artists.)

SoHo Booking (Offers booking to a curated list of dance, performance, and musical artists and companies. Also provides project management for a select list of artists in various disciplines.)

Volunteer support

Business Volunteers for the Arts/Chicago

Business Volunteers for the Arts/Florida (Provides bookkeeping, planning/budgeting, tax assistance, insurance analysis, marketing, and public relations.)

Business Volunteers for the Arts/NY (BVA/NY)—a program of Arts and Business Council (Service organization for NYC arts groups and businesses. Consultants from the business community available to assist arts groups on pro bono basis with specific management problems. Projects are usually longer term; however, volunteers may be available for specific projects related to crisis issues such as cash-flow analysis, budget development, personnel, crisis-response teams, and credit-related areas.)

City-as-School—Executive Internships Program (Places and pays students for 30 hours per week in the summer, and provides credit for 10 hours per week in the winter.)

City University of New York—Office of Student Financial Assistance

Jobs for Youth (Provides workshops for dropouts ages 16–25 and provides full-time jobs during the summer.)

Mayor's Voluntary Action Center (New York, NY) (Places high school to retired people, skilled and unskilled workers.)

Interns

Barnard College (No college credit.)

Brooklyn College (Part-time and full-time internships available; students receive college credit.)

Columbia Student Enterprises/Columbia University (No college credit.)

Graduate Program in Arts Administration/Teachers College, Columbia University (Options range from short-term "practicums"—a few days for specific projects—to long-term programs.)

Great Lakes College Association (Coordinates semester-long, full-time internships; students receive credit.)

Hunter College (Offers college credit.)

Marymount Manhattan College—Career Development Office (Offers college credit.)

New York University—Dance Education Department (No college credit.)

New York University—Gallatin Division, University without Walls (Nontraditional B.A. and M.A. programs provide credit for individually tailored projects.)

New York University—Graduate Performing Arts Administration Program (Flexible programs; university strongly suggests a stipend be provided.)

For information about volunteer and internship programs in your area, contact your local arts service organization, or call your area colleges and universities.

Structure of Your Operations

Arts Action Research (formerly FEDAPT) (Consulting and research group focusing on assisting established organizations to restructure and reconceptualize themselves.)

Government Financial Services

American Woman's Economic Development Corp. (AWED) (Business counseling service for women starting or running a business. Services include bookkeeping, planning/ budgeting, buying work space, credit cards, tax assistance, and more.)

Food Stamp Program

Fund for the City of New York (Nonprofit computer exchange; organizational workshops and consulting.)

Social Security Benefit Information

Supplemental Security Income

Support Services Alliance (SSA)

Unemployment Insurance

Welfare

Publications

The Artist's Tax Guide and Financial Planner.

"Request for Earnings and Benefit Estimate Statement." Form used to obtain an estimate of Social Security benefits earned.

Legal Issues

American Civil Liberties Union (Defends individuals whose First Amendment rights have been violated through arts censorship.)

Art Law Line (See Volunteer Lawyers for the Arts/NY below.)

Arts Resource Consortium Library—joint project of American Council for the Arts and Volunteer Lawyers for the Arts (Library staff will assist arts managers and individual artists with inquiries over the phone, by fax, and by mail. Library may be used in person on appointment basis. Information on art law and nonprofit arts management.)

Business Volunteers for the Arts (Provides bookkeeping, planning/budgeting, tax assistance, insurance analysis, marketing, and public relations.)

California Lawyers for the Arts

Colorado Lawyers for the Arts

Community Action for Legal Services

Connecticut Volunteer Lawyers for the Arts

Copyright Office/Library of Congress

Council of New York Law Associates

Cultural Council Foundation

Dance Bay Area

Entertainment Arts and Sports Law Section—The Florida Bar (Contract negotiations, copyright, occupational hazards, and taxation.)

Foundation for Independent Artists/Pentacle

Georgia Volunteer Lawyers for the Arts

Lawyers for the Creative Arts (Chicago)

Legal Advocacy & Resource Center (LARC) (Boston)

National Campaign for Freedom of Expression (NCFE) (Membership. Coalition of artists, organizations, and individuals aimed at protecting the First Amendment and freedom of expression. Chapters across the United States. Legal defense for artists.)

National Coalition Against Censorship

Nebraska Advocacy Services

Ocean State Lawyers for the Arts

People for the American Way (Constitutional liberties organization; advocates for freedom of expression; technical assistance.)

Philadelphia Volunteer Lawyers for the Arts

St. Louis Volunteer Lawyers & Accountants for the Arts

Texas Accountants & Lawyers for the Arts

Utah Lawyers for the Arts

Virginia Lawyers for the Arts

VLAA—Cleveland Bar Association

Volunteer Lawyers for the Arts (Maine)

Volunteer Lawyers for the Arts New Jersey

Volunteer Lawyers for the Arts (VLA) (New York) (Legal services for artists and arts organizations; works to protect and improve artists' rights; 44 national affiliates; publications; operates an Art Law Line. Also, VLA sells Model Independent Contractor contracts and Instructional Guidelines for choreographers, scenic designers, makeup artists, lighting designers, electricians, carpenters, builders, and property builders.)

Volunteer Lawyers for the Arts/Lawyers Committee for the Arts (Washington, DC)

Volunteer Lawyers Project (VLP) (Boston)

Volunteer Legal Services Project of Monroe County (NY)

Washington Volunteer Lawyers for the Arts

If you live outside New York, contact your local arts council or VLA in New York City for information on low-cost legal services in your area.

Publications

Board Liability: Guide for Nonprofit Directors. A complete guide that identifies board responsibilities and helps directors avoid liability. Issues covered include proper board structure, conflict of interest, and indemnification and insurance.

The Buck Starts Here: Enterprise and the Arts, a Survival Guide for Arts Organizations. Addresses such urgent issues as analyzing not-for-profit potential, legal restrictions on earned income, setting up subsidiary organizations, real estate transactions, and more.

"Employers Guide to Unemployment Insurance."

The Green Book: Official Directory of the City of New York.

Handbook for Employers: A Guide to Employer Rights and Responsibilities under the New York State Unemployment Insurance Law.

"How the New York State Labor Law Protects You."

"New York State Unemployment Insurance for Claimants."

This Way Up: Legal & Business Essentials for Nonprofits. A summary of recent VLA national conference of nonprofit arts organizations. Topics include employees vs. independent contractors, IRS and labor regulations, board liability, insurance, loans, sponsorship, and merger/dissolution.

To Be or Not to Be: An Artist's Guide to Not-for-Profit Incorporation. Explains the pros and cons of corporate status, legal responsibilities and requirements, and alternatives to incorporation. Also covers applying for tax-exempt status and initial structure of board of directors.

U.S. Congress Handbook. Guide to and listing of congressional representatives and senators, their committees, and the White House.

VLA Guide to Copyright for the Performing Arts

Budgeting

Accountants for the Public Interest (National network of accountants who volunteer to nonprofit organizations, small businesses, and individuals who cannot afford professional accountant services.)

Accountants for the Public Interest/Support Center of New York (Bookkeeping, budgeting, tax assistance, workshops, referrals.)

Funding

International

Arts International, Fund for U.S. Artists at International Festivals and Exhibitions (See description below under "The International Marketplace.")

United States Information Agency, Arts America Program (See description below under "The International Marketplace.")

National

Economic Development Administration

Federal Council on the Arts and Humanities

National Endowment for the Arts (see the Directory for individual program phone numbers) (Programs: Advancement; Dance; Design Arts; Expansion Arts; Folk Arts; Inter-Arts; International Activities Office; Media Arts: Film/Radio/Television; Music; Opera–Musical Theater; Special Constituencies Office; Theater; Visual Arts.)

National Endowment for the Humanities

Smithsonian Institution, Performing Arts Program

U.S. Department of Education

U.S. Department of the Interior

National organizations that can provide information about state and local government funding agencies:

National Assembly of Local Arts Agencies (NALAA) (Assists the executive and volunteer leadership of the nation's local arts agencies to promote the arts at the local level through professional development, information publications, national arts policy development, and increasing public awareness of the arts.)

National Assembly of State Arts Agencies (NASAA) (A nonprofit membership organization of state arts organizations whose goals include enhancing growth of the arts, developing an informed membership, representing the collective needs and concerns of the member agencies, and providing forums for the review and development of national arts policy.)

Publications

"Annual Report of the NEA." Lists grants and program panelists.

The Arts and 504. A handbook for making the arts accessible to disabled people.

Guide to the National Endowment for the Arts. An overview of NEA programs.

State arts funding agencies (alphabetical by state/geographic entity)

Alabama State Council on the Arts and Humanities
Alaska State Council on the Arts and Humanities

American Samoa Council on Culture, Arts, and Humanities
Arizona Commission on the Arts
Arkansas Arts Council
California Arts Council
Colorado Council on the Arts and Humanities
Connecticut Commission on the Arts
Delaware State Arts Council
District of Columbia Commission on the Arts and Humanities
Arts Council of Florida
Georgia Council for the Arts and Humanities
Guam Council on the Arts and Humanities
Hawaii State Foundation on Culture and the Arts
Idaho Commission on the Arts
Illinois Arts Council
Indiana Arts Commission
Iowa State Arts Council
Kansas Arts Commission
Kentucky Arts Council
Louisiana Department of Culture, Recreation, and Tourism
Maine Arts Commission
Maryland State Arts Council
Michigan Council for the Arts
Minnesota State Arts Board
Mississippi Arts Commission
Missouri Arts Council
Montana Arts Council
Nebraska Arts Council
Nevada State Council on the Arts
New Hampshire State Council on the Arts
New Jersey State Council on the Arts
New Mexico Arts Division
New York State Council on the Arts
North Carolina Arts Council
North Dakota Council on the Arts
Northern Mariana Islands Commonwealth Council for Arts and Culture
Ohio Arts Council
State Arts Council of Oklahoma
Oregon Arts Commission
Commonwealth of Pennsylvania Council on the Arts
Institute of Puerto Rican Culture
Rhode Island State Council on the Arts
South Carolina Arts Commission
South Dakota Arts Council
Tennessee Arts Commission
Texas Commission on the Arts
Utah Arts Council
Vermont Council on the Arts, Inc.
Virginia Commission for the Arts

Virgin Islands Council on the Arts
Washington State Arts Commission
West Virginia Arts and Humanities Commission
Wisconsin Arts Board
Wyoming Council on the Arts

Local arts funding agencies (alphabetical by locality)

These are just a few: Contact your local arts service organization for more organizations.

Boston Arts Commission
Chicago Department of Cultural Affairs
Metropolitan Dade County Cultural Affairs Council
DC Commission on the Arts and Humanities
Cultural Arts Council of Houston
City of Los Angeles Cultural Affairs Department
Milwaukee Artist Foundation
Minneapolis Arts Commission
Minneapolis Community Development Agency
New York City Department of Cultural Affairs
New York Foundation for the Arts (New York Artist Fellowships)
San Francisco Arts Commission
Tacoma Arts Commission
Cultural Alliance of Greater Washington

Foundation resources

Associated Grantmakers of Massachusetts

California Community Foundation, Funding Information Center

Donors Forum (Chicago)

Foundation Center (New York, San Francisco, and Washington, DC) (See Directory for toll-free number for referrals to cooperating collections.)

Grants Information Service (Dallas)

Minneapolis Public Library

Publications

Below are listed selected publications that are important fund-raising tools. Many of these books are expensive, but they can be found in Foundation Center libraries as well as in the reference rooms of large public libraries.

Comsearch: Broad Topics.

The Foundation Directory. Published annually.

Foundation Fundamentals: A Guide for Grant Seekers.

The Foundation Grants Index Quarterly.

Foundation Grants to Individuals.

Foundations News. A bimonthly magazine.

National Guide to Funding in Arts and Culture. Published every 2 years.

Sources of Foundation Grants to Individuals.

Taft Foundation Reporter. There is a newsletter associated with this publication called the *Foundation Giving Watch.*

Corporate resources

Arts and Business Council, Inc. (This organization's Business Volunteers for the Arts matches volunteer business executives with arts organizations and provides resource information.)

Business Committee for the Arts, Inc. (BCA) (Counsels arts organizations on more effective ways to enlist corporate involvement in, and support of, their activities.)

National Corporate Fund for Dance, Inc. (This national not-for-profit organization seeks general operating support from the business community for major American dance companies and provides special service programs for dance companies throughout the United States.)

Publications

The Chronicle of Philanthropy. Biweekly newspaper on nonprofit organizations, private foundations, and corporate philanthropic programs.

Corporate Philanthropy Report. Monthly newsletter with trends and issues affecting corporate philanthropic programs.

Events Clearinghouse Calendar. Published monthly. Call to check a date or register your gala event fund-raiser.

Guide to Corporate Giving IV. Each listing includes names and addresses of contributions officers, application procedures, requirements, deadlines, type and level of support offered, criteria used in judging requests, awards dates, and more.

Money for Performing Artists. A guide to grants, awards, fellowships, and artist-in-residence programs available to individual artists, including information on 250 funding organizations in 50 states.

Sponsorship and the Arts. A practical guide to corporate sponsorship of the performing and visual arts.

Loans

Alliance of Resident Theatres/NY (ART/NY) (Provides bridge loans up to $3,000 based on grant letter, contract, or other collateral at no interest charge to member organizations.)

Artists Community Federal Credit Union (ACFCU) (Provides loans to members. Artists and people employed in arts community are eligible for membership.)

Commercial Banks (Bridge loans to tide you over until your grant arrives also can be obtained from some commercial banks. Policies vary, so you'll need to talk with an officer at the place where you regularly do business.)

Fund for the City of New York (Makes cash-flow loans against approved but delayed payments on specific government contracts and, occasionally, foundation or corporate grants to New York City not-for-profit groups. To be eligible for a loan, an organization must have a confirmed grant or contract. There is a 2 percent service charge for the use of these funds; however, if the loan is repaid within 2 months, half the service charge is refunded. Loans are usually repaid within 3 months. There is sometimes a waiting list.)

New York City Economic Development Corp. (Loan program to help smaller nonprofit organizations with capital and cash-flow financing at prime interest rates.)

New York Foundation for the Arts Revolving Loan Program (Provides short-term cash flow loans for arts organizations based on pending public agency or, occasionally, foundation grants.)

Parachute Fund through Dance Bay Area (Serves members of the Bay Area dance community who are facing life-threatening illness and have demonstrated financial need.)

S.A.F.E. (Special Arts Fund for Emergencies)

Theatre Development Fund, Inc. Executive Director's Discretionary Loan Fund (Last resort lender to TDF program participants. Program currently in abeyance.)

THE MARKETPLACE

Any Fool can paint a picture, but it takes a wise man
to be able to sell it.—Samuel Butler

■ I got into producing other people through self-producing. I realized early on that my talents were best used helping artists rather than being one, but I do identify with the struggle inherent in producing one's work, in New York in particular. My first word of advice is, do not wait for someone to discover you. It isn't a reflection on your work that the ten or so producers of experimental dance in New York City don't know who you are or what you do. You must learn the art of gentle harassment. Don't call the producer(s) at home at midnight twice a week, but do be persistent, and don't be shy if the opportunity arises to talk about your work or to invite someone to see it. In addition to making your work, you have to get comfortable with your own brand of self-promotion, which has to do with being articulate, and even more to do with passion and conviction than with high-tech videos and press packets. What happens in the dancing is what really matters. And there's personal taste: No two producers have the same point of view. Unfortunately, the community is so small that almost everyone talks, wanting to know, or to tell, who's "hot." That's the marketplace, and it is worth understanding.—Elise Bernhardt, producer, "Dancing in the Streets" ■

The National Marketplace
Ivan Sygoda

From the opening night gala at Lascaux until the early seventies, performing arts touring was an arduous and haphazard nonsystem of one-night stands. You performed where they let you, got paid if you could, and did a fair amount of schlepping. When your tour was finally over, they buried you in unconsecrated ground. Despite the rigors of such a life—with a little help from friends and patrons and a lot of moxie—Bournonville, Petipa, Duncan, Wigman, Dunham, Graham, Balanchine, Cunningham, and the rest of the pantheon survived and created their legacy of work.

By the seventies, however, a great evolution had occurred that profoundly altered the context in which American cultural endeavor takes place. On the one hand, the establishment of the National Endowment for the Arts (and, eventually, today's network of local, state, and regional arts councils) redefined the relationship between artists and the public: Taxpayer support of the arts became public policy. On the other hand (the outstretched one), artists organized their professional lives in new ways in order to be eligible for this largess: whence the rise of the not-for-profit corporation and all it entails.

The Market Terrain

It would seem logical to divide the market terrain into two parts: "here" and "there" or "home" and "away." This binary division, however, encourages unproductive thinking because it becomes too easy to equate "home" with your more or less annual "home season" and "away" with everything else. Also, "touring" and "the marketplace" are by no means synonymous. "Touring" is a catchall word that covers everything from an experimental "downtown" artist going north of Manhattan's 14th Street, to a five-week, ten-nation Far Eastern tour, to a four-month residency as guest faculty at a university. Yet there is a marketplace for your art at home that is independent of your annual home season and that doesn't involve going out on the road at all. This is important because, if you're like many choreographers, you tend to devalue the kinds of work you get to do locally. Next to your big home season, where you premiere new pieces before friends and critics, other local work tends to pale in prestige and visibility. This attitude is counterproductive. The hard work you do locally and the audience you carefully build in your own community are a more reliable shield against the vagaries of funding and fashion in the so-called mainstream marketplace than anything else. "Home" and "away" involve a continuum of concentric circles emanating from wherever home base is.

Convenient geographic divisions are the following:

The local marketplace, where you can perform and/or teach without having to stay overnight. Because, usually, no per diems (daily allowances for food and lodging) and only minimal transportation expenses are incurred in one's local marketplace, there are cost advantages that bring certain kinds of activities within the range of certain kinds of presenters, activities that would be less feasible for them to purchase from nonlocal artists. The limits of "local" may vary depending on whether there is convenient and reliable public transportation, whether you own a car or other suitable vehicle, and local custom. Manhattanites often act as if Brooklyn were overseas. Out West, people think nothing of driving for two hours.

The regional marketplace, which is basically one's home and neighboring states. Both geographic and political factors define one's "natural" region. In particular, the territory defined by each of the six regional arts organizations can have a greater effect on your possibilities than mere physical proximity. This is because the National Endowment's Dance on Tour (DOT) program places a premium on engagements involving artists and companies brought in from outside the region. To the degree that programming decisions are influenced by funding possibilities, and all other things being equal, it may prove easier for a New York–based company to secure an engagement in North Carolina than one in New Jersey. Conversely, if your state or region has a statewide or in-region touring program, your chances of getting bookings may be influenced by other political factors. Does the program have a roster? Does the roster consist of in-state or in-region companies? Are you on the roster?

The national marketplace, which is usually defined as the touring circuit served by well-established companies of national renown and involving major festivals, auditoriums, and performing arts centers. It may include a major presenter who happens to be located in your home town, where you may or may not ever have been invited to perform.

The international marketplace, which is otherwise known as the rest of the planet. The international marketplace is as fragmented and diverse as the local, regional, and national marketplaces. It ranges from the opera house circuit booked by impresarios with gold chains to alternative spaces that specialize in everything from ballet to the experimental. [See the next article, "Foreign Intrigues."]

The film and video marketplace, which includes both commercial and non-commercial enterprises, broadcast and cable television, and even videos for purchase or rental by home consumers. This marketplace can be as local as the video store around the corner or as international as the known universe. It changes as rapidly as the technologies on which it is based.

The Local Terrain

The concept of market fragmentation is crucial. Each of the above divisions contains many different sorts of actual and potential dance presenters with differing needs and expectations. One occasionally hears choreographers lament what they perceive to be limited thinking by presenters. The latter want only, or think they want only, certain kinds of companies. But choreographers can be guilty of the same lack of imagination. They limit their list of targeted presenters to the relatively short roster of active venues that book companies everyone has heard of. Yes, it would be naive to maintain that these are not generally considered the best gigs. But it's time for an attitude check. Are you dancing for presenters or for people? People are everywhere, even in your own backyard.

Your local community offers a challenging mix of problems and opportunities. Sometimes the two are synonymous. If you live in one of the urban agglomerations where there are many dance artists and companies, it will seem that there is a lot of healthy competition for the available work.

Remember the concept of market fragmentation. Not only are the various companies in your area likely to be quite different from one another, but the various communities within your community are also heterogeneous. For every dance troupe there is an audience that will appreciate its unique mix of movement style, thematic concerns, choice of music, workshop activities, and choreographic personality. To use another marketing phrase, your first task is to discover your "niche." The word comes from the Old French for "nest" or "nook," but you've got to get over the idea that a niche is ineluctably small or even permanently comfortable. Nonetheless, it is a kind of home.

The elemental niche, of course, is dancing for Aunt Ida in your living room. If you danced in high school or college, then the school community was your next niche. Dozens of concentric circles follow, but your willingness to acknowledge or mine them depends on your attitude about yourself: who you are, where you are, and where you come from. Religious and ethnic communities are the most obvious, even if you're not about liturgical dance or traditional dance forms. It may be enough that your work references traditions, values, music, or historical events relevant to that community. Furthermore, that community is likely to have either facilities or occasions for your work. Each such group may have developed a system or network for taking care of its own—day care, elders centers, and such—that offers opportunities for classes, workshops, and lec-dems, if not for performances.

You must not underestimate the amount of meaningful dance activity that goes on nationwide in this way. It's just that much of it is less visible because it is publicized only to the intended target audience in "niche" publications.

Here again, problem and opportunity are synonymous: There are no widely distributed lists of these opportunities complete with contact names and facility descriptions. You have the onus or opportunity to create the marketplace, but once you do, it's really yours.

Another local market involves government and quasi-government agencies that deliver social services to groups within the community. The targeted groups may be the same kinds of religious or ethnic communities as those alluded to above, or they may cut across these lines to focus on different kinds of groups: children, seniors, the physically or mentally challenged, the incarcerated, the hospital bound, the homeless, refugee groups, halfway houses. However, the people in charge may not yet realize the kind of contribution you can make. They may never have offered a performance or workshop. They may not understand the ways in which your art can engage, challenge, and validate its audience. You have to sell them on the idea, after a process whereby you define these goals for yourself.

Not all such local activity focuses on special-interest groups. Parks departments, community-development agencies, civic associations, even real-estate developers can celebrate a place or event with performing arts activities meant to have wide appeal. Many communities have established programs to bring art and artists to citizens who are not ordinarily exposed to them. In general, however, there are few ready-made contact lists. Three approaches suggest themselves. First, really investigate your own community. Is there some place, situation, or event that might be enhanced by what you do? Recognize—or, if need be, invent—and define the need your presence might fulfill, and then find out who or what has jurisdiction. Expect this part of your task to be difficult, especially if a performing arts event was not originally part of the concept. Second, you can start with the phone book, that most useful and underutilized resource of artists and administrators. Examine the government listings, often grouped in a special section. Check out parks departments, school districts, development authorities, chambers of commerce. Be efficient in the explanation of what you're looking to learn or do because you want to keep the attention of the person who answers and because you'll have to explain all over again the dozen times your call is passed through channels. Jot down the name of each person you talk to. Chances are rather good that you'll cycle back to her/him.

Third, keep your eyes and ears open. Information about performances that might have been yours is on, in, or near every lamppost, wall, kiosk, bulletin board, dance studio changing room, newspaper, house organ, church bulletin, aerobics class, and chiropractor's office and everywhere else some other clever choreographer thought to tape up a notice. Let what you see inspire you. In other words, steal ideas shamelessly.

Ideally you will convince someone to pay you for what you do. Otherwise, you may have no choice but to split the gate, if there is one. Or you may simply decide to invest in your own visibility and exposure. Or, within the limits of good citizenship, you may elect to perform when and where you weren't invited. Who says you can't march in the Memorial Day parade or invade the food fair or dance on the village green? Well-planned guerrilla action can advance the art form and your own career.

The business world represents a largely unworked terrain, beyond the more obvious and visible sponsored events in corporate plazas and shopping malls. Put yourself in the shoes of the manager of a commercial enterprise.

She/he has the task of energizing a group of people, forging them into a team, getting them to work together more productively, more effectively. You know all about that process. You do it every day in rehearsal. Well, perhaps you can help that manager do her/his job. A lunch-hour movement class can be a metaphor for what the manager is trying to accomplish the rest of the working day. Make a deal. Teach classes there for a fee, or get the firm to subsidize your next performance or buy a hundred tickets to it for distribution to employees. Does the company have branches? Do it again. Perhaps there is a way to do a miniperformance at the factory. If the firm has day care, offer kiddie classes, and then pin concert invitations to each kiddie. One way or another, there may be a way for you and your company to be in residence at Los Angeles Tool and Die just as interestingly as you might be at the Krannert Center.

There are other sorts of commercial opportunities the focus of which is not necessarily concert dance but that do offer honest dance employment, albeit less altruistically. These range from entrepreneurs who run commercial dinner theaters and nightclubs to producers of fashion shows, industrials, and advertisements.

Of course, it generally reads better than it plays, but these are the kinds of things dance companies can and have made happen for themselves. Furthermore, these are areas where the agent you think you need generally has little experience or aptitude. You yourself, as the one who knows most about your company, have the best chance of making it happen because you have the quickest reaction time and the most creative enthusiasm in relation to your own possibilities.

The point, which could be made at any of a dozen junctures in this text, is worth emphasizing. There are myriad opportunities for you to market yourself, your company, and your art in your home community that are best ferreted out and realized by you yourself. An agent, manager, or other third party would have to be wedded to you in ways that money can't buy to transmit these intangibles as effectively as you could. Finally, don't forget that you are allowed to be looking for work while you are on unemployment, should it come to that.

Arts-in-Education

Arts-in-Education is an immense area of concern and endeavor. In this country, it is usually under local jurisdiction, as is our educational system. This means that resource lists have to be ferreted out locality by locality. We have the space here to offer only a few thoughts to help orient your own thinking about how you might fit in.

For reasons both good and bad, often both at the same time, it seems that arts resources in this country are today being focused on arts-in-education. On the one hand, it's "safer" to devote tax dollars to the delivery of a known artistic product to a quantifiable number of school-age people than it is to risk investment in the creation of work that may prove provocative, offensive, erotic, or merely unsuccessful. On the other hand, we are finally and collectively realizing how profoundly we have failed to build audiences for our art form.

The field of arts-in-education is still wide open, in part because, with a few notable exceptions, we have not attracted the best and the brightest to it. "We" is collective here: we-all, the society at large that has failed to establish arts programs intelligently and to fund them adequately, and we-all in dance who have ignored the field with all its problems and opportunities. Some choreographers wouldn't be caught dead doing work in the schools because they see it as some sort of limbo from which one can never return. Others seek it out, albeit unenthusiastically, because work in education seems to be part of the dues one pays to get other kinds of local funding.

Dance/USA, the national service organization for nonprofit professional dance, recently inaugurated a task force to study arts-in-education as it relates to the art form. We can expect that the very role of dance in the schools will be reexamined. Are we building dancers or audiences for dance? Is dance a participatory, possibly recreational, activity, or is it a means of expression? Is dance expressive of a culture or of an individual's unique sensitivity? Given one's answers to such questions—and there is great validity to each point of view—what sort of artist should be doing what sort of work with which students? To put it bluntly, the larger dance agenda is at stake. The field of serious concert dance, realizing where resources will be directed in the years to come and motivated by enlightened self-interest, means to reclaim the turf it had more or less abandoned for a decade. The process will be challenging because it will involve attitude adjustment on all sides. We may learn that the artists we consider our most creative and innovative choreographers are not necessarily our most inventive and effective dance educators. We may learn to recognize a wider array of excellences among our colleagues and discover new kinds of respect for their efforts. The education establishment will be challenged to make room for us, literally and figuratively. Dance takes time and space and energy, all of which cost money.

You should join the debate, if only because your livelihood is ultimately at stake. Just as you must define your unique aesthetic mission to succeed in the performing marketplace, you must discover and articulate your educational mission to hold your own in the developing school marketplace.

What do you have to offer, and why is it important? Who are you, and why should I let you near my kids? We already have a phys ed program, thank you. We do arts and crafts. Go away.

As you can see, as a community we've got a lot of work to do. [See "On Arts Education" in chapter 6.]

The Regional and National Marketplaces

We finally get to the place where most artists most often think they want to be most of the time—on tour, showing their work under the proper technical circumstances to houses full of discriminating and appreciative concert-goers, and getting paid well enough that there's money left over to put in the kitty for the next piece.

We should start with some basic definitions. Presenters are usually organizations (though they can be individual entrepreneurs) and usually not-for-profit (though they can be commercial enterprises or government agencies) whose raison d'être is the presentation of live performing arts attractions to their communities. Call them professional presenters, if you will, to underline the distinction between their ongoing commitment to presentation and that of nonpresenters—the church group that hires you for its fund-raiser and so forth.

Presenters are incredibly varied in their budget size, facilities, level of activity, operational structure, curatorial structure, relationship to community, and taste in dance. Some are huge, such as the Brooklyn Academy of Music and UCLA. Some are small, such as Pyramid in Rochester, New York, or the Sushi Gallery in San Diego. Some, such as Cal Performances at UC/Berkeley, present dozens if not hundreds of events per year in all imaginable performing arts disciplines. Twenty or thirty others, such as the Pittsburgh Dance Council and a number of the major summer festivals, are dance specific. Some have made spaces out of converted warehouses, bingo halls, and churches, not to mention the proverbial barn. Some have multiple facilities, such as the Broward Center for the Performing Arts in Fort Lauderdale, Florida. Some have no facilities at all, such as Ruth Felt's San Francisco Performances and Dance Umbrella in Boston, but rent an appropriate venue for each presentation. Some presenters are independent organizations. Others function within a large context, such as a college or a university or an art museum. Some are run as benevolent dictatorships, with curatorial authority invested in one person. Others are structured like New England town meetings, with programming decisions reached by consensus. Still others have programming committees.

How is one to get a handle on such a diverse universe of presenters? If the issue on the table is where you are likely to get bookings, binary oppositions like those enumerated above don't help much. Big presenters book small companies. Small presenters have been known to splurge on big companies. This is not to say that common sense doesn't apply. Financial considerations aside, the New York City Ballet won't fit into the Sushi Gallery. Categorizing types of presenters is a thing that can be done, and we shall do it here, but it really is an exercise of limited usefulness.

Colleges and universities offer many performance and residency opportunities. However, it is usually a mistake to assume that a particular college or university is a presenter. Rather, it may be three or even more independent presenters, all operating on one campus.

The most visible of these is usually the performing arts series. This is, typically, a multidisciplinary subscription series that takes place in the main auditorium and is targeted at both students and the surrounding community, or town and gown, as they say. The facility and the programming that happens within it are usually overseen by a professional staff person, although there may be committee structures involved. By "staff person," we mean that the individual rarely has faculty status, a fact that can be of consequence for the programming mission. When artists emerging into the marketplace refer to booking conventions and to the kinds of opportunities they hope to find there, it is most often these series and the people who run them that they are thinking of. (To put things in perspective, colleges and universities constitute only about 35 percent of the membership of the Association of Performing Arts Presenters.)

The student activities office on the same campus can program attractions more actively than the performing arts series and may have access to different halls. Its budget may even be larger. But it is a different budget controlled by different structures overseen by different staff and committees. It is even likely to participate in a different booking circuit, the National Association of Campus Activities (NACA). To generalize grossly, student-activity programming focuses less on concert dance as a means of artistic expression than on attractions with more immediately evident entertainment and accessibility values.

A third locus of dance activity on campus is, or can be, the dance department (if one exists; dance is often housed in physical education). Dozens of degree-granting dance departments across the country have the budgets and wherewithal to invite visiting artists to perform and offer workshops. Again, a different budget, a different decision-making structure, and a different time frame. Although there are professional organizations for dance educators, there are no booking conventions that focus on them. However, since most dance educators are dancers and former dancers who have fanned out across the country, their booking decisions tend to be made on the basis of personal contact, artist to artist. *Dance Magazine* publishes a biennial *College Guide* that lists the chair of each such dance department and gives a capsule description of its activities. Note that this is also a national marketplace where agents are of little use. You're the one with the personal connections that can turn into engagements.

Occasionally, other departments on a campus may sponsor dance events: the music department, especially if its own musicians are involved; the theater department, especially if dance is housed therein; special studies departments, such as religious studies, women's studies, black studies, Asian studies, etc. Similarly, special interest clubs in these or other areas may find the means to sponsor you, perhaps as a fund- or consciousness-raiser. Finally, and especially when an educational institution focuses special efforts on issues of cultural equity and community relations, an independent council or commission chaired by a dean or faculty member may have the budget and desire to present your work.

The majority of presenters are not college or university based. Performing arts centers and theaters, often owned and operated by cities or development authorities to serve a wide variety of community needs, include impressive new facilities as well as restored vaudeville houses and renovated movie palaces. Inspired by successes like New York's Lincoln Center, many municipalities used performing arts facilities to help revitalize neighborhoods and spark development. It remains to be seen in the more spartan nineties whether programming visions and budgets will follow the architectural dreams of the eighties.

Dance and performing arts festivals large and small provide excellent visibility for the companies they host and an exciting environment in which ideas can be exchanged and links forged—links between artist and artist and between artist and presenter. These engagements are therefore among the most desirable, which also means that they are among the hardest to obtain.

Much innovative and influential programming happens under the aegis of art museums and galleries. Presentations can occur in the institution's own theater or at theaters off-site in the community. They can also occur in gallery spaces, sometimes in relation to a particular exhibition, or in sculpture gardens. Symphony orchestras occasionally host dance, and not only *The Nutcracker.* There is room in their tradition and budget for guest artists. Since much dance uses music that orchestras like to play and subscribers to hear, all kinds of possibilities exist for soloists and ensembles. Some classic drama, such as Shakespeare and Molière, allows for dance interludes. So does some contemporary work. Also, if the stage is suitable, and if the next production doesn't involve an invasive set, a theater company can present a dance company between subscription events.

Dance companies themselves are presenting other dance companies with increasing frequency. When you think about it, it makes perfect sense. Picture a company that, either instead of or in addition to touring, has come to depend on multiple home seasons during the year for income and stability. That company has a frightening amount of dance to create or acquire if it's to keep the audience members coming back repeatedly. Putting another company on your subscription series or sharing a program with it is a creative solution. It varies the menu, attracts new audience members, and challenges existing ones.

A variation on the above theme involves what amounts to barter among dance companies. Let's say you're a company based in Seattle and a colleague whose work you value is based in San Diego. You would each like to show your work to new audiences, but no established presenter is inviting you to San Diego, and no presenter in Seattle will book your friend. So book each other. Depending on budgets, fund-raising success, your accumulation of frequent-flyer miles, your ability to house and feed one another, and other such factors, the exchange might involve anything from your doing your new solo on your friend's concert and vice versa to a trade of full companies. You're both securing a hall and taking care of public relations and box office anyway. The frustrating thing about this idea is that it's not fundable: Hardly any cash changes hands.

In the years since its inaugural season in 1985–86, the National Performance Network (NPN) [see the Appendix] has grown into a pace-setting consortium of fifty-one presenters in twenty-six cities. The primary sponsors who together compose the network are united in their commitment to innovative work in dance, performance, music, theater, and puppetry by emerging, non-mainstream, and culturally diverse artists from all over the land. The annually updated NPN brochure, which lists artists selected to tour on the network, contains important information about ancillary NPN programs such as the co-commissioning creation fund and SURFF, a special project to seed innovative artist-community partnerships.

Now, having gone through this census of presenter types in the regional and national marketplaces, we must try to ascertain what we have accomplished. Have we delineated areas that will help you focus your limited and therefore precious booking resources? What makes these presenters "regional" or "national" anyway, where is the dividing line, and does it matter?

Let's define "national" presenters as those with the history and means of engaging artists and companies that interest them regardless of where in the country these originate. This in itself says nothing about taste, prestige, influence, visibility, fundability, desirability, or any other ability except that of selecting companies from a wide spectrum of possibilities and of paying them enough for an engagement to prove viable. Regional presenters do exactly the same thing, except that they don't cast their nets quite so far. Following this reasoning, regional and national form part of the same continuum. Do presenters in the West get some sort of national merit badge or certificate the first time they bring a troupe across the Rockies? Sure, if you insist. Why are we engaged in this verbal gavotte? Because of the perceived prestige of New York City companies in the American dance world. Most choreographers across the country would define "national," and therefore "prestigious," in absolute terms and equate both with the presenters that have a history of presenting the biggest or best-known troupes from the East Coast. If you want to run on that race course, that's your business, but then accept your share of the responsibility for laying it out that way.

Remember that each so-called national presenter can also be a local presenter. None of them exists in a vacuum. Each is enmeshed in a complex web of relationships with other presenters in that community, funders in that community, choreographers and other performing and creative artists, audiences, even nonattenders. Some have a commitment to local artists that is as rich and varied as their commitment to nonlocal artists. Others won't give local artists the time of day. This can be a source of great frustration.

Why Tour?

Which brings us back to an important point. Given our working definition, what is there about these national presenters that makes you pin so many hopes on getting booked by them? Why are you willing to expend so much time, money, and energy to get their attention? Why are you so willing to go into hock to do these gigs, which never seem to pay enough, no matter how decent the fee?

There are many answers, but what are your answers? Do you really want to tour at all? And if you think you do, are you sure this is not merely a reflex answer, a conditioned response based on models that may not really apply to you?

There are many good reasons for touring, both artistic and financial. If opportunities to perform at home are limited, you may need to tour simply to perform more. You may need this additional public exposure to perfect your craft or to rework a particular piece and try out the results. Or a particular group of dancers you work with may insist on a certain level of activity (financial considerations aside, for the moment) if they are to remain with you, and may need them because it takes so much time to get your movement inside their bodies. Touring can help pay the rent if performance and residency fees truly reflect your costs. They rarely do, these days. For many companies without the resources or connections to do effective fund-raising, touring may be the only way to pay bills and match state or federal grants. Finally, it may simply be your own ego or ambition that dictates your decision to seek tour engagements. If that's the case, then bravo! and full speed ahead. It's as good a reason as any other, and perhaps more likely to remain valid and motivating throughout the vagaries of your professional and personal life.

These considerations may seem self-evident, but they are by no means trivial. The decisions you reach about entering the national marketplace will have an extraordinary impact on your company's budget and on your allocation of precious time and energy. You cannot tour without a considerable investment in all three of these areas. There are dozens if not hundreds of companies going after the same gigs you want. And there are hundreds if not thousands of presenters who could book you instead of someone else, if only—what? It's rarely sufficient to be simply a very good choreographer with a very good company. You need to narrow your focus on presenters and to persuade them to focus their efforts on you. This takes a lot of homework.

Before you start researching lists and addressing packets, you have to sit quietly and think about who you are and about who these presenters are. You will then be able to understand better what happens to you in this marketplace, why you get certain bookings, and why you don't get others. You will make better decisions about your marketing and promotional materials. You will collaborate more effectively and humanely with whoever helps you get bookings.

John Killacky, currently director of performing arts at the Walker Art Center in Minneapolis, does two mind-opening exercises at performing arts workshops and seminars. Exercise 1: He reads or distributes two parallel lists. One column lists ten or so well-known and highly regarded dance companies. The other column lists the sort of review extracts that everyone puts on flyers and in press packets. The object of the exercise is to match the companies in column A with the corresponding quotes in column B, the ones the companies themselves extracted to characterize the work for the benefit of presenters and audiences. Well, absolutely everyone and his brother is "stunning!" "moving!" "exciting!" "energetic!" and "wonderful!"

Exercise 2: The artists and managers take out a blank piece of paper and write their mission statement on it, unsigned. Then the papers are folded and tossed onto the table. One by one, the participants read the other statements out loud. The object is to identify which mission statement belongs to whom. Ideally, your mission statement is your verbal DNA, the expression of your unique artistic signature. It's depressing how few of these statements are correctly identified, even by people who are familiar with the work that supposedly corresponds to the mission statement.

The Mission Statement

Your mission statement is the key to everything that follows. It is *not* the bland, politically correct, and inoffensive prose that you stick in your funding applications and press materials because you were instructed to do so:

> Joe Schmendrake and Dancers exists to provide a forum for the artistic director to develop his unique choreographic vision using a cohesive company of highly and specifically trained dancers, and a means to present that work in the most optimal circumstances to the widest possible audiences in our home community and throughout the known universe.

You can substitute the name of any choreographer you've ever heard of for good old Joe. This kind of mission statement affirms everything and says absolutely nothing.

The mission statement we're talking about here isn't necessarily one you'd even type up for publication, although the discipline of committing it to paper is invaluable. Call it your credo. It's your affirmation, to yourself before anyone else, of why you make the work that you make and why you make it the way you make it, who you make it for and why you make it for them, and why they should care and why you care even if they do not.

If you've never attempted to do this, your first attempts will make you heave in disgust. Don't edit! No one will see what you write until you want or need them to. You've got to get beyond sincerity to specificity, and for most mortals it's not an easy road.

You make work to express yourself! Express what, and how? You make dance because it's the only language that doesn't lie! Lovely. What have you got to say in that language? You're expressing universal human longings! Gimme a break—so's the homeless person on the corner. You're making beauty! Hmm. You're exposing the plight of the disenfranchised, the disinherited, the dispossessed! Are you indeed becoming the "other," that most difficult and magical of artistic feats that enables the audience to shed its skin with you? Or are you simply exploiting the already exploited for their plot value? Don't imagine for an instant that you'll be comfortable with your answers. This questioning is an ongoing process, and the answers are perpetually provisional.

When you get through this exercise, a lot of other things will begin to fall into place. Where do you fit in? Are you really trying to develop a distinctive, idiosyncratic movement vocabulary? Some presenters and their audiences value that above all else, yet it's the sort of idea that would make most people's eyes glaze over. Are you really about elegant, gorgeous dancing? Then don't be afraid to say it. Do you go right for the political jugular vein? Then stake your claim. It's all part of accepting responsibility for your goals.

The above process applies most of all to your art, to the work you put onstage. But it also applies to your other professional activities, particularly to the classes, workshops, lec-dems, and other "outreach" activities you probably offer as income-producing events at home and as residency activities on the road. Each such activity should be animated by its own mission statement, its own raison d'être. Many touring artists have experienced how dreary it can be when some class that was scheduled turns out to be merely a space filler. The regular teacher gets a free period. You're faced with a bunch of kids who have no idea who you are or why you're there. And you yourself begin to forget why. The mission statement for that class—the technique, how it relates to the participants, what they're likely to get out of it, can get you centered again. This in turn can make it possible for you to overcome endemic entropy and actually accomplish something. You won't always succeed, but at least you'll be measuring success by your own yardstick.

Finally, and at the risk of overdramatizing, each residency you are asked to do at home or away should have its own mission statement. Many such engagements entail community activities. Increased ticket sales are but one of many goals involved. Building an effective residency involves a partnership between you, the guest artist who brings talent and expertise into the community, and the presenter, who knows that community. This means merging your artistic mission statement and the presenter's mission statement into shared means and objectives. Just as there are trite artistic mission statements, there can be nonspecific, pro forma residency mission statements that are little more than lists of ingredients—a class for this group, a lec-dem for that, a talk here, a workshop there—that add up to nothing special. Anyone can make a shopping list. It takes work to turn the ingredients into a memorable meal.

Your mission statement is what keeps you centered when you're offstage. As you enter the marketplace, you have a thousand decisions to make. Some may seem momentous: Should you find an agent, and which one? Others are more quotidian: This photo or that? Should we reprint that review? Your mission statement can inform these choices. It can help you sort out priorities and alternatives, and it can orient the efforts of those around you, whatever constellation of paid staff members, volunteers, consultants, and board members you've put together to further your career. [See "Promoting Your Performance" in chapter 2.]

Establishing Fees

Back in the days of the National Endowment for the Arts Dance Touring Program (DTP)—dismantled in the early eighties—all-inclusive company fees for half- and full-week residencies were published in the annual DTP directory. To account for airfare differences, companies usually divided the country at the Mississippi or into concentric geographic regions around their home base. Depending on which of various programmatic revisions were in effect any given year, these fees were either nonnegotiable or slightly (10 percent) negotiable. Everything was out in the open.

Since then the situation has changed considerably. Money and budgets are cause for anxiety all around. Most people will tell you with whom they sleep before they'll tell you what they earn a year. And so it's not surprising that the process of setting and then negotiating company touring fees has become "remystified." The goal of this section is to demystify the topic as much as possible.

The problem with fee sheets can be summarized as follows. Fee sheets lack the flexibility you may want and need when dealing with particular situations. A number of things seem axiomatic: If you list the high fee you want on your fee sheet, presenters with limited budgets might assume you mean it and not pursue the engagement because you're out of their league. If you don't mean it, or almost never mean it, then you shouldn't say it. On the other hand, in the absence of any obvious mitigating factors, it is extremely difficult to get so much as one dollar more than the fee you have stated in writing. What you state about your fees in your marketing packet—indeed, whether you include such a document at all—is therefore a matter for discussion.

We've all experienced how indistinct a television picture can become when competing signals interfere with each other on the same channel. The same kind of interference can happen concerning company fees. Three separate figures must be determined: what your company is "worth," how much it will actually cost you to do the gig, and how much it will actually cost the presenter to present you.

Worth is intangible, inextricably wound up with everyone's attitudes toward the object of interest—you and your work. Look at it one way: You're worth whatever you can get, not a penny more. Look at it another way: You're worth the cost in blood, sweat, time, and tears of a lifetime of dedication. In other words, you're worth your weight in diamonds, and you're worth your weight in coal. The only things to be gleaned from this line of reasoning are the notions of scarcity and desirability. This is why we keep harping on the uniqueness and focus of your artistic and programmatic mission. Are you unique in some identifiable way and therefore rare, or are you interchangeable with other artists and companies? Will presenters and audiences believe that you are the sole source of something desirable, or is it a buyer's commodity market where competition among essentially equivalent or interchangeable products drives the price down?

Scarcity and desirability. You may well position yourself as the only living exponent of work pioneered by the nineteenth-century Nebraskan choreographer Laurinda Schmendrake, but the light of that late, lamented artist is hidden under many bushels indeed. You have your work cut out for you.

Sooner or later, of course, you'll have to tell the presenter what you charge. The best way to begin figuring it out is to investigate what it costs you to fulfill an out-of-town engagement. We'll use a hypothetical company and do the math a few different ways.

The Royal American Dance Company, under the artistic direction of Tamara Schmendrake (Laurinda's great-granddaughter), tours with six dancers, including Tammi, and a technical director. They're based in Lincoln, Nebraska. Presenter Ron Bowlin at the Lied Center there told John Killacky how wonderful they are, and John has invited them to give a single performance at the Walker Art Center in Minneapolis, filling in on a Tuesday for a group that had to cancel. The accompanying table and paragraphs that follow show how these costs can be calculated.

Personnel. Tammi generally tries to pay her dancers at the prevailing union (AGMA) rates, approximately $450 per week. If the company is on the road only two days, it feels like a single performance engagement, and she feels that $200 is the minimum compensation. If they go Saturday, she will consider it a

Category	Travel Monday	Travel Saturday
Personnel:		
Tammi	@ 250 250	@ 300 300
5 dancers	@ 200 ... 1,000	@ 225 ... 1,125
Tech. Dir.	@ 250 250	@ 300 300
7 persons	1,500	1,725
Fringe benefits	@ 25% 375	@ 25% 431
Airfare:		
7 round-trips	@ 540 ... 3,780	@ 208 ... 1,456
Hotel:		
3 doubles	2 nights @ 70	2 nights @ 60
		2 nights @ 70
Subtotal	420	780
1 single	2 nights @ 50	2 nights @ 45
		2 nights @ 50
Subtotal	100	190
Total	520	970
Per diems:		
7 @ 35.	2 days 490	4 days 980
Misc. expenses	350	400
Total direct expenses	7,015	5,962

Figures are in dollars.

"half-week" engagement, hence the higher salary. Her TD gets a bit more in recognition of her prep work, besides which, she won't do it for less. Tammi gets a bit more on general principle.

Fringe benefits. These are a fixed percentage of salaries. [See "Budgeting" in chapter 3.] The exact percentage varies by state and experience rating.

Airfare. The difference between regular coach fare and discounted (super-saver) fares can be astonishing, over 60 percent in this case. The magnitude of the saving is what prompts Tammi to consider going to Minneapolis on Saturday. A good and patient travel agent can be the artist's best friend.

Hotel. The price differential between single rooms and double rooms can vary. Weekend rates are frequently less because there are fewer business travelers. Always request a theatrical discount and determine what taxes will be added to the room rate. The local presenter is the best source of information about suitable housing.

Per diems. This is the prevailing union rate for food per diems.

Miscellaneous expenses. These are the direct expenses incurred in planning and executing this one engagement: long-distance calls, the cost of publicity materials, postage, costume cleaning, gels and tech supplies, transportation to and from the airport at each end, a six-pack for the crew, the pay-per-view movie they'll watch in the hotel, etc., etc.

The performance is planned for a Tuesday evening in October. John asks Tammi to quote an all-inclusive fee. She does the necessary research, the results of which are summarized in the accompanying table.

In a world where no one has money to throw away, it is important to realize that the process of setting fees cannot be entirely divorced from the give and take involved in negotiating a contract. The example we are using is a perfect case in point, mainly because of the extreme difference in the two airfare quotes. In essence, the artist (Tammi) and the presenter (John) need to collaborate in determining the parameters of the engagement. Tammi depends on John to steer her toward the cheapest or most convenient housing: Is there any free housing available? If not, where do visiting artists usually stay? Does the hotel offer a theatrical rate? (She also needs to contact the hotel and confirm rates and room availability.) Will the Walker staff volunteer to get the company back and forth from the airport? If not, what kinds of public transportation are available, and what do they cost? The same questions apply regarding travel between the hotel and the theater. Tammi needs to describe the ideal technical schedule, and John needs to tell her if that schedule is feasible. Perhaps there is an event in the theater the previous evening such that the performance will have to be a day-in. Decisions about travel depend on the answer. Perhaps only the technical director should travel out in advance. Housing and per diem costs will change accordingly.

The most important question that Tammi needs to ask John is whether the performance can be Saturday or Sunday evening instead of Tuesday, so that it can make sense to stay over the Saturday evening. It can't be, because it's a Tuesday series, because subscription tickets have already been sold, because John can't get the theater on the weekend, etc. Too bad. But Tammi, bolstered by the adventurous spirit she inherited from her great-grandmother, was clever enough to pursue the option of traveling on Saturday anyway. As the budget shows, it would save over $1,000, despite increased salary, fringe, housing, and per diem expenses.

But Tammi still has to deal with another sort of expense before she will be ready to quote a fee—the Royal American Dance Company's general overhead. Ideally, as the article on budgeting reminds you, the whole year's income should equal the whole year's expenses. Since contributed income for companies like Tammi's usually goes to fund the creation of new work, earned income from engagements such as the Walker is often the only source of revenue to "amortize" the ongoing expenses of simply being open for business: phone, utilities, postage, desk space, a typewriter or word processor, rehearsal space, office supplies, perhaps even clerical help.

There are a number of ways to estimate what should be added to the direct expense totals listed in the budget to cover some reasonable share of yearly overhead. The most accurate way would be to take the previous year's total overhead or the current year's projected total overhead and then divide it among the current year's confirmed and very probable engagements. But if your company is relatively young or growing rapidly, the number you come up with might not prove reliable.

The easiest way is to adopt the $1,500 administrative line item allowed for in the standard National Performance Network (NPN) engagement agreement. It's a plausible figure and has the moral suasion, so to speak, of NPN usage behind it:

NPN method	Travel Monday	Travel Saturday
Total direct expense	7,015	5,962
Administration line item	1,500	1,500
Fee	8,515	7,462
Rounding off	8,500	7,500

You'll notice that $1,500 is approximately 15–20 percent of the total fee. Were your own math to result in significantly higher or lower numbers, the percentage represented by $1,500 would vary widely. Since it is often true that overhead is in some sort of direct relationship with budget size, it would make sense to use a percentage (say, 20 percent) instead of an absolute number. In other words, you want to quote a fee such that, when you subtract 20 percent (0.2) of it for administrative overhead, you are left with the original direct expenses total. We're solving for x, the fee you quote. Here's the way the math would have looked on the junior high school blackboard:

Percentage	Travel Monday	Travel Saturday
Total direct expenses	$x - .2x = 7,015$	$x - .2x = 5,962$
Restated	$.8x = 7,015$	$.8x = 5,962$
Restated	$x = 7,015/.8$	$x = 5,962/.8$
Gross fee	$x = 8,768$	$x = 7,452$
Rounding off	8,800	7,500
Administrative overhead	1,785	1,538

Finally, Tammi could engage in the following bit of mathematical reasoning. A different seven-member troupe hoping to perform at the Walker would perforce have computed its expenses in much the same way, all other things being equal. Say the other troupe had a booking agent to deal with who gets a 15 percent commission. If the Royal American Dance Company needs to charge in the neighborhood of $7,500 or $8,500, so does the other company. In other words, the other troupe's booking agent needs to quote a price such that, when the 15 percent commission is subtracted, the troupe is left with one or the other number. The math works the same way as above, except that now we're solving for the fee the agent must quote so that the company nets the above amounts:

Booking Agent Fee	Travel Monday	Travel Saturday
Fee to company	$x - .15x = 8,800$	$x - .15x = 7,500$
Restated	$.85x = 8,800$	$x - .15x = 7,500$
Restated	$x = 8,800/.85$	$x = 7,500/.85$
Gross fee	$x = 10,352$	$x = 8,824$

In theory, since there are companies out there with booking agents to compensate, the Royal American Dance Company should remain "price competitive," even at the above rates. Also, if Tammi acquires in-house help with booking or enters into a relationship with a professional booking agent, she would have to start factoring in the expense this way.

Before revealing what happened with Tammi's Walker engagement, we need to massage the above numbers one last time:

	Travel Monday	Travel Saturday
Gross company fee	10,352	8,824
Subtract airfare	−3,780	−1,456
Net fee	6,572	7,368

This suggests a completely different way to estimate fees. Remember that Tammi travels with seven people: five dancers, herself, and the technical director. Both the above numbers are within spitting distance of the following formula for a "half-week" engagement: $1,000 per person traveling plus airfare. Here's how that formula would play itself out in our example:

Formula	Travel Monday	Travel Saturday
7 × $1,000	7,000	7,000
Add airfare	+3,780	+1,456
Total fee	10,780	8,456
Rounding off	10,750	8,500

Following this line of reasoning, a quick and dirty way to calculate a reasonable one-week residency fee would be to allow $2,000 per person traveling plus the actual cost of the airfare. If two or more presenters shared a week of the company's time, the airfare could be divided among them. Finally, one could extrapolate further, and, assuming that a single tour performance is really a two-day residency (three of which can be crammed in a six-day week, unless you're keen to travel, tech, dress, and perform all on the same day), then a fine price to quote for such a single is (let's round up a teeny bit to compensate for the extra wear and tear on your body) $700 per person plus transportation. Indeed, if the business about the Tuesday evening and super-savers hadn't fouled things up, Tammi could have done the Walker gig for ($4,900 + $1,456 = $6,356, which she probably would have rounded up to) $6,500.

So, were the Royal American Dance Company to include a fee sheet in its booking packet, it would look something like this:

Royal American Dance Company
List Prices

Full-week residency	$14,000 plus transportation
Half-week residency	7,000 plus transportation
Single performance	5,000 plus transportation

So what fee should Tammi quote to John when she calls him back? There is a bit of a dilemma here. This is the biggest, most prestigious engagement her company has been offered so far, and she wants it desperately. Every single one of the numbers her calculator has spit out feels inordinately large. She's never dared ask for even $5,000, not to mention $7,500. Surely John will laugh in her face. Surely no one will believe she's worth $10,000. But her calculator doesn't lie. This is what things cost.

Also, since the Saturday option has the company out from Saturday afternoon until Wednesday morning, is it entirely reasonable to call it a single performance? Wouldn't it be fairer to base the Saturday option on the half-week fee, which would bring the quote up to the $8,500 range? Who should reap the benefit of the company's willingness to inconvenience itself, the Royal American Dance Company or the Walker Art Center? What if the super-saver fare were suddenly abolished or if some happenstance made it impossible to ticket the flight the required twenty-one days in advance? Perhaps two of the dancers have to attend a wedding that Sunday.

Having shared the mathematical experience of the past few pages, we know for a fact that there is no fat here, no matter which fee Tammi eventually quotes, and that the above numbers truly reflect Tammi's expenses. If her company tours for significantly less, and if she still persists in paying her dancers and technician, the company will lose money, or, rather, Tammi will lose money.

What will probably happen is this: Tammi will quote a fee of $8,500 all-inclusive, hoping (a) that John will say yes and (b) that circumstances will permit the company to fly out on Saturday. John, whose budget is tight, will say he can't afford that much. The group that had to cancel was going to get $7,500, and that's the number that got locked in. Tammi looks at her own budget and realizes that she can accept the engagement at that fee but explains that this would obligate the company to arrive on Saturday. John is totally understanding and has the excellent idea to contact Kim Konikow at the Minnesota Dance Alliance to suggest that she arrange a Sunday afternoon community workshop with the company, for which they would be paid a fee, or at least a percentage of the class admissions. Everyone is content and feels that she/he was dealt with fairly. It really doesn't matter that, in her heart of hearts, Tammi would have done the gig for $7,000 or that, if pressed, John would have gone up to $8,000.

The Negotiating Process

If you think back on the preceding pages, you might realize that we have quite thoroughly discussed the topic of negotiation. You've reassessed who you are and what your work is about. You've thought about what you do and what you don't do. You've analyzed what resources you require to do what you do effectively, and you have a realistic sense of what it all costs. You've begun to gauge where compromise is possible and where it isn't. You've even authorized yourself to think creatively about travel and other options. The only other information you need is the reminder that presenters have significant presentation expenses over and above your performance or residency fee: crew and other tech costs, marketing costs, and the same kinds of general overhead expenses that you do. If a presenter is paying you x thousands of dollars, then it is safe to assume that she/he is paying another x thousands of dollars in ancillary expenses. Your fee is but the half of it, if that much. Also, presenting organizations of all stripes are as beleaguered by funding cuts and diminished resources as artists are. When they plead poverty, they are not lying.

Once in a while, a presenter will give you the impression that she/he actually takes offense when you turn down an unmanageable fee, as if your refusal indicated your lack of commitment to Art itself. Feel free to remind that person, politely but firmly, that your contribution to the cause of Art is the making of it, not the funding of it, and that you already subsidize your Art with long hours and low pay.

Ultimately, it's got to be the artist's decision. You are allowed to say no. But so is the presenter. If a thing just can't work, whether because of money or technical limitations or time or any other reason, it is professional to recognize reality and to deal with it. It is also a kindness. Hanging on in an untenable situation, as if the morrow would bring a miracle, is disruptive and unproductive for all concerned.

Getting Help

Up to this point, we have been assuming that the artist her/himself has been at the center of booking efforts. Given the inevitable frustrations to be endured in pursuing and negotiating engagements, most artists dearly want to find someone to do this for them so that they can get back in the studio and concentrate on the work.

The solicitation of bookings is an act of communication involving a human being at each end. Your company's success depends to a certain degree on the quality of that communication. The choice of a third party to represent you in these transactions is thus very important.

Booking is accomplished either in-house by someone on staff who works for you and you alone or out-of-house by an agency or individual who is contracted to provide this service for you and for other artists as well. The choice involves questions of finances as well as of temperament. Some large companies book in-house because they can afford the expertise. On the other end of the quantitative scale, many small or emerging companies are also booked in-house, often out of sheer necessity. Perhaps no one besides the artistic director and her/his lover/spouse/parent/child is willing to do the task at a price the company can afford, that is, zero. Some companies distribute the burden among company members and turn booking into a cooperative venture.

Every permutation has been tried somewhere, with varying degrees of success: full- or part-time, dancer or nondancer, professional or amateur, unsalaried, salaried, commissioned or combination payment by bed and board, etc. The most important factor seems to be the enthusiasm and perseverance of the person doing the work. An artistic director working on her/his own behalf can sometimes do better than a professional booking agency, for which your company is not as financially interesting as larger companies on the roster. (If you are relatively unknown or small, and therefore command a lower fee, then obviously the booking agent's percentage of that fee is correspondingly lower, yet the work involved in getting the booking is just as hard.)

But expense isn't the only factor involved. Even if you are successful in getting engagements, you will have spent time and energy that you would rather have devoted to the work itself. Sooner or later you are likely to seek assistance.

There are more options than you may think. The field of arts management has a certain amount of glamor attached to it: show biz and all that. Many schools have programs in arts administration, for instance. There are dozens if not hundreds of people, ranging from the rankest amateurs to graduates with M.B.A.s and Ph.D.s, who want to break into the field in various capacities. Their demands range from minimal (interns from universities and private citizens more interested in work experience than financial remuneration) to quite high (experienced professionals who expect and possibly deserve salaries of $30,000 to $50,000 or higher).

There is no guaranteed formula for success. An intangible factor independent of salary level is involved. Something has to click between you and your art, on the one hand, and the person doing the booking, on the other. Call it empathy, which is not to be confused with blind optimism and yea-saying.

As an artist, your business is communication. Out there where your craft gives way to your powers of inspiration, you have learned to trust your intuition. You should trust it in this matter, too.

Booking Agents

It is a kind of luxury to have in your employ a person whose sole job is to look after your interests—in this case, booking. If you can't find or afford one, the solution is to engage an agent or agency that specializes in booking performing arts groups. Many artists assume that having a professional booking agent is the solution of choice. The following list enumerates the most frequently cited reasons for thinking this way.

Every item on this list can be true in the case of any particular booking agent. There are even some booking agents of whom it can be said that all these items are true. But no one of these items is necessarily true of any prospective agent. Booking agents don't take courses or have to pass qualifying exams. You have to consider their reputation and experience—and your intuition.

—Booking agents, because of their experience in the field, have a better sense than you of how to target efforts. There are over forty-five hundred presenters listed in the Pentacle/Dance Theater Workshop National Performing Arts Mailing List. Agents know which few dozen are the most likely to be interested in your work.

—Booking agents know the "players." They have met or previously dealt with the presenters on the targeted list. Their calls will be taken. They will be listened to. Your brochure will be read. Your videotape will be screened.

—Booking agents have "clout," or are perceived to have it. You may benefit from the fact that presenters may call an agency they trust when "shopping" for their next season. You may be able to ride on the coattails of more established companies on the roster.

—Booking agents have a better sense of the budgets and facilities of these presenters. They know what other artists have been booked by them and under what terms. They stand a better chance of commanding the highest possible fee, the most optimum working conditions.

—Booking agents are more inured to rejection and stress. They are better able to cope with the anxieties of the process and are more practiced at negotiating. They also have more time for it. It's what they do.

—Booking agents attend booking conferences, which are thoroughly daunting to the uninitiated, and they have learned to cope with them. These are annual convocations of presenters, united by geography or membership status, who meet to exchange information, discuss common problems, trade success and failure stories, talk about work, learn about new programs and grants, and generally hobnob with their fellow wizards. In the midst of all this there is made available for their examination the "exhibit hall" or "resource room," affectionately known as the Pit. This is invariably the basement or grand ballroom of the convention hotel, transformed for the occasion into a maze of booms and cross-rods from which draperies are suspended and signs hung so as to define "booths" of varying sizes, each furnished with a skirted table and chairs. These booths are rented by artists, managers, and agents, each representing from one to dozens of attractions and decorated and accoutered in the most varied means imaginable. Some agencies spend thousands of dollars for commercially designed displays complete with blinking lights and four-color posters. Some dress mannequins in costumes representative of their style of dance, theater, or puppetry. There are slide projectors, video monitors, toothy smiles, and extended hands everywhere. The effect is visually cacophonous. Artists attending such conventions for the first time usually feel like the proverbial gangling teenager at the junior prom, all hands and no place to put them.

—Booking agents have more access to adequate contracts and other resources. They know from experience which terms and conditions should be included in a contract to protect the artist's interests. They know the precedents and usages.

—Booking agents can run interference for the artist in case problems arise. They are better at renegotiating contract terms and have a better sense of limits and possibilities.

There are trade-offs to consider. The agency may represent other exponents of your art form, and you may feel you are being placed in direct competition with them. You might feel ambiguous about the perceived quality of other artists on the roster and worry that this could reflect poorly on you. The sheer size of the roster may make you wonder to what degree the agency will be able to focus on you.

Most booking agents are honest, hardworking folks who are dedicated to Art and to Artists. They probably make a better living than you do, but few of them grow rich in this business. Which means that the sharks and the con artists stay away. But since they do have to make ends meet, they select their rosters with care. It isn't enough for them simply to "like the work." They have to feel a connection to it, and they have to feel that they can talk about it intelligently and persuasively to people who are not yet familiar with it. They have to believe that they can sell it to enough presenters so that both you and they feel that your mutual investment has been worthwhile. They want to waste neither your money nor their time. They also know how you will answer the question you will ask yourself if results are slow in coming: "Is it that my work is no good or that my booking agent is no good?" You get two guesses, and the first one doesn't count.

Given the ratio of performing artists who want to tour and the number of agents in business, most artists will not succeed in getting themselves placed on a roster, period. It's a fact; there's no shame to it. But that doesn't mean you shouldn't try. The skills needed to obtain a hearing by an agent who interests you are not unlike those needed to get bookings. You have to do homework. Does the agent specialize in your art form? Which artists are on the agent's roster? What do these artists have to report about their experience of the agent? (And will any of them put in a good word for you?) Are there other artists on the roster of the same approximate size, price, and reputation as yourself? Will you stand out or get lost? What about artists who have left the roster? What were their reasons for their departure? Can you articulate what your work is about and the ways in which it is unique? Why do you think the agent might be right for you?

Just because there is a scarcity of agents ready, willing, and able to take you on doesn't mean you have to jump at the first opportunity that may present itself. There are many kinds of agencies for you to investigate. They may be either commercial or not-for-profit. Some are large corporations; others are small one- or two-person shops. Some are unfailingly businesslike; others are chatty and folksy and always have time to shoot the breeze with you. Some have enormous rosters; others have small ones.

You need to feel comfortable and confident about the deal. Will channels of communication be good? Will you feel that the agent understands your work, your needs, your ambitions? Will you be apprised as time goes on about what efforts are being made on your behalf? If these efforts are not as fruitful or as quick in coming as you had anticipated, will you be given satisfactory explanations?

Contract terms differ widely regarding retainers, commissions, reimbursements, and the scope of services offered. It is your right and your responsibility to understand what is included and what it will cost.

Some agencies simply deliver signed contracts to you and expect you to do the follow-up work yourself, that is, tour management and the exchange and revision of technical information. Others fully manage the engagement in partnership with you. Some, particularly the nonprofit ones, offer other management services that complement the booking process per se, such as grant writing and fund-raising for ambitious touring projects or co-commissions.

A retainer is a payment made regularly, often monthly, to the agent to retain the services offered. Don't forget that the agent has ongoing business expenses just as you do: office rent, utilities, taxes, etc. Given the lead times involved in the booking process, the agent is unlikely to see commission income from you for at least a year. The retainer enables her/him to get to work in the meantime. Retainers can be structured as a guarantee against future commissions, which means they function as a deposit for which you will eventually see a credit, or they may be independent of future commissions.

A commission is a percentage of the fee received for an engagement that the agent subtracts and keeps as payment for her/his efforts in getting you the gig. This percentage can range anywhere from 10 to 30 percent, depending in part on the traditions and practices pertinent to the branch of show business involved. Another variable involves how any set percentage is actually computed. Some agents subtract certain expenses, such as transportation, before computing the commission owed. Some exempt certain kinds of engagements, such as home seasons. Some have different commission structures for performance residencies, teaching engagements, and choreographic commissions. Some, given the fixed-line item for administration, place a cap on the commission that can be collected for National Performance Network engagements.

You should expect to be billed regularly by the agent for certain kinds of expenses incurred on your specific behalf. Such reimbursements include long-distance phone charges for calls to presenters and the cost of faxes, postage, express delivery, messenger service, and copying and other reproduction expenses involved in distributing your materials. Some agents also expect you to pay your pro rata share of advertisements and booking conferences. You have the right to require adequate documentation of all billed expenses, and you would be smart to get estimates of what such expenses might add up to.

Finally, the agent may insist that you provide her/him with certain quantities of photographs, videotapes, booking brochures, press kits, posters, and/or flyers at the outset. This may cause cash-flow problems, especially if some of these materials have to be redesigned to meet specifications set by the agent. In particular, the agent may demand that the agency's contact information be printed on all materials and that an ad be placed at your expense in *Stern's Performing Arts Directory* or a similar publication.

Given the cash-flow problems that performing artists have, most agents end up "floating" an artist, especially at the beginning of a booking relationship. This rarely means fronting money for marketing materials. Rather, it often means deferring reimbursements until commission income starts to come in. Although the artist will rightly appreciate the courtesy and the confidence thus extended, a word of caution is in order. This is a kind of debt that can become a habit and be abused just like credit card debt. Also, when many agencies issue contracts for artist engagements, it is the agency that is the payee. In other words, the presenter pays the agency, which first subtracts the commission and any other payments that are in arrears and then remits the remainder to the artist. Almost all agency-artist contracts give the agency the right to do this, even though the right is not always exercised. But if the debt gets out of hand, or if the booking relationship starts to sour, the agent will indeed do what is necessary to ensure payment. The wrong kind of insouciance can thus cause the artist to lose control over earned income.

Many artist-agent relationships are as enduring as good marriages. A few never survive the honeymoon. Others start off well and then become dysfunctional. Perhaps a few years down the line a newer "hot" company may join the roster and seem to bump you from your privileged spot. Therefore, on entering a booking relationship, it is prudent and reasonable to understand the procedures by which one or the other party can get out of it when and if the time comes. Most agency contracts provide for their own renewal, usually on an annual basis. The juncture is usually in the late spring, before agency rosters for the following season are printed, ads placed in professional directories, and so forth. This is also the time when other agencies confirm new additions to their rosters. "Divorces" at any other time are likely to be messier. Any artist leaving a roster should expect to pay the commissions owed on engagements contracted by the agent but not yet completed.

The National Association of Performing Arts Managers and Agents (NAPAMA) [see the Appendix] is a trade organization of approximately one hundred of the most active artist representatives working in the performing arts (classical and new music, dance, performance, and theater). It strives to promote high standards of professionalism and to facilitate effective communication among presenters, managers, and artists. NAPAMA's "Guidelines for Ethical Behavior" outlines what each of these should reasonably expect of the others in the process of booking and presenting artists. Artists might profit from reading what this pamphlet has to say about the subject, even if they are representing themselves. It covers such topics as convention etiquette and the proper procedures for holding dates and dealing with cancellations.

Don't be surprised at the use of the word "etiquette." Common courtesy involves nothing less than sending your message out truthfully and clearly, respecting the right of other messages to be heard, and really listening to the messages you receive. Yes, in some respects, the marketplace can be a jungle where Darwinian laws apply and where only the fittest adapt and survive. However, in many respects it is not a jungle but a community of dedicated professionals working in partnership with one another to ensure that artists with something to say to the public have the means and the opportunity to say it.

Support for Touring

The most accessible financial support for touring generally comes from governmental sources [see "Funding" in chapter 3]. Most of it takes the form of specific amounts awarded to presenters and earmarked to subsidize company fees for specific engagements. It is much rarer for touring companies to receive such targeted support directly, although this is how Dance/USA's new American Dance Touring Initiative (ADTI) is structured (see Appendix). Some government funding, such as the various NEA programs to which presenters apply, support presenters' programming in general, based on the distinction of their track record. Artists and companies can also apply for general tour support, but most choose to use their grants for the creation of work. The upshot is that, to the degree that a subsidy is a "carrot" that can help shape behavior, it is by and large presenters who hold the stick. They have to make the decision to book you before targeted subsidy becomes a possibility.

As this book is going to press, National Endowment for the Arts support for presenters in the various disciplines (Dance, Inter-Arts, Music, Theater, Opera–Musical Theater) has been consolidated within the Inter-Arts Program, renamed the Presenting and Commissioning Program. The new program will continue to administer the Dance on Tour program within the NEA. The transition has been taking place in stages, with Dance being folded in in fiscal 1994.

It is too soon to determine how this transition might affect the parameters of existing touring and commissioning programs. Chances are that, if funding levels remain stable, current programs of interest to creative artists and presenters will simply be reshuffled administratively. However, if political and financial pressures force revision of priorities, other scenarios are possible. Artists serious about maximizing their chances of securing subsidized engagements should monitor developments affecting both themselves and presenters. It's a good idea to request and study current guidelines for all the relevant programs.

The same advice applies to state arts councils. Many of them are under financial stress, but you may find that programs directed at "underfunded counties" or special constituencies have been better protected than direct support to artists.

Foreign Intrigues: Artistic Opportunity and Realpolitik in the International Marketplace
David R. White, with Ann Rosenthal

Overview: Art in the Land of Elsewhere

From afar, the rest of the world appears to offer independent dance and theater artists everything that the United States does not: festivals and municipal theaters whose directors look first at the process and quality of work rather than at its ability to unleash ticket sales; a tradition of massive government arts subsidy that in turn has fertilized a further tradition of festival structures and other cultural opportunities; and a public that is perceived to welcome and thrive on the experience of unfamiliar artists in order to satisfy a wide-ranging intellectual appetite. These appearances suggest that civilization, so-called, must be alive and well and living abroad, a far cry from the marginal recognition too often accorded American artists at home. Or so the wishful, wistful thinking goes.

But the reality of international artistic opportunity has shifted irrevocably from the 1970s and early 1980s, when independent American artists and almost entire American art forms—notably modern dance and jazz and experimental music—found regular work, significant income, and startling acclaim abroad, particularly in the countries of Western Europe. The 1990s find Western Europe looking inward, preoccupied with its changing identity under gradual political and economic integration; East Central Europe and the former Soviet Union opening their borders and cultures to the world at large while struggling with rising nationalist pressures that threaten social disruption and cultural conflict; and the cultures of Latin America, Asia, Africa, and the Caribbean within the United States powerfully asserting their values and histories within the rapidly transforming U.S. demographic landscape and therefore within the country's domestic and international artistic priorities. Further complicating the map is the tension between the economic haves and have-nots, the result of a gap between countries that are capable of supporting their own artists and cultural activity (and its interaction with the world) and those that cannot.

Perhaps the most difficult complication of all involves the legacy of U.S. isolationist posture toward the rest of the world's cultures. While the attitude and activity of certain key government agencies, notably the U.S. Information Agency (USIA) and the National Endowment for the Arts [see the Appendix for details on agencies mentioned in this article], have improved with regard to helping independent artists and companies travel overseas—for example, the cooperation of the USIA and the NEA with the Rockefeller Foundation and the Pew Charitable Trusts in creating the Fund for U.S. Artists at International Festivals and Exhibitions, now administered by Arts International—there is still scant official attention to and compassion for the sensitive issue of *reciprocity.*

Since the 1980s, a number of U.S. producers and presenters—among them the Jacob's Pillow Dance Festival, the Brooklyn Academy of Music, the American Dance Festival, the Caribbean Cultural Center, the Los Angeles Festival, the Walker Art Center, Miami-Dade Community College, Philadelphia's Movement Theater International, Seattle's On the Boards and other members of the National Performance Network, and the Suitcase Fund of Dance Theater Workshop—have independently undertaken to secure international artists a permanent, visible presence at the table of American culture and to help them build sustained relationships here with colleagues and communities of particular interest to them. Joining such pioneers as New York's LaMama and Baltimore's Theater Project, these and other organizations have sought to demonstrate that the world *is* welcome in the United States and that ongoing contact with the cultural histories and contemporary artists of other countries is fundamental to American self-knowledge and equitable nurturing of its own immigrant, pluralistic character.

In recent years, a more ominous shadow has been cast across this long-overdue normalization of cultural relations by the Kafkaesque maneuverings around visa issues of the Immigration and Naturalization Service (INS) and the Office of Management and Budget (OMB) in Washington, DC. It is absolutely essential that independent artists in the United States understand that the question of visas for their international peers coming to the United States is vital to their own needs and aspirations. Artist and politician alike must recognize and address the crucial element that both defines and inhibits an open international marketplace: In order to ensure an ongoing forum for Americans in other countries, the United States must find ways to assist substantively in making the work of foreign artists available and visible in this country, without placing intolerance and obstruction in their path. In international culture, as in the international politics that surrounds and permeates it, there is no such thing as a one-way street.

For the artist who is simply thinking about touring, bookings, and the pros and cons of self-producing in the Edinburgh Fringe, it is clearly time for both a new perspective and a new vocabulary. If a true marketplace of ideas and the means to realize them are to exist, that marketplace will have to embrace a broader expanse of countries and cultures than ever before and dramatically different ways of building working relationships with host communities and peer artists throughout the world. That means that the artist, already creator and for the most part self-manager, now must become in equal parts social historian, international economist (or at least black marketeer), and cultural diplomat. Most important, the artist must take the lead in researching, instigating, and structuring these new relationships. "Touring" is a term that too often seems to imply a perception of other cultures as places merely to be scheduled and passed through, passive stages to perform on and to leave, check in hand. "Collaboration and partnership" might better define the artist's task in the years ahead, the responsibility to engage the world in joint creative venture in search of enduring interaction rather than transient tourism.

Western Europe: Points of Departure

By any measure of sheer cultural *traffic,* Western Europe is the center of the international marketplace, providing the greatest concentration of festivals and production sponsorships. Ironically, Western Europe's colonial past has left it an important threshold into the cultural structures of Asia, the Middle East, and various parts of Africa.

There is no question of the crucial nurturing role that the region has played in the development of contemporary American arts in this century, both creatively and economically. Until the early 1980s, the presentation of modern dance by European sponsors was virtually synonymous with the presentation of American artists. From Loie Fuller and Isadora Duncan to Trisha Brown and Dana Reitz, free spirits have found both shelter and laboratory in France or Germany or Holland. From Merce Cunningham, who was awarded France's prestigious Legion d'Honneur, to Alwin Nikolais, who was once promised an apartment in the Louvre if he would relocate his company to Paris, from the Jazz Tap Ensemble to Bill T. Jones and Stephen Petronio, the list is long and varied. Certainly Western Europe has supported a range of more traditional dance making, but it was to an inclusive idea of progressive experimentalism that its producers made their firmest commitment, from France's Festival d'Automne and Holland's Springdance to Berlin's Akademie der Kunste and London's Dance Umbrella and The Place theater.

That reality is now literally history. The rise of conservative governments and the corresponding reduction of formerly luxurious national cultural subsidies; the emergence of a new and hungry generation of European artists who legitimately command a substantially greater share of official patronage and available funding; and an inexorable tide of European cultural nationalism that has paralleled the economic union of the twelve most powerful Western European nations in 1992 and has been further stirred by the precipitous opening of East Central Europe—these are the forces that pose a major challenge to American artists in the festival and theater networks. In the case of theater, this has had little effect since language facility still largely limits an American theater dependent on words to the United Kingdom, Holland, and Germany. But, in the case of dance, it has turned a once-familiar world upside down.

Opportunities will not disappear, however: dance has become a dominant interest in the region, supplanting theater even in formerly theater-only festivals. Despite active artist communities around them, young producers in France, Belgium, and Spain are showing renewed interest in certain American artists. Teaching remains an area where Americans are in demand, from Holland's experimental Schools for New Dance Development in Amsterdam and Årnhem to France's Centre National de Danse Contemporaine and Berlin's Tanzfabrik. American contemporary dance is first and foremost about movement invention, whereas much European work is imagistic, concerned more with dramatic scenography than kinetic vocabulary: Artists must exploit the difference. For performance artists, an active demimonde of clubs and pro-gressive theater venues, from Glasgow's Third Eye Center and its periodic "National Review of Live Art" to Zürich's Die Rote Fabrik (The Red Factory), offers a foothold. Visual theater, as demonstrated by the success of such art-ists as Robert Wilson, Ping Chong, the Wooster Group, and San Francisco's Soon Three, can also rely on a continuing welcome in a number of coun-tries, assuming the economics of such freight-heavy projects can be resolved. Smaller companies in general must look past the most entrenched festivals (unless you have an electric reputation or a visible genetic heritage, such as Karole Armitage did relative to Merce Cunningham or Stephen Petronio to Trisha Brown) and go off-road, searching the countryside and smaller cities for unfamiliar venues where one can still build a personal relationship.

Inflation and a perpetually weaker dollar abroad, along with the abnormally high costs of traveling internally in Western Europe, will continue to weigh heavily on American artists. The notion that international touring can bring in a surplus of much-needed income for creative projects at home is no longer realistic; simply breaking even on expenses, not to mention artistic salaries, is a respectable goal in a post-1992 Europe, if you can avoid the traffic.

To truly avoid the traffic, it's time to see the world as it exists beyond our habits with Western Europe and in tandem with what U.S. cultural behavior will be in the coming century. Here are some previews of coming attractions in the years to come.

Central Europe and FSU (Formerly the Soviet Union): Unblocking the East

The key to understanding the Eastern reaches of Europe (remember that former Soviet governments used to call the Soviet Union an integral part of Europe and that Leningrad—now St. Petersburg—was universally seen as a European city) is knowing that, whatever the lockstep political systems that preceded the remarkable revolutionary period of 1989, the so-called Eastern Bloc of Warsaw Pact nations was a bloc in name and enforced ideologies only. Progressive cultural activity was largely suppressed and relegated to under-ground status, isolated from one country to the next by both repressive travel and emigration policies and unworkable economics and currencies. Com-munication was often nonexistent, within and between countries, and general artistic information and exchange was for decades in extremely short supply. A few organizations such as the International Theater Institute (ITI) provided a valuable information drop and artistic lifeline through local chapters within a number of these countries. Poland somehow managed to sustain certain critical nonofficial structures that maintained a fragile contact with the world outside, such as the Meeting of Open Theater in Wroclaw, an experimental theater festival now over thirty years old. And the former Yugoslavia, not part of the Eastern Bloc collapse but ultimately fractured by deadly and irreversible ethnic disputes, saw active festivals in Ljubljana, Zagreb, and Belgrade. But while art forms like literature and music and scripted theater might travel by means of *samizdat* manuscripts and bootleg tapes through the underground, others such as dance and visual theater could not. And as glasnost opened a window on artistic imaginations and processes that had been hidden away, in Russia, for instance, one could see among young artists an immediate, nostalgic return to the techniques of 1920s constructivism—the last remembered period of sheer creative invention, revisited as if six decades of oppression had never intervened—rather than a concern with contemporary forms and ideas.

Uncertainty covers the ground in the postrevolutionary period. Despite the leadership of theater artists in the now separate Czech and Slovak republics or poets in Romania in galvanizing the profound political changes within the region's societies, the arts were initially left behind in the rush toward social democratization and the consumerist Oz of a "market economy." Roiling nationalist movements and ethnic rivalries threaten to burst into the cultural arena and to upset a number of governmental applecarts, as they have so terrifyingly in what used to be Yugoslavia. But an active grass roots of independent organizers and producers is beginning to make itself known, struggling to create from scratch, with minimal resources, an "alternative" system of support not unlike the movement of independent spaces in the United States. While funding (and fees) will remain a tremendous problem as these devastated economies are rebuilt out of near bankruptcy, the profound need for long-denied information will create real opportunities for artistic partnership. Arts International and the Dance Theater Workshop (DTW) Suitcase Fund, among others, have undertaken major projects to explore how these opportunities can be supported and extended into serious reciprocal programs.

Already artists Bill Young and Donald Byrd have built ongoing relationships with such producers as Budapest's Gyorgy Szabo, a young entrepreneur who has worked out of a Hungarian youth center, underwriting his enthusiasm for contemporary dance by producing rock concerts and other events. No matter the good intentions and local capabilities of the new crop of producers, the likelihood of pocketing anything more than basic expenses (even the best organizers can offer only their version of room and board and local transportation) is unrealistic until economic conditions change radically. So subsidize thyself, travel light (including your expectations), and always carry your credit card and a stash of hard currency for emergencies. In the eyes of people like Szabo, regular teaching and choreographic residencies are a priority, stimulating local artists and students with face-to-face training experiences and choices previously denied them. In dance and other performance disciplines, there is simply a lot of learning time to make up for. And teaching residencies, allowing an artist or team of artists to spend a substantial period in a country at relatively modest cost, can open up significant relationships for the future. When choreographer Monica Levy found herself in Budapest for personal reasons, she set out on her own to find suitable studio space for classes when none was apparently available. Within a year, she was choreographing for two local companies, one ballet, the other modern, as well as for Hungarian state television. At the same time, she offered local independent artists a model of energetic resourcefulness, stepping out to find her own solutions in a difficult environment rather than waiting for them to come to her.

The universe that was the old Soviet Union references the new central Europe and more: The diversity of former and current member republics encompasses Asian culture and fundamentalist Islam. Ukraine borders Poland, Moravia borders the Czech and Slovak Federated Republic, and Armenia borders Turkey. The now independent Baltic states of Lithuania, Latvia, and Estonia have a more open cultural terrain, owing in part to their historic relationship to Scandinavia. As in Central Europe, theater and cabaret traditions are well developed throughout these emergent states. Modern dance, as of this writing, doesn't really exist as a descriptive term, much less as a community; instead, isolated pockets of activity exist with perhaps the most possibilities in the Baltics, sometimes linked to ballet organizations, but generally located in university or conservatory settings. Some dance artists have set up shop in studio theaters, finding the institutional dance world too restrictive. The American Dance Festival and Jacob's Pillow Dance Festival have both established programs to train Russian choreographers and dancers at home and in the United States.

Prior to the cataclysmic changes of 1991, the Soviet Union of Theater Workers was the primary country-wide agency charged with supporting all import and export of theater and dance. Combining branch offices in each of the republics with two central Moscow offices, the Union figured prominently in the structuring of most undertakings, demonstrating an interesting mix of essential information, bemused encouragement, and bureaucratic opacity.

In the aftermath of the changes, the central office and organization have dissolved along with the Soviet governing structure. But it appears that the "local" offices will retain their roles within the independent republics (Russia's is by far the richest and most powerful) and most likely in the emergent independent nation-states.

Among the American artists who have recently found their way in despite the difficulties have been A Travelling Jewish Theater and The Talking Band. New York's Irondale Ensemble designed a provocative *Uncle Vanya* project in collaboration with the St. Petersburg Salon Theater. Choreographers Tamar Rogoff and Marika Blossfeldt and director Bonnie Stein have developed ongoing projects in Lithuania and Estonia. A triumvirate of San Francisco dance companies—Margaret Jenkins, ODC/San Francisco, and Contraband—have gone to Russia, as have such major figures as Alvin Ailey, Trisha Brown, and Paul Taylor. Contraband's trip was part of an ambitious exchange project arranged by The Lab in San Francisco, which brought together writers, poets, and other contemporary artists. That effort was largely supported by a San Francisco–based U.S.-Soviet friendship society, and therein lies the wrinkle. Even if the door is open, and even with official sanction, the burden of financing this activity falls largely on the artist or company. At best, an allowance in rubles, or other local currencies, for internal travel, housing, and per diems can be provided by agencies in these countries (though, with hotels throughout the different countries and republics now demanding hard currency in payment, the internal bureaucracies will generally *not* pay full hotel costs); at the very least, the artist must find the funds for international travel and artist fees.

Latin America, Africa, and Asia: The True New World

Global village or not, from the U.S. artist's point of view the world remains largely unexplored, and nowhere more so than across the grand geographies of Central and South America, Africa, and Asia. It is not an overstatement to say that the future cultural character of the United States will depend on a greater practical interaction with those complex societies and heritages out of which a significantly different U.S. population has emerged. But working in and with those cultures presents the artist with a formidable investigative task. Across these continents, many countries are intractably poor, struggling to feed their people; they are not worrying about subsidizing cultural relations with the rest of the world. Even those countries with substantial economies generally have not created the kind of cultural infrastructure characteristic of Western Europe, even in support of their own artists. Accordingly, theater and producing networks, along with festivals, are mostly nonexistent. Geographic and political isolation from the United States in many cases only compounds what has been an enormous lack of information here about many of these cultures and the possibilities for cooperation and dialogue.

In Latin America, contemporary artists in a number of countries have begun to take issues of cultural policy into their own hands, navigating a course between municipal theaters and established folkloric celebrations. In Paraty,

Brazil, theater artists Marcos and Rachel Ribas have led an effort to link up independent organizers in various parts of Latin America to create a network for support of regional independent work, which will also eventually provide the basis for a process of international exchange. Venezuela has a long-standing international theater festival based in Caracas; dance artists David Zambrano and Livia Daza Paris have undertaken projects to bring more independent artists to Caracas to perform and work with Venezuelan choreographers and dancers. In Lima, Peru, Luciana Proano decided to create a continuing series of workshop residencies, inviting such artists as Pat Hall-Smith, Merian Soto, and Mary Luft. Luft, a Miami-based choreographer and performance artist who also became a local producer to ease Miami's isolation from contemporary artistic activity, has pioneered a number of dance and new music projects in Peru and Brazil, based on her own personal explorations.

Africa is a different matter altogether. Northern and Southern Africa, East and West Africa—colonial, political, religious, and tribal histories have long kept the continent a house divided. Relations and communications among neighboring countries have often been extremely difficult, with the result that there are few visible networks. With help from the Rockefeller Foundation, however, a new pan-African performing arts institute has been established in Zimbabwe, following extensive planning by representatives from a variety of African nations. Universities occupy an important place in most societies, and there are constantly strengthening ties among African scholars. In the United States, organizations like the Council for the International Exchange of Scholars (CIES) are avenues into the rarified universe of scholarly exchange, some of which touches on cultural issues. Another important bridge to African culture may lie in Unesco, the cultural arm of the United Nations headquartered in Paris. As indicated earlier, the colonial African past has left in its wake a number of key organizations in cities like Paris and London dedicated to nurturing and promoting indigenous African cultures.

Without a doubt, personal research and travel is a fundamental prerequisite for designing projects in and with Africa. At home, one of our most knowledgeable human resources is choreographer Chuck Davis, whose own research and company—the African-American Dance Ensemble, based in Durham, North Carolina—have for years taken him back and forth to Africa.

Asia is also vast and disparate. Certain capitals that are becoming the world's economic engines into the next century—Tokyo, Seoul, Taiwan, Hong Kong, and Singapore—will clearly anchor the geography of exchange and partnership in the region. Unlike Latin America and Africa, funding exists in a number of Asian countries for certain kinds of cultural activity, although usually at a conservative institutional level. The emphasis is on "national treasures," the gifted guardians of centuries-old traditions, rather than on upstart experimentalists who question the social order. The larger question is the nature of the cultures themselves, the venerability and inward focus that in some cases views both contemporary artistic exploration and involvement with foreign cultures with suspicion and skepticism (for the most part, a historically justifiable point of view).

Learning and accepting the context and defining characteristics of the host culture on its own terms is crucial to an artist's pursuit of creative opportunity. A good beginning in looking at particular countries is to contact the Asian Cultural Council (ACC) and the Asia Society, both in New York City. The former provides funding for fellowships for both Asian and American artists, while the latter has been instrumental in introducing the United States to a host of traditional and contemporary Asian artists. The Japan Society, also in New York, is an equally considerable source of concrete information and insightful perspective regarding the current Japanese cultural environment. Despite the distances and financial difficulties involved, a number of independent artists have managed to undertake major projects. Choreographer Ruby Shang has created teaching and choreographic residencies in both Japan and China. H. T. Chen has put together tours for his company to Hong Kong, Taiwan, and mainland China; with assistance from DTW's Suitcase Fund, he is helping link up a series of alternative theaters in those countries as well as in Singapore to provide structural opportunities for regional and international artists. And percussionist and movement artist Keith Terry, from Berkeley, California, collaborated with Balinese dance artist I Wayan Dibia for several years, beginning with an ACC fellowship that took Terry to Bali. That relationship culminated in the elaborate *Body Tjak* project, for a company of over twenty American and Balinese performers, which premiered in San Francisco and Bali in 1990.

Canada, Mexico, and the Caribbean: Coda for the Border

The luck of geography has allowed the United States to live in splendid, often arrogant isolation from most of the world. Nevertheless, its economic and population bulk casts a long shadow over its immediate neighbors. The "open borders" imperative of the free-trade zone created in the early 1990s among the United States, Canada, and Mexico only underscores the need to make up for lost time and inadequate relationships along the cultural frontier. Canada offers an extremely active terrain,with major communities working in dance, theater, and music and an economy that parallels that of the United States. Despite strong territorial, at times adversarial distinctions in the contemporary aesthetics of French-speaking and English-speaking Canada, artists move freely among the three most active urban communities—Montreal, Toronto, and Vancouver. In the United States, a number of pilot projects have been implemented—among them those of Arts Midwest, a regional arts agency located in Minneapolis, and of the National Performance Network directed by DTW—to increase the frequency of artist exchange between the two countries.

Mexico and the island nations of the Caribbean basin are the wellspring of a complex meeting of the African and Hispanic/Latino diasporas, both of which extend into Central and South America. Through immigration, sanctioned and otherwise, their cultures have assumed an increasingly prominent place in the life of the United States, most visibly across the southern tier from Miami to Los Angeles but just as importantly in regions such as New England and in major Midwestern cities such as Chicago. The Chicano/Mexican-American community has been extremely active in opening the border to Mexico. Among the organizations that have led the way are San Antonio's Guadalupe Cultural Center and San Diego's Centro Cultural de la Raza as well as theater companies such as El Taller in San Francisco and interdisciplinary artist collectives such as the Border Arts Workshop, also based in San Diego. In New York, visual artist Pepon Osorio and choreographer Merian Soto have long collaborated (under their organizational name, Pepatian) in creating work about and establishing working relationships between the Nuyorican and Puerto Rican communities. They joined with other independent Latino artists in the late 1980s in designing "Tour de Fuerza," a cooperative performance and touring program supported by DTW's Suitcase Fund. Out of that original partnership have emerged a number of subsequent projects, including the marathons known as "Rompeforma" (Broken Form) of contemporary dance and performance that take place annually in Puerto Rico—an ongoing effort that led Pepatian and such Puerto Rico–based artists as Viveca Vazquez and Petra Bravo to shape a new public climate for such work on the island. Finally, the foremost activist organization dealing with the cultures of the Caribbean and the African diaspora, both as a presenting/exhibition center and as a scholarly catalyst, is the Caribbean Cultural Center in New York City, led by Marta Moreno Vega, a powerful spokesperson for this country's obligation to reexamine and fundamentally alter its inequitable cultural behavior and hierarchies, both internally and externally, as we turn the corner on the coming century and a new cultural reality.

Making Connections: Opening Gambits

In the manner of Mary Luft, Ruby Shang, and Keith Terry, you must use imagination in building the kind of relationships that will result in meaningful creative projects. Again, personal investigation is an absolute necessity: Individual fellowship programs such as the Fulbright Program or those available to particular countries through such agencies as the NEA, as well as those already mentioned, may well be the best way to lay the groundwork for the future. Through the USIA, a variety of programs ranging from cooperation with independent binational centers to long-term cultural residencies may provide another resource, although they must generally originate with a request from the local U.S. embassy (when you travel to countries of interest, make sure to meet with the embassy or consulate's cultural officer). And, of course, establishing strong partnerships with individual artists in various countries is the surest way to find your way in.

Establishing your work in the international arena is first and foremost a question of information—how to gather it about the cultural organizers, presenters, and festivals that might be interested and how to get it out in order to make yourself and your interests known to them.

There is no question that personal familiarity, credible references, and the support of key American presenters and other professional colleagues are among the main criteria by which international presenters make their decisions. In general, mass mailings of promotional materials are a highly expensive and largely ineffective means of gaining entry to the international marketplace. A more manageable approach begins with developing a finite list of presenters most likely to be interested in your work (think about and talk to artists whose work is similar in scope to your own who have already found sponsorship abroad) and then communicating with them on a regular basis. Send them not only your latest press kit but also letters of interest, performance announcements, good reviews, tour schedules, and so on. If you are planning a trip (or vacation), or if a tour with another company takes you in the vicinity of any of these sponsors, call and ask for an appointment. More often than not, foreign presenters are very open to meeting with visiting artists. Such encounters are crucial to putting a face to a name, and a personal relationship can give rise to a predisposition to appreciate your work.

It should be pointed out that theater and festival directors, in Western Europe, South America, and elsewhere, travel frequently (far more than their American counterparts) and are accustomed to seeing work live before making program decisions. They have come to trust videotapes more recently in order to familiarize themselves with the increasing volume and variety of work that comes their way and to decide whether to make a trip to see an artist or company in performance or rehearsal. Be sure to understand the different video formats (NTSC, PAL, and SECAM are the basic systems in different parts of the world). If you are serious about working abroad, it is a worthwhile investment to convert good tapes of recent performances into the system appropriate to the producers you wish to reach.

Many festival and theater directors make periodic visits to the United States at times of dense activity, during which they immerse themselves in live performances, showings, and video screenings over a period of one to two weeks. If you have been in touch with an international presenter, most likely your name will be on her/his list to inquire about or visit. For the most part, however, the visitors rely on their producing counterparts in the United States—for example, the directors of such spaces as Baltimore's Theater Project, the Kitchen, P.S. 122, or DTW—or on certain management groups such as Pentacle to help build their schedules around artists of particular interest. It should be pointed out that, for a variety of reasons, for many of these producers, coming to the United States usually means staying in New York City; only rarely does a visitor make it to Minneapolis, Chicago, or the West Coast, much less Miami or Austin. Sometimes it's a question of not being able to afford the additional travel costs; sometimes it's simply ignorance and laziness and a tendency to see, from a European perspective anyway, New York as the United States. The USIA's international visitor program, which underwrites key individuals, including producers, to come to the United States at the suggestion of various American embassies, does require individuals to travel to multiple American cities. And DTW, through the Suitcase Fund, invites a number of foreign organizers and presenters to the annual meeting of the National Performance Network. That meeting, which takes place in a different city each year, always showcases both artists local to that city and videotapes from around the country brought by the NPN's member presenters.

Increasingly, these producers have come to trust the judgment of their American colleagues in directing their attention to artists they should be considering. Therefore, it is important to recognize that alternative American presenters are now firmly a part of the international network that you are trying to reach. The NPN annual meeting, the yearly conference of the Association of Performing Arts Presenters (APAP), and, abroad, the Informal European Theater Meeting, as well as numerous festivals, all have become regular opportunities for this international communication, much of which is directly concerned with the exchange of information about specific artists. You must make use of this informal "circle of opinion" wherever possible. A good working relationship with local presenters and managers, whether at home or at sites such as those in the NPN, can translate into a persuasive argument that will kindle foreign interest. Let producers and booking managers know about your desire to work abroad. Ask them for help in developing your mailing list of likely international producers. Ask them to let you know in advance when a visitor is coming to town. And ask them to suggest your work, show a videotape, or provide a strong reference.

To begin the research, if not the pursuit, start with colleagues who've had international experience. Where did they go? Who or what was instrumental in making the connection? If you are interested in a particular country, especially in those parts of the world that are off the beaten track, contact the cultural office of that country's embassy or local consulate in Washington, New York, and occasionally other American cities. They should have up-to-date information and can indicate if and when someone will be coming to the United States to investigate work and exchange. Also, contact the cultural officer in the American embassy or consulate in that country (or have the local organization that's interested in you contact the local American representative). Remember that, if it's possible for the USIA to help, the request for support of your work must originate from inside the country and be transmitted to Washington from the American embassy.

Nothing happens without individual initiative and doggedness. And nothing works better than face-to-face communication with the culture and organizations that you are interested in. Get a copy of DTW's constantly updated "International Presenters" list, do some background reading, take a "working vacation" (tax-deductible to the extent allowed by law), and go introduce yourself. You'll be surprised how often a seemingly inscrutable world will welcome you in if you demonstrate a sincere desire to learn and collaborate.

See the Appendix for a list of key individual consultants and organizations that may help you on your way.

Brass Tacks: Negotiation, Organization, and Contract

Once you've found someone interested in your work, you'll need to establish a fee, negotiate contracts and technical riders, and make travel arrangements. Organizing an international tour makes special demands, demands due to differences in styles of doing business, language, monetary systems, and technical facilities.

Establishing a fee. There are two ways of setting your fee: The first is a performance fee plus expenses, that is, hotel, transportation (including freight), and sometimes per diem; the second is an all-inclusive rate. In order to quote an all-inclusive fee you will need to have the entire tour mapped out and to know exactly how much freight you will be carrying. Seasonal variations in airfares and hotel rates alone can break your tour budget if not taken into account when setting your fee. The always-fluctuating rate of exchange makes it even more difficult to project daily expenses while on tour. Companies starting out, therefore, usually choose the first option, whereby a fee is paid to the artist, with hotel and transportation charges paid directly by the sponsor and per diems paid out in local currency. If you are just breaking into international touring, it is advisable, as when touring domestically, to select a performance program that is easily manageable in terms of the number of people on the road, amount of freight, and complexity of technical requirements.

There are particular expenses incurred only while touring abroad, and there are budget categories common to all touring that become more expensive on a foreign tour. For example, the single performance fee you are accustomed to quoting domestically will leave you short overseas unless it is part of a longer tour. A single performance anywhere in Europe will involve one week on the road since you will need to include two long travel days and jet lag recovery time. Salaries, per diems, and hotel expenses need to be calculated on a weekly basis. Daily expenses such as food, hotels, and local travel will vary from country to country. While the $35.00 per diem you pay dancers on a U.S. tour might be fine in Portugal, it will be hard to get by on in Italy. Consult with artists who have just returned from the country you're going to about prices for food, local travel, and hotels. The presenter is not always the best judge of what these costs are and will sometimes assure you that the per diem she/he is offering is more than adequate, without taking into account that you and your dancers will be needing late-night taxis and won't always have the time to search out the most inexpensive restaurants. Your administrative costs for a foreign tour will be much higher than for domestic touring: Overseas telephone calls made during peak hours, overseas postage, translation services, packages sent by courier services, special visas, work permits, and inoculations if necessary are all costs that must be budgeted. If you are traveling with freight, you'll need to include the cost of customs documents and possibly a customs broker's fee in your tour budget.

To avoid confusion and conflicts later, be clear when quoting your fee to the presenter that it is a "net" fee and that no deductions for taxes or any other purpose can be made. In many countries, value-added taxes (VAT) can take a huge bite (up to 30 percent) out of your fee, so be very straightforward and firm about the fee you must take home with you. While it is possible to have these taxes reimbursed, it is a bureaucratic and paperwork nightmare. In most cases the presenter can have the tax reduced or waived, but you will need to supply proof of nonprofit, tax-exempt status and that Social Security and other specific taxes are paid in the United States. These documents usually will have to be written in a particular format and notarized. Find out from the presenter exactly what is needed to gain an exemption, and follow those instructions precisely.

Contracts, payments, and technical requirements. It is in your best interest to initiate a contract on your end rather than to wait for the foreign presenter to send one that will more often than not include key clauses you will want to have stipulated. Some presenters insist on signing a version of the contract that they have had translated into their native language. This is often an official governmental requirement by which you will have to abide. Before you sign, have it translated back into English so that you can confirm that all the clauses have been included and that no alterations have been made. Ask the presenter to sign both versions of the contract and technical rider.

Payments. If you have quoted and agreed on a fee in American dollars, you should expect to be paid in dollars. If you receive payment in local currency, you risk that the rate of exchange could leave you with a significantly lower fee. Be clear in your contract exactly how, when, and in what currency payments are to be made. If some part of your fee is going to be paid in foreign currency, set out in your contract exactly what rate of exchange it should be paid at and how much fluctuation from that rate is permissible. It is fairly standard to receive 25–50 percent of the entire fee four to six weeks in advance of the tour. If you receive 25 percent in advance, it is fair to request 50 percent on arrival and the balance on the day of, but prior to, the final performance. If the presenter is to reimburse you for airfares, get approval of the fare before purchasing tickets, and ask for the full amount due to be wired to your bank account. If per diems are to be paid in local currency, request that they be given to you in cash to disperse to the company on your arrival in the city. The most reliable and safest way to accept payments is by wire transfer in U.S. dollars directly to your bank account. For transfers that are made while you are on tour, ask for the papers that verify that the transfer has been made. You will need to provide the presenter with the following information: bank name, address, account name and number, ABA number (ask your bank for this), and the bank officer to whose attention the transfer should be made.

For model contracts and sample clauses governing payment arrangements and schedules, you can contact the Suitcase Fund office of Dance Theater Workshop, Pentacle, or International Production Associates, among others.

Technical requirements. The technical rider should state very clearly every-thing—*everything*—you expect the sponsor to provide. If you can have the rider translated into the appropriate language, do so. It will help the overseas technical director understand your needs. Remember that equipment and electrical currents are different overseas and that what is readily available here may be a rare and expensive item abroad. Include in your contract that the sponsor must provide at least one translator throughout the engagement. One translator must have knowledge of technical theater terms and be present and available to your technical director during load-in, setup, focusing, all stage rehearsals, and performances. A second translator, if possible, should be available to the rest of the company.

Customs documents. The ATA carnet is a special customs document de-signed to simplify and streamline customs procedures for people who wish to take professional equipment into countries overseas. This is absolutely indispensable for dance companies with set materials or electronic or musical instruments. If you have a substantial amount of equipment being taken overseas, you will need to obtain a carnet from the U.S. Council of the International Chamber of Commerce (1212 Ave. of the Americas, New York, NY 10036). If you will be going to more than one country, it can be helpful to hire a customs broker to prepare the carnet and other documents that will be needed for crossing borders and obtaining customs clearances.

APPENDIX THE MARKETPLACE

Addresses and phone numbers of the following resources may be found in the alphabetized Directory at the end of the book.

The National Marketplace

Funding for national touring

Government

The most accessible financial support for touring generally comes from governmental sources in the form of awards to presenters earmarked to subsidize company fees for specific engagements.

National Endowment for the Arts support for presenters in the various disciplines has been consolidated within the Presenting and Commissioning Program, and the parameters of existing touring and commissioning programs will probably be altered.

Artists serious about securing subsidized engagements should monitor developments affecting both themselves and presenters. It's a good idea to request current guidelines from the National Endowment for the Arts and the state or local arts councils within the region you would like to tour. (See listings under "Funding" above.)

Regional

The following six regional arts councils administer the Dance on Tour program. Each region distributes the guidelines and administers the subsidy program for the presenters in that region. Artists should request these guidelines.

Arts Midwest (Illinois, Indiana, Iowa, Michigan, Minnesota, North Dakota, Ohio, South Dakota, Wisconsin.)

Mid-America Arts Alliance (MAAA) (Arkansas, Kansas, Missouri, Nebraska, Oklahoma, Texas [associate member].)

Mid-Atlantic States Arts Consortium (MASAC) (Delaware, District of Columbia, Maryland, New Jersey, New York, Pennsylvania, Virginia, West Virginia.)

New England Foundation for the Arts, Inc. (NEFA) (Connecticut, Maine, Massachusetts, New Hampshire, Rhode Island, Vermont.)

Southern Arts Federation (SAF) (Alabama, Florida, Georgia, Kentucky, Louisiana, Mississippi, North Carolina, South Carolina, Tennessee.)

Western States Arts Foundation (WSAF) (Alaska, Arizona, California, Colorado, Hawaii, Idaho, Montana, Nevada, New Mexico, Oregon, Utah, Washington, Wyoming.)

Presenting consortia

These organizations offer subsidies to their presenter members across the country. The efficiencies of routing their coordinated efforts can save significant amounts of money for all involved, including the artist.

California Presenters

Consortium for Pacific Arts & Cultures (CPAC) (American Samoa, Guam, Northern Marianas.)

Dance Theater Workshop's National Performance Network

Dance/USA's American Dance Touring Initiative

Green Mountain Consortium

Pacific Northwest Arts Presenters

Southwest Performing Arts Presenters

Foundation and corporate touring support

Foundations and corporations occasionally focus support on touring, but such support is usually targeted at a very small and select list of artists. One such program is that of the AT&T Foundation. Occasionally, the marketing division of a corporation can be convinced that subsidizing a particular artist in particular locations (in return for very visible credit) can benefit that corporation's image. It's a long shot, to say the least. A little less unlikely would be to get an airline to donate the tickets for your tour.

Backyard support

Ask your board, friends, relatives, and supporters to support your tour this year. Especially for an emerging company, a tour or prestigious engagement can be as galvanizing as a home season.

National touring information resources (that provide information and assistance with regional touring)

American Association of Museums

American Symphony Orchestra League

Association of Performing Arts Presenters (formerly ACCUCA) (Membership of presenting organizations, artists, and artists' managers. Provides membership services, including advocacy work. Annual booking conference in December.)

International Society of Performing Arts Administrators

National Association of Campus Activities

National Association of Performing Arts Managers and Agents

National League of Historic Theaters

New England Presenters

Publications and mailing lists:

Guidelines for Ethical Behavior.

Musical America Directory. Listings of presenters.

National Performance Network Brochure.

Pentacle/Dance Theater Workshop National Performing Arts Mailing List. A computerized list of over 4,500 U.S. presenters.

Stern's Performing Arts Directory (formerly *Dance Magazine Annual Performing Arts Directory*).

The International Marketplace

Resources

A sampling of U.S. and international resources for working abroad

Arts America Program
(See U.S. Information Agency below.)

Arts International (A division of the Institute of International Education. Administers the Fund for U.S. Artists at International Festivals and Exhibitions, which is supported by the Rockefeller Foundation, the Pew Charitable Trusts, the NEA, and the U.S. Information Agency. The staff is developing a data base to provide information on international festivals and the experiences of grantees at various festivals. Arts International is also updating its resource guide for artists working internationally, including information on financial support and residency opportunities. It also administers the Collaborative Works Program funded by the Annette Kade Endowment and created to encourage the creation of new work or new international collaborations among French and U.S. or German and U.S. artists from all disciplines.)

Asian Cultural Council (Awards individual fellowship grants in support of cultural exchange in the visual and performing arts between the United States and the countries of Asia. While most of these grants enable artists, scholars, and specialists from Asia to pursue research and creative activity in the United States, some awards are available for Americans to travel to Asia, primarily Japan. The Asian Cultural Council can also provide useful contact information and advice about working in Asia.)

Asia Society and Japan Society, Inc. (Both organizations have been instrumental in bringing numerous performing arts events and residencies by Asian artists to the United States. They have extensive contacts in Asia and can provide valuable information about the cultural environment in various Asian countries and how and whom to approach about working in the region.)

British Music Worldwide

Caribbean Cultural Center (A major U.S. presenter of African and Afro-Caribbean artists that has extensive information about the arts in the Caribbean and throughout Africa.)

Council for International Exchange of Scholars (CIES) (A private organization that facilitates international exchange in higher education. Under a cooperative agreement with the U.S. Information Agency, CIES works with the Institute of International Education to administer the Fulbright Scholar Program: Grants for Faculty and Professionals. In order to apply for a Fulbright from CIES, you must hold a doctoral degree. This is not the case for the Fulbright Program, which is administered by the Institute of International Education; see below.)

Chuck Davis/African-American Dance Ensemble (Choreographer Chuck Davis's research and study have taken him and his company to Africa on an annual basis. Davis also facilitates an open cultural arts "safari" for two to four weeks every summer, which brings dancers, musicians, and others to various African countries to learn the origins of traditional dances. Artists wishing to begin exploring the possibilities in Africa can write to or call Davis, who is willing to share his extensive contacts or refer you to others who can be of assistance.)

Dance Theater Workshop (DTW) (A production/service organization with extensive international contacts. In 1985 Dance Theater Workshop established The Suitcase Fund: A Project of Ideas and Means in Cross-Cultural Artist Relations, to encourage artists and producers to work across cultural and geographic boundaries and to stimulate the research and implementation of specific artist projects that grow out of these investigations. DTW has an exhaustive, constantly updated list of international presenters, service organizations, and residency opportunities that is available to members and nonmembers at a nominal fee.)

David Eden (A native Russian who is based in New York and works as an independent producer and consultant concentrating on projects with Russia and Israel. Working independently and as a facilitator with a number of organizations in the United States, including Jacob's Pillow Dance Festival, the American Dance Festival, the New York International Festival, and DTW's SUITCASE FUND, Eden has masterminded a number of projects that have brought U.S. and Russian artists into contact with each other through workshops, residencies, and performances. Eden's intimate knowledge of what it takes to get things done there make him an invaluable resource for artists attempting to understand how the arts function in the former Soviet Republics and how to begin to develop and sustain contacts there.)

Informal European Theater Meeting

Institute of International Education (IIE) (An international educational and cultural exchange organization. IIE has administered the USIA's Fulbright Program, which it coadministers with the Council for International Exchange of Scholars, since the founding of the program in 1946. Fulbright fellowships are awarded primarily for graduate study and academic research, but artists are also eligible for fellowships to work abroad. Approximately fifty graduate-level and professional artists are supported by the Fulbright Program every year. The Fulbright Program also offers a small number of Travel Grants to supplement awards from non-IIE sources. IIE's network is active in regional offices throughout the United States and in Mexico City, Bangkok, Jakarta, Budapest, and Sri Lanka.)

International Research and Exchanges Board (IREX) (Guarantees access by American scholars to research resources in the former Soviet republics, Europe, and the Mongolian People's Republic, and encourages scholarly cooperation with the region, especially in the humanities and social sciences. IREX arranges reciprocal research exchanges as well as bilateral and multilateral special projects. In the past, IREX administered a small Creative Arts Program that supported artist exchanges and residencies in Russia and Central Europe, but this program was discontinued in 1991 owing to lack of funding. Nevertheless, IREX can provide resource information on the artistic environment in the region.)

International Theatre Institute/US (ITI) (Publishes a quarterly newsletter that lists upcoming international festivals, meetings, symposia, and workshops. Its library, which receives current information on festivals worldwide, is open to the public. There are seventy-nine ITI centers throughout the world, which can be contacted for information on performance and residency opportunities in particular countries.)

Movement Theater International (MTI) (A very active presenter of international work with a major focus on mime, clown, puppet theater, and circus arts. Movement Theater International has been developing contacts with international artists and producers since 1979 and has brought many artists to the United States, particularly from Southeast Asia, Indonesia, and Africa. MTI can provide information and advice about the arts in many parts of the world, but in particular in Eastern Europe, Southeast Asia, and central and southern Africa. MTI is developing an exchange program with Zaire that will involve teaching and joint workshops. A similar program is in the works with Russia.)

National Endowment for the Arts, International Activities Office (Although the International Activities Office of the NEA does not have a large grants budget, it can be helpful in providing information and contacts for working abroad and in facilitating discussions with cultural attachés from various countries. Also has a guide to funding opportunities for international projects within the National Endowment for the Arts.)

Pentacle (A management/service group with some experience in European booking and touring conditions for small companies)

The Suitcase Fund
(See Dance Theater Workshop above.)

Tigertail Productions/Mary Luft & Company (Mary Luft is a choreographer and independent producer who has done extensive research in South/Central America—with a particular focus on dance and music in Brazil and Peru. She acts as a facilitator for artists coming to the United States from South America, organizes projects in South America, and is compiling a resource directory of South American cultural organizers and artists that is scheduled for completion in 1993. Luft can provide limited information about key individuals in Brazil and Peru who could be helpful in arranging residencies.)

Two Continents Arts Exchange (An organization that serves as program consultant and artistic adviser to several large and small Western European theaters and festivals. Two Continents also serves as a facilitator/liaison between a number of Western European theaters and the U.S. artists they present. Artists can contact Two Continents Arts Exchange for current information on performing opportunities, especially in France and Spain. Two Continents is continually reviewing the work of U.S. artists who might be of interest to European theater and festival directors.)

United States Information Agency (USIA) Arts America Program (The USIA is charged with overseas cultural affairs for the federal government. In recent years it has had $2–$3 million to spend worldwide on the export of visual and performing American works and artists, through its Arts America Program. The USIA generally targets existing funds at parts of the world of geopolitical concern to the U.S. government—that is, where the United States wants to create influence and gain political goodwill—particularly countries with limited access to examples of American culture. It does not sponsor programs in Japan, Australia, or Western Europe.

The process of applying for and receiving support from the USIA can be cumbersome and bureaucratic, but persistence can pay off. Proposals are considered only in response to requests from American embassies abroad. Final decisions are made by the staff in Washington, DC, from among those artists "favorably endorsed" by NEA-organized panels. To be reviewed by a panel, you need to submit a "Fact Sheet for Performing Artists Touring Privately" and a videotape, press kit, and publicity material. The form, which is available from the DC office of Arts America, can be submitted at any time during the year. The panels meet only once or twice a year, however, so if you are considering touring abroad, it would be wise to submit the fact sheet and have your work reviewed. Although Arts America is not a grant application program, it does try to keep the embassies informed of artists planning overseas tours. It is a good idea to keep the Washington, DC, office and the appropriate foreign office informed of your plans—as far in advance as possible. At the request of the cultural affairs officer at the local U.S. embassy, tours can be fully or partially subsidized. Arts America can also provide assistance in the form of referrals and contacts.

Arts America also runs a program through which it sponsors "cultural specialists" to be in residence abroad for two to six weeks to teach or work with a local company. Again, the request for support must come from the American embassy abroad. That embassy can request a particular artist for a residency, or the request can be very general, for example, for a choreographer to work with a particular local dance company in Caracas. Again, only artists who have been endorsed by the NEA-organized panel are eligible for assistance; the Arts America office in Washington, DC, makes selections from that list. Generally, the program supports travel expenses, a modest honorarium, accommodations, and living expenses. Those interested in the program should contact the embassy cultural affairs officer in the country they wish to work in and request her/his assistance.)

U.S. Council of the International Chamber of Commerce

Publications

Guia Teatral de España. A biannual publication with exhaustive listings and summaries of theaters, festivals, government cultural agencies, and artists throughout Spain.

International Festival Guide. An up-to-date list of theater and dance festivals throughout the world. It contains basic information about nearly 500 international festivals (addresses, phone and fax numbers, frequency, directors) as well as short descriptions of the festivals.

International Presenters and Festivals List. An up-to-date list of international present-ers, service organizations, and residency opportunities available through Dance The-ater Workshop.

Performing Arts Yearbook for Europe.

Organizations and consultants

A sampling of key organizations and consultants abroad who may be able to pro-vide resources and answer questions about performing arts opportunities in various countries:

Ardani-Moscow Theater Agency (Founded in June, 1990, in Moscow by a group of professional arts managers, it has become one of the first private arts agencies in Russia. The agency provides touring both of foreign companies in Russia and of Rus-sian companies abroad. Its primary interests are in ballet, jazz, and classical music.

Artcelona and New African Connection (A production/promotion company that has considerable information on Spanish theaters and festivals and their programming interests. In recent years, it has also developed extensive contacts in Africa.)

Canada Arts Presenters Association (CAPACOA) (An association of Canadian presenters from all ten provinces and the Yukon that is organized much like the Association of Performing Arts Presenters in the United States. Members also include government cultural agencies, arts councils, artists, and artist managements. Its presenter mem-bers' theaters range in size from 200 to 3,200 seats. CAPACOA was established to pro-mote the presentation of the arts in Canada and to encourage the touring of artists throughout the country. CAPACOA's mailing list is available for purchase, and artists can also contact the Ottawa office for advice/information on how and whom to approach about touring in Canada.)

Canada Council Touring Office (Within Canada's equivalent to the NEA, a comprehen-sive source of information concerning sponsors and touring networks in Canada.)

Dance Umbrella (United Kingdom) (In addition to producing the London Dance Um-brella Festival and festivals in Leicester and Newcastle, Dance Umbrella has also cre-ated networks with regional arts centers to help tour dance artists throughout En-gland.)

DANCEWORKS (The Canadian national office for the U.S./Canada Performance Initiative, a bilateral project designed to increase performance, residency, and creative opportu-nities for U.S. and Canadian artists of all cultural backgrounds in dance, music, theater, performance art, and puppetry. The U.S./Canada Performance Initiative is a program of DTW and DANCEWORKS in cooperation with similarly dedicated organizations in the United States and Canada. DANCEWORKS is a valuable source of information on dance presenters across Canada, and its dance curator is the spokesperson for CanDance, a loose affiliation of Canadian dance presenters who join forces in lobbying efforts on behalf of the dance community and its interests.)

Laura Kumin (See also Consejeria de Cultura in the Directory) (An American who has been living and working in Madrid for a number of years and who has a wealth of information on who's who in Spain and how and when to approach them. In addition to organizing and producing a national choreographic competition (the Certamen Coreografico de Madrid), which showcases emerging Spanish dance companies and promotes new work, Kumin is a dance adviser to the Comunidad de Madrid.)

Netherlands Dance Institute (NID) (Primarily a service organization for professional dance, the NID collects and disseminates current information about dance in the Netherlands. The NID houses an international dance library, a photo archive, and a video dance library and works in close collaboration with the Netherlands Theatre Institute (see below) and the Netherlands Mime Centrum. On request, the NID can provide lists with information about dancers, companies, theaters, festivals, workshops, and dance schools. Questions by mail or phone will be answered by NID staff or referred to other individuals or organizations.)

Netherlands Theater Institute (A truly activist branch of the International Theatre Institute that acts as a service and information center for Dutch theaters and festivals. The Netherlands Theater Institute can also provide information on Dutch theaters, festivals, and agents interested in foreign artists. It also publishes *Theatre and Dance from the Netherlands,* a quarterly newsletter that features articles on Dutch dance, mime, and theater artists as well as on Dutch festivals.)

Office National du Diffusion Artistique (ONDA) (An agency that assists French presenters [in some instances with subsidy] in creating block-booked tours for performing groups, both local and foreign. Also a prime mover, with the Netherlands Theater Institute, in developing coordination among a large number of European presenters.)

Tanztendenz München (The official institution for the support of Munich-based dance, this nonprofit organization is a key resource for information on dance in Germany. It also houses dance studios, represents several independent dance companies, and provides a range of services that promote and strengthen the Munich dance community.)

Unesco (United Nations Educational, Scientific, and Cultural Organization) (One of fifteen intergovernmental agencies of the United Nations. Its activities are coordinated by the U.N. Economic and Social Council, which is the humanitarian policy arm of the United Nations. In the field of culture, it facilitates international exchange of information on different aspects of cultural policies and enables bilateral and multilateral relations to be established through international exchanges. It sponsors seminars and meetings, training internships, and professional exchanges and funds a wide variety of initiatives ranging from multidisciplinary projects that bring professional and amateur artists together to study grants for young artists to support of regional training programs and the creation of multicultural centers. In addition to providing financial support for particular projects, Unesco can provide information about cultural policies and programs worldwide. Be aware that the United States is not a member of Unesco, so many of its programs will not be open to you; its informational resources will be of the most value.)

Union of Theater Workers of the USSR (Prior to August 1991, the Union of Theater Workers included in its membership theater unions in all the Soviet republics and developed and supported exchange projects, festivals, and performances with Soviet and foreign theater artists. The Union also represented the interests of Soviet theater abroad. In the "postrevolutionary" period we can only assume that the theater unions in each republic will continue to operate independently, perhaps under different names, and support a variety of projects by national and international artists.)

Vlaams Theater Institut (VTI) (VTI is a center for research, documentation, advice, and promotion for the performing arts and is an important information resource about the Flemish arts community. VTI also houses a specialized data bank for the performing arts and extensive documentation—printed and video—about international performing arts companies and theaters. It is an excellent source of information on European theaters and festivals, and it is open to receiving materials on international companies, which are made available to visitors. The international department of VTI answers questions about Flemish and foreign theater.)

Organizers

Cultural organizers in eastern/central Europe who can provide valuable insight and information about working in the region or point you to other key individuals in specific countries (see Directory for contact information):

Ondrej Hrab (Ondrej Hrab was an active participant in the alternative political and cultural movement in Czechoslovakia in the 1970s and 1980s and produced illegal and semilegal performances of international artists in Prague and other cities. Since 1989, Hrab has served as secretary of the Theater Community and is working on proposed models for state arts policy and on creating new international relations for Czech theater art. The primary concern of the Theatre Community is to support the preservation and expansion of theater arts in Czechoslovakia, to protect the interests of the theater from commercial and political oppression, and to aid in the country's reemergence as an active participant in the global theater community. The Theater Community also provides organizational, promotional, and limited financial support for theater activities of all kinds, including workshops, festivals, and performances by emerging Czech artists as well as performances by artists from abroad.)

Gyorgy Szabo, Performing Arts (Gyorgy Szabo is the programming director of performing arts at the Petofi Csarnok, a multidisciplinary "youth center" that presents innovative theater, new music, and dance along with rock and jazz concerts and commercial discos. But Szabo's work extends far beyond the walls of the Petofi Csarnok: He is a leading, outspoken, and tireless advocate for independent dance artists in Hungary. Despite limited resources, he has been instrumental in bringing Western choreographers and their companies to Budapest to perform and teach and has been an integral player in developing an informal network of cultural organizers throughout Eastern/Central Europe.)

H E A L T H

We are bound to our bodies like an oyster to its shell.

—Plato, *Phaedrus*

■ So we will hold each other. We'll build new works. We will deepen our relationships. We'll disagree. And we'll do what we do best, which is build and struggle.—Bill T. Jones, choreographer ■

AIDS Explained
Michael Lange, M.D.

AIDS, the acquired immunodeficiency syndrome, is felt to be an end stage of a progressively weakened immune system. At the point at which a patient develops AIDS, her/his immune system can no longer fight certain infections or the development of certain malignancies (cancers). This progressive destruction of the immune system is believed to result from infection with the human immunodeficiency virus (HIV). A person usually becomes infected with HIV either by intimate sexual contact with an HIV-infected person or by contamination with HIV-infected blood (needle sticks, needle sharing, etc.). Generally, two to six months following the infection, the HIV-infected person will develop antibodies to HIV (i.e., she/he becomes HIV seropositive). From seroconversion (the time at which someone becomes HIV seropositive) until the development of AIDS, a varying time period elapses (generally eight to ten years), during which the HIV-infected person has no symptoms at all and, hence, is asymptomatic. The time period from seroconversion to the point of developing signs and symptoms of physical sickness (AIDS-related complex, also known as ARC, and, finally, AIDS) depends on the rate at which a certain subset of lymphocytes (white blood cells known as T-helper, or CD4, lymphocytes) is destroyed. This rate of destruction varies greatly from one person to the next. The shortest time period from seroconversion to the development of AIDS has been only a few months; on the other hand, there are some individuals (an estimated 20 percent of seropositives) who still feel perfectly healthy twelve years after being infected. In view of this time variation, what should you do?

First of all, it is necessary to face the possibility that you may have been infected. To determine that, you should get tested for the HIV antibody. If you are found to test positive for the HIV antibody, you should seek medical advice. In order to be able to deal with the potential knowledge of being HIV positive, it is important to understand a few basics of the disease process (also known as HIV pathogenesis).

HIV Testing

Testing for the HIV antibody in New York State, for example, can be done only with a patient's consent. There are several laboratories run by the city health department where you can be tested absolutely anonymously. When you go to such a clinic, you receive counseling and are given a number. You do not give your name. Your blood is first tested by the ELISA method for the HIV antibody; if positive, a confirmatory test called a Western Blot is performed. Only if your blood tests positive by both methods are you considered to be HIV positive. You will return to the laboratory approximately one week after giving your blood, present your number, and be told your test result. If you tested positive, you will receive a further counseling session and be advised to see a doctor.

On Being HIV Positive

If you find out that you are HIV positive, it is important to find out how much destruction of your immune system has already occurred. The simplest, most accurate way of achieving this is to have your CD4 positive lymphocytes (T-helper lymphocytes) measured. Unfortunately, the CD4 count can fluctuate considerably (from 50 to 100 points). It is common clinical practice to divide HIV patients into three main categories based on the CD4 count; generally, a lower CD4 count means that more damage has already occurred to the immune system.

I. CD4 count under 200
At this level, your immune system is so weak that you are at risk of developing opportunistic infections (OI). If you develop one of these OIs or develop Kaposi's sarcoma or lymphoma (both of which may also occur with higher CD4 counts), you then have AIDS, according to the definition of the Centers for Disease Control (CDC-AIDS). With a count of less than 200 you are considered at risk of developing AIDS and should be prescribed prophylactic (preventive) medication against pneumocystis pneumonia. At this stage, many clinicians also prescribe prophylactic medication against cytomegalovirus (CMV), a herpes-related virus that can cause blindness. Some also give prophylaxis

against other opportunistic infections, but the value of this course of action has not yet been proved. The majority of clinicians feel strongly that you should receive antiviral (anti-HIV) medication at this stage (see below).

2. CD4 count between 200 and 500

The majority of patients whose T-helper count is within this range are asymptomatic (i.e., they feel healthy). Some develop milder symptoms such as fatigue and malaise, low-grade fever, loss of weight, and/or chronic diarrhea. These somewhat vague symptoms are collectively referred to as AIDS-related complex (ARC) and usually occur in the lower range (CD4 count below 300). Many clinicians prescribe anti-HIV medication for this group of patients, although this practice remains controversial. It is felt that, if no treatment is given during this period, a patient has a 50 percent chance of developing clinical disease during the next three years.

3. CD4 count above 500

Almost all HIV-seropositive patients with CD4 counts above 500 are asymptomatic and will remain so for years. No studies have demonstrated any benefit to taking any medications at this early stage.

Limitations of Following CD4 Counts

It is important to realize that CD4 counts give limited information. They do indeed tell you whether you are at risk of getting opportunistic infections. But a CD4 count is a measurement at one point in time; it does *not* tell you at what rate the CD4 count will decline. We do know that one person whose CD4 count is 350 today may have five CD4 cells in three years, while another may retain 350 after the same three years. A lot of research is being done to find tests that would predict the rate of decline of CD4 cells (these tests are called "surrogate markers"), but so far none of the commercially available tests have been very useful.

It is therefore advisable, particularly in the earlier phases of HIV infection (CD4 counts of 200–500 or greater than 500), to measure your CD4 count at regular intervals and to have regularly scheduled visits with your doctor. I recommend that if your CD4 cells are above 500, you should test your CD4 count every three months for the first year, and that if four measurements show relative stability, testing every four to six months is adequate. If, on the other hand, you see a steady decline in CD4 counts or marked fluctuations, it is advisable to continue regular follow-up visits with your doctor at two- to three-month intervals.

Antiviral Therapy

The most widely held concept about the progression of HIV infection attributes the destruction of the CD4 lymphocytes directly to HIV infecting and destroying these cells. Although there is considerable controversy as to how—whether directly or indirectly—the CD4 cell destruction occurs, the principle of present treatment is to suppress the multiplication of HIV. By this hypothesis, arrest of HIV multiplication will lead to the decrease or absence of new virus particles being produced, resulting in fewer or no further CD4 cells being infected and destroyed.

Zidovudine (AZT)

A number of different agents will inhibit the multiplication of HIV in the laboratory setting. One of these, AZT, also known as Zidovudine, has been approved by the U.S. Food and Drug Administration (FDA) since 1987 to be used in treating AIDS. It has been demonstrated to improve quality of life and to decrease the incidence of opportunistic infections in patients with fewer than 200 CD4 cells. The efficacy of this drug in this situation, however, appears limited, and it is not clear that AZT as such prolongs survival if you start taking it when your CD4 count is less than 200. More recently (in 1990), the approved use of AZT was extended to HIV-positive patients with CD4 counts between 200 and 500. This approval was based on a study in which the drug was taken for an average of only twelve months. Since just a small minority of patients with this CD4 count range develop ARC or AIDS if they are not taking any drugs, and as the previous studies had shown an improvement that generally did not last longer than six months, it is not clear that it is advisable to recommend that everyone in the 200- to 500-cell category should take AZT. Indeed, a follow-up of three years for this group has not been able to show that it prolongs life. A further (now 2.5 years) study where physicians and patients are blinded as to whether the patient is taking placebo or AZT is continuing in France and England. Known as the Concord Study, the results of this study bear watching.

In addition, AZT is associated with a considerable number of toxicities. These can be divided into short-term toxicities, appearing within a few weeks of starting AZT (bone-marrow suppression, severe anemia), and long-term toxicities, generally appearing after a year (neuropathy, muscle degeneration) or several years (lymphoma). The incidence of short-term toxicities that initially led to about 50 percent of patients taking AZT having to stop the drug during the first year has been greatly reduced since 1990, when it became clear that the beneficial effects of AZT could be achieved with one-third the dose given in the initial studies. It is not known at this time if lower dosing will result in lower incidence of the long-term toxicities or if they will just take longer to appear. During 1991–92, two other nucleoside analogs (antiretroviral related to AZT) have been approved by the FDA. Of these, DDC (Dideoxycytidine) has been approved for combined use with AZT in situations where the benefit of AZT appears to be on the wane. The other, DDT, (Didanosine or Videx) can be used alone. Both are associated with a fairly high incidence of peripheral neuropathy (numbness, tingling, or pain in hands and feet) and DDT rarely results in severe pancreatitis, which can be fatal. Trials are also under way to use these drugs in various combinations or in rotations.

The above discussion emphasizes the fact that much remains unknown about how AIDS develops or about good treatment for HIV infection. It is important for patients to realize that therapy (i.e., treatment) for HIV infection is a rapidly changing field and that attitudes and opinions may have changed by the time this article appears in print. A number of "alternative therapies" are also in wide use. Of these, several are based on published literature, demonstrating an anti-HIV effect in the test tube or an immunological effect in test tube, animal model, or preliminary human study. Examples of these include N-acetylcysteine (NAC) and Diethyldithiocarbamate (DDTC).

How then can the HIV-infected person stay on top of this rapidly changing field? If she/he is lucky, the treating physician is well informed and stays on top of the situation. Since there is much discussion and difference of opinion, even among physicians taking care of HIV-infected patients, as to the best approach to the disease, many patients feel more comfortable gathering as much information about the disease as they can and then discussing the pros and cons of therapy with their physicians. Information that is intelligible to laypeople can be had from a number of organizations: Gay Men's Health Crisis (GMHC); the Persons with AIDS Coalition (PWA); and the American Foundation for AIDS Research (AMFAR), which puts out a treatment directory that tries to list every available experimental treatment in the world (it is highly informative but does not attempt to prioritize the treatments as to which are most likely to provide help).

Regular Contact with Doctors

Physicians who are well informed about and acknowledged experts on HIV infections are generally overloaded, and it may be difficult to get an immediate appointment. If you cannot find an "AIDS expert" to be your primary-care physician, you should find a good internist. Remember, the opportunistic infections (OIs) are what kill most AIDS patients, and for most of these there is very specific treatment. With the exception of tuberculosis, you will not develop OIs unless your CD4 count is well below 200. It is important to realize, however, that, if you fall into this category, it is necessary to check with your doctor if you get symptoms suggestive of flu-like illness. Visual disturbances, headaches, fevers, diarrhea, sinusitis, and cough, particularly when associated with shortness of breath, deserve a doctor's visit if they persist for three or more days. You want to make sure that these symptoms do not represent early manifestations of an OI, as it is clear that early treatment of an OI is associated with a much better rate of recovery.

Prevention

HIV infection—and its end stage, AIDS—is primarily a sexually transmitted disease. That it first appeared in the United States predominantly among gay people and intravenous drug users seems to have been coincidental. At this stage even larger numbers of heterosexuals are becoming HIV infected. Women now compose the most rapidly growing group of newly infected HIV-positive people.

As we have no cure for AIDS and HIV infection, it is important to practice "safe sex." Condoms are highly useful, although not an absolute guarantee of preventing HIV transmission. Birth control pills, foams, and IUDs do not prevent transmission. Remember that sleeping around is dangerous and that it takes only one sex act to become infected. Although HIV is not highly infectious (some uninfected people have had regular unprotected sex with an HIV-positive person for years), you don't know at what point you may pick up the HIV virus. If you do have relations with a known HIV-positive person, it has been shown by gay persons practicing "safe sex" [see "What Is Safer Sex?" in this chapter] that HIV transmission can be reduced to a negligible incidence if you adhere to the rules.

Be careful! No one is immune to contracting AIDS.

Life Support Systems
Phyllis Lamhut

I have anxiety sweats, depressions coupled with an overwhelming sense of wanting to take this round thing they call the world and toss it. I donate as much money as I can for AIDS research, take care of my friends who are ill, support those who remain after losing their loved ones, and attend many funerals mourning the beautiful and talented souls who have had their lives snuffed out by a plague whose name is taboo because it is associated with drugs and sex in a country manipulated by politicians with public puritanical ethics and secret private domains.

I can do no more at this time. I have to turn to my art and push those inner voices and nightmares into a shape. Without being self-indulgent, I decided to choreograph a piece emanating from the AIDS environment in which I live.

I interviewed a number of AIDS patients, mostly dancers, since they dominate my world and as a choreographer I cannot function without them. I tried to understand how odd rhythms overtake their lives, their heroic sense of self as their bodies heave and deteriorate, knowing that dying is a possibility and hoping for a cure before their time comes.

I invited five mature male artists who are not often seen in New York to dance: Clay Taliaferro, Eleo Pomare, Manuel Alum, Robert Small, and Ben Hazard (who is also my composer). I call the work *MAN*. It consists of five solos. I needed dancers who are so experienced in their expressive values that no gesture would be wasted. I decided not to do the work for men only. Three women are present: Natasha Simon, Andrea Borak, and Lorn MacDougal. They are a life-support system—mothers, relatives, friends. They mourn deeply for those lost and are bright birds of spirit. I think they are me.

What Is Safer Sex?

[*The following information has been provided by the Gay Men's Health Crisis. See the Appendix for the* GMHC *Hotline information.*—Eds.]

Safer sex is just common sense. Since we know that the AIDS virus is transmitted by body fluids entering another body, the sensible way to prevent infection is to block their entrance. Wear a condom (rubber) when you have sex, so semen cannot get inside the mouth, vagina, or anus (in oral, vaginal, or anal sex). Put the rubber on as soon as the penis gets hard; the virus that causes AIDS could be present in preseminal fluid.

Latex condoms have been proved to be the most effective in preventing HIV infection. Lambskin and other "natural membrane" products are not as good as latex. They may allow HIV to pass through. The use of spermicidal (sperm-killing) lubricants, especially those with nonoxynol-9, may increase your protection. But they should always be used with a condom and never instead of a condom. Many condoms are prelubricated, some with spermicides, but you will probably want to use unlubricated condoms when engaging in oral sex. Condoms still provide the greatest protection and relieve you of the worry about the risk involved.

Both men and women should learn how to use condoms properly. Make them an integral part of sex and not an embarrassing, fumbling intermission. Here are the basic steps: When the penis is hard, roll the condom down all the way to the base, leaving some space at the head. Be sure to squeeze out any air bubbles. In vaginal or anal intercourse, use plenty of water-based lubricant, like KY or ForPlay. (Crisco, baby oil, hand lotions, and petroleum-based products like Vaseline can break down the latex within minutes.) This will reduce the risk of breaking the rubber or injuring body tissue, which could leave an opening for infection. Condoms seldom break when used correctly, but it's still a good idea to pull out before coming. The condom should be rolled off (not pulled) after coming and before losing the erection.

In oral sex with women, dental dams may be used. (However, they have *not* been tested for protection against HIV.) A dental dam is a six-inch-square piece of thin latex that's available in dental and medical supply stores. You can make a homemade dam by cutting a rolled condom to the center and opening it. It should be rinsed first, to remove any talc or other substance, and then dried. The dam should cover the entire vulva and should be held at both edges. Be very careful not to turn the dam inside-out during oral sex since this will totally defeat its purpose. Dental dams can also be used for oral-anal sex by both men and women.

Remember: Never reuse condoms or dental dams.

HIV Testing

[*The following information has been provided by the Gay Men's Health Crisis. See the Appendix for help in locating an HIV-testing center in your area.*—Eds.]

There are several reasons to consider taking the HIV-antibody test. If you suspect that you have been infected with HIV, you should consider taking the test as a first step toward adopting a healthier life-style and taking control of your health. Several new therapies have shown promise in delaying the onset of AIDS in people who have been infected with HIV. These experimental treatments, which suppress the virus and strengthen the immune system, may be most effective at the early stages of the disease. Therefore, it is often best to begin these therapies as early as possible after HIV infection.

Knowing that you are HIV positive will, in most cases, reinforce positive changes in sexual behavior. This is important since repeated exposure to the virus seems to play a large role in the development of AIDS and ARC (AIDS-related complex).

You should consider taking the HIV-antibody test if you are considering having a child and think that you or your partner may be infected. Confirming that you are HIV negative before conceiving a child will reduce the chance of transmitting HIV to the child before or at birth.

To assist you in coping with your reactions to your test results, it is extremely important that you set up a support network of people you trust before taking the test.

Also, you should discuss your questions and fears about the HIV test and AIDS with a trained counselor both before and after you take the test. The purpose of pretest counseling is to make sure that you understand what the test will and will not tell you and whether or not you should take it. Pretest counseling will help prepare you in case you test positive.

Posttest counseling will help you deal with any negative reactions. Eventually, with the help of friends and family, you will feel better. Then you can begin to take control of your health by improving your life-style and, if appropriate, beginning preventive medicines.

It is important to remember that if you have not developed antibodies to the virus, you are HIV negative. However, a negative test result does not guarantee that you are virus free. Your body can take anywhere from six weeks to a year after infection with the AIDS virus to produce antibodies. If you take the test after you have been infected with HIV but before your body has had enough time to produce antibodies, you will test negative. A negative test result does not mean that you cannot transmit the virus to someone else. You need to be retested periodically in the following year, while continuing to practice safer sex. Even if HIV negative, intravenous drug users should never share needles.

INSURANCE

Health Care: A User's Manual
Jonathan Lorch, M.D.

Case 1. You're rehearsing with Elizabeth Streb and slip. You crash into a colleague and now have a five-inch gash above your left eye that is bleeding profusely. Someone gets a cloth and presses the wound to stop the bleeding temporarily and then takes you to the local emergency room. You are asked for your insurance coverage and answer, "None." The clerk peers over her glasses and tells you to have a seat. The friend accompanying you suggests you request a plastic surgeon because "it's a big cut and you don't want to be left with any ugly scar." You question the clerk, and she says, "You have no insurance coverage, and a cut like that will cost at least $1,000 to have a plastic surgeon sew up."

Case 2. You finally make it into "Fresh Tracks" at Dance Theater Workshop. (And you thought it was rigged!) It's the night before your New York premiere in a Pepatian production. After your final tech you go to a nearby Thai restaurant for a bowl of Tom Yom soup. The shrimp looks a tad old, but you're hungry and want to get home quickly for some sleep. At 4:00 A.M. you are awakened by severe stomach cramps, nausea, and vomiting. Dread sets in! An hour later diarrhea starts, and when you finally leave the bathroom twenty minutes later, you are weak and dizzy. At 10:00 A.M. you can hardly get out of bed, but the diarrhea continues. Your performance work is a solo piece, and the dread now mutates to panic that you won't be able to perform unless you get medical help. You have no insurance and don't know any doctor in *all* of New York.

Twenty-five years ago these kinds of problems rarely had a tragic end. New York City was a mecca for physicians and a haven for the ill. The public hospital system was vast (the security force, alone, for the city's public hospitals was larger than the entire police department of the city of Los Angeles!) and, though maybe not in the best physical shape, was staffed with superb doctors and nurses. One could walk into any of the city's hospitals and receive excellent and compassionate care at minimal or no cost other than the wait. Even physicians in private practice donated their services at city hospitals. Unfortunately, the geography of New York health care has changed dramatically over the years, without question for the worse. What happened?

The factors leading to the lamentable decline in available, affordable, and compassionate health care in New York City include the usual human frailties of greed, anger, hopelessness, and illusion, compounded by a staggering number of people with AIDS and drug-related problems. The results are fewer public and private hospitals, all of which are overcrowded, underfunded, poorly staffed, and verging on bankruptcy. Doctors and nurses are abandoning the city, and training programs no longer attract the best-qualified physicians. In fact, some don't attract any physicians at all. Physicians' fees have become exorbitant, insurers are paying them less, and because their office rents are astronomical, they are less likely to accept nonpaying patients. Finally, health insurance has become virtually unaffordable to most independent artists of modest means. The picture is bleak. But with some thought, finesse, and planning, health care *is* obtainable, and the above cases might have happy endings.

Therefore, the first day you are on your own as an artist, start considering your health care. If you are young (under fifty), your chances of needing to be admitted to the hospital are small. More likely you will need to see a physician in her/his office and have an X-ray or lab tests, all as an outpatient. If you are a dancer, the need for physical therapy is almost a certainty. A visit to a doctor's office, a few common lab tests, and an X-ray can easily cost $300; a follow-up visit, an additional $65–$100. Physical therapy starts at $65.00 per treatment session. If you are a woman, there are other concerns. Are you planning to have a child? The cost of this can be $5,000–$8,000! A woman needs routine gynecological exams and, at certain times in her life, mammograms. These services can be expensive. Having realized the cost of medical care, people either decide they are immortal and in need of no coverage or blindly buy whatever they can afford without examining exactly what they are purchasing. There are, however, alternatives. None of them is perfect, and each has certain quirks that may make it inappropriate to you.

1. You can remain uninsured, which makes you *self-pay*. This is traditional medical care, in which you pick your doctor and just pay the bills when they come due. (Cases 1 and 2 fall into this category.) This is not insurance but a gamble that you will never have a calamity like my two imaginary performers above or wind up in a hospital bed costing $500–$750 per day! Worse yet, any urgent care you may need will probably be provided by an emergency room. This is expensive and can take six to eight hours if you are not literally at death's door.

2. Another option is a *health maintenance organization* (HMO), for which you pay a fee and everything is included. What's the catch? You must use the HMO's doctors and hospitals. If you don't like the doctors or the hospitals to which you will be fed, you have no recourse. In addition, HMOs rarely have physicians who specialize in the problems of artists. Also, most HMOs are located only in certain major cities, so if you tour a great deal, getting emergency care approved and paid for may be a problem. Though a raspy voice could be a career-ending catastrophe for a singer, some HMOs don't consider it an emergency and won't pay for a visit to an ER.

3. *Major medical* is considered by some the pinnacle of insurance. It covers office visits to a doctor of your choice, hospitalization at the hospital of your choice, lab tests, X-rays, and often medications. What's the catch? This coverage can cost up to $600 a month! There may be a yearly deductible, which can range from $100 to $1,000—which means you must pay this amount first before the insurance company pays anything. Plus, these policies usually cover only 80 percent of what the insurer thinks a service is worth. This means that if you are a violinist with tendinitis of your fingering hand and you visit the world's greatest specialist, who charges $500 a visit, the insurer will pay what

it thinks the visit is worth, say 80 percent of $100, and you must pay the other $420.

4. *Managed care* is a recent innovation that really combines an HMO with major medical. Though limited, your choice of physicians is usually greater than with an HMO, and you would be admitted to the hospital with which your physician is affiliated. How much you pay for each office visit can vary from 80 percent to nothing. What's the catch? Again, the specialist you need may not participate in this plan, or you may have to pay for emergency care while on tour.

5. *Medicaid* is a state- and federally funded assistance program for the poor and disabled, the former being the category into which most artists, unfortunately, fall. It covers hospitalization, outpatient care, and medication, usually without any cost to you. What's the catch? The outpatient coverage can be used only at a hospital clinic because it pays about $12.00 to a physician for an office visit and no reputable private doctor can accept such a low fee. However, if you have a chronic condition that requires you to have expensive medication or long-term physical therapy, it may be worth the aggravation to obtain Medicaid. To be eligible in New York City, a single person must earn less than $500 per month and have less than $3,000 in savings. (You are allowed to keep $1,500 in savings for funeral expenses!) If you work "off the books" and your tax return from last year shows less than this amount, you can go to a city Human Resources center to apply. If you earn more than $500 per month, it still may be worth applying. Medicaid is an assistance program, so if you earn $600 per month and are also spending $300 per month on medication and physical therapy, you will pay $100, and Medicaid will pay the rest. Again, remember, with Medicaid only, you will have to get your treatments or care at a hospital clinic. But it can be at the hospital of your choice, so you may find just the care you require. However, be prepared: If you go to Human Resources, it is a long and depressing experience.

6. Yet another option is *workers compensation.* If you have injured yourself during a rehearsal or performance at an institution or with a company that has paid for workers' comp, you can be seen by a doctor for this injury at no cost to you. This type of insurance covers work-related accidents only. If you get pneumonia during your run, you are in the same category as Cases 1 and 2, which is uninsured. Ideally, if you are a part of a company or employed by an institution, some coverage will be provided. However, because of the cost of these policies and the declining funding for the arts, the coverage may be minimal. You should study the policy and, if it is not adequate for your needs, investigate further.

7. Finally, there is *supplemental coverage.* This is coverage that pays for additional services not included in your basic policy. It is much more afford-

able than primary coverage and can often be tailored to your needs. If you are a woman planning to have a child, check your basic policy regarding the coverage of pregnancy. Also, inquire as to whether the plan covers routine gynecological exams and mammograms. Another, and a not-to-be-ridiculed, possibility is to find someone who has good insurance coverage through her/his work and has an interest in becoming a "family." These days the word "family" has a broad connotation and does not necessarily require a marriage license. Different insurers have different definitions of what constitutes a family, but they are all accommodating since the cost of family coverage will be passed on to your partner's employer.

These are not trivial choices. Health coverage may affect your life expectancy. A study has recently been published documenting that uninsured patients admitted to the hospital die at a higher rate than insured patients and get referred less often for certain types of expensive tests than do those who are insured.

The truth is that, after your rent, food, clothes, and classes have been paid for, any type of coverage except Medicaid may be unaffordable. What then?

Here is where improvisation and creativity come in. The least expensive place to obtain care is at a hospital clinic, not a hospital emergency room. These clinics are staffed by residents who are overseen by established physicians who have completed all their training. The fee will be based on your income and is at most $75.00 per visit. This fee includes all required X-rays and diagnostic tests but not medications. Now you might be thinking it wise to investigate the private and public hospitals in your city to find the one that has the best care for your needs. In this case, the best clinic care may be very expensive. To obtain the basic rate, you may have to be seen at the hospital in your "catchment area." Your catchment-area hospital is the hospital closest to where you live. Unlike with Medicaid, if you go to any other but your catchment-area hospital with cash (and you will be asked for proof of your address), you may be charged the basic fee as well as for any tests and X-rays that are performed, just as with a private physician. Be sure to ask exactly what you will be charged. For those who have never been seen at a New York City hospital clinic, the experience may conjure up a vision of a Brueghel painting. This is just not true! With a little finesse you can get excellent care.

There is no question that the wait to be seen in a hospital clinic can be interminable, but as an artist with an interesting history and a problem that you seriously want to resolve, you may be treated differently. Most physicians who work in hospital clinics are overburdened with patients whose diseases are intertwined with seemingly incurable social ills. It is difficult and frustrating work. Physicians in this setting dream of seeing an articulate, energetic person with an exciting profession who seems in control of her/his life. You can receive excellent, compassionate care in a clinic if you learn how to be an excellent, compassionate patient. This does not mean passive! For example, learn how to give a good history:

> Doctor: Tell me, what is your problem today?
> Dancer: Well, I had just been invited to an audition with the Bill T. Jones/ Arnie Zane Company, and I was speaking with Arthur Aviles, who described to me how the company works—the touring schedule and some of the lighting plots they use. Then I was asked to dance in a small piece with Heidi from their last performance in Brussels, which was a great success. The music started. It's by John Zorn—do you know him? Anyway, I was moving stage right. . . .

This is the start of a nightmare for you and your doctor. The physician is now thinking how to get you to the point and be finished rather than about your problem. You will be frustrated because the physician will be anxious to leave and will devote less time to explaining the cause and treatment of your problem. Rather, try this:

> Doctor: Tell me, what is your problem today?
> Dancer: Well, I was performing a jump the day before yesterday and heard a pop in my right foot, felt a sharp pain, and had to stop dancing. I went home, rested the foot, and applied some heat and ice, but the pain has gotten worse, and now I can hardly stand on it.

Nothing extraneous. No waste of time. The whole appointment will be about your problem, and both you and your doctor are on the way to a satisfying professional relationship.

If you have more than one problem to discuss, say so at the beginning of the appointment: "I have a foot pain and a rash." Don't wait until the end of your appointment to say, "Oh, by the way, I have a rash." Buy a thermometer. Being sick can make you feel like you have a fever when you really don't, and fever is an important sign of disease. Having a friend feel your forehead is no more reliable than your intuition. If you say, "Doctor, I have a cough and a fever," your doctor will always ask, "What is your temperature?" Answering, "I don't know. I just feel hot," is no help. Instead try, "Last night it was 103; this morning it was 99." These are obvious things, but they make you a valued patient, and that is exactly what you want to be. If you are asked to have a test or take a medication, either do it, or tell the physician you don't intend to. Coming back for your next visit having done nothing that was suggested will not be appreciated. Also, keep in mind that physicians in training are overworked and rarely appreciated. They love it when people say, "Thanks. I appreciate your time." If you like your doctor and can afford it, offer her/him tickets to your next performance or opening. Physicians are intensely proud when patients think enough to offer them a gift, plus, you never know, you could be grooming an "angel."

If the clinic system is not appealing, there are other approaches, especially for acute problems. Cases 1 and 2 are acute problems. Once the cut is closed or the food poisoning runs its course, you will be back to normal. A chronic problem is something that either keeps coming back or never goes away. You can see a private physician. There are many in the city who enjoy taking care of artists and do so for reduced fees. Friends are the best source of names. A few hints: Don't call Friday night during dinner or Saturday at midnight for a problem you've had for a week. If in doubt and the week is ending, call early and say, "I didn't want to bother you this weekend. This is my problem, do you think I need to be seen?" Such thoughtfulness is deeply appreciated and makes you a valued patient. Don't be shy to bring up the fee. Say, "I am short of money now, can I pay you $10.00 a week?" Remember, however, physicians have no control over the charges of labs or X-ray facilities, and these people will hunt you to the ends of the earth to collect. So if you need a lot of tests, again, consider a hospital clinic. No one will tell you this, but you can be seen at a hospital clinic, get the tests done, and bring the results back to your private doctor.

There are two more possibilities for care, but these need to be arranged in advance. If you are part of a company, try to find a physician to become doctor to the company. This may sound difficult, but if you look in many performance programs, you will see a listing for "house physician." Don't be shy; call and ask. You may be surprised.

Finally, if you are really nervy, you can try to call a physician who is doctor to another company. You can tell a white lie or embellish the truth by saying that you are part of the company, or that the company referred you because of your problem, or that someone from the company recommended the doctor because "you are so wonderful!" (Flattery is nothing to be shunned when dealing with large egos.)

So far, I have discussed only types of insurance and obtaining outpatient care. Suppose you are admitted to a hospital and have no insurance or money. What happens to you? If you are in New York City, there won't be much of a problem. As soon as you are admitted and it is appropriate, you will be seen by a social worker who will put in an application for Medicaid. A hospitalized artist rarely has any savings and usually is making less than $500 per month, so eligibility is not a problem. If you are outside New York City, the rules are different. But if you are sick and are taken to any hospital, they must treat you, irrespective of your financial status.

Though the picture for health care in New York City is bleak, great care is still available. Still, do think about your health care needs before a problem arises. Begin to develop a list of physicians and therapists who work with artists. Find out the name of the hospital in your catchment area. When seeing any medical care provider, be a valued patient. Be brief, specific, and, if necessary, keep a diary so your history is accurate. Don't forget, health professionals consider artists special people and an honor to care for.

Action Medical Insurance for the Arts
Meyer Braiterman

Surveys indicate that about two-thirds of artists and other art workers in New York State have medical insurance, and, of those, many are being forced to give up their insurance because of increasing costs. The costs affect both self-employed individuals and employee groups. In addition to expense, arts organizations have been faced with growing discrimination by insurers who do not want to insure their employees. As nonprofit organizations, they have had as much trouble obtaining insurance as are businesses like toxic waste dumps, logging and mining operations, used car dealers, and bars, all of which have traditionally had a hard time getting employee insurance.

When thousands of companies, including a number of arts organizations, had their rates increased by Guardian in 1988, they had to shop for less expensive insurers. In the process of shopping, Dance Theater Workshop approached six insurers for bids. Four did not even want to look at the bid request. One company, Phoenix Mutual, had profitably insured DTW for five years, from 1977 to 1982. They increased their rates for all "small" groups back then by over 80 percent. In 1988, they would not bid for DTW's coverage "due to the nature of the industry." DTW then joined an association of employers, mostly in the publishing industries, and got coverage at the same rates they had originally had with Guardian. Following relatively nominal rate increases in 1989 and 1990, they then had a whopping 40 percent increase in 1991, which sent them shopping again.

While it has been a long-standing policy of many insurers of employer groups to review nonprofit organizations for a determination as to their major sources of funding (insurers believe that the income of organizations funded primarily by the government is unreliable), the new policy is to deny insurance to nonprofit organizations regardless of their funding sources, and some insurance companies now explicitly exclude theaters, galleries, and museums, even if they are *not* nonprofit. However, there are still plans available from some companies for most arts organizations. It is also important to recognize that this discriminatory situation in many states exists for employee groups only—not for individual insurance policies.

Responding to citizen pressure, New York State recently passed a law making it illegal for insurance companies to exclude industries or individuals from their policies. We have yet to see if this change will keep soaring insurance costs at bay.

People tend to see the increasing cost of medical insurance as the problem rather than the increasing cost and profits of the hospitals, pharmaceutical companies, and myriad other industries making more and more off the illnesses of people. A national medical *insurance* program along the lines of Medicare would only perpetuate the problem. Even if the entire arts community were to write their congressional representative this week, it could still take years for a true national *medical* plan to be passed. Our current hope is for a national or state program that will meet the needs of arts workers and other people in the same boat and at the same time help the beleaguered arts organizations and other employers. Had we demanded from our legislatures and elected officials a real medical program for people twenty years ago, we would have such a program in place now. Let's start demanding.

STAYING WELL

Psychological Issues for the Dancer
William Sommer, M.D.

If work and love are the arenas of life's great endeavors, the way to operate within those arenas is to balance control and spontaneity. For a dancer, work and control dominate. The physical training demands single-minded commitment, which in turn often distracts from the arena of love and the expression of spontaneity. Certain dance styles, especially ballet, have specific shapes to the movement and to the bodies in motion—an abstraction of an ideal, an image of perfection—that dictate precisely the nature of the training. Those ideal forms, however, occur in nature only rarely. What usually happens in order to conform to the ideal is that the developing shape of the body— especially the female body—is controlled or hindered.

Even for performers involved in dance forms less fused to a specific technique (those incorporating improvisation or language, for example), the performers still express themselves primarily in the corporeal. This demands physical discipline of a different, but hardly less stringent, order. In both cases, by literally embodying an art form, the dancers must learn to live in very specific ways. These demands create rewards and problems.

The artistic rewards in dancing are, of course, paramount, but they can be elusive, intangible, and often difficult to sustain. The material rewards are likewise limited and inconsistent. Therefore, the physical rewards hold special gratifications. The sheer exhilaration of moving precisely, elegantly, vigorously, is unparalleled in usual mortal undertakings. But to achieve these moments of physical ecstasy, dancers have to spend a disproportionate amount of time in rigorous training and rehearsal—activities outside the mainstream of the developing lives of most young adults. The physical "highs" are there, but other things must yield to sustain them.

Dancers and athletes are unique in that they have to maintain iron discipline—the mind controls the body to bring it into shape. The danger is that the mind, in directing the body, may disallow the body's reciprocal influence on the mind. For instance, the initial danger signal of pain in tendinitis may be mentally overridden. Rather than mind and body being partners, the apparent unity can sometimes be a case of master/mind over slave/body. The most basic needs of the body—for nourishment, for holding, for sexuality, for rest, for maturation—are either put to the service of dance or ignored. Far from unifying mind and body, the technical endeavors can sometimes treat the body as an object, an "other." Even in embracing the holistic life-style approach to mind/body issues, the dancer may focus more attention on what's going on with the body than on what's driving the mind.

This disproportionate influence of some dancers' minds over their bodies can become a paradigm for their relationships to others—just as it might reflect their parents' relationships to them as children. It may be simplistic to make this triple equation: (1) The way one responds to and cares for one's body mirrors (2) the way one was responded to and cared for by parents; this in turn shapes (3) the way one is able to respond to and care for others. The psychological ramifications of a lopsided relationship between mind and body can affect personal relationships profoundly. This lopsidedness finds a parallel in the hierarchical nature of the teacher/choreographer relationship to the student/dancer, in which all the power flows in one direction. How often and in how many ways does a dancer hear, "Just do what you're told"?

Because it is the primary focus, the body can also become the locus for expression of unfulfilled personal needs. Symptoms develop in the body. These symptoms can involve issues that have no direct connection to the body yet find a home there. Such diverse issues as conflicts over work, authority, independence/dependence, and love may utilize the well-traveled pathway of bodily expression for symptom formation. Anxiety, depression, and anger may manifest themselves as problems linked with bodily needs: nutrition (as eating disorders), skin sensations (as dermatological problems), sensuality/ sexuality (as sexual inhibitions and dysfunctions), recuperative rest (as stress injuries), and growth (as difficulties coping with the normal aging process).

Since the body can often seem the source of all problems, the obvious cure can seem to be through the body as well—with diets, massages, sexual experimentation, rest cures, exercises—all of which do help in significant ways. Dancers strive to "listen" to their bodies and to respond to them with sensitivity and ingenuity. Therapeutic body work is successful because it lets the body unveil its secrets. This process of body listening is parallel to that part of the psychotherapeutic process of listening to one's hidden emotional life bubble up into conscious awareness. However, these body-healing techniques have the additional, attractive feature of furthering dance work.

This feature can, however, perpetuate the old proposition of putting the body through its paces, albeit "therapeutic" paces, as the restorative process segues into a working process. This nearly secret strategy can become the very antithesis of recuperation and can also serve as a major resistance to dealing with personal and interpersonal problems. With these difficulties, ameliorating symptoms and behavior can be most successful by directing efforts away from the body and shifting the focus onto the mind. And the most effective way to establish that focus is through psychotherapy.

The "talking cure" must surely seem strange, especially to those devoted to exploring bodily rather than verbal expression. Yet psychotherapy is the most direct route to uncovering, for instance, this internal mental tyrant that tries to dominate body, self, and others.

One way to describe how psychotherapy works is that the therapist becomes one of those other people. The dancer and therapist develop a relationship. It is an odd one. Both concentrate on the sole task of understanding just one of them—and that understanding comes through their interaction. In the exchanges, the dancer, while developing trust in the therapist, will simultaneously develop fear of "the worst" in the therapist (criticism and rejection)—which gets projected onto the therapist. The therapist "takes on" the dancer's inner harshness as well as the harshness the dancer experiences both from people currently in her/his life and from people significant in the past. As the dancer and therapist grapple with each other in the task of understanding, the sources of these fears and frustrations become clearer. The "unacceptable" parts of the dancer—whether aggression or vulnerability or both—get uncovered and accepted. And, in the process, gradual alterations and integration occur.

This description of therapy—sometimes called "psychodynamically oriented" or "psychoanalytically oriented" psychotherapy—may make the process seem difficult and complicated. It isn't easy. One must be in considerable emotional pain to commit the required time, money, and self-scrutiny. Yet let me hasten to add that psychotherapy does help. It helps sort out feelings, symptoms, work blocks; it can be exhilarating and challenging and can unveil the most amazing things. In addressing, then tempering, the tyrannical part of the controlling mind, psychotherapy can also open up great areas of emotional as well as physical spontaneity. It can complement other forms of healing and free the mind to work with the body.

In other words, the "talking cure" is not a "mind game," irrelevant to the body; rather, it is grappling with personal feelings that shape the sense of self, one's interactions with others, and one's view of the world.

Besides psychotherapy, other modes of treatment for psychological difficulty include behavior modification, hypnosis, psychotropic medication, and psychoanalysis.

Behavior modification employs relaxation techniques (including light self-hypnotic trance states) that are then used to lessen certain troubling symptoms. This method can be fast and effective for certain well-circumscribed difficulties (such as simple phobias), but it specifically does not engage the whole personality. Its straightforwardness appeals to dancers in a way similar to body-training techniques; it has the same disadvantage as well—keeping things compartmentalized rather than trying to integrate them.

Psychotropic medications are very helpful in relieving specific distresses. The important categories are as follows: antidepressants (including the popular Prozac, and requiring steady, year-long use generally); minor tranquilizers (including benzodiazepines such as Valium and Ativan, which are currently in disrepute because of their potential for addiction); major tranquilizers (such as Thorazine, for severe anxiety accompanied by disordered thinking); and sleep medications (addicting and therefore not recommended). Lithium is a unique and exceedingly effective medication for treating people with clear-cut manic-depressive or major depressive disorders.

Psychoanalysis is the most intensive psychological treatment and is available at surprisingly minimal cost at training institutes. Its aim is to understand one's personality structure in order to modify deeply ingrained detrimental patterns of functioning and relating that repeat themselves in one's life. Psychoanalysis, most often conducted with the patient lying on a couch, usually requires a time commitment of three years, three to four times per week, in order to achieve the intensity and freedom of relating needed to illuminate lifelong hidden emotional patterns.

Psychotherapy is what most people choose. First, the basic questions: When? How? Who? Where? How Much?

When? Ideally, one should approach psychotherapy with calm delibera-tion, as one might approach beginning work with a movement instructor, choreographer, or body trainer. Taking time to secure the best psychothera-pist for yourself, even if you're feeling distressed, is *essential.*

How? Choosing a therapist has to be an active endeavor, which means a lot of research, a lot of shopping! Be a consumer, not a sheep. Some dancers have trouble with this because they are so accustomed to being instructed and bullied in training that they will often take whoever will accept them. A rule of thumb is to have a minimum of two consultations with three different thera-pists before settling on the one for you.

Who? The criteria for choosing a therapist for psychodynamic treatment are, to me, the following: (1) The therapist should have formal training (in-cluding supervision and personal treatment) in a well-established psychologi-cal discipline. The three best-established professional disciplines are psychi-atry (with an M.D. degree), clinical psychology (with a Ph.D. degree), and clinical social work (with master's plus diplomate status). (2) The therapist should demonstrate, during the consultation, broad psychological knowl-edge and the flexibility to address your questions specifically. These might include feminist issues (such as active career roles for women, not neces-sarily including marriage and children), sexual issues (such as gay and les-bian choices being an alternative life-style, not psychopathology), and cre-ativity versus psychotherapy (is being a little crazy necessary for creativity, and might therapy interfere?). (3) The therapist should give you a sense of rapport, of having made a definitive emotional connection to you.

If the initial consultation session leaves you feeling uneasy about some aspect of the therapist or depressed and bad about yourself, heed those reactions while acknowledging that therapists do not work just to make you feel good. There has to be, however, some sense of excitement, some interest in the therapist's remarks about you, some general feeling of shared optimism regarding your impending work together. If you're inclined to have specific preferences regarding gender, age, and ethnicity for your therapist, state them outright and clearly.

Where and for how much? Private therapists are the most readily accessible and generally have the most experience. However, costs can be prohibitive. Private fees for forty-five-minute sessions in the New York City area, for exam-ple, currently range about as follows: psychiatrists (from whom medications, if necessary, can be obtained), $90–$150; clinical psychologists, $70–$120; clinical social workers, $40–$100. Some negotiation is always possible, even below these "usual fees," especially if more than once-a-week sessions are recommended.

Advanced-training or postgraduate institutes are institutes for licensed psychotherapists and are often good places to get excellent treatment on a sliding scale. Especially recommended are those institutes that have substantial requirements for candidates, such as professional degrees and experience in the field; some institutes take anyone who will pay the tuition, regardless of prior degrees or experience. The standards for therapist admissions should be secured from the institute. Do not hesitate to shop, even within the institutes or clinics. The therapist to whom you are assigned after the intake interview does not have to be the one you're stuck with. If the beginning sessions don't feel right, first discuss this matter with the therapist, then go back to the initial interviewer and insist on a consultation with someone else.

Outpatient psychiatric clinics affiliated with hospitals are a source of low-cost, competent treatment; the therapy is generally done by people who are in training for professional degrees, such as psychiatric residents or psychology interns. Because therapists will be completing their training and graduating, the length of time for the treatment may be limited. Also, most hospitals can accept only patients who reside within their geographic district. Here, too, charges are assigned on a sliding scale.

A sliding-scale fee is one determined by your income or, more precisely, by your income tax return from the previous year. The minimum fees at advanced-training institutes in New York City are usually about $15–$25 per session, with the initial screening interview costing about $30. Hospital psychiatric clinics can often reduce their fees even further, especially for a "good" psychotherapy case (which you are). You should anticipate sustaining psychotherapy for at least a year. Once you've committed your time and money, you should secure a reciprocal commitment from your therapist to be available to you for at least that duration. Ideally, of course, you should continue therapy as long as you find it useful.

One final word about finding the right place and the right therapist. Ask around—friends, colleagues, mental health directories. If you're in a new city, you should seek recommendations from the health service (mental health division or counseling service) of any college or university and the director of clinical (or psychiatric) social work at the nearest training hospital.

To address psychological issues for *any* artist at this point in history without discussing the special impact of HIV infection and AIDS is unthinkable. This continuum of illnesses and symptoms has so many unknown and unpredictable factors that the specter of it in oneself or in one's loved ones is almost unbearable. For artists from whom so much self-discipline and body control is demanded, the prospect of this capricious, physically debilitating force intruding into one's life can be extremely daunting. It is an enemy that can bring out the best in individuals and communities (and also the worst). The fight against it has been unconscionably limited by the government. This means that the most essential weapon for the individual in this battle is to overcome feeling helpless. This becomes more crucial in seeking effective medical treatment, even without symptoms—in fact, especially *before* symptoms. The greatest psychological challenge is getting help to strategize about getting *better* help. Psychotherapeutic support and coping strategies should be sought in as many different ways and with as much unstinting determination as humanly possible. [See the Appendix for a listing of recommended psychological facilities in several cities around the country.]

How Should an Injured Dancer Look for Medical Care?
William G. Hamilton, M.D.

Traditionally, this has been a problem in areas outside the major cities in America that have resident companies. Fortunately, the situation is improving, thanks to the dance explosion that has taken place in this country over the last two decades. Dance medicine has become a subspecialty within the field of sports medicine, and seminars on the injured dancer are now a part of the annual meetings and CME (continuing medical education) courses offered by the various sports medicine societies. More and more papers are appearing in the medical literature about problems unique to dancers, and several textbooks have been published in this field, so local M.D.s have something to refer to if their experience with dancers is limited.

Dancers who live in the major cities of America generally know who in the local medical community is familiar with injuries. If not, they should call up the local dance company and find out who usually cares for their injured performers. In areas outside the major cities, a good place to start is with the local sports medicine doctor; she/he is the one most likely to be familiar with your problem. After all, tendinitis is the same in a dancer as it is in a football or baseball player. It may be in an odd location, but the pathology is the same. A sports medicine doctor is also the most likely source of a good physical therapist, and good "PT" usually plays an essential part in the treatment of dance injuries.

Most of all, be an informed consumer. Get references, ask around. Talk to the local sports teams. Find out who is good—and who isn't—and how many dancers she/he sees. Don't be misled by fancy advertising and hype. Dancers are notoriously poor, and most doctors in the field of dance medicine see them out of a love for the arts and the artists, so ask about reduced fees.

Maintenance—How to Stay in Shape for Dancing

The best physical conditioning for dancers is usually obtained by dancing. This sounds redundant, but the point is that dancers vary tremendously in what they are trying to do, their body types and sizes, their assets and liabilities, and especially the type of dancing they do: ballet, modern, jazz, tap, show dancing, ethnic dancing, etc., etc.

Of course, everyone strives for that perfect balance between strength, flexibility, and timing. If a dancer is naturally tight, then she/he should spend time on flexibility. Strength is a different matter. There are special circumstances where strengthening is important: trying to stay in shape while injured, recovering from an injury, or trying to correct a specific weakness. Swimming is the best overall conditioning exercise for dancers; with the modern "fiberglass" casts (they usually aren't really fiberglass), the injured dancer can often swim in a health club pool while healing. For other situations it is best to let a sports-oriented doctor or physical therapist outline a proper exercise regimen based on your specific needs.

Dancers have benefited greatly from a specific set of exercises called the Pilate's Method, a series of exercises with springs that allows the dancer to work in the turned-out position of function—that is, in ballet positions in full turnout. Until recently, there were few of these studios outside New York City, but the method is gaining in popularity, so try to find out if one is available in your area.

Last of all, in many forms of dancing, especially ballet, physical problems may be due to poor training, placement, and technique or to trying to get perfect technique from a not-so-perfect body. Because of these factors, I often recommend to injured dancers that they spend some time during their recovery with a technique coach or movement analyst to see what part these factors may be playing in their injury.

APPENDIX HEALTH

Addresses and phone numbers of the following resources may be found at the end of the book in the alphabetized Directory.

HIV and AIDS Information and Services

ACT-UP (AIDS Coalition to Unleash Power) (Offices in Boston, Chicago, Los Angeles, Miami, Minnesota, New York, and San Francisco.)

AIDS Action Committee

AIDS Foundation of Chicago

AIDS Information Hotline

AIDS Project LA

American Foundation for AIDS Research (AMFAR)

Columbia Presbyterian HIV Clinical & Behavioral Center

Gay Men's Health Crisis (GMHC)

Human Resources Administration AIDS Service Line

Jewish Board of Family and Children's Services

Kansas City Free Health Clinic (Provides a variety of services for patients with AIDS.)

Lesbian & Gay Community Switchboard/Arizona AIDS Information Line

Minnesota AIDS Project

National AIDS Hotline/National HIV and AIDS Information Service (Good for referring people to AIDS services within their own locale.)

National AIDS Information Clearing House

New York City Department of Health—AIDS Information

Parachute Fund through Dance Bay Area (Serves members of the Bay Area dance community who are facing life-threatening illness and have demonstrated financial need.)

Project Inform

PWA (Persons with AIDS) Coalition

San Francisco AIDS Foundation

South Florida AIDS Network

Insurance

American Dance Guild (Membership health insurance.)

American Guild of Musical Artists (Membership health insurance.)

Artist Trust (Request a copy of their pamphlet "Access to Affordable Health Care." Some of it is written for residents of Washington State; other information is more general.)

Arts Family Association (Insurance for disability, health, life, pension, dental, and vision. Referral service for legal or health needs. Also provides credit and career counseling.)

Blue Cross/Blue Shield
(Nonprofit insurance companies located in each state.)

Citizens for a National Health Program (Ask for national directory of organizations in support of a national health plan. Cost is $1.50.)

Co-op America (Membership health insurance.)

Empire Blue Cross/Blue Shield (in New York)

Gay Men's Health Crisis (Insurance seminars second Tuesday of every month.)

Health Benefit Information

Health Insurance Association of America

National Insurance Consumers' Helpline

National Organization for Women (NOW) (Membership health insurance. Plans not available in every state.)

New York State Medicaid

Support Services Alliance (Offers an insurance program especially designed to meet the needs of small organizations and self-employed individuals.)

Contact your local arts service organization for further referrals.

Staying Well

Mental health

*Recommended New York City psychological facilities
for performing artists*

Institute for Performing Artists

Kathryn and Gilbert Miller Health Care Institute for Performing Artists

For psychodynamic psychotherapy

Institute for Contemporary Psychotherapy

Institute for Performing Artists (Mental health care for music and theater artists.)

Metropolitan Center for Mental Health

Musicians Emergency Fund, Inc. (Alternate care, emergency funds, and inpatient rehabilitation for music artists.)

New York Freudian Society Psychoanalytic Consultation Service

Specialty clinics

Eating disorders: Bulimia Treatment Associates, Center for Study of Anorexia and Bulimia

Career counseling: Artists Career Planning Service, Career Transition for Dancers

General health

Alaska Sports Medicine Clinic

Arts Medicine Center

Center for Safety in the Arts (COH)

Cleveland Clinic Foundation

Doctors for Artists (Referral service.)

Michel Fokine Fund of the New York Community Trust (Underwrites medical expenses.)

Harkness Center for Dance Injuries (Providers of quality care for dancers with muscular-skeletal injuries; sliding-scale billing.)

Kathryn and Gilbert Miller Health Care Institute for Performing Artists (Offers comprehensive health-care services to artists, including women's health-care and psychological counseling.)

New Mexico Physical Therapy & Rehab Center

ODPHP National Health Information Center (Health services include accident, alternate care, art hazards, hotline, hospital-clinic, mental health, performing arts medicine, specific diseases.)

Performing Arts Physical Therapy

Planned Parenthood Federation of America, Inc.

Sports Therapy for Athletic Rehabilitation & Treatment (START)

UCSF Health Program for Performing Artists (Provides a full range of treatments to performing artists, including mental, dental, orthopedic, physical therapy, psychotherapy, and surgical intervention.)

University of Washington Sports Medicine Clinic

Women's Sports Foundation

Contact your local arts service organization for further referrals.

Publication

Dealing with Healing.

C O M M U N I T Y:
THE BODY POLITIC

Action is the only reality, not only reality but morality
as well.—Abbie Hoffman

■ What is your role, as an artist and a citizen, in the local arts community and in the greater community in which you live and work? What is your role in the national arts community, or as a member of an ethnic community, or as a voter and a taxpayer?

These questions may never have definitive answers, but by posing them to yourself from time to time, they can be used as a tool to help you make decisions that affect your future and the future of those around you, whom you touch.

Some artists see themselves as disconnected from the lives of ordinary people. Many feel nonartists view them as "different." Yet artists are ordinary people who just happen to be creating not-so-ordinary things. Ordinary people involved in creating on a day-to-day basis have a unique worldview. A great possibility for change exists if every artist, and all those in the extended arts community, would read, discuss, form opinions, and vote, on the basis of her/his vision of the future.

See the Appendix for organizations that provide information, resources, and a sense of community to performing artists who wish to participate as public advocates.—Tia Tibbitts Levinson, arts worker ■

■ How useful can dancing be when everywhere we look we are reminded of the notion that it is of so little use to care for one another?—DJ McDonald, choreographer ■

for women who dance:
thoughts about body image
Dana Reitz

while speaking with many women
who have made a life in the field of dance
some retired
some still involved
the subject of body image was discussed
along with difficulties of life changes
transitions, injuries, etc.
we understood the payments many have made
physically, emotionally, psychologically
in a field so run by image
this article is written in encouragement
of those women who want to learn
about their bodies and minds within the dance world
and it is written in the hope that any self-image
that develops is used as a tool rather than a prison

it occurs to me once in a while
that there is no law of choreography
no law of dancing
there are historical precedents
there are knee joints
there are teachers and tapes
schools of thought
training sessions, books
photographs, reviews
and performances right in front of your eyes

and somewhere in your mind is an image of you
body perfect
ready to fit
needing only permission to start
approval for the effort
a break

the main questions for the next years to come, i think
are who's driving the bus

who is in charge of your training
your dancing
and what happens when your body and mind do not fit
the image created, for you, by you
that basic belief you have invested so much in
what happens when the world changes?

since the future is unknown
it seems a strange ritual
to invest in an outer directed image an idea that may keep one
    enclosed and
unfamiliar with survival tactics
it seems strange that dance—
that which has to do with movement—
is often tied to a static image of the dancer
it seems strange that dancers—those who move—
are often tied to a static image of youth
a particular body perfection that does not accept age
it seems strange that many women who dance
are tied to a static image
of weight, size, look
often that of a very young female,
sometimes close in appearance to a young male
given this, it does not seem strange that
many women who dance have a very hard time with body change,
weight shift
hormonal fluctuation, changing needs and desires
and further, it does not seem so strange that
women who dance succumb to a variety of health problems
starting in the alphabet with amenorrhea
anorexia nervosa, and arthritis

i can see the willful drive for physical excellence
the passionate desire to sing with the body
the need to be heard, be paid attention to
be taken seriously
the desire to be accepted
then—there can be the craving to rise above
a bit
to succeed

to become historically significant
in whatever way
the way of the belief
the way of the land
the way of the current kingdom . . .

this all seems similar to the search for the holy grail
what's needed is a good horse to start with
and a lot of indestructible armor
and some guy out front saying this is the way
but the question may rise at some point along this trail
just whose holy grail is this
and what if i feel like taking the next left turn?

CHAOS, FEAR, THE UNKNOWN
and that oh so uncomfortable TRANSITION
interesting
maybe very interesting
and very much in need of support
for
there appears to be no glory in transition
no prize for taking care of oneself
no advertisement for a decision to take time out
to think, repair
no big parties
no grand public recognition for a change of direction

if one has painted oneself into an image corner
and has obeyed the dictum "the show must go on"
one can feel like audience fodder
the willfulness to achieve the image
rather than live in the process of working
may help to create a brittle image that can shatter
and the glorification machinery cannot help
pick up the pieces

women who dance
are women
who must deal with food, housing
sexuality, age
dancing will not cure sexually transmitted diseases
the ravages of a bad diet

or bad living conditions
dancing will not prevent difficult relationships
will not fix emotional upheaval
will not repair leaky roofs
HOWEVER
dancing can lead to an incredible amount of self-awareness
women who dance
are women
who have access to a great store of physical knowledge
who have the opportunity to uncover and
develop the body and mind together
who can embark on great adventures into unknown territories
fully prepared to take care of themselves

if images are needed
then women who dance
could use living ones
moldable, breathable
adjustable ones
that guide not rule
not dead ones
not ones painted by outsiders
not ones without ground

we need a variety of images
rather, a variety of experiences
that include the real body
real hormones, real organs, real glands
real thoughts
real age
and real differences
then
i think
dancing
in its most exhilarating manner
includes us
our most complete being
and we with full acceptance
can continue to include dancing
in our living

Cross-Cultural Performance Strategies

Guillermo Goméz-Peña

I am a writer in Mexico, where writers are respected and heard, and a performance artist in the United States, where writers are marginalized. My activities have always bounced back and forth between my writing and my performance work: What I can say as a journalist I don't perform, and vice versa. My journalistic voice is balanced and logical. My performance voice is frantic and fractured.

Performance is the most flexible language I've found. I use it to analyze and articulate political, artistic, sexual, and spiritual desires and frustrations. When I write, I combine social and cultural commentary with quotes, memories, excerpts of conversations, and bilingual poetry. Because of this, my performance work is based heavily on text and filled with direct references to my sociocultural environment.

My writings and my performances have the same epic tone; I believe that the contemporary Mexican-American drama, framed by diaspora, economic exile, police persecution, and cultural exclusion, is of epic dimensions.

I crisscross from the past to the present, from English to Spanish, from the fictional to the autobiographical. I fuse prose and poetry, sound and text, art and literature. My writings are simultaneously essays and manifestos, performance texts and social chronicles, poems and radio pieces. And, in them, I try to exercise all the freedom that my two countries have denied me.

I see my work in relation to other artists and thinkers. My personal paradigm is valid only when intersected with history. "I" often means "we." And, depending on the context, "we" means either the border citizens (the Mexicans outside Mexico, the Latin Americans) or the "nonaligned," experimental artists who are involved in the creation of a new cultural topography.

The notion of multicontextuality is very important to me. As a cross-cultural artist, I feel responsible to audiences in both Mexico and the United States. I see no difference between performing for a prestigious museum or theater, a university, or a farm work center. In fact, my most memorable performances have taken place in nonartistic settings. And it is within those settings that I obtain direct information to understand the Mexican-American community—who they are and what they ache for.

My two studios (one in Mexico and one in the United States) are my bases of operation. The photos, postcards, messages, and texts that hang on their walls are constantly changing to reflect the political dynamics of the various ideas, projects, and activities I'm involved in.

I rehearse, but not as much as other performance artists. I can do it only for an hour every now and then. In fact, my true rehearsals are my constant trips, my long writing nights, my journalistic assignments, my political activities, the books I read, and the conversations I have. And it is within these activities that my work finds substance, texture, and form.

I am not a "high artist" but a countercultural practitioner, and I'm always dying to go back to the world, to be, and to work, in the world.

The right to have a public voice, not fame, is rarely fought for by artists. The mainstream art world has managed to persuade us that "good art" is not to be appreciated by everyone, and we have swallowed it. If we want to be makers of the culture in the nineties we have to fight for the right to have a public voice outside the art world.

Today, more than ever, we must speak from the center, not the margins, and we must do it in large-scale formats and for large audiences. It is essential to challenge the anachronistic myth that as "multicultural artists" we are meant to work only within "community contexts" or marginal, leftist milieus. Our place is the world, and our communities are multiple.

The Parachute Fund
David Gere

Imagine this scenario: You're young. You're a dancer. Your body is your livelihood. One day, a simple test confirms your worst fear: You're "positive," you've come in contact with the HIV virus that causes AIDS.

Finding out that you are in danger of developing full-blown AIDS is devastating news under any circumstances. But that devastation is compounded if your life revolves around dancing. Most dancers in the United States can't afford health insurance, or the coverage they *can* afford is minimal. (Only the most established companies provide health benefits, and, in the late 1980s, the cost of maintaining those benefits skyrocketed.) Disability insurance? You've got to be kidding. Savings? Hah! So the question is, Who can you depend on when you're in critical need?

In 1988, an ad hoc AIDS Response Group was formed under the auspices of Dance Bay Area—a group whose members include choreographer Joe Goode, arts administrator Linc King, Dance Bay Area executive director Lillian Goldthwaite, and myself. We were empowered by our peers to create a safety net for dance community colleagues confronting not just AIDS but life-threatening illnesses of any kind. We called it the Parachute Fund. [See the Appendix.]

Who would be eligible? Dancers, dance students, choreographers, administrators, writers, technicians—virtually anyone who could substantiate her/

his participation in the dance community. How much money would be made available per person? Up to $1,500, payable over any three months of a calendar year. What could it be spent on? Medical expenses or monthly insurance premiums were obvious priorities. But, just as important, we wanted this money to be used to pay for a massage, to buy a VCR, or, in the best of all possible worlds, to rent studio time to continue dancing. Creative pursuits, we reasoned, could be as life sustaining as the most powerful drugs. Last but not least, where would the money come from? We would go out and raise it ourselves.

Over the last three years, over a hundred generous artists and friends of the arts have contributed to the Parachute Fund, which is maintained by the San Francisco Foundation, a community-based philanthropy, at no fee. Organizations ranging from the Della Davidson Company to the Bay Area Dance Series have donated proceeds from benefits or contributed a percentage (for example, 3 percent) of box office receipts for an entire season. ODC/San Francisco dancer Ney Fonseca organized Dancing against Indifference, a performance of AIDS-inspired work to benefit the fund and the political action group ACT-UP. Hundreds of people had to be turned away at the door, and the Parachute Fund was suddenly several thousand dollars richer.

Precisely because the Parachute Fund has been embraced by the community at large, building it up and maintaining it have been relatively easy tasks. Ironically, the hard part has been convincing our friends who are sick to use it. In a profession that equates health and youth with a sense of personal worth, many are reluctant to admit—even privately—that they are struggling with disease. They dissemble, even to their closest colleagues. Or, worse yet, they quietly retreat and disappear from the scene altogether. Part of the task of operating a fund like this is to make it extremely simple to use and completely accessible. This message is our mantra: "We're here when you need us."

You might be wondering how the Parachute Fund got its name. First off, the image of a big, beautiful, billowy cloud of cloth that saves your life in an emergency seemed right for the kind of fund we had in mind. But, for me, the name was doubly significant. In January of 1988, my friend Joah Lowe, a performer and movement therapist who was just starting to make his name as a choreographer, landed in the hospital with pneumocystis pneumonia. After a harrowing eight-day plunge, he was dead.

At his home, after he died, I found this hand-scrawled passage from the Russian poet Yevgeny Vinokurov among a stack of poems and bits of wisdom Joah had copied onto note cards:

When you try at the rip cord,
And the parachute does not open,

And there beneath you lie endless forests,
And it is plain that you will not be saved,

And there is no longer anything to cling to,
No longer anyone to be met on the way,
Spread your arms softly, like a bird,
And enfolding space, fly.

There is no way back, no time to go balmy,
And only one solution: the simplest,
For the first time to compose yourself,
And to fall with the universal void in your embrace.

I Am Encouraging People to Really Feel
Karen Finley

[*The following is an excerpt from a talk Ms. Finley presented in December 1990 during the Association of Performing Arts Presenters Conference in New York City.*—Eds.]

When you are sitting next to someone, you do not know what has happened to them in life. In urban areas especially we are getting away from feeling. I think the country is in a state of mourning. There is a sense of apathy because we think someone else is going to take care of "it." There are many people, even liberals, who feel they are not part of the society that is committing the atrocities. But we *are* the population, all of us, contributing to these conditions.

I go to Grand Central Station and see everyone going to work, walking over the homeless. We feel powerless. We are not taking people and gassing and killing them. We are doing it in a very slow way in our forgotten subways, corners of hospital rooms, classrooms. We have to take direct action ourselves and become more politically involved. It should go hand in hand with eating, going to the bathroom, making love, and watching television.

What really move me are the letters I receive or meeting people after a performance who have experienced what I talk about. Whether it is a mother whose child has died of AIDS or rape or incest victims—each moves me to think my work is in some way from their own life. I have a public sculpture in New York at Houston Street and First Avenue, with a poem, "The Black Sheep." Someone came up to me and said, "I live under your sculpture." The subway is underneath it. That hits my heart in a big way.

On Arts Education
Victoria Marks

If it is our goal to educate children to become sentient human beings capable of handling complex problems, then art must play a role in that education. While our institutions train students to survive in the material world, they offer no guidance as to the quality of that survival. Children are given skills so that they become good international competitors and market consumers, but they are not given the resources to make moral and ethical decisions. The arts are a link to our inner life, to what is not concrete, not fact. They give voice to the questions that cannot be answered by science or math but are at the same time essential to perspective in those fields.

The arts—the performing arts in particular—are about the body. Current education is about the authority of the mind over the body. By challenging the theory that knowledge resides in the mind alone, the arts license children to be at one with thought and feeling. They are empowered.

Working with an artist, a student might be asked to play a character by accessing an unfamiliar part of her/himself or, more fantastically, be asked to fly. In bargaining with the "real" world and with "real" experience, this child learns that each is fluid and that there is power in her/his subjective experience.

Artists' relationships with schools take many forms and are most successful when that relationship is defined by the circumstance and the needs of the school, the neighborhood, the teachers, and the artist. As an artist, I am not in the schools to find talented youngsters who, with training, will enter my field. Nor is it my purpose to build audiences for art or to assist with a history or math lesson. If one of those things occurs while I am working, I am delighted. But my most immediate purpose is to give children an opportunity to express themselves as artists.

In 1983, I began working as a teaching-artist for the Lincoln Center Institute. Through that program I worked in many New York City schools as an artist in the classroom and as a performer of choreographic work. I also conducted intensive hands-on study sessions for public school educators who were involved in the Lincoln Center program.

While investigating participation in an extended residency in one school, I became involved with the education program of the New York Foundation for the Arts (NYFA). With NYFA's financial support, I have worked in Eastchester High School for the past four years, watching students develop as artists. The relationship between artist and educator is extremely important. This kind of residency would not have occurred without the collaboration of a teacher in the school.

Since 1989, I have been working as a liaison for educators and artists in the Pentacle/Arts in Education project. This program focuses primarily on District 3 in Manhattan. Because we began working with an already overburdened system, where educators were enormously overworked and underappreciated, and where the arts were seen as just one more thing that kept teachers from getting done what had to be done, we created a special kind of partnership in the classroom. We took the teacher's curriculum for communication skills and planned artist-led classes that supported their education agenda. The teachers were able to observe, through direct classroom experience and teacher-artist meetings, the value of the arts in the classroom. We have tacitly made arts supporters of the classroom educators.

Not all artists belong in the schools. Some cannot communicate well with adolescents and children, while others are working with ideas and material that are inaccessible to these communities. For those of us who have some facility in this area and who do not feel we compromise our work by sharing it with children, there is enormous need.

■ A big part of the artist's job now is to connect with people at the crisis points of our society. Where a few years ago artists were so worried about some strange thing called the "cutting edge," the challenge today is to deal with a culture in pain. The Border Arts Workshop/Taller Arte Fronterize in San Diego/Tijuana and the variety of artists responding to the AIDS crisis are good examples of a creative response to crisis. Important work is being done all over this country, dealing with the homeless, multicultural expression, aging, and lesbian and gay issues. This can and must happen everywhere; it reconnects the performing artist to society. It may also reveal new strategies for how an artist can create a way to make a living. There are many programs like the California Arts Council's Artists in Residence project, which supported a work by performance artist John Malpede (another ex–New Yorker). The strength and beauty of this work—developed in collaboration with homeless people on skid row—garnered the Los Angeles Poverty Department a New York Dance and Performance Award (Bessie) in 1989.—Tim Miller, performance artist, teacher, and cultural organizer ∎

∎ The message I get in this country is don't experiment—and it is partially a personal thing since I've had the experience of doing work that was deemed a hit one year, lost all my NEA funding the next, then got it back the next year because the powers that be declared my new work a hit. Although I am making pieces that are ambitious and making choices that are somewhat drastic, my powerful work may not come until I'm forty. But if it's been undermined by a "this works now" mentality, we're not going to go anywhere. The other thing we're going to cut out is the assimilation of the avant-garde, of new ideas that finally go into the mainstream that feeds Broadway. I just hope that, slowly, I can shake things up.—Tere O'Connor, choreographer ∎

Multiculturalism: A Double-Edged Sword
Chiori Santiago

On the face of it, companies that produce multicultural dance face the same problems as any other production company. For a company working out of a non-Western tradition in America, the staging of classical forms is difficult. "Dances from Asian traditions don't always lend themselves to a proscenium stage," says Gail Nishikawa of San Francisco's Asian American Dance Collective (AADC). "They were intended to be performed in an outside environment or in a circle." Nishikawa cites a recent festival where groups offered Brazilian capoeira and Balinese-influenced dance that had been modified to suit the proscenium. "The choreographers were pretty sophisticated about staging, and the performances went over well," she says. But when an American Indian dance group chose to replicate their circle dance, viewers complained that it was boring.

Unfortunately, standards for judging multicultural dance are still based on Western notions about form and staging. "When you do something outdoors in San Francisco, it's not considered 'art' anymore," Nishikawa says. Instead, the dance is often dismissed as a community cultural event akin to a YMCA talent show. To maintain credibility, she chooses to present concerts on mainstream, proscenium stages.

Simply making that choice limits or changes the type of dance that audiences finally see. Presenting in a Western format can eliminate many worthwhile performers. Notes Lily Kharrazi of City Celebration, which produces San Francisco's annual Ethnic Dance Festival: "There are certain assumptions you can't ignore when you're asking people to sit in a theater. You want to offer a panorama, show the integrity of the form. Yet those with the most integrity often don't have the most razzle-dazzle."

One dancer who auditioned for the Ethnic Dance Festival performed a traditional Japanese dance that was excruciatingly slow and exacting, with very little obvious movement. "She wasn't chosen, not because she wasn't good, but because the dance was not up to the judges' standards," Kharrazi says. "After you've seen, say, half an hour of energetic West African dance, it takes a real shift to watch fifteen minutes of an articulated foot."

That can leave producers scratching their heads over how far to take their allegiances to dance traditions versus the reality of the marketplace. "You don't want to end up with the Kodak Hula Show," says Nishikawa, who has staged dances by Chak Sam Pa, a Tibetan group, as part of the Asian Pacific dance festival produced by AADC. "Chak Sam Pa does religion-based artwork, and it was very uncomfortable asking them to do it differently; you need to respect the sacred source. Luckily, their artistic director was interested in having the work seen." The collaboration was well received by viewers.

Simply defining oneself as "multicultural" can be a double-edged sword. A non-Asian company might include an Asian-based dance in a program and qualify for funding as "multicultural," while a company such as AADC, Nishikawa says, is often seen by funders as "ethnic specific," although their programs include dances from many Asian cultures. And does using dancers of many races mean a failure to preserve the culture and intent of a dance?

"I don't think its wrong to put a white person who is competent into a black dance, or vice versa, although I believe many of my colleagues would disagree," says Halifu Osumare, a choreographer and instructor in the dance department at Stanford University and founder of Oakland's Everybody's Creative Arts Center in 1974 (now Citicentre Dance Theatre). "At this point in the global power shift, blacks are protective of what we do best. But I don't think anyone should be excluded from learning or performing any form she or he chooses."

In order to better acquaint audiences with non-Western forms, many choreographers spend a great deal of time on research, use extensive program notes, and often a strong story line. More prosaic production concerns include such technical details as lighting and makeup. "The wrong lighting with dark-skinned people can make them look ghostly," Osumare says. "Technicians of color who've had experience working with people of color are more sensitive to those issues."

Perhaps the only solution to many of these concerns is time. Developing a multicultural aesthetic is not, according to Nishikawa, "a ten-minute deal." But those in the field believe that it *is* happening, if slowly. "People have bought into the idea of a multiracial society, but not into a multicultural one," Osumare says. "But I really do see dance as developing past the local, petty level of competition and politics; I see it in relation to a new world paradigm. Multiculturalism in dance begins to acknowledge the world we live in."

Talking Dance
Liz Lerman

This piece is about dancers and talking—not talking onstage, but talking about our work. When I began studying dance in earnest—an impressionable child in Milwaukee—I first heard the idea, strongly stated by those responsible for my early dance education, that if you can talk about it, it must not be a dance.

As I entered my teenage ballerina years, I noticed that suddenly everyone in the dressing rooms had become stupid. We could talk about our aches and pains, and about our teachers and choreographers, but nothing else. It seemed that some of our teachers' and choreographers' requests to leave our brains outside the studio had seeped mysteriously into our beings. I learned to be quiet.

Later I discovered, through the words of a critic, that program notes, too, were unfashionable. A paraphrase of that long-ago review would go something like this: Those lengthy notes were so unnecessary; if you can write about it, don't dance it. Later still, I learned that to be a true artist I had to have a manager protecting me from everyone and talking for me to everyone. A sign of artistic success was to be left in isolation in my studio making art while everyone around me did the describing, the naming, the pleading, the encouraging, and the talking.

I have come to see this as a great lie and a great mistake. It is a lie because, in fact, to survive we need to talk. And it is a mistake because our talking is empowering for us and for those in direct contact with us. I don't mean that we have to talk all the time. Management is crucial, program notes *can* be redundant, and sometimes an artistic process is better served by silence. But I think our silence is part of the reason for our marginalization. Not just the marginalization of the arts within the rest of American society, but the marginalization of the artist within the art world.

I think we need to be able to communicate to people why we dance, for whom, and to what ends. If we cannot do this, if we depend on others such as managers, writers, and presenters to do it for us, the message will get muddled, and the needs of artists will be misunderstood.

I once made a list of all the people I have to talk to in order to be understood. Everyone does not need to hear the same story or the same version of the story. That would be boring for all of us. Some need to be inspired, others need details, others get history, current events, missionary zeal, or the facts of life. The list was incredibly long and went something like this: dancers, funders, writers, government people, teachers, parents and families of the dancers, neighbors, peers, volunteers, students, collaborators, presenters, staff, board people, my father (who at seventy-one has heard all the stories but still wants to know when I will accept a university job), and my daughter (who is almost three and asks me every day why I go to dance).

Two things consistently surprise me as I step gingerly into the world of talking at meetings, panels, and symposiums. The first is how much I have still internalized the notion that somehow I will be taken more seriously if I remain remote. The second surprise is how happy everyone is when we take time to talk. The dancers in the company are happier knowing what is going on. The funders are excited just to talk about the field. The writers are trying to keep up with all the changes and need these conversations. And, certainly, the presenters need to hear from us directly. It is one way for artists to be more engaged in the delivery of art to those who will see it.

So let's break the silences.

■ The arts are political, whether they like it or not. If they stay in their own realm, preoccupied with their proper problems, the arts support the status quo, which in itself is highly political. Or they scream and kick and participate in our century's struggle for liberation in whatever haphazard way they can, probably at the expense of some of their sensitive craftsmanship, but definitely for their own souls' sake.—Peter Schumann, puppeteer ■

APPENDIX COMMUNITY: THE BODY POLITIC

Addresses and phone numbers of the following resources may be found in the alphabetized Directory at the end of the book. (Thanks to the New York Foundation for the Arts for compiling many of the following political/arts advocacy/arts community resources.)

National

Actors' Equity Association (AEA) (Trade union of professional actors and stage managers.)

AFL-CIO Department of Professional Employees (Council of unions of technical, professional, and white-collar workers, including those in arts and entertainment.)

Alliance for Arts Education (AAE) (Network of arts education organizations.)

Alternate Roots (Association of artist-run organizations.)

American Arts Alliance (AAA) (Represents major museums, dance, and opera companies, presenters, orchestras, theaters, and service organizations. Helps shape national arts agenda.)

American Association of University Professors (AAUP) (Membership. Represents college and university faculty; academic freedom division; publications.)

American Council for the Arts (ACA) (Sponsors National Advocacy Day, monitors legislation, publications. Operates a free information hotline to help artists with questions about funding, housing, insurance, health, and law.)

American Council of Learned Societies (ACLS) (National organization in humanities scholarship and teaching; publications and conferences.)

American Federation of Musicians

American Federation of Television and Radio Artists (AFTRA)

American Guild of Musical Artists (AGMA) (Arts union for dance, music, opera–musical theater.)

American Guild of Variety Artists (AGVA) (Arts union for music and theater.)

American Music Center (Membership. Promotes American contemporary music; library, publications, services.)

American Society of Composers, Authors and Publishers (ASCAP) (Licenses the nonexclusive rights to perform music in public.)

American Symphony Orchestra League (ASOL) (National service organization for orchestras; maintains government affairs office.)

Artswire (Links the arts community nationwide through an electronic wire service.)

The Association of American Cultures (TAAC) (Membership. Advocates for arts issues of diverse populations.)

Association of Hispanic Arts, Inc. (AHA) (Serves primarily Hispanic artists and arts organizations; provides staff advice and referrals in management areas.)

Chamber Music America (Serves ensembles and presenters; advocacy information and resources.)

College Art Association (CAA) (Furthers teaching of art and art history; publications, conferences, advocacy information.)

Cultural Alliance of Greater Washington

Dance/USA (Membership. Information on issues affecting dance.)

Federation of State Humanities Councils (Membership. Sponsors annual Humanities on the Hill—advocacy.)

Hospital Audiences, Inc. (HAI) (Advocates for arts access for the disadvantaged, people with disabilities, people at risk, and the frail elderly.)

League of Resident Theatres (LORT)

League of Women Voters (Great resource for all voter needs; sponsors forums on issues and candidates; voter registration, information, and support.)

Meet the Composer (Publications and advocacy network for American composers.)

National Artists' Equity Association

National Assembly of Local Arts Agencies (NASAA) (Arts policy development and advocacy.)

National Association of Artists' Organizations (NAAO) (Membership of alternative organizations and artists, publications, networks.)

National Cultural Alliance (Membership. A national marketing project aimed at promoting a better public understanding and changing public opinion about the arts and humanities.)

National Gay and Lesbian Task Force (Advocates on behalf of lesbians and gay men; addresses censorship issues.)

National Humanities Alliance (Membership. Monitors issues affecting scholarship, teaching, and other activities.)

People for the American Way (Advocates on behalf of freedom of expression and civil liberties issues)

Religious Action Center of Reformed Judaism (Active in freedom of expression struggle.)

Screen Actors Guild (SAG)

Society of Stage Directors & Choreographers (SSD&C) (Arts union for dance and theater.)

Theater Communications Group (TCG) (Membership. Communications and advocacy efforts on behalf of theater artists and companies. Publications include *American Theater Magazine and ArtSearch*.)

United Scenic Artists Local 829 (Arts union for dance, theater, opera–musical theater, media arts.)

Visual AIDS

At the State Level

Alliance of New York State Arts Councils

Media Alliance (Membership. Advances independent media arts in New York State; publications, conferences, and resources; advocacy action committee.)

New York State Alliance for Arts Education (Membership. Programming, networks, and resources.)

New York State Arts and Cultural Coalition (NYSACC) (Represents artists and cultural institutions, monitors legislation in Albany, sponsors Arts Advocacy Day.)

At the Local Level

ACT-UP (AIDS Coalition to Unleash Power)/New York (See other major city listings under ACT-UP in the Directory.) (Action in response to the AIDS crisis. Meetings are on Mondays at 7:30 P.M. at the Lesbian and Gay Community Services Center, 208 W. 13th St., N.Y.)

Alliance for the Arts (Research and policy on arts issues.)

Alliance of Resident Theatres/New York (ART/NY) (Advocates for NYC nonprofit theaters; network and resources.)

Arts Coalition of Independent Democrats (Membership. Voter registration, endorsement of candidates and platforms, legislative support for free-lance artists, and dissemination of information on candidates, legislation, and city policy with an impact on the arts community.)

Chicago Artists Coalition (Documents censorship incidents nationally; committee for artists rights and service organization for visual artists.)

Get Smart/The Ad Hoc Artists Group (Action for artists' rights and against censorship.)

Greater Chicago Citizens for the Arts

New York City Arts Coalition (Membership. Focus on city, state, and federal budgets and other public policy issues; advocacy network; publications.)

New York City Art Teachers Association/United Federation of Teachers (Labor union for public school teachers and other school employees. Extensive advocacy network, publications, and services. Chapter in each school; five borough offices.)

Parachute Fund through Dance Bay Area

San Francisco Arts Democratic Club (Membership. First successful club of its kind in recent years. Gets the artists' vote out in SF.)

MANY PLACES,
MANY DREAMS

All the world's a stage.—William Shakespeare, *As You*

Like It

Austin, Texas
John Job

The list of dance soloists, dance theater groups, performance artists, ballet companies, ethnic dance companies, and specialty groups that have graced Austin's stages over the last five years would be the envy of even the largest American cities. From the multivenue Performing Arts Center at the University of Texas, to downtown's landmark Paramount Theater, to Dance Umbrella's Synergy Studio, Austin has established itself as a must on every performer's touring itinerary. The city's hip, laid-back sense of itself, its nationally envied music scene, and the physical attraction of the Texas Hill Country make it a place many people have difficulty leaving. In fact, many of Austin's artists came here first on tours with other groups and never left.

The city boasts a wealth of independent, native, and inherited ethnic, ballet, modern, and new dance ensembles and soloists, complementing a vigorous dance program at the university. Dance Umbrella functions as a coordinating hub and, in collaboration with other service organizations like Women and Their Work and the Black Arts Alliance, connects Austin to the National Performance Network, the National Endowment for the Arts' Dance on Tour programs, the Mid-America Arts Alliance, and other presenting entities.

Dance Umbrella also provides grant preparation and administrative services, publicity help, and full production services for local and Texas-based dance artists, publishes a monthly newsletter, presents performances and workshops by national and international artists, and operates a rehearsal and performance studio. And it is the principal conduit for municipal, state, and foundation grants for local dancers and choreographers.

Florida
Demetrius A. Klein

When I first began making work in Florida (late in 1986), I was naive as a choreographer. My work tended to be mostly surface-level movement to music. The thing that Florida gave me was time, space, and people with whom to work. My dancers, for the most part, were adult beginner students. And they were the key to my development as a choreographer, enabling me to work uninterrupted with a raw but devoted group of people.

I tried renting theaters and presenting concerts, but that proved to be financially disastrous. My real breakthroughs came when I began doing work in my, then, very small space. This let me put the work first, without worrying about box office, lighting, and other such things. We performed to five or six people at a time in a hot, un-air-conditioned studio. We also began to self-produce, successfully, at small performance spaces in New York. Eventually we were able to get a larger space in which to rehearse and perform.

Most of this would have been impossible in New York or any other major metropolitan area. First of all, I didn't grow up in such an area and really don't feel comfortable in large cities. Then there is the financial issue. Space was, and is, relatively cheap in Florida. My wife and I have been able to teach dance classes in order to survive and to work undistracted.

The dance community here is small but mighty. Artists such as Leslie Neal, Dale Andree, Mia Michaels, Jane Carrington, Gary Lund, and Lynne Wimmer do good work, period. Geography should have nothing to do with the evaluation of its quality. The Florida Dance Festival, which takes place in Tampa every year, is an enormous asset as well. Quite honestly, attending the festival in 1986 persuaded me to stay in Florida. I was able to study composition from Ralph Lemon for two summers in a row, and he was a powerful influence on my work.

All in all, what can Florida offer an artist that other areas cannot? I don't think it can provide unmatched service organizations or marketing or any other such thing. What it can offer is an opportunity to put the work first, to dig in and develop it for a small but enthusiastic audience, and the chance to live a relatively sane life.

North Carolina's Triangle
Lee Wenger

Durham, North Carolina, might surprise performers from more metropolitan areas with the diversity, quality, and level of support given to the arts. In the Triangle area alone (Durham, Raleigh, and Chapel Hill), there are fifteen diverse dance companies and ten theater groups. Each city has an art center that offers courses, rents performance space, and awards grants. In addition, there are four universities and several private colleges that offer dance programs, award North Carolina teaching certificates, and present performing arts series.

North Carolina has a strong state and local arts council system as well. The North Carolina State Arts Council (NCAC), located in Raleigh, offers grants to performance groups and individuals, sponsors a visiting artist program, and supports a touring subsidy program. The two major touring companies in North Carolina are North Carolina Dance Theater, located in Charlotte, and African American Dance Ensemble, based in Durham and directed by Chuck Davis. Several smaller modern dance companies are also listed on the NCAC touring roster, including Wall Street Danceworks, in Asheville, and my company, New Performing Dance Company.

North Carolina is home to two prominent training institutions. The North Carolina School of the Arts, located in Winston-Salem, trains dancers on the high school and college levels. In Durham, the American Dance Festival (ADF) provides local dancers with opportunities to study with an outstanding selection of instructors during its six-week summer program.

ADF has developed a broad-based, sophisticated modern dance audience and given local critics valuable experience reviewing major dance companies. As a result, local companies have increased attendance at their events and received well-written reviews. ADF's concert series has also placed local companies in a national context, giving our community a new respect for "local" artists.

The state of North Carolina has a professional dance organization, N.C. Dance Alliance, which promotes the art of dance through advocacy and an annual event that includes a showcase of dances by many of the state's choreographers. This organization serves both professional dancers and dance educators.

Teaching dance in public or private schools, universities, private studios, or public art centers is the best way to earn a steady income through dance. Except for the major companies, most companies can pay neither rehearsal salaries nor performance honorariums. Almost all of us hold other jobs.

Durham is also unusual for its quality and variety of body therapies and sports medicine services. Both Duke Hospital and Chapel Hill Memorial hospital have sports medicine programs. There is also an excellent massage school in Chapel Hill, and many of its graduates work in this area.

Washington, DC

Jennifer Poulos and Kim Chan

There is a lot more to Washington, DC, than the National Endowment for the Arts. The performing arts community in Washington includes a variety of artists who have legitimate pride in their work as well as a commitment to making Washington a city where artists can choose to live and survive. There are a number of artist-run organizations in various arts genres whose continual efforts to create working environments and centers for artists have done much to enhance the quality of artistic life in the city.

All types of dance can be found in DC—modern, ballet, and African are the most visible. There are also large swing and percussive dance followings, but jazz dance aficionados may be disappointed. For those whose interest is in theater, there is a thriving small-theater district.

Washington-based dance companies will find that, although the artist community here is fairly supportive, the prospects of support from area presenters and other types of sponsors can seem discouraging. The D.C. Commission on the Arts and Humanities and surrounding county arts councils have grant programs for individual artists who reside within their jurisdictions.

The dance grapevine in DC is small; talking to people in class will turn you on to most auditions and work opportunities. Audition notices and other information are posted at most local studios and occasionally in the *Washington Post,* where you can buy listings. If you're versatile, you can join the Actors' Center, which has a phone line listing audition notices, workshops, and other information for actors.

Because of the volume of high-profile companies that come through DC, it can be difficult to get press attention for your work. Rely on the grapevine, paid advertising, and mailings to do your advertising—though, if you're organized and work well in advance to inform them, the area dance press can be supportive. (The dance press is actually more supportive of DC dance artists than the other performing arts press is of area music and theater.)

The Cultural Alliance of Greater Washington is a membership organization for individuals and metropolitan area arts organizations that offers a variety of services, including health, life, and dental insurance, a JOBank, and TICKETplace (half-price day-of-the-show tickets). Its membership directory is a guide to the metropolitan area arts community, from performing groups to public funding agencies to education programs.

Rehearsal space is always difficult to find. Because Washington has never been an industrial center, there are few large empty lofts or warehouses waiting to be used for classes or by resident companies. Dance Coalition is a small membership organization that offers rehearsal and performance space on Capitol Hill (contact Diane Hunt at 301/270-4445). However, it cannot accommodate a large number of choreographers and dancers without losing its availability to serve as a dependable space for its members. Dance Place's second studio, Hot Feet, features a floor designed for percussive dance and is also available as a rehearsal space.

Dance performances abound, mostly by touring companies. Washington has one of the largest dance presenting seasons on the East Coast outside Manhattan, thanks primarily to Dance Place (capacity 199; it is also a studio), which has performances almost every weekend year-round by emerging and established artists drawn from the community and from out of town. Dance Place is a National Performance Network presenter, and you can sign up to usher and see the performances for free.

At the Kennedy Center, dance is presented by both the Washington Performing Arts Society (WPAS) and the Center itself. In addition to their own presentations, the two organizations copresent a modern dance series for major touring companies that periodically features Washington companies. Here you will see the major international ballet and modern dance companies and the Washington Ballet, which self-presents regular seasons at two of the theaters.

As part of a plan to develop DC as a cultural center, theaters capable of accommodating a variety of artistic styles will be opening—economy willing—throughout the metropolitan area within the next five to ten years. Until then, the other performance venues in town are rental spaces: the Warner Theatre and George Washington University's Lisner Auditorium and Marvin Center. Just outside the city, dance can be seen at P. G. Publick Playhouse in Hyattsville, Maryland, and George Mason University in Fairfield, Virginia. The amount of dance seen at these theaters will depend on the amount of dance any given presenter is planning to schedule into its season.

The Mount Vernon College Florence Hollis Hand Chapel has an excellent series booked by its Performing Arts department and is also available for rental. From time to time, the Smithsonian will have dance concerts as well. There are several other colleges with dance departments within the immediate area that present student, faculty, and resident company concerts but do not have active dance concert calendars by touring companies.

Most likely, you won't make a living working as a dancer. There are just a handful of companies with much national visibility and regular touring seasons. Yet, as the dance community establishes itself, more artists are finding DC an attractive and affordable place to live as well as a city to which they can make a significant artistic contribution.

Brooklyn, New York
Elise Long

Over the last ten years, like many independent artists, I have had the opportunity to wear an infinite number of hats: choreographer, performer, graphic
designer, arts administrator, fund-raiser, coach, writer, teacher, sound engineer, lighting designer, seamstress, photographer, consultant, janitor, secretary, accountant, word processor, construction worker, general contractor,
community organizer, wife, and producer. Though I continue to wear most of
these hats on an ongoing basis, I have never really thought of myself as
anything other than a creative artist.

One of my primary jobs as a creative artist is to discover and make new
things; this job also includes presenting old things in a new light. I enjoy
creating environments in which people, materials, and ideas can interact. The
outcome of this creative interaction may be a dance, a painting, a code of
ethics, or a community. I regard the sharing of this alchemy with the general
public as the professional artist's social responsibility; my work is the greatest contribution I can make toward creating a healthier and more humane
society. And I give it gladly.

Space and money—or, rather, a gigantic lack of both—coupled with an increasing desire to upgrade the quality of my personal life and physical surroundings, spurred me to seek a home and work outside Manhattan. Brooklyn
is by no means a land of milk and honey; it suffers from the same obscenities
as other urban centers, and then some. But it has stores of raw energy to tap
and vast frontiers to explore. It is a place largely unencumbered by fashion,
rich in human resources, and percolating with history and local color—and it
seems able to tolerate people of my age and their ilk who consider raising
children and making art as legitimate and not mutually exclusive adult activities. Moving here has allowed me to pursue my art and life with an almost
always empty pocket, yet I have been able to purchase my own apartment and
a beautiful dance space within walking distance of my home. Brooklyn has
enabled me to know my neighbors, students, fellow artists, and audience in
more than a casual or cursory way. In return, I feel inspired to provide Brooklyn with a performance alternative that might be just a little more humane, a
little more daring, and ultimately more honest than many larger mainstream
presenting institutions can afford.

From Lower Manhattan to Central Ohio
Stuart Pimsler

Suzanne Costello and I drove from New York City to Ohio in August 1983. We had spent the previous six years in lower Manhattan, living and working in a loft space we named the Parkfast Dance Stadium. I had spent the majority of my childhood in Manhattan and believed that the best of everything was on that frenetic island. Nevertheless, I spent hours walking and bicycling through Manhattan in search of some quiet, unpopulated space. When my company started to tour throughout the country, I was ready to look for a new home.

After a residency at Denison University, we were invited to return the following year for an extended period. Denison sits on top of the only sizable hill in Granville, a quaint, upscale village within an hour's drive of Columbus, where we found a diverse community of artists and dancers. My company was encouraged to apply for funding from the Ohio Arts Council. I was amazed at the amount of art being created in Columbus, as well as throughout Ohio, and found kinships with other choreographers (many of whom had worked in New York). Ironically, I was attending more performances in Ohio than I had in New York, particularly at the Dance Hall in Cincinnati (a National Performance Network [NPN] site) and the Wexner Center in Columbus. For the past four years I have shared ideas with other members of the Chester Group, which is composed of seventeen movement artists from various parts of the country who meet annually at the Yellow Springs Institute in Chester Springs, Pennsylvania.

State and city support have enabled me to pay my company members throughout a ten-month season. An active touring schedule (including ten presentations at NPN sites throughout the United States), annual home seasons, and return engagements to New York City have provided me with a broad range of audience perspectives.

But before you pack your bags, there are some concerns. National funding patterns and media analysis continue to pass over the quality and quantity of work being created in the center of the country. This pattern perpetuates a stigma of artistic inferiority that is out of sync with the kind of work being created. Inevitably, the compelling diversity of choreographic voices at work in the Midwest will be considered a vital part of the national dance panorama.

Ohio
Vicky Dummer

Numerous dancers and choreographers with national reputations have come from Ohio or through Ohio's colleges and universities. Ohio State University has the reputation for supplying half the dancers in New York City. When these dancers tire of fighting for recognition, funding, and affordable living and working space in the city, they come back to Ohio.

Ohio is a logical place for many artists to turn to because of its thriving arts community. The state boasts six major dance companies, over eighteen colleges and universities offering courses in dance, over fifteen modern dance companies, several professional ethnic companies, several liturgical dance companies, and dozens of community-based traditional companies. Dance presentation is also booming in Ohio, with four National Performance Network sites, approximately fifty presenters (those that apply to the Ohio Arts Council for support), and the annual Performance Art Festival in Cleveland.

Under the visionary leadership of Dr. Wayne Lawson, the Ohio Arts Council (OAC) provides monumental support for the arts. By putting dollars behind artistic vision first, organizational structure and fiscal responsibility second (although a close second), artists are allowed to explore and go beyond the traditional boundaries of their form. Consider the New Steps Project between the Ohio Ballet and the Cleveland Ballet, which allows dancers from these companies to create new ballet choreography, or outreach efforts from companies like Dancing Wheels, where physically handicapped dancers collaborate with able-bodied dancers to create work and build self-esteem.

A simplified version of the OAC funding structure as it applies to dance can be broken down into three categories: Major Institutional Support, distributed biannually on a percentage basis to organizations with budgets greater than $500,000; Project Support, open to all dance-movement organizations and individuals for one-time project awards; Technical Assistance, which provides funds (up to three $2,000 awards per organization) for consultancies and workshops.

Coordinators at the OAC contribute greatly to the success of the program areas. The Artist in Education Program coordinators have been instrumental in promoting dance to the Ohio Department of Education as a content area in the educational system. Dance certification was approved in Ohio in 1987 through their efforts, with the assistance of OhioDance and the Ohio Alliance for Arts Education. A dance education degree program is now in place at two Ohio colleges, and four more are in various stages of development. A K–12 dance curriculum has been developed for a pilot project in the Columbus City School System.

Everything isn't perfect in Ohio. Smaller companies and individual performers continue to have difficulty hiring appropriate and affordable management. Dance currently being presented in the state tends to be the most accessible or popular. Presenters seem to be more interested in selling seats than in stretching their audiences. There is a great need to educate presenters about other possibilities within the form so that they can develop and educate their audiences. Ohio also lacks informed dance critics. We have some very talented writers. Unfortunately, only two are associated with newspapers.

Ohio has a fine reputation for dance, yet our artists struggle for recognition from the National Endowment for the Arts in terms of funding and from *Dance Magazine* for national press coverage. More needs to be done to show off the wealth of talent within the state. Until that time, we will continue to harbor and care for our New York City refugees.

Chicago
Lisa Tylke

Chicago has always been a place where grass-roots initiatives can develop, grow, and flourish. The performing arts community is a living example of the city's ability to nurture the creative spirit. Home to more than thirty-eight companies, Chicago's dance community provides a wealth of cultural activities throughout the year, including public performances, in-school residencies, and student and teacher training programs.

The strength of the dance community lies in its diversity. Local artists work in modern, jazz, ballet, tap, traditional African, East Indian, American Indian, Spanish, Latino, and sacred dance forms. Muntu Dance Theatre (a company dedicated to performing traditional and contemporary African dance) and Natyakalalayam (carrying on the rich tradition of classical Indian dance) are two examples of nationally recognized culturally specific companies.

The city has also provided the setting for local companies, such as Mordine and Company Dance Theater and Joseph Holmes Chicago Dance Theater, to develop from choreographer-driven pick-up groups into major performing companies. The Hubbard Street Dance Company (established in 1974) is recognized internationally for its performances of works by Twyla Tharp, Bob Fosse, Daniel Ezralow, and founder and artistic director, Lou Conte.

Performance venues are limited. The greatest need is for a midsize theater.

The community is fortunate, however, to have the Dance Center of Columbia College. A National Performance Network primary sponsor, the Dance Center serves as a major venue for local and national companies and artists and offers showcase opportunities for emerging choreographers.

Larger venues include the Civic Stages Chicago, which presents the Spring Festival of Dance, offering performances by national touring companies such as the American Ballet Theatre, the Joffrey Ballet, and the Dance Theatre of Harlem as well as by local companies like the Hubbard Street Dance Company, the Chicago Repertory Dance Ensemble, and the Joseph Holmes Chicago Dance Theater. The Auditorium Theater presents national and international dance companies.

Chicago has several alternative performance spaces. Beacon Street Gallery, the Blue Rider Theater, Links Hall, and Puszh Studios present dance and performance programming as well as renting their spaces to self-presenting artists. These venues provide a point of entry for new and emerging artists. Some, such as Randolph Street Gallery, also offer technical and financial assistance to local artists.

Touring provides local artists with the majority of their performing opportunities. Most companies tour regionally through programming from Arts Midwest and the Illinois Arts Council. The National Endowment's Dance on Tour program provides assistance to Illinois companies for national touring, and Chicago Artists Abroad (a private foundation) supports touring abroad. Support for in-school residencies and performance throughout Illinois is available to artists through Urban Gateways and the Illinois Arts Council.

Dancers have opportunities to study with master teachers such as Gus Giordano (jazz), Larry Long (ballet), Tommy Gomez (Dunham technique), Shirley Mordine (modern), Nana Shineflug (modern), and Jimmy Payne (tap). High-caliber professional classes can be found at several studios, including the Ruth Page Foundation, the Lou Conte Studios, the Dance Center of Columbia College, Dancespace, and the Boulevard Arts Center. Chicago is also home to one of the nation's few performing arts high schools—the Chicago Academy for the Arts. Columbia College, Northwestern University, and Northeastern Illinois University offer degrees in dance.

The Chicago Dance Coalition (CDC) is the service organization for Chicago's dance community. CDC's programs and services include technical assistance and promotional and human resource services for members, the Dance Hotline (a twenty-four-hour telephone service listing area dance performances and events), the monthly *Performance Calendar,* the annual *Dance Instruction Directory,* and the semiannual *Chicago Dance Magazine.* CDC also sponsors an annual conference and workshop series as well as the Ruth Page Awards, which honor excellence in local dance.

Minneapolis
Sharon Varosh

I thought I had been exiled to Siberia when I moved from Washington, DC, to Minneapolis in 1976. The seventy-below-zero windchills made me fear for my fingers and toes during interminable bus waits. And Chicago was four hundred miles away.

Minneapolis and I have grown on each other over the last sixteen years. At age forty-two, newly married, and about to start a family, I find I have discovered a place where I am valued as a mature dancer and where I can be a total person in a total community.

In 1976, Loyce Houlton's Minnesota Dance Theater combined ballet, Graham technique, and pure "Houlton" for the highest profile in town. Nancy Hauser's Wigman-influenced modern dance company (which I danced with for five years) made a cozy home for the counterculture on the Mississippi's West Bank. These two leaders would provide fascinating dancers to top companies for a generation: Melanie Lien to Pina Bausch, Lise Houlton to the American Ballet Theatre, Erin Thompson to Nina Weiner, Lise Friedman to Merce Cunningham, Sara and Jerry Pearson to Murray Louis, Bill Harren to Alwin Nikolais, Gail Turner to Meredith Monk, and Ralph Lemon, who danced with Nancy Hauser and went on to become the director of his own company.

The Minnesota Independent Choreographer's Alliance soon challenged this isolation. Formed in 1979 to give area choreographers a sense of community, today's renamed Minnesota Dance Alliance (MDA) is one of the foremost dance service organizations in the country. It funds choreographers, dancers, and companies, provides rehearsal and performance space, mediates discussion of controversial issues, and produces a monthly newsletter.

Through MDA's Visiting Artist Program, I had one of the most sublime experiences of my life. Laurie Van Wieren, Marcella Kingman, and I helped conceive and dance a piece with Eiko and Koma. *Canal* later metamorphosed into *Passage,* which won Eiko and Koma a Bessie Award. Danced nude, lying in six inches of water, the grueling and absorbing improvisation forged a shared excitement and respect that are a dancer's greatest joy.

Though opportunities to work with master artists are surprisingly abundant, the community feels the lack of resident master teachers and critics. Generally, local choreographers are reviewed only if they already have the imprimatur of New York critics—a shame because choreographers like Georgia Stephens, Van Wieren, Lovice Weller, and Diane Elliot continue to develop honest, quirkily intellectual works.

Minnesota
Louise Robinson

Minnesota has an active and growing arts community. There exists a strong infrastructure, ranging from major institutions to small experimental performing groups to independent artists. For the independent artist, a number of service organizations provide information and resources. In addition to the Minnesota Dance Alliance, such organizations include the Minnesota Composer's Forum, Playwrights' Center, The Loft, Intermedia Arts, Film in the Cities, and the Minneapolis College of Art and Design. Funding resources are slightly more plentiful and varied than in other communities. However, demand far exceeds supply, so an image of abundance is misleading.

The dance community is unique in several ways. We are a community without a "major institution" since our ballet company closed its doors more than two years ago. The full effect of this situation is as yet unknown. And we have only a handful of dance companies, including the Zenon Dance Company, the Nancy Hauser Dance Company, the New Dance Ensemble, the Ethnic Dance Theatre, the Ballet of the Dolls, and Zorongo Flamenco. To balance this, we have a wealth of artists working independently and cooperatively. This unusual mix, I believe, results in a community that is not particularly segmented. Some camps exist, but the flow in and out of them is quite loose, creating an interactive and supportive environment.

To a large extent, the Dance Alliance acts as a focal point for the community, providing communication tools that are heavily accessed, extensive information and networking resources, funding in the form of fellowships and project support, and performance opportunities. Other resource organizations exist as well, providing extensive artistic and managerial services. An example is United Arts, which offers counseling and workshops on grant writing and other administrative concerns.

I must mention that we have a strong community of presenters in the Twin Cities, the Walker Art Center and Northrop Auditorium among them. There is a growing number of presenters throughout the state, some affiliated with colleges and universities and some operating as independent civic organizations. Of particular note is the cooperation among these presenters. Two, three, or more presenters will often copresent and even cocurate events. Opportunities also arise in which dance companies and independent artists are brought into the mix—evidence of the healthy dialogue that exists here on many levels.

San Francisco
Joe Goode

The San Francisco Bay Area is the alternative life-style center of the world. It is a gay/lesbian mecca and a hotbed for leftist political activism and alternative forms of medicine, spirituality, and psychology. As you can imagine, this spirit of freedom and experimentation affects the art and artists produced in this region. I think it is safe to say that much of the art produced here is of a socially conscious, if not outright political, nature.

On my arrival in San Francisco in 1978, I began to spew forth a series of bloody solo works in which I demanded that the viewer acknowledge the content of the material as well as its formal structure; I was tired of the formalist movement in dance and, frankly, enraged by the insistence (in the formalist camp) on keeping the performer faceless and detached. I expected little more than a bemused acceptance of first steps in a new form. What I found, however, was an unabashed zeal for this style of confessional, content-driven dance.

Perhaps I was in the right place at the right time, but I think it was more than that. I was drawn to San Francisco because of its reputation for social, political, and artistic experimentation. I was looking for a place to combine my interests as a choreographer, actor, and writer. I was also looking for acceptance (perhaps from myself) as a gay man. My voice continues to be shaped by this community.

San Francisco Bay Area
Lillian Goldthwaite

The Bay Area is noted for the diversity of its ethnic communities. There are over twelve flamenco companies, fourteen African dance companies, and countless companies of Asian and Southeast Asian backgrounds. Juergas, Pow Wows, and Contact Improvisation "jams" are found in equal numbers, as are concert performances in one-hundred-seat lofts and larger theaters.

The performance art community comes from a long Bay Area tradition, ranging from experimental theater grounded in political activism to Beat-era coffeehouse readings and open-mike comedy houses. The best work, as always, defies categorization and is just as likely to occur under freeways and in abandoned housing projects as in dance studios and theaters.

The various art communities function within fairly discrete "neighbor-hoods." Service organizations such as Dance Bay Area [see the Appendix] and Theater Bay Area work with local presenters to increase communication. The most disheartening limitations to the Bay Area arts community remain the overall lack of resources to support the vast quantity of activity—specifi-cally in terms of funding, media coverage, and presenting opportunities.

There are only two foundations that consistently provide small grants to the vast number of individual artists and unincorporated groups, and the funds they distribute are minuscule in relation to the enormous number of requests they receive. Other sources of contributed income are limited and generally flow to the well-known, big-budget companies.

The larger presenters include San Francisco Performances (Herbst Theater, San Francisco), Cal Performances (Zellerbach Hall, U.C. Berkeley campus), and the Lively Arts at Stanford University. They focus on larger companies like Merce Cunningham, Paul Taylor, and Alvin Ailey. Of these, Cal Performances has now begun presenting local companies on a more regular basis.

The small, alternative dance presenters (houses with a capacity of fewer than four hundred seats) have one by one ceased presenting "seasons." They are financially limited to coproducing or copresenting, that is, waiving or discounting their space rental fees, and providing in-kind production and marketing services.

Out-of-town companies wishing to be seen in the Bay Area, for the most part, must self-produce. Local groups find themselves in the same position, with the exception of the following presenting opportunities: the Bay Area Dance Series presents ten to fifteen groups in a three-month season at Laney College in Oakland; the Furious Feet Festival is produced annually by Dance Brigade; Footwork, in San Francisco's Mission District, presents the work of two or three local choreographers during its Spring Series and Edge Festival, and provides other opportunities in its Summer Bread and Butter series; the Ethnic Dance Festival produced by City Celebration showcases up to twenty-three ethnic dance companies over two weekends at the Palace of Fine Arts in San Francisco; the African Music and Dance Festival presents six African dance companies during three multiple-bill evenings at Calvin Simmons The-ater in Oakland; and the Pacific Asian Performing Arts Festival presents six or more companies whose work is grounded in Pacific Rim cultures; and The-ater Artaud's Summer Dance Project runs from mid-July through early Sep-tember featuring works by local contemporary choreographers and perfor-mance artists.

It is important to note that there is a wealth of supporting service organiza-tions to call on for help ranging from general information to health and per-formance liability insurance; fiscal agency; discounted equipment rentals, legal counsel, and management assistance; small grant programs; and perfor- mance opportunities.

Dance Bay Area can provide referrals and assistance in all these areas. Its monthly newsletter, *In Dance,* keeps members informed about dance perfor- mances, funding, and other useful resources.

West Coast
Elizabeth Zimmer

New York may no longer be the mecca for performers that it was twenty years ago, but to paraphrase an old saying, it's still way ahead of whatever's in second place. The structures that draw artists to the Big Apple simply do not exist in anything like equivalent strength elsewhere in the country, and people planning to relocate, tour, or simply stay put outside Manhattan need to do their homework.

The differences in scope and strength among the various West Coast dance centers are enormous. San Francisco, a city less than half the size of Los Angeles, has easily twice as much dance, more presenters, reasonably sensi- tive media, and a sophisticated dance service organization with a genuinely useful and attractive monthly newspaper—in short, a serious and entrenched dance culture that is beginning to reverberate nationally.

Los Angeles, the country's second-largest city in the most populous state, anchors a county with a population of about six million. Covering 4,069 square miles, the county is almost two-thirds the size of Kuwait. Negotiating this vast expanse, especially if your destinations are more than one a day, requires lots of driving. People nest in their segregated neighborhoods or crawl the roads in individual tin boxes. Most dance artists must work de- manding jobs to support a car, fuel, and insurance as well as the other neces- sities that keep them alive.

Finding time in a day to take a dance class, gather with colleagues and create, or even attend concerts is a struggle that dance generally loses.

Whispers of publicity about regional performance are drowned out by the hugely financed roar of the film industry. Except by a few practitioners and a couple of critics, new local choreography is neglected. The local alternative paper, the *LA Weekly,* has no regular dance writer; its editors don't feel the community's productions brook attention. The *Los Angeles Times,* which bills itself as the largest metropolitan daily paper in the United States, also ignores local dance and performance art; to the city's journalistic power structure, America's most important choreographer is Paula Abdul.

At the tip of a peninsula four hundred miles north, San Francisco's forty-nine square miles are crisscrossed by an efficient network of public transportation. It's possible to get around on foot or to hop a bus; rapid transit bridges the water to nearby cities. It appears to this frequent visitor that, in San Francisco, the best local dance emerges from, and speaks for, the tight communities, charting the gritty experience of living in a world under siege from AIDS, from urban poverty, from the earth's own unstable crust. There is still the legendary California sunlight, but Bay Area dancers clearly understand the importance of a finely tuned physical being and a sharp intelligence. They also grasp the utility of well-promoted annual series, of awards programs, of sophisticated lobbying efforts.

The matter of infrastructure is clearly a major issue. Sad as it may seem, choreographic talent and technical brilliance are not enough to sustain a dance career in the nineties. Critical to survival are the institutions that are the root structure for the artist: the state and city funders, the nonprofit arts managers, the presenters, publicists, and entrepreneurs. I find myself wondering whether, if you could clone presenters like David White of Dance Theater Workshop and Mark Russell of P.S. 122, they'd be able to set up in Los Angeles operations paralleling their own in New York and what effect that would have on the generally limp local situation.

Several West Coast cities benefit from healthy, working infrastructures. San Francisco's is centered around Dance Bay Area and the gorgeous facilities of the San Francisco Ballet. Seattle, a much smaller city, hosts the Pacific Northwest Ballet, a strong alternative presenter at On the Boards, and several innovative choreographers who genuinely like the town.

San Diego, not often renowned as an arts center, in fact has a sophisticated gallery and presenting operation at SUSHI as well as a local dance alliance; it has a ballet company of its own and serious modern dancers attempting to put down roots [like the relocated John Malashock, formerly of Twyla Tharp Dance; see the article following this one].

Mention Los Angeles to dance professionals across the country, and they immediately ask about the Dance Gallery. Widely touted for almost fifteen years, with plans drawn up and a site chosen, this lifelong dream of Bella Lewitzky's is at the moment a ghost institution. A skeleton staff in a downtown office valiantly works at fund-raising and organizes presentations ranging from concerts by William Forsythe's Frankfurt Ballet (which, despite packed houses, managed to lose money) to a quite excellent informal series of Sunday afternoon events that offer dancing, refreshments, and performer-audience interaction. But the Dance Gallery has not become the center that local citizens have hoped for. Its Guild, formed to encourage generous donors through offers of sociable interactions with dance-world luminaries, doesn't exactly "get down" with local artists, and the entire undertaking yields little in the way of direct day-to-day impact.

The Dance Resource Center, a service organization recently emerged from the bankrupt rubble of the Los Angeles Area Dance Alliance, makes its headquarters at the Dance Gallery's office, but it is understaffed, underfunded (with perhaps a tenth the resources of its sister organization in San Francisco), and unsure of its mandate. It desktop publishes a wan bimonthly newsletter and holds occasional poorly attended meetings, but without a strong body of artists and managers the scene remains relentlessly amateur.

Los Angeles dance is mired in the fifties. If styles of dance are bound up with styles of living, and I'm coming to think that they are, then it's important to remember that in Southern California the living is easy, sunny, motorized. Movement lacks urgency and irony. The choreography meanders, taking its sweet time to get to elusive, trite, or obvious points. Stage pictures are often pretty but unresonant.

Divisions are less sharp here between "downtown" and "mainstream" choreographers, even as the landscape is sprawling and diffuse. People who would be "mainstream" if they had the drive, the money, or the managerial resources share programs with experimenters; the result, too often, is confused audiences.

Rumor has it that San Francisco built its opera house before it paved its streets, and serious devotion to the living arts is evident everywhere. Even in dank, drizzly weather, audiences find their way to remote industrial districts where rents are low and spaces huge; Los Angeles dancegoers worry about where they'll park the Mercedes, and too often just stay home.

The Los Angeles scene consists primarily of people who grow up here, go to university here, graduate, and start performing. For the most part, they do not expose themselves to contemporary developments elsewhere in the country, and local presenters offer little help in this regard. Leading-edge dancers from the East Coast often play San Diego, Santa Barbara, and San Francisco, skipping LA entirely; in two years we have been skirted by Susan Marshall and Steven Petronio, to name only two. Even when artists do show up, unsophisticated publicists too frequently fail to mobilize audiences; Bebe Miller's local debut, in 1989, was painfully underattended.

It's hard to find good classes, and too few dancers take them. The result is a dilution of technical standards that only compounds the conceptual emptiness. I used to take a ballet class, taught by an alumna of the Ballet Russes, into which several students—mostly affluent matrons in Beverly Hills—insisted on bringing their large dogs.

Even when it is stridently political and attempts to speak from a community base, Southern California performance art verges on the cute. Protest demonstrations targeted at the NEA and other agents of censorship draw a small, ragtag band with little skill at garnering media attention.

Highways, a gallery for new performance and visual works by artists and a center for intercultural collaboration, was founded in May 1989 by Tim Miller and Linda Frye Burnham. They've had a startling success, aiming their almost-nightly programming primarily at the region's gay, lesbian, black, and Latino arts constituencies. "We've found that our audience is far more interested in local artists than in those from out of town. . . . This means, unfortunately, that Highways must turn down most out-of-town proposals because, at this point, we rely so heavily on ticket sales to stay alive," noted the directors in a 1991 newsletter. Although Santa Monica is twenty miles from downtown Los Angeles, it is more multicultural than neighboring West LA, and Highways draws a diverse crowd; the performing space is small, more suited to solo or duet work than to ensemble dancing. Highways is part of the 18th Street Arts Complex, which also contains the offices of *High Performance* magazine and several nonprofit arts and video groups. It's the closest thing to an arts community to be found in the region, and greatly welcome.

California, it should be said, has one of the worst records in the country for funding the arts. Economic instability leaves even new, well-endowed municipal programs facing lean times. And LA has specifically announced that its funding mandate will favor representatives of traditionally underserved communities. The city receives only about 5 percent of the federal dance funding made available to New York.

The bottom line is, dancers go where they can work. The jazz and commercial dance scene is quite lively here, fed by the demand from MTV and similar programming. But unless and until a serious contemporary engine gets fired up, new dance in Southern California will remain vestigial. LA is now mainly a jumping-off point for athletic performers catapulting toward the New York City or San Francisco Ballets and an egocentric playground for refugees from clubs.

San Diego
John Malashock

In 1984, I left New York for all the right reasons and moved back to San Diego for all the wrong reasons.

Ten solid years of performing, and exhausted. Five good and hard years with Twyla Tharp. Touring more and more each year. My last year with the company I was on the road almost six months, with a wife and son left behind. New York was losing its charm, especially as a place to raise a child. I felt the need to be in more humane surroundings. More important, when I left New York at age twenty-nine, I thought I was done with dance.

We moved back to San Diego, where I grew up. I thought it would be good to go "back home." Duncan could have his grandparents. Nina and I could have a more "normal" life. I would take up some other line of work.

I spent two years beating my head against that fantasy. First of all, moving back to where our parents lived required some major, and often painful, readjustments. Then, working in a field that just wasn't right for me provided some unbelievable obstacles. Dancers and briefcases just don't mix.

You learn a lot when you deny yourself the things that are most elemental to your being. Dance came back to me with a vengeance. In an incredibly short time I went from dabbling in the studio to operating a full-time, year-round professional company.

In San Diego? Well, let's talk about this regional thing. Though San Diego's arts audience appreciates high-caliber work, like many regional audiences it still buys into the "if it's from New York, it's better" attitude. The critics, on the other hand, are hungry for good, locally produced work. Not many people know that San Diego is the sixth-largest city in the country—that's a lot of people to try to reach.

It has been somewhat ideal for me here. Certainly it helps that I fit into the "hometown boy makes good and returns" role; and because San Diego has been known as a place that talented dancers *more often leave* than gravitate to, it certainly turned a few heads when I moved back. The dance writers in the region were eager to play up a new professional game in town, and, of course, the fact that I had worked with Tharp made it easier for me to attract good dancers.

All that said, there's still nothing easy about forging a new path in the dance world. Every plus here has a minus. There are not enough trained dancers. San Diego is a hard town in which to raise money. It's harder to get the New York dance mafia to sit up and take notice of what's happening here.

Yet, the truth is, I can't imagine trying to have a dance company in New York these days. I'm not saying that everyone should get out of New York, but rather that I've appreciated being in a supportive working atmosphere and want dancers to know that there are serious artists and opportunities elsewhere. When someone has the need to work, and work hard, they will do it anywhere. Even in San Diego.

APPENDIX   MANY PLACES, MANY DREAMS

Addresses and phone numbers for the following resources may be found in the alphabetized Directory at the end of the book.

Dance (and Related Performance) Service Organizations

African American Arts Alliance of Chicago
Alabama Dance Council
Alliance of Resident Theatres/New York
Allied Arts Council of Southern Nevada
American Dance Guild (New York)
Artists Foundation (Boston)
Artist Trust (Seattle)
Artreach-Dallas, Inc.
Arts & Humanities Council of Florence (Omaha, NE)
Arts/Boston
Arts Council of New Orleans
Arts Extension Service (Amherst, MA)
Association of Hispanic Arts (New York)
Association of Independent Video & Filmmakers (New York)
Austin Federation of Musicians
Bloomington Area Arts Council
Boston Dance Alliance
Bronx Council on the Arts (New York, NY)
BACA/Brooklyn Arts and Culture Association (New York, NY)
Center for Contemporary Arts (CCA) (Santa Fe, NM)
Chicago Artists Coalition
Chicago Dance Coalition
City of Raleigh Arts Commission
Contemporary Art Center
Dallas Dance Council
Dallas Federation of Musicians
Dance Alliance—Capital Saratoga Region
Dance Bay Area (San Francisco, CA)
DanceCleveland
Dance Council of Central Pennsylvania
Dance Giant Steps (Brooklyn, NY)
Dance Resource Center (Los Angeles)
Dance St. Louis
Dance Services Network (Hartford, CT)
Dance Theater Workshop (New York, NY)
Dance Umbrella Boston, Inc.
Dance Umbrella, Inc. (Austin)
Dansource (A national clearing house for choreographers, consultants, designers, per-
formers, scenery rentals, and other services for the performing arts)

Diverseworks (Houston)
Downriver Council for the Arts (DCA) (Wyandotte, MI)
Downtown Art Co. (New York, NY)
The Field (New York, NY)
Florida Dance Association
Greater Columbus (Ohio) Arts Council
Greater Louisville Fund for the Arts, Kentucky
Kuumba House (Houston, TX)
League of Chicago Theaters
Los Angeles Contemporary Exhibitions (LACE)
Lower Manhattan Cultural Council (New York, NY)
Mayor's Council on the Arts (Burlington, VT)
Memphis Black Art Alliance
Metropolitan Arts Commission (Portland, OR)
Metropolitan Arts Council (Omaha, NE)
Metropolitan Dance Association (Washington, DC)
Mid-America Arts Alliance (Arkansas, Kansas, Missouri, Nebraska, Oklahoma, Texas)
Mid-Atlantic Arts Foundation (Delaware, DC, Maryland, New Jersey, New York, Pennsylvania, Virginia, West Virginia)
Milwaukee Artist Foundation
Movement Research (New York, NY)
New York Foundation for the Arts
OhioDance
Pentacle (New York, NY)
Performing Arts Resources, Inc. (New York, NY) (Membership or per-service fee. Job referral service for technical and administrative assistance, consultation, and resource library. Also conducts seminar series and provides information on dance floor construction.)
Philadelphia Dance Alliance
Pittsburgh Dance Council
Queens Council on the Arts (New York, NY)
Santa Barbara Dance Alliance
Santa Fe Council for the Arts
Staten Island Council on the Arts
Texas Arts Council
Texas Composers Forum
United Arts (St. Paul, MN)
Washington (DC) Performing Arts Society
Wisconsin Dance Council

Publications

Blasted Allegories. An anthology of fictional and critical writings by contemporary artists.

The Graywolf Annual Five: Multi Cultural Literacy, Opening the American Mind. Thirteen essays toward a broader, more inclusive vision of U.S. culture.

Out There: Marginalization and Contemporary Cultures.

The Predicament of Culture: Twentieth-Century Ethnography, Literature, and Art. An ethnography that explores the boundaries of what is termed a "culture"; an important voice in the emerging conversation between anthropology, cultural criticism, and literary theory.

Reimaging America: The Arts of Social Change.

The Signifying Monkey. A critical approach to African-American literature through an examination of black vernacular tradition and history in Africa, Latin America, and the Caribbean.

DIRECTORY

The Directory is a listing of contact information for the organizations referred to in the text and in each chapter's Appendix as well as bibliographic or ordering information for the publications mentioned.

Acadia Scenic, Inc.
130 Bay St.
P.O. Box 197
Jersey City, NJ 07303

"Access to Affordable Health Care."
Available from Artist Trust
(see below). Free.

Accountants for the Public Interest
1012 14th St., Suite 906
Washington, DC 20005
202/347-1668

Accountants for the Public
Interest/Support Center of New York
36 W. 44th St., Rm. #1208
New York, NY 10036
212/302-6940

Actors' Equity Association (AEA, Equity)
165 W. 46th St., 15th Fl.
New York, NY 10036
212/869-8530

ACT-UP (AIDS Coalition to Unleash
Power)/Boston
P.O. Box 483
Kendall Square Station
Cambridge, MA 02142

ACT-UP (AIDS Coalition to Unleash
Power)/Chicago
P.O. Box 579002, Suite 275
Chicago, IL 60613
312/509-6802

ACT-UP (AIDS Coalition to Unleash
Power)/Los Angeles
P.O. Box 26601
Los Angeles, CA 90026
213/669-7301

ACT-UP (AIDS Coalition to Unleash
Power)/Miami
c/o Body Positive
187 N.E. 36th St.
Miami, FL 33137
305/787-1131

ACT-UP (AIDS Coalition to Unleash
Power)/Minnesota
P.O. Box 50201
Loring Park Station
Minneapolis, MN 55405

ACT-UP (AIDS Coalition to Unleash
Power)/New York
135 W. 29th St., 10th Fl.
New York, NY 10001
212/564-2437

ACT-UP (AIDS Coalition to Unleash
Power)/San Francisco
2300 Market St., Suite 68
San Francisco, CA 94114
415/563-0724

Adwar Video
2370 Merrick Road
Belmore, NY 11710
516/785-1200
Fax: 516/785-1345

AFL-CIO
Department of Professional Employees
815 16th St. N.W.
Washington, DC 20006
202/223-4446

African American Museum of Fine Arts
3025 Fir Street, Suite 27
San Diego, CA 92102
619/696-7799

African American Arts Alliance of
Chicago
1809 E. 71st St.
Chicago, IL 60649
312/288-5100

African American Museum of Fine Arts
4901 Morena Blvd., Suite 125
San Diego, CA 92117
619/27-AAMFA

Agora de la Danse
840 Cherner
Montreal, Quebec H2L 1H4
514/525-7575
Fax: 514/525-6632

AIDS Action Committee
131 Clarendon St.
Boston, MA 02116
617/437-6200
800/235-2331

AIDS Foundation of Chicago
1332 North Halstead St., Suite 303
Chicago, IL 60622
312/642-5454

AIDS Information Hotline
U.S. Department of Health & Human
Services
Public Health Service
800/342-AIDS (Hotline)

AIDS Project LA
6721 Romaine St.
Los Angeles, CA 90038
213/962-1600
800/922-2437

Alabama Dance Council
2716 Cherokee Road
Birmingham, AL 35216

Alabama State Council on the Arts and
Humanities
Division of Cultural Affairs
One Dexter Ave.
Montgomery, AL 36130
205/242-4076

Alaska Sports Medicine Clinic
255 E. Fireweed
Anchorage, AK 99503
907/276-7277

Alaska State Council on the Arts and
Humanities
411 W. Fourth Ave., #1E
Anchorage, AK 99501-2343
907/279-1558

Alcone Co., Inc.
5-49 49th Ave. (5th St.–Vernon)
Long Island City, NY 11101
718/361-8373

Alliance for Arts Education (AAE)
Education Department
Kennedy Center for the Performing Arts
Washington, DC 20566
202/416-8800

Alliance for the Arts
330 W. 42nd St., Suite 1701
New York, NY 10036
212/947-6340

Alliance of New York State Arts Councils
1002 Breunig Rd.
Steward Int'l Airport
New Windsor, NY 12553
914/564-6462

Alliance of Resident Theatres/New York
(ART/NY)
131 Varick St., #904
New York, NY 10013
212/989-4880; 212/989-5257

Allied Arts Council of Southern Nevada
3750 South Maryland Parkway
Las Vegas, NV 89119
702/731-5419

Altmann Stage Lighting and Rentals
57 Alexander St.

Yonkers, NY 10701
212/569-7777; 914/476-7987

Alverno College: Alverno Presents
P.O. Box 344922
3401 South 39th St.
Milwaukee, WI 53234-3922
414/382-6150
Fax: 414/382-6354

American Arts Alliance (AAA)
1319 F St. N.W., #307
Washington, DC 20004
202/737-1727

American Association of Museums
1225 Eye St. N.W., Suite 200
Washington, DC 20005
202/289-1818

American Association of University
Professors (AAUP)
1012 14th St. N.W., # 500
Washington, DC 20005
800/424-2973

American Civil Liberties Union
132 W. 43rd St.
New York, NY 10036
212/944-9800

American Council for the Arts (ACA)
1 East 53rd St.
New York, NY 10022
212/223-2787
800/232-2789 (Information Hotline)

American Council of Learned Societies
(ACLS)
228 E. 45th St.
New York, NY 10017
212/697-1505

American Dance Festival
P.O. Box 6097, College Station
Durham, NC 27708
919/684-6402
1697 Broadway, Suite 1201
New York, NY 10019
212/586-1925

American Dance Guild
33 W. 21st St.

New York, NY 10010
212/627-3790

American Federation of Musicians
(AF of M)
1501 Broadway
New York, NY 10036
212/869-1330

American Federation of Television and
Radio Artists (AFTRA)
260 Madison Ave.
New York, NY 10016
212/532-0800

American Foundation for AIDS Research
(AMFAR)
1515 Broadway
New York, NY 10036
212/719-0033

American Guild of Musical Artists
(AGMA)
1727 Broadway
New York, NY 10019-5284
212/265-3687

American Guild of Variety Artists (AGVA)
184 Fifth Ave.
New York, NY 10010
212/675-1003

American Harlequin Corp.
311 West Burbank Blvd.
Burbank, CA 91505
800/642-6440 or 818/846-5555
Fax: 818/846-8888
also
406 Montchanin Rd.
Box 300
Montchanin, DE 19710
215/388-0666
Fax: 215/388-0555

American Music Center
30 W. 26th St., #1001
New York, NY 10010
212/366-5260

American Samoa Council on Culture,
Arts, and Humanities
Office of the Governor
P.O. Box 1540

Pago, American Samoa 96799
9011-684-633-5613

American Society of Composers,
Authors, & Publishers (ASCAP)
One Lincoln Plaza
New York, NY 10023
212/595-3050

American Symphony Orchestra League
(ASOL)
777 14th St. N.W., Suite 500
Washington, DC 20005
202/628-0099

American Theater. Available from
Theater Communications Group
(see below).

American Woman's Economic
Development Corp. (AWED)
641 Lexington Ave., 9th Fl.
New York, NY 10022
212/692-9100

Angel Sound
1600 Broadway, Rm. 310
New York, NY 10019
212/757-1401

"Annual Report of the NEA."
Washington, DC:
National Endowment for the Arts (see
below).

Ardani-Moscow Theater Agency
Tverskkoj Blvd. 23
103009 Moscow
Russia
(7) (095) 203-42-21
Fax: (7) (095) 213-87-58

Arizona AIDS Information Line,
see Lesbian & Gay Community
Switchboard

Arizona Commission on the Arts
417 West Roosevelt
Phoenix, AZ 85003
602/255-5884; 602/255-5882

Arkansas Arts Council
The Heritage Center, Suite 200
255 East Markham St.

Little Rock, AR 72201
501/324-9337

Artcelona and New African Connection
Placa Regomir 3
08002 Barcelona
Spain
34-3-315-2698

Artists Career Planning Service
7 E. 30th St., #3
New York, NY 10016
212/460-8163

Artists Community Federal Credit Union
(ACFCU)
155 Avenue of the Americas
New York, NY 10013
212/366-5669

Artists Foundation
8 Park Plaza
Boston, MA 02116
617/227-2787

*The Artist's Tax Guide and Financial
Planner.* New York: Lyons & Burford.
Available from Volunteer Lawyers for the
Arts (see below). $16.95.

Artist Trust
512 Jones Building
1331 3rd Ave., Rm. 517
Seattle, WA 98101
206/467-8734

Artist Trust
1402 Third Ave., Suite 1415
Seattle, WA 98101
206/467-8734

Art Law Line, see Volunteer Lawyers
for the Arts (New York)

Artreach-Dallas, Inc.
P.O. Box 191266
Dallas, TX 75219
214/526-3513

Arts Action Research (formerly FEDAPT)
205 S. Patrick St.
Alexandria, VA 22314
703/739-2722

Arts Administration, Graduate Program
in Teachers College
Columbia University
Box 78
New York, NY 10027
212/678-3271; 212/678-3268

Arts America Program, see U.S.
Information Agency

Arts and Business Council, Inc.
25 W. 45th St., Suite 707
New York, NY 10036
212/819-9287

*The Arts and 504. Government Printing
Office, Superintendent of Documents,*
Washington, DC 20402. Specify stock
number 036-000-00047-3. $3.75.

Arts & Humanities Council of Florence
P.O. Box 12003
Florence Station
Omaha, NE 68112
402/455-6871

Arts/Boston
100 Boylston St., Suite 735
Boston, MA 02116
617/423-4454

Arts Coalition of Independent Democrats
P.O. Box 119
New York, NY 10113-0019
212/691-6500; 212/732-1201

Arts Council of New Orleans
821 Gravier St., Suite 600
New Orleans, LA 70112
504/523-1465

ArtSearch. Available from Theater
Communications Group (see below).

Arts Extension Service
Division of Continuing Education
University of Massachusetts
Amherst, MA 01003
413/545-2360

Arts Family Association
14715 Mesa Vista Dr.
Houston, TX 77083

713/879-6657
800/736-5787

Arts Interactive Multi Media (AIM)
152 Mercer St.
New York, NY 10012
212/925-7771

Arts International
809 United Nations Plaza
New York, NY 10017
212/984-5370
Fax: 212/984-5574

Arts Medicine Center
1721 Pine St.
Philadelphia, PA 19103
215/955-8300

Arts Midwest
528 Hennepin Ave., Suite 310
Minneapolis, MN 55403
612/341-0755
(Illinois, Indiana, Iowa, Michigan,
Minnesota, North Dakota, Ohio, South
Dakota, Wisconsin.)

Arts Resource Consortium Library
1285 Ave. of the Americas, 3rd Fl.
New York, NY 10019
212/245-4510
Fax: 212/245-4514

Artswire
c/o New York Foundation for the Arts
5 Beekman, #600
New York, NY 10038
212/233-3900
also
811 First Ave., #403
Seattle, WA 98104
206/343-0769

Asian Cultural Council
280 Madison Ave.
New York, NY 10016
212/684-5450
Fax: 212/684-8075

Asia Society
725 Park Ave.
New York, NY 10021

212/288-6400
Fax: 212/517-8315

Asociacion de Musicos Latino
Americanos
P.O. Box 502 96
Philadelphia, PA 19132
215/727-5428

Associated Grantmakers of
Massachusetts
294 Washington St., Suite 840
Boston, MA 02108
617/426-2606

The Association of American Cultures
(TAAC)
1225 19th St. N.W., #340
Washington, DC 20036-2411
202/463-8222

Association of Hispanic Arts, Inc. (AHA)
173 E. 116th St.
New York, NY 10029
212/860-5445

Association of Independent Video and
Filmmakers (AIVF)
625 Broadway, 9th Fl.
New York, NY 10012
212/473-3400

Association of Performing Arts
Presenters
1112 16th St. N.W., #620
Washington, DC 20036
202/833-2787

Association of Theatrical Press Agents
and Managers (ATPAM)
165 W. 46th St.
New York, NY 10036
212/719-3666

AT&T Foundation
550 Madison Ave.
New York, NY 10022-3297
212/605-6734

Audio Force
630 9th Ave., Rm. 1012
New York, NY 10036
212/262-2626

Audio Visual Workshop
333 W. 52nd St. (8th–9th)
New York, NY 10019
212/397-5020

Austin Federation of Musicians
200 Academy Dr., Suite B
Austin, TX 78704
512/440-1414

BACA/Brooklyn Arts and Culture
Association
200 Eastern Parkway
Brooklyn, NY 11238
718/783-3077

Barnard College
Office of Career Services
3009 Broadway
New York, NY 10027-6598
212/854-2033

H. Barnett Associates, Inc.
545 8th Ave., Suite 401-113
New York, NY 10018
212/279-1980

Bay Area Video Coalition (BAVC)
1111 17th St.
San Francisco, CA 94107
415/861-3282

Best Audio East, see Theatre Technology

Big Apple Lights
533 Canal St.
New York, NY 10013
212/226-0925

Black Arts Alliance
1157 Navasota St.
Austin, TX 78702
512/477-9660

Blasted Allegories. Ed. Brian Wallis. New
York: New Museum of Contemporary
Art; and Cambridge, MA: MIT Press;
800/356-0343. $16.95 paperback, $30.00
hardcover.

Bloomington Area Arts Council
202 East Sixth St.
Bloomington, IN 47408
812/334-3100

Blue Cross/Blue Shield (nonprofit
insurance company): Look in phone
book under "Blue Cross."

*Board Liability: Guide for Nonprofit
Directors.* Daniel L. Kurtz. Moyer Bell,
Ltd. Available from Volunteer Lawyers
for the Arts, New York (see below).
$12.95 Paperback.

Boston Arts Commission
Boston City Hall, Rm. 608
Boston, MA 02201
617/725-3245

Boston Dance Alliance
P.O. Box 1151
Back Bay Annex
Boston, MA 02117
617/695-0955

Box Office Management International
(BOMI)
333 E. 46th St., Suite 1B
New York, NY 10017
212/949-7350

Thomas Bramlett & Associates, Inc.
219 Grand St. (2nd–3rd)
Hoboken, NJ 07030
201/659-3565

Brett Theatrical
91 Beach Road
Bristol, RI 02809
401/274-7458

British Music Worldwide
Rhinegold Publishing Ltd.
241 Shaftesbury Avenue
London WC2H 8EH
44-71 240-5749

Broadcast Musicians, Inc. (BMI)
320 W. 57th St.
New York, NY 10019
212/586-2000

Bronx Council on the Arts
1738 Hone Ave.
Bronx, NY 10461
212/931-9500

Brooklyn Academy of Music (BAM)
30 Lafayette Ave.
Brooklyn, NY 11217
718/636-4100

Brooklyn College
Performing Arts Management
Bedford Ave. and Ave. H
Brooklyn, NY 11210
718/780-5292

Brooklyn Dance Consortium
G.P.O. Box 022503
Brooklyn, NY 11202-0052
718/797-3116

Brooklyn Museum Costumes and Textile
Department
200 Eastern Parkway and Washington
Ave.
Brooklyn, NY 11238
718/638-5000

Bryant Park
Music and Dance Tickets Booth
6 E. 43rd St., Rm. 2100
New York, NY 10017
212/382-2483

*The Buck Starts Here: Enterprise and the
Arts, a Survival Guide for Arts
Organizations.* Available from Volunteer
Lawyers for the Arts, New York (see
below). $11.95 Paperback.

Bulimia Treatment Associates
88 University Place, Suite 505
New York, NY 10003
212/989-3987

Business Committee for the Arts, Inc.
1775 Broadway, Suite 510
New York, NY 10019
212/664-0600

Business Volunteers for the
Arts/Chicago
55 E. Monroe, Suite 3705
Chicago, IL 60603
312/372-1876

Business Volunteers for the Arts/Florida
Museum Tower
150 West Flagler St., Suite 2500

Miami, FL 33130
305/789-3590

Business Volunteers for the Arts/NY
(BVA/NY)
25 W. 45th St., #707
New York, NY 10036
212/819-9361
212/819-9287 (General Information)

California Arts Council
2411 Alhambra Blvd.
Sacramento, CA 95817
916/739-3186

California Community Foundation
Funding Information Center
606 South Olive St., Suite 2400
Los Angeles, CA 90014-1526
213/413-4042

California Lawyers for the Arts
Fort Mason Center
Building C, Rm. 255
San Francisco, CA 94123
415/775-7200
315 West 9th St., Suite 1101
Los Angeles, CA 90015
213/623-8311

California Presenters
c/o Performing Arts University of
California
Riverside, CA 92521
714/787-4629

Canada Arts Presenters Association
432 Besserer St.
Ottawa, Ontario K1N 6C1
Canada
613/234-6803
Fax: 613/234-6803

Canada Council Touring Office
99 Metcalfe St.
P.O. Box 1047
Ottawa, Ontario K1P 5V8
Canada
613/598-4395
Fax: 613/598-4390

Capezio Dance Theatre Shops (see also
Dance Factory Outlet)

1655 Broadway
New York, NY 10019
212/245-2130
and
177 MacDougal St. (8th St.)
New York, NY 10011
212/477-5634

Capezio East
136 E. 61st St.
New York, NY 10021
212/758-8833

Career Transition for Dancers
1727 Broadway, 2nd Fl.
New York, NY 10019
212/581-7043

Caribbean Cultural Center
408 W. 58th St.
New York, NY 10019
212/307-7420
Fax: 212/315-1086

Carver Community Cultural Center
226 North Hackberry
San Antonio, TX 78202
210/299-7211

Center for Contemporary Arts (CCA)
291 East Barcelona Road
Santa Fe, NM 87501
also
P.O. Box 148
Santa Fe, NM 87504-0148
505/982-1338

Center for Non-Profit Management
2900 Live Oak
Dallas, TX 75204
214/826-3470

Center for Safety in the Arts (COH)
5 Beekman St., Rm. 1030
New York, NY 10038
212/227-6220

Center for Study of Anorexia and Bulimia
Institute for Contemporary
Psychotherapy
1 W. 91st St.
New York, NY 10024
212/595-3449

Centre Firearms Company
10 W. 46th St.
New York, NY 10018
212/244-4040

Centro Cultural de la Raza
2130-1 Pan American Plaza, Balboa Park
San Diego, CA 92101
619/235-6135
Fax: 619/595-0034

Chamber Music America
545 Eighth Ave.
New York, NY 10018
212/244-2772

Character Generators
152 Mercer
New York, NY 10012
212/925-7771

Chicago Artists Coalition
5 West Grand Ave.
Chicago, IL 60610
312/670-2060

Chicago Dance Coalition
67 E. Madison, Suite 2112
Chicago, IL 60603
312/419-8383

Chicago Department of Cultural Affairs
78 East Washington
Chicago, IL 60602
312/744-6630

Chicago Prop Finders Handbook.
Available through Broadway Press, 12
W. Thomas St., Box 1037, Shelter Island,
New York, NY 11964-1037. 800/869-6372.
$55.00, plus $4.80 shipping, handling,
and tax.

The Chronicle of Philanthropy (biweekly).
Chronicle of Philanthropy, 1255 23rd St.
N.W., Washington, DC 20037;
202/466-1200. $57.50 per year.

Chuck Davis/African-American Dance
Ensemble
One Saturn Court
Durham, NC 27703
919/596-0713; 919/596-2729

Circuit Network
25 Taylor St., #616
San Francisco, CA 94102
415/346-9963

Citizens for a National Health Program
15 Pearl St.
Cambridge, MA 02139
617/868-3246

City-as-School
Executive Internships Program
16 Clarkson St., Rm. 405
New York, NY 10014
212/741-1152

City University of New York
Office of Student Financial Assistance
2 Pennsylvania Plaza
New York, NY 10121
212/868-6018

Classical Performing Arts Management
7758 Ludington Place
La Jolla, CA 92037-3806
619/456-3878

Cleveland Clinic Foundation
Medical Center for the Performing Arts
9500 Euclid Ave.
Cleveland, OH 44195
216/444-3903

College Art Association (CAA)
275 Seventh Ave.
New York, NY 10001
212/691-1051

College Guide. Dance Magazine, 33 W.
60th St., New York, NY 10023;
212/245-9050

Colorado Council on the Arts and
Humanities
Grant-Humphreys Mansion
750 Pennsylvania St.
Denver, CO 80203
303/894-2617

Colorado Dance Festival
Box 356
Boulder, CO 80306
303/442-7666

Colorado Lawyers for the Arts
938 Bannock, #227
Denver, CO 80204
303/892-7122

Columbia Presbyterian HIV Clinical &
Behavioral Center
212/740-0046

Columbia Student Enterprises
Box 4535 CMR
Columbia University
New York, NY 10027
212/854-4535

Columbia University, Graduate Program
in Arts Administration, see Teachers
College

Community Action for Legal Services
335 Broadway
New York, NY 10013
212/431-7200

Comsearch: Broad Topics. New York: The
Foundation Center (see below). $55.00.

Connecticut Commission on the Arts
227 Lawrence St.
Hartford, CT 06106
203/566-4770

Connecticut Volunteer Lawyers for the
Arts
Connecticut Commission on the Arts
227 Lawrence St.
Hartford, CT 06106
203/566-4770

Consejeria de Cultura
Comunidad de Madrid
Plaza de España, 8, 3
28008 Madrid
Spain
34-1-580-2678

Consortium for Pacific Arts & Cultures
(CPAC)
2141c Atherton Road
Honolulu, HI 96822
808/946-7381
(American Samoa, Guam, Northern
Marianas.)

Contemporary Arts Center
900 Camp
P.O. Box 30498
New Orleans, LA 70190
504/523-1216
Fax: 504/528-3828

Contemporary Dance Theater, Inc.
The Dance Hall
P.O. Box 19220
Cincinnati, OH 45319
513/751-2800

Co-op America
2100 M St. N.W., Suite 403
Washington, DC 20063
800/424-2667

Cooper Square Theatre
50 E. 7th St.
New York, NY 10003
212/228-0811

Copyright Office
Library of Congress
Washington, DC 20559
202/707-9100

Corporate Philanthropy Report (monthly).
Craig Smith, 2727 Fairview Ave. East,
Suite D, Seattle, WA 98102. $150 per year;
$128 per year for nonprofit
organizations.

Costume Collection
601 W. 26th St.
New York, NY 10001
212/989-5855
212/221-0885, Administrative Office

Costume Institute of the Metropolitan
Museum of Art
1000 Fifth Ave. and 82nd St.
New York, NY 10028
212/879-5500

Council for International Exchange of
Scholars (CIES)
3007 Tilden St. N.W., Suite 5M, Box GPOS
Washington, DC 20008-3009
202/686-4000
Fax: 202/362-3442

Council of New York Law Associates
36 W. 44th St.
New York, NY 10036
212/840-1541

Creative Costume, Inc.
330 W. 38th St.
New York, NY 10018
212/564-5552

Creative Time
66 West Broadway
New York, NY 10007
212/619-1955

CTL Electronics
116 West Broadway
New York, NY 10013
212/233-0754

Cubiculo
414 W. 51st St.
New York, NY 10019
212/265-2138

Cultural Alliance of Greater Washington
410 8th St. N.W., Suite 600
Washington, DC 20004
202/638-2406

Cultural Arts Council of Houston
1964 West Gray, Suite 224
Houston, TX 77019-4808
713/527-9330

Merce Cunningham Dance Studio
55 Bethune St.
New York, NY 10014
212/691-9751

Dallas Dance Council
P.O. Box 740511
Dallas, TX 75374-0511
214/348-4116; 214/373-7753

Dallas Federation of Musicians
11029 Shady Trail, Suite 114
Dallas, TX 75229
214/358-4447

Dallas Alliance—Capital Saratoga Region
417 Eastline Road
Ballston Spa, NY 12020
518/885-7838

Dance and Theatre Collection of the New
York Public Library, see Library for the
Performing Arts

Dance Bay Area
44 Page St., Suite 604 C
San Francisco, CA 94102
415/252-6240

Dance Brew, Inc.
P.O. Box 622
Fort George Station
New York, NY 10040
212/724-0288

Dance Center of Columbia College
4730 North Sheridan Road
Chicago, IL 60640
312/271-7804
Fax: 312/271-7046

DanceCleveland
1148 Euclid Ave., #311
Cleveland, OH 44115
216/861-2213

Dance Council of Central Pennsylvania
821 Farmingdale Road
Lancaster, PA 17601
717/393-7395

Dance Factory Outlet (see also Capezio
Dance Theatre Shops)
One Campus Road
Totowa, NJ 07512
201/790-9768

Dance Giant Steps
1040 Park Pl., #C5
Brooklyn, NY 11213
718/773-3046

*Dance Magazine Annual Performing Arts
Directory,* see *Stern's Performing Arts
Directory*

Dance Notation Bureau
31 W. 21st St., 3rd Fl.
New York, NY 10010
212/807-7899

Dance Place
3225 8th St. N.E.

Washington, DC 20017
202/269-1600

Dance Resource Center
P.O. Box 6299
Los Angeles, CA 90055
213/668-2755

Dancer's Collective of Atlanta, Inc.
4279 Roswell Road, Suite 604-335
Atlanta, GA 30342
404/233-7600

Dancers' Studio West
1892 14A St., S.E.
Calgary, Alberta T2G 4Z3
Canada
403/264-2689
Fax: 403/269-7320

Dance St. Louis
634 North Grand St., #1102
St. Louis, MO 63103
314/534-5000

Dance Services Network
30 North Arbor St.
Hartford, CT 06106
203/233-8012

Dance Theater Workshop
219 W. 19th St.
New York, NY 10011-4079
212/691-6500
Fax: 212/633-1974

Dance Umbrella (United Kingdom)
c/o Riverside Studios
Crisp Road
London W6 9RL
United Kingdom
44-81-741-4040
Fax: 44-81-846-9039

Dance Umbrella Boston, Inc.
380 Green St.
Cambridge, MA 02139
617/492-7578
Fax: 617/354-1603

Dance Umbrella, Inc. (Austin)
P.O. Box 1352
Austin, TX 78767
512/477-1064; 512/322-0227

Dancer's Collective of Atlanta, Inc.
4279 Roswell Road, Suite 102-335
Atlanta, GA 30342
404/233-7600
Fax: 404/255-4465

Dance/USA
777 14th St. N.W., #540
Washington, DC 20009
202/628-0144

Danceworks
1087 Queen St. West, 4th Fl.
Toronto, Ontario M6J 1H3
416/534-1523
Fax: 416/531-1922

Dancing in the Streets
131 Varick St., Rm. 901
New York, NY 10013
212/989-6830

Danskin
111 W. 40th St., 18th Fl.
New York, NY 10018
212/764-4630

Dansource
P.O. Box 15038
Dallas, TX 75201
214/520-7419

Danspace Project
St. Mark's Church in-the-Bowery
131 E. Tenth Street
New York, NY 10003
212/674-8112

D.C. Commission on the Arts and
Humanities
410 8th St. N.W., 5th Fl.
Washington, DC 20004
202/724-5613

Dealing with Healing. New York: The
Field (see below).

Delaware State Arts Council
State Office Building
820 North French St.
Wilmington, DE 19801
302/577-3540

Design Laboratory
Fashion Institute of Technology
227 W. 27th St.
New York, NY 10001
212/760-7708

District of Columbia Commission on the
Arts and Humanities
410 Eighth St. N.W., 2nd Fl., Suite 500
Washington, DC 20004
202/724-5613

DiverseWorks
1117 East Freeway
Houston, TX 77002
713/224-7960

Dixon Place
258 Bowery
New York, NY 10012
212/219-3088

Doctors for Artists
105 W. 78th St.
New York, NY 10024
212/496-5172

*Doing it Right in LA: Self-Producing for the
Performing Artist.* LA Fringe Festival/
CARS, 1653 18th St., #1, Santa Monica,
CA 90404, 213/315-9444. $12.00.

Donors Forum
55 West Jackson Blvd.
Chicago, IL 60604
312/431-0260

Downriver Council for the Arts (DCA)
2630 Biddle
Wyandotte, MI 48192
313/281-2787

Downtown Art Co.
280 Broadway, Rm. 412
New York, NY 10007
212/732-1201

Durham Arts Council, Inc.
120 Morris St.
Durham, NC 27701
919/560-2716

Eagle Lace Dying
315 W. 35th St., 8th Fl.

New York, NY 10001
212/947-2712

Eaves & Brooks Costume Company
21-07 41st Ave.
Long Island City, NY 11101
212/729-1010

Eclectic Encore Studio
620 W. 26th St., 4th Fl.
New York, NY 10001
212/645-8880

Economic Development Administration
c/o U.S. Dept. of Commerce
14th and Constitution Ave. N.W.,
Rm. 7810
Washington, DC 20230
202/377-2000, ext. 5113

Eden, David
155 Henry St., #9G
Brooklyn, NY 11201
212/629-0500
Fax: 212/269-0508

Eden's Expressway
537 Broadway
New York, NY 10012
212/925-0880

El Centro Su Teatro
4725 High Street
Denver, CO 80216
303/296-0219

Emanu-El Midtown YW-YMHA
344 E. 14th St.
New York, NY 10003
212/674-7200

Empire Blue Cross/Blue Shield
622 Third Ave.
New York, NY 10017
212/476-1000

*Employers Guide to Unemployment
Insurance.* New York State Dept. of Labor,
Office of Communications, W. Averell
Harriman State Office Building Campus,
Rm. 511, Albany, NY 12240-0012;
518/457-5519.

Entertainment Arts and Sports Law
Section
The Florida Bar
600 Apalachee Parkway
Tallahassee, FL 32399-2300
904/222-5286

Ethnic Folk Arts Center
Performance Space:
179 Varick St.
New York, NY 10014
212/691-9510
Office:
131 Varick St., Rm. 907
New York, NY 10013
212/620-4083

Eulipions, Inc.
2715 Welton Street
Denver, CO 80205
303/295-6814

Events Clearinghouse Calendar
(monthly). New York: Alliance for the
Arts (see above).

Evolving Arts Dancespace
622 Broadway
New York, NY 10012
212/777-8067

Excellent Floors
191 Spring St.
New York, NY 10012
212/226-5790

Extrapolating Studio
Performance Space:
220 E. Fourth St.
New York, NY 10009
212/533-9585
Mailing address:
c/o Judy Trupin
143 Ave. B, #12 A
New York, NY 10009

FEDAPT, see Arts Action Research

Federal Council on the Arts and
Humanities
1 McPherson Sq.
Washington, DC 20005
202/456-6200

Federation of State Humanities Councils
1012 14th St. N.W., #1007
Washington, DC 20005
202/393-5400

Festival de Theatre des Ameriques
C.P. 7, Succursale E.
Montreal, Quebec H2T 3A5
Canada
514/842-0704
Fax: 514/842-3795

Fiber Built Cases, Inc.
601 W. 26th St. (11th–12th)
New York, NY 10001
212/675-5820
Fax: 212/691-5935

Fibrecase and Novelty Company, Inc.
708 Broadway (4th–Waverly)
New York, NY 10003
212/254-6060; 212/477-2729

The Field
131 Varick St., #909
New York, NY 10013
212/691-6969

Field Studios, Inc.
232 6th Ave.
Brooklyn, NY 11215
718/855-4431

Film Video Arts
817 Broadway (12th St.), 2nd Fl.
New York, NY 10003
212/673-9363

Firehall Arts Centre
280 East Cordova St.
Vancouver, British Columbia V6A 1L3
Canada
604/689-0691
Fax: 604/682-6710

Florida, Arts Council of
Division of Cultural Affairs
Department of State
The Capitol
Tallahassee, FL 32399-0250
904/487-2980

Florida Dance Association
Miami-Dade Community College

Wolfson Campus
300 N.E. Second Ave., Suite 1412
Miami, FL 33132
305/347-3413

Flynn Theatre for the Performing Arts, Ltd.
153 Main Street
Burlington, VT 05401
802/863-8778
Fax: 802/863-8776

Michel Fokine Fund
New York Community Trust
2 Park Ave., 24th Fl.
New York, NY 10016
212/686-1000

Food Stamp Program: Look in telephone book under (State) Social Services Department.

Foundation Center, referrals
800/424-9836

Foundation Center
312 Sutter St., Rm. 312
San Francisco, CA 94108
415/397-0903

Foundation Center
1001 Connecticut Ave. N.W., Suite 934
Washington, DC 20036
202/331-1401

Foundation Center
79 Fifth Ave., 8th Fl.
New York, NY 10003-3050
212/620-4230

The Foundation Directory (annual). New York: The Foundation Center (see above). $140 Paperback; $165 Hardcover.

Foundation Fundamentals: A Guide for Grant Seekers. Ed. Judith B. Margolin. New York: The Foundation Center (see above). $19.95.

Foundation Giving Watch, see *Taft Foundation Reporter*

Foundation Grants Index Quarterly. New York: The Foundation Center (see above). $60.00 per year.

Foundation Grants to Individuals. New York: The Foundation Center (see above). $40.00.

Foundations News (a bimonthly magazine). The Council on Foundations, 1828 L St. N.W., Washington, DC 20036; 202/466-6512. $5.00 per issue; $29.50 per year.

14th Street Stage Lighting
869 Washington St. (near 14th St.)
New York, NY 10014
212/645-5491

Freed of London Ltd.
922 W. 58th St. (7th Ave.)
New York, NY 10019
212/489-1055

Fund for the City of New York
121 Ave. of the Americas,
Sixth Floor
New York, NY 10013
212/925-6675

Fund for U.S. Artists at International Festivals and Exhibitions, see Arts International

Gay Men's Health Crisis (GMHC)
129 W. 20th St., 3rd Fl.
New York, NY 10011
212/807-6664
212/807-6655 (AIDS Hotline);
212/645-7470 (TDD for the hearing impaired)

Georgia Council for the Arts and Humanities
2082 East Exchange Pl., Suite 100
Tucker, GA 30084
404/493-5780

Georgia Volunteer Lawyers for the Arts
34 Peachtree St. N.W., #2330
Atlanta, GA 30303-1131
404/525-6046

John R. Gerardo Luggage
30 W. 31st St.
New York, NY 10001
212/695-6955

Gerritts International
R.R. #1
950 Hutchinson Rd.
Allentown, NJ 08501
609/758-9121

Get Smart/The Ad Hoc Artists Group
64 E. 4th St.
New York, NY 10003
212/732-1201

Gowanus Arts Exchange
295 Douglass St.
Brooklyn, NY 11217
718/596-5250

Grants Information Service
Dallas Public Library
1515 Young St.
Dallas, TX 75201
214/670-1468

The Graywolf Annual Five: Multi Cultural Literacy, Opening the American Mind. Ed. Rick Simonson and Scott Walker. Graywolf Press, 2402 University Ave., Suite 203, St. Paul, MN 55114; 612/641-0077. $8.95 Paperback; add $3.00 postage per order.

Greater Chicago Citizens for the Arts
P.O. Box 146237
Chicago, IL 60614
312/280-1025

Greater Columbus Arts Council
55 East State St.
Columbus, OH 43215
614/224-2606

Greater Louisville Fund for the Arts
623 West Main St.
Louisville, KY 40202
502/582-0100

Great Lakes College Association
305 W. 29th St.
New York, NY 10001
212/563-0255

The Green Book: Official Directory of the City of New York. Available at Citybooks, Rm. 2223, Municipal Building, New York, NY 10007. $8.50.

Green Mountain Consortium
P.O. Box 172
Woodstock, VT 05091
Contact: Judi Simon-Bouton
802/457-3592

GSD Productions, Inc.
P.O. Box 79
Locust Valley, NY 11560
516/671-1360

Guadalupe Cultural Arts Center
1300 Guadalupe Street
San Antonio, TX 78207
210/271-3151
Fax: 210/271-3480

Guam Council on the Arts and Humanities
Office of the Governor
P.O. Box 2950
Agana, Guam 96910
001-671-477-7413

Guia Teatral de España (biannual). The Centro de Documentacion Teatral, Calle Capitan Haya 44, 28020 Madrid, Spain. 34-1-270-51-99 (subscriptions) 34-1-270-57-49/279-32-96/279-82-27/ 279-46-86 (information)

Guidelines for Ethical Behavior. Available from National Association of Performing Arts Managers and Agents (NAPAMA) (see below).

Guide to Corporate Giving IV. Ed. Robert Porter. New York: The American Council for the Arts (see above). $25.00.

A Guide to L.A. Performing Venues. LA Fringe Festival/CARS, 1653 18th St., #1, Santa Monica, CA 90404; 213/315-9444.

Guide to the National Endowment for the Arts. Washington, DC: National Endowment for the Arts (see below).

Handbook for Employers: A Guide to Employer Rights and Responsibilities under the New York State Unemployment Insurance Law. Dept. of Labor, 1 Main St., Brooklyn, NY 11201.

Hands On
131 Varick St., Rm. 909
New York, NY 10013
212/627-4898

J. C. Hansen
423 W. 43rd St.
New York, NY 10036
212/246-8055

Harkness Center for Dance Injuries
301 E. 17th St.
New York, NY 10003
212/598-6022 or 598-6146

Harmonic Ranch
59 Franklin St.
New York, NY 10013
212/966-3141

Harvard University Theatre Collection
Wadsworth House
Cambridge, MA 02138
617/495-3650

Harvestworks, Inc., Studio PASS
596 Broadway, #602
New York, NY 10012
212/431-1130

Hawaii State Foundation on Culture and
the Arts
335 Merchant St., Rm. 202
Honolulu, HI 96813
808/548-4145

Haywood-Berk Floor Company
414 W. Broadway
New York, NY 10012
212/226-4024

Health Benefit Information
800/562-9400 (Hotline)

Health Insurance Association of America
1025 Connecticut Ave., Suite 1200
Washington, DC 20036
202/223-7780

Helena Presents (formerly Helena Film
Society)
Myrna Loy Center
15 North Ewing

Helena, MT 59601
406/443-6620

Heritage Village Arts
336 South Virginia Lee Road
Columbus, OH 43209
614/253-7261

Highways Performance Space
1651 18th St.
Santa Monica, CA 90404
213/453-1755
Fax: 213/453-4347

Home for Contemporary Theatre and
Art
61 E. 8th St., Suite 315
New York, NY 10003
212/529-9218

Hospital Audiences, Inc. (HAI)
220 W. 42nd St., 13th Fl.
New York, NY 10036
212/575-7660; 212/575-7676

*How the New York State Labor Law
Protects You.* New York State Dept. of
Labor, Office of Communications,
W. Averell Harriman State Office Building
Campus, Rm. 511, Albany, NY
12240-0012; 518/457-5519.

How to Run a Small Box Office. Kirsten
Beck. New York: Alliance of Resident
Theatres/New York (see above). $12.00;
20% discount for members of ART/NY or
DTW.

Hrab, Ondrej
Divadelni Obec Theatre Community
Valdetejnske nam 3
118 00 Prague 1 - Mala Strana
Czechoslovakia
(42) 2-539-257
Fax: 42-2-539-256

Human Resources Administration AIDS
Service Line
212/645-7070

Hunter College
Inservice Learning Program
615 Park Ave.

New York, NY 10021
212/772-4000

Idaho Commission on the Arts
304 West State St.
c/o Statehouse Mail
Boise, ID 83720
208/334-2119

Ideal Wig Co., see Playbill Cosmetics

Illinois Arts Council
State of Illinois Center
100 West Randolph St.
Suite 10-500
Chicago, IL 60601
312/814-6750

Independent Feature Project—Florida
660 Ocean Dr.
Miami, FL 33139
305/538-9478

Independent Feature Project—Midwest
30 N. Michigan Ave., Suite 508
Chicago, IL 60602
708/377-5421

Independent Feature Project—New York
132 W. 21st St., 6th Fl.
New York, NY 10011
212/243-7777

Independent Feature Project—North
1401 3rd Ave. South
Minneapolis, MN 55404
612/870-0156

Independent Feature Project—Northern
California
P.O. Box 460040
San Francisco, CA 94146
415/826-0574

Independent Feature Project—West
5550 Wilshire Blvd., Suite 204
Los Angeles, CA 90036
213/937-4379

Indiana Arts Commission
402 W. Washington St., Rm. 072
Indianapolis, IN 46204
317/232-1268

Informal European Theater Meeting
143 Boulevard Anspach
1000 Brussels
Belgium
Contact: Hilde Teuchies
32-2-514-5676
Fax: 32-2-514-9193

Inquilinos Boricuas en Acción
405 Shawmut Avenue
Boston, MA 02118
617/262-1342
Fax: 617/536-5816

Institute for Contemporary
Psychotherapy
1 W. 91st St.
New York, NY 10024
212/595-3444

Institute for Performing Artists
Postgraduate Center for Mental Health
124 E. 28th St.
New York, NY 10016
212/689-7700, ext. 290, 291; 212/889-0102

Institute of International Education (IIE)
809 United Nations Plaza
New York, NY 10017-3580
212/984-5328
Fax: 212/984-5452

Institute of Puerto Rican Culture
Apartado Postal 4184
San Juan, Puerto Rico 00905
809/723-2115

Institute of the Arts at Duke University
109 Bivins Building
Durham, NC 27708
919/684-6654
Fax: 919/684-8906

International Alliance of Theatre Stage
Employees (IATSE)
1515 Broadway, Suite 601
New York, NY 10036
212/730-1770

International Chamber of Commerce, see
U.S. Council of the International
Chamber of Commerce

International Festival Guide. Available at five centers of the European Network of Information Centers for the Performing Arts, located in Brussels, Amsterdam, Madrid, and Paris. In Belgium, contact the Vlaams Theater Institut (see below).

International Research and Exchanges Board (IREX)
126 Alexander St.
Princeton, NJ 08540-7102
609/683-9500
Fax: 609/683-1511

International Presenters and Festivals List. Contact Dance Theater Workshop (see above)

International Society of Performing Arts Administrators
6065 Pickerel Dr.
Rockford, MI 49341
616/874-6200

International Theatre Institute/US (ITI)
220 W. 42nd St., 17th Fl.,
New York, NY 10036
212/944-1490
Fax: 212/944-1506

Iowa State Arts Council
State Capitol Complex
1223 East Court Ave.
Des Moines, IA 50319
515/281-4451

Japan Society, Inc.
333 E. 47th St.
New York, NY 10017
212/832-1155
Fax: 212/755-6752

Jewish Board of Family and Children's Services
120 W. 57th St.
New York, NY 10019
212/582-9100

Jobs for Youth
1831 Second Ave.
New York, NY 10128
212/348-1800

Jomandi Productions
1444 Mayson St. N.E.
Atlanta, GA 30324
404/876-6346

Joyce Theater
175 Eighth Ave.
New York, NY 10011
212/691-9740
Fax: 212/727-3658

Junebug Productions, Inc.
1061 Camp Street #D
New Orleans, LA 70130
504/524-8257
Fax: 504/529-5403

Kansas Arts Commission
Jayhawk Towers, Suite 1004
700 Jackson
Topeka, KS 66603
913/296-3335

Kansas City Free Health Clinic
5119 East 24th St.
Kansas City, MO 64127
816/231-8895

Bob Kelly Cosmetics, Inc.
151 W. 46th St., 9th Fl.
New York, NY 10036
212/819-0030

Kentucky Arts Council
31 Fountain Place
Frankfort, KY 40601
502/564-3757

The Kitchen
512 W. 19th St.
New York, NY 10011
212/255-5793
Fax: 212/645-4258

The Knitting Factory
47 E. Houston St.
New York, NY 10012
212/219-3006

Kumin, Laura
Calle Imperial 3-2, Izq.
28012 Madrid
Spain
34-1-265-7037

Kuumba House
3414 LaBranch
Houston, TX 77004
713/524-1079

Laban Institute of Movement Studies
31 W. 27th St., 4th Fl.
New York, NY 10001
212/689-0740

Lawyers for the Creative Arts
213 W. Institute Pl., Suite 411
Chicago, IL 60610
312/942-ARTS

League of Chicago Theaters
67 East Madison St., Suite 2116
Chicago, IL 60603
312/977-1730

League of Women Voters (NY)
817 Broadway
New York, NY 10003
212/674-8484

Legal Advocacy & Resource Center
(LARC)
14 Beacon St.
Boston, MA 02108
617/742-9279

Lesbian & Gay Community Switchboard/
Arizona AIDS Information Line
P.O. Box 16423
Phoenix, AZ 85011-6423
602/234-2752

Library for the Performing Arts
Lincoln Center
111 Amsterdam Ave.
New York, NY 10023
212/870-1657

Library of Congress
Independent Ave. at First St. S.E.
Washington, DC 20540
202/707-5000

Life on the Water
Fort Mason Center, Bldg. B
San Francisco, CA 94123
413/885-2790
Fax: 415/885-4257

Lighting Design Handbook. Lee Watson.
New York: McGraw-Hill, Inc.

Lighting Dimensions Directory. Available
from Lighting Dimensions Associates,
135 Fifth Ave., New York, NY 10010-7193.
212/677-5997.

Lincoln Center Dance and Theatre
Collection, see Library for the
Performing Arts

Lincoln Center Out-of-Doors
Community Relations Department
Lincoln Center for the Performing Arts
70 Lincoln Center Plaza
New York, NY 10023
212/877-1800

Little Red Book and Producers Guide.
Newsletter about theater and Theatre
Development Fund also available. New
York: Theatre Development Fund (see
below).

Longacre Hardware
801 Eighth Ave. (48th–49th)
New York, NY 10019
212/246-0855

City of Los Angeles
Cultural Affairs Department
433 South Spring St., 10th Fl.
Los Angeles, CA 90013
212/485-2433

Los Angeles Contemporary Exhibitions
(LACE)
1804 Industrial St.
Los Angeles, CA 90021
213/624-5650
Fax: 213/624-6679

Louisiana Department of Culture,
Recreation, and Tourism
Division of the Arts
P.O. Box 44247
Baton Rouge, LA 70804
504/342-8180

Lower Manhattan Cultural Council
42 Broadway, Rm. 1749
New York, NY 10004
212/432-0900

Maine Arts Commission
55 Capitol St.
State House Station 25
Augusta, ME 04333
207/289-2724

Make-up Center, Ltd.
150 W. 55 St.
New York, NY 10019
212/997-9494

Maryland State Arts Council
15 West Mulberry St.
Baltimore, MD 21201
301/333-8232

Marymount Manhattan College
221 E. 71st St.
New York, NY 10021
212/517-0475
Career Development Office, 212/517-0567

Master Dyeing Company
24-47 44th St.
Long Island City, NY 11103
718/726-1001

Mayor's Council on the Arts
City Hall
Burlington, VT 05401
802/658-9300

Mayor's Voluntary Action Center
61 Chambers St.
New York, NY 10007
212/566-5950

Media Alliance
356 W. 58th St.
New York, NY 10019
212/560-2919

Meet the Composer
2112 Broadway, #505
New York, NY 10023
212/787-3601

Memphis Black Art Alliance
985 South Fairview
Memphis, TN 38106
901/948-9522

Messmore and Damon
530 W. 28th St.

New York, NY 10001
212/594-8070

Metropolitan Arts Commission
1120 South-West Fifth Ave., Rm. 1023
Portland, OR 97204
503/796-5111

Metropolitan Arts Council
Box 1077 Downtown Station
Omaha, NE 68101-1077
402/341-7910

Metropolitan Center for Mental Health
130 W. 97th St.
New York, NY 10025
212/864-7000

Metropolitan Dade County
Cultural Affairs Council
111 Northwest First St., Suite 625
Miami, FL 33128
305/375-4634

Metropolitan Dance Association
4201 16th St. N.W.
Washington, DC 20011
202/829-3300

Miami-Dade Community College, Wolfson
Campus
300 N.E. 2nd Ave., Suite 1403
Miami, FL 33132
305/347-3768
Fax: 305/347-3645

Michigan Council for the Arts
Cultural Affairs
1200 Sixth St.
Detroit, MI 48226
313/256-3731

Mid-America Arts Alliance (MAAA)
912 Baltimore Ave., Suite #700
Kansas City, MO 64105
816/421-1388
(Arkansas, Kansas, Missouri, Nebraska,
Oklahoma, Texas.)

Mid-Atlantic States Arts Consortium
(MASAC)
11 E. Chase St., Suite 2-A
Baltimore, MD 21202
301/539-6656

(Delaware, District of Columbia, Maryland, New Jersey, New York, Pennsylvania, Virginia, West Virginia.)

Kathryn and Gilbert Miller Health Care Institute for Performing Artists
425 W. 59th St., #6A
New York, NY 10019
212/523-6200

Kathryn Bach Miller Theatre
Columbia University
200 Dodge Hall
New York, NY 10027
212/854-1643

Milwaukee Artist Foundation
820 E. Knapp St.
Milwaukee, WI 53202
414/276-9273

Minneapolis Arts Commission
City Hall, Rm. 200
Minneapolis, MN 55415
612/673-3006

Minneapolis Community Development Agency
Arts Economic Development Specialist
105 5th Ave. South, Suite 600
Minneapolis, MN 55401-2538
612/673-5018

Minneapolis Public Library
Sociology Department
300 Nicollet Mall
Minneapolis, MN 55401
612/372-6655

Minnesota AIDS Project
2025 Nicollet South, Suite 200
Minneapolis, MN 55404
612/870-7773
800/870-0700 (Hotline)

Minnesota Dance Alliance
528 Hennepin Ave.
Minneapolis, MN 55403
612/340-1900

Minnesota State Arts Board
432 Summit Ave.
St. Paul, MN 55102
612/297-2603

800/652-9747 (Toll-free within Minnesota)

Mississippi Arts Commission
239 N. Lamar St., Suite 207
Jackson, MS 39201
601/359-6036

Missouri Arts Council
Wainwright Office Complex
111 North Seventh St., Suite 105
St. Louis, MO 63101
314/340-6845

Money for Performing Artists. Ed. Susan Niemeyer. New York: American Council for the Arts (see above). $14.95.

Montana Arts Council
48 North Last Chance Gulch
Helena, MT 59620
406/444-6430

Movement Research
28 Avenue A
New York, NY
Mailing address:
P.O. Box 794 Village Station
New York, NY 10014
212/477-6635

Movement Theater International (MTI)
3700 Chestnut St.
Philadelphia, PA 19104
215/382-0600
Fax: 215/382-0627

MPCS Video Industries, Inc.
514 W. 57th St.
New York, NY 10019
212/586-3690

Mulberry Street Theatre
179 Varick St.
New York, NY 10014
212/691-5788

El Museo del Barrio
1230 Fifth Ave.
New York, NY 10029
212/831-7272
Fax: 212/831-7927

Museum of Contemporary Art (MOCA)
250 South Grand Ave.
Los Angeles, CA 90012
213/621-2766
Fax: 213/620-8674

Musical America Directory
825 Seventh Ave., 8th Fl.
New York, NY 10019
212/887-8383

Music Gallery
1087 Queen St. West
Toronto, Ontario M6J 1H3
Canada
416/534-6311

Musicians Emergency Fund, Inc.
16 E. 64th St.
New York, NY 10021
212/578-2450

Mutual Hardware Corp.
5-45 49th Ave.
Long Island City, NY 11101
516/361-2480
Fax: 718/729-8296

NADA (formerly Theatre Club
Funambules)
167 Ludlow St.
New York, NY 10002
212/420-1466

National AIDS Hotline/National HIV and
AIDS Information Service
800/342-2437
800/344-7432: Spanish
800/243-7889: TTY/TDD

National AIDS Information Clearing
House
800/458-5231

National Artists' Equity Association
P.O. Box 28068
Central Station
Washington, DC 20038
202/628-9633

National Assembly of Local Arts
Agencies (NALAA)
1420 K St. N.W.

Washington, DC 20005
202/371-2830

National Assembly of State Arts
Agencies (NASAA)
1010 Vermont Ave. N.W., Suite 920
Washington, DC 20005
202/347-6352; 202/544-0660

National Association of Artists'
Organizations (NAAO)
918 F St. N.W.
Washington, DC 20005
202/347-6352

National Association of Campus
Activities
13 Harbison Way
Columbia, SC 29212
803/732-6222

National Association of Performing Arts
Managers and Agents (NAPAMA)
c/o Beverly Wright
157 W. 57th St., Suite 1100
New York, NY 10019
212/333-7735

National Black Theatre
2033 Fifth Ave.
New York, NY 10035
212/427-5615

National Campaign for Freedom of
Expression (NCFE)
P.O. Box 21465
Washington, DC 20004
202/393-2787

National Coalition against Censorship
2 W. 64th St.
New York, NY 10023
212/724-1500

National Corporate Fund for Dance, Inc.
250 W. 57th St.
New York, NY 10107
212/582-0130

National Cultural Alliance
1225 Eye St. N.W., Suite 200
Washington, DC 20005
202/289-8286

National Endowment for the Arts
Nancy Hanks Center
1100 Pennsylvania Ave. N.W.
Washington, DC 20506
Main number: 202/682-5400
Advancement: 202/682-5436
Challenge Grants: 202/682-5436
Dance: 202/682-5435
Design Arts: 202/682-5437
Expansion Arts: 202/682-5443
Folk Arts: 202/682-5444
International Activities Office:
202/682-5422; Fax: 202/682-5602
Media Arts: Film/Radio/Television:
202/682-5452
Music Program: 202/682-5445
Opera–Musical Theater Program:
202/682-5447
Presenting & Commissioning Program:
202/682-5444
Special Constituencies Office:
202/682-5531, -5532; 202/682-5496
(Voice/TDD)
Theater Program: 202/682-5425
Visual Arts: 202/682-5448

National Endowment for the Humanities
Nancy Hanks Center
1100 Pennsylvania Ave. N.W.
Washington, DC 20506
202/786-0438

National Gay and Lesbian Task Force
1734 14th St. N.W.
Washington, DC 20009-4309
202/332-6483

National Guide to Funding in Arts and Culture (biennial). New York: The Foundation Center (see above). $125.

National Humanities Alliance
1527 New Hampshire Ave. N.W.
Washington, DC 20036
202/328-2121

National Insurance Consumers' Helpline
800/942-4242

National League of Historic Theaters
1511 K St. N.W., #923

Washington, DC 20005
202/783-6966

National Organization for Women (NOW)
1000 16th St. N.W., Suite 700
Washington, DC 20036
202/331-0066 (NOW office)
800/255-4432 (insurance information)

National Performance Network
c/o Dance Theater Workshop
219 W. 19th St.
New York, NY 10011
212/645-6200 (NPN office only)
212/691-6500 (general office)

"National Performance Network Brochure." Contact Dance Theater Workshop (see above).

National Performing Arts Mailing List. Contact Dance Theater Workshop (see above).

Nebraska Advocacy Services
522 Lincoln Center Building
215 Centennial Mall S.
Lincoln, NE 68508
402/474-3183

Nebraska Arts Council
1313 Farnam-on-the-Mall
Omaha, NE 68102
402/595-2122

Netherlands Dance Institute (NID)
Herengracht 174
1016 BR Amsterdam
The Netherlands
31-20-623-7541
Fax: 31-20-626-44-33

Netherlands Theater Institute
P.O. Box 19304
1000 GH Amsterdam
The Netherlands
(31) 20-23-51-04

Nevada State Council on the Arts
329 Flint St.
Reno, NV 89501
702/688-1225

New England Foundation for the Arts,
Inc. (NEFA)
678 Massachusetts Ave.
Cambridge, MA 02139
617/492-2914
(Connecticut, Maine, Cambridge,
Massachusetts, New Hampshire, Rhode
Island, Vermont.)

New England Presenters
Connecticut College, Box 5331
270 Mohegan Ave.
New London, CT 06320
203/447-1911

New Hampshire State Council on the
Arts
Phoenix Hall
40 North Main St.
Concord, NH 03301
603/271-2789

New Jersey State Council on the Arts
4 North Broad St., CN306
Trenton, NJ 08625
609/292-6130

New Mexico Arts Division
228 E. Palace Ave.
Santa Fe, NM 87501
505/827-6490

New Mexico Physical Therapy & Rehab
Center
2607 Wyoming Blvd. N.E., Suite A & B
Albuquerque, NM 87112
505/296-9521

New York City Arts Coalition
155 Avenue of the Americas, 14th Fl.
New York, NY 10013
212/366-6900, ext. 206

New York City Art Teachers Association/
United Federation of Teachers
260 Park Ave. South, 3rd Fl.
New York, NY 10010
212/777-7500

New York City Dept. of Cultural Affairs
2 Columbus Circle
New York, NY 10019
212/974-1150

New York City Dept. of Finance
Office of Legal Affairs
1 Centre St., Rm. 500
New York, NY 10007
212/566-2574

New York City Dept. of Health—AIDS
Information
455 1st Ave.
Brooklyn, NY 11232
718/485-8111

New York City Economic Development
Corp.
110 Williams St.
New York, NY 10038
212/341-5900

New York Foundation for the Arts
155 Avenue of the Americas, 14th Fl.
New York, NY 10013
212/366-6900
Fax: 212/366-1778

New York Freudian Society
Psychoanalytic Consultation Service
21 W. 86th St.
New York, NY 10024
212/873-7029

New York State Alliance for Arts
Education
9B38 Cultural Education Center
Empire State Plaza
Albany, NY 12230
518/473-0823

New York State Arts and Cultural
Coalition (NYSACC)
1002 Breunig Rd.
Stewart Int'l Airport
New Windsor, NY 12553
914/564-6462

New York State Council on the Arts
915 Broadway
New York, NY 10010
212/387-7000
800/GET-ARTS

New York State Medicaid
1 Commerce Plaza

Albany, NY 12234
718/291-1900

New York State Unemployment Insurance for Claimants. New York State Dept. of Labor, Office of Communications, W. Averell Harriman State Office Building Campus, Rm. 511, Albany, NY 12240-0012; 518/457-5519. Also available at Dept. of Labor, 1 Main St., Brooklyn, NY 11201.

The New York Theatrical Sourcebook. Ed. by the Association of Theatrical Artists and Craftspeople. Published by Broadway Press, 12 West Thomas St., Shelter Island, NY 11964; 800/869-6372. $30.00, plus $3.25 shipping, plus $2.74 NYS sales tax.

New York University
Dance Education Department
Education Building, Rm. 675
35 W. 4th St.
New York, NY 10003
212/998-5400

New York University
Gallatin Division
University Without Walls
715 Broadway, 6th Fl.
New York, NY 10003
212/998-7370

New York University
Graduate Performing Arts
Administration Program
239 Greene St., Suite 300
New York, NY 10003
212/998-5500

North Carolina Arts Council
Department of Cultural Resources
Raleigh, NC 27601-2807
919/733-2821

North Dakota Council on the Arts
Black Building, Suite 606
Fargo, ND 58102
701/239-7150

Northern Mariana Islands
Commonwealth Council for

Arts and Culture
Convention Center
Capitol Hill, Saipan
P.O. Box 553, CHRB
Commonwealth of the Northern Mariana
Islands MP96950
011-670-322-9982

Novelty Scenic
40 Sea Cliff Ave.
Glen Cove, NY 11542
516/671-5940
718/895-8669

Ocean State Lawyers for the Arts
P.O. Box 19
Saunderstown, RI 02874
401/789-5686

ODPHP National Health Information
Center
P.O. Box 1133
Washington, DC 20013-1133
202/429-9091
800/336-4797

Office National du Diffusion Artistique
(ONDA)
66, rue de la Chaussee d'Antin
75009 Paris
France
33-1 42-80-28-22

Ohio Arts Council
727 East Main St.
Columbus, OH 43205
614/466-2613

Ohio Theater
66 Wooster St.
New York, NY 10012
212/966-4844

One Night Stand
c/o LaMama
74A E. 4th St.
New York, NY 10003
212/254-6468

On the Boards
153 14th Ave.
Seattle, WA 98122
206/325-7901

Open Eye NEW STAGINGS
270 W. 89th St.
New York, NY 10024
212/769-414

Oregon Arts Commission
835 Summer St. N.E.
Salem, OR 97301
503/378-3625

*Out There: Marginalization and
Contemporary Cultures.* Ed. Russell
Ferguson, Martha Genver, Trinh Minh-he,
and Cornel West. Cambridge, MA: MIT
Press; 800/356-0343. $14.95 Paperback;
$29.95 Hardcover.

Oxford Fibre Sample Case Corp.
762 Wythe Ave.
Brooklyn, NY 11211
718/858-0009

Pace Downtown Theater
One Pace Plaza
New York, NY 10038
212/346-1398, -1715

Pacific Northwest Arts Presenters
P.O. Box 55877
Seattle, WA 98155
206/365-4143

Painted Bride Art Center
230 Vine St.
Philadelphia, PA 19106
215/925-9914
Fax: 215/925-7402

Parachute Fund through Dance Bay
Area, see Dance Bay Area

Commonwealth of Pennsylvania Council
on the Arts
Finance Building, Rm. 216
Harrisburg, PA 17120
717/787-6883

Pentacle
104 Franklin St.
New York, NY 10013
212/226-2000
Fax: 212/925-0369

People for the American Way
2000 M St. N.W., #400
Washington, DC 20036
202/467-4999

Performance Mix
New Dance Alliance, Inc.
182 Duane St.
New York, NY 10013
212/226-7624

Performance Space 122 (P.S. 122)
150 First Ave.
New York, NY 10009
212/477-5288
Fax: 212/353-1315

Performing Arts Physical Therapy
2121 Broadway, Suite 201
New York, NY 10023
212/769-1423

Performing Arts Resources, Inc.
270 Lafayette St., Suite 809
New York, NY 10012
212/966-8658

Performing Arts Yearbook for Europe. Arts
Publishing Ltd., 4 Assam St., London E1
7QS, United Kingdom; 44-71 247-0066.

Philadelphia Dance Alliance
1315 Walnut St., Suite 1500
Philadelphia, PA 19107-4719
215/545-6344

Philadelphia Volunteer Lawyers for the
Arts
251 South 18th St.
Philadelphia, PA 19103
215/545-3385

Pinay Flooring Products
563 Court St.
Brooklyn, NY 11231
718/858-4000

Pittsburgh Dance Council, Inc.
719 Liberty Ave.
Pittsburgh, PA 15222
412/355-0330
Fax: 412/355-0413

Planned Parenthood Federation of America, Inc.
2010 Massachusetts Ave. N.W.
Washington, DC 20036
202/387-6556
also
810 Seventh Ave.
New York, NY 10019
212/541-7800 (Main switchboard for National Office Planned Parenthood Federation of America)

Playbill Cosmetics/Ideal Wig Co.
37-11 35th Ave. (37th–38th)
Astoria, NY 11101
718/361-8601

The Predicament of Culture: Twentieth-Century Ethnography, Literature, and Art. James Clifford. Cambridge, MA: Harvard University Press; 617/495-2600. $15.95 Paperback; $34.95 Hardcover.

PREGONES Theater
295 St. Ann's Avenue
Bronx, NY 10454
718/585-1202
Fax: 718/585-1608

Present Music
1840 North Farwell Ave., Suite 301
Milwaukee, WI 53202
414/271-0711

Production Arts Lighting
636 Eleventh Ave.
New York, NY 10036
212/489-0312

Progressive Fibre Products, Inc.
708 Broadway, 10th Fl.
New York, NY 10003
212/254-6025

Project Inform
800/822-7422 (Hotline)

ProMix, Inc.
111 Cedar St.
New Rochelle, NY 10801
914/633-3233 or 212/944-7685

Props for Today
121 W. 19th St., 3rd Fl.

New York, NY 10011
212/206-0330

P.S. 122, see Performance Space 122

Puerto Rican Culture, see Institute of Puerto Rican Culture

PWA (Persons with AIDS) Coalition
212/532-0568 (NYC Hotline)
800/828-3280 (National Hotline)

Queens Council on the Arts
161-04 Jamaica Ave.
Jamaica, NY 11432
718/291-1100

City of Raleigh Arts Commission
305 South Blount St.
Raleigh, NC 27601
919/831-6234

Randolph Street Gallery
756 North Milwaukee Ave.
Chicago, IL 60622
312/666-7737
Fax: 312/829-3858

Reimaging America: The Arts of Social Change. Ed. Mark O'Brien and Craig Little. New Society Publishers, 4527 Springfield Ave., Philadelphia, PA 19143. $18.95 Paperback; $49.95 Hardcover, plus $2.50 postage ($0.75 each additional book).

Reliance Audio Visual
623 W. 51st St.
New York, NY 10019
212/586-5000

Religious Action Center of Reformed Judaism
Union of American Hebrew Congregations
2027 Massachusetts Ave. N.W.
Washington, DC 20036

"Request for Earnings and Benefit Estimate Statement."
800/772-1213

Rhode Island State Council on the Arts
95 Cedar St., Suite 103

Providence, RI 02903-4494
401/277-3880

Riverside Theatre Dance Festival
Theatre of the Riverside Church
Riverside Church Rental House
120th St. and Riverside Dr.
New York, NY 10027
212/864-2929

Rivoli Shoe Repair
166 W. 50th St.
New York, NY 10011
212/247-4850

Rosco Labs
36 Bush Ave.
Port Chester, NY 10573
914/937-1300

Rose Brand Textile Fabric
517 W. 35th St. (10th–11th)
New York, NY 10001
212/594-7424

St. Joseph's Historic Foundation, Inc.
801 Fayetteville St.
P.O. Box 543
Durham, NC 27702
919/683-1709; 919/682-7216

St. Louis Volunteer Lawyers &
Accountants for the Arts
3540 Washington
St. Louis, MO 63103
314/652-2410

S & S Hosiery
135 W. 50th St.
New York, NY 10019
212/586-3288

San Francisco AIDS Foundation
25 Van Ness Ave.
San Francisco, CA 94102
415/864-5855
415/863-2437 (Hotline)

San Francisco Arts Commission
25 Venice, Rm. 240
San Francisco, CA 94102
415/554-9671

San Francisco Arts Democratic Club
P.O. Box 460524
San Francisco, CA 94146-0524

San Francisco Performing Arts Library
and Museum
399 Grove St.
San Francisco, CA 94110
415/255-4800

Santa Barbara Dance Alliance
P.O. Box 22256
Santa Barbara, CA 93121
805/962-9163

Santa Fe Council for the Arts
806 Falda de la Sierra
Santa Fe, NM 87501
505/988-1878

Schomburg Center for Research in Black
Culture
515 Malcolm X Blvd.
New York, NY 10037
212/491-2200

Screen Actors Guild (SAG)
1515 Broadway, 44th Fl.
New York, NY 10036
212/944-1030

Several Dancers Core
P.O. Box 2045
Decatur, GA 30031
404/373-4154
Fax: 404/377-1815

The Signifying Monkey. Henry Louis
Gates, Jr. Fairlawn, NJ: Oxford University
Press.

Silver and Sons Hardware Corp.
711 Eighth Ave. (44th–45th)
New York, NY 10036
212/247-6969

Smithsonian Institution
Performing Arts Program
Museum of American History, Rm. 310
Washington, DC 20560
202/357-4173; 202/357-2696

Kenneth Snopes Engineering and Design
6240 B Lake Worth Blvd.

Forth Worth, TX 76135
817/237-9390

Society of Stage Directors &
Choreographers (SSD&C)
1501 Broadway, 31st Fl.
New York, NY 10036
212/391-1070

SoHo Booking
Downtown Art Co.
280 Broadway Rm. 412
New York, NY 10007
212/732-1201
Fax: 212/732-1297

South Carolina Arts Commission
1800 Gervais St.
Columbia, SC 29201
803/734-8696

South Dakota Arts Council
108 West 11th St.
Sioux Falls, SD 57102
605/339-6646

Southern Arts Federation (SAF)
1293 Peachtree St. N.E.
Suite 500
Atlanta, GA 30309
404/874-7244
(Alabama, Florida, Georgia, Kentucky,
Louisiana, Mississippi, North Carolina,
South Carolina, Tennessee.)

South Florida AIDS Network
Jackson Memorial Hospital
1611 N.W. 12th Ave.
Miami, FL 33136
305/549-7744

Southwest Performing Arts Presenters
San Antonio Performing Arts
Association, #230
110 Broadway
San Antonio, TX 78205
210/224-8187

Space Chase. New York: The Field.

Space for Dance. Partners for Livable
Places, Livability Clearing House, 1429
21st N.W., Washington, DC 20036;

202/887-5990, 1984. $19.50 Hardback,
plus shipping.

Spaces for the Arts. New York: Pentacle
(see above).

A Space to Create and Showcase Primer.
New York: Alliance of Resident
Theatres/New York (see above).

Spartan Flame Retardants
345 East Terrra Cotta Ave.
Crystal Lake, IL 60014

Sponsorship and the Arts. Ron Bergin.
Entertainment Resources Group, P.O.
Box 6487, Evanston, IL 60202.

Sports Therapy for Athletic
Rehabilitation & Treatment (START)
3400 Main St.
Springfield, MA 01105
413/788-6195

Stage Lighting. Richard Pilbrow. New
York: Von Nostrand Reinhold Co., 1970.

Stagestep, Inc.
P.O. Box 328
Philadelphia, PA 19105
800/523-0961

State Arts Council of Oklahoma
Jim Thorpe Building, Rm. 640
2101 North Lincoln Blvd.
Oklahoma City, OK 73105
405/521-2931

Staten Island Council on the Arts
1 Edgewater Plaza, Rm. 311
Staten Island, NY 10305

Stern's Performing Arts Directory
(formerly *Dance Magazine Annual
Performing Arts Directory*)
33 W. 60th St. 10th Fl.
New York, NY 10023
212/245-8937; 212/458-2845

The Suitcase Fund, see Dance Theater
Workshop

Supplemental Security Income: Look in
telephone book under (U.S.)
Social Security Administration
800/772-1213

Support Services Alliance (SSA)
P.O. Box 130
Schoharie, NY 12157
518/295-7966

Sushi Performance and Visual Art
852 Eighth Ave.
San Diego, CA 92101
619/235-8466

Symphony Space
2537 Broadway (at 95th St.)
New York, NY 10025
212/864-1414

Synergy Productions
874 Broadway, Suite 901
New York, NY 10003
212/673-5139

Syracuse Scenery & Stage Lighting Co.,
Inc.
1423 North Salina St.
Syracuse, NY 13208
315/474-2474

Gyorgy Szabo, Performing Arts
Petofi Csarnok
Zichy Mihaly utca 14
Budapest H-1146
Hungary
36-11-224-434
Fax: 36-11-423-358

Tacoma Arts Commission
747 Market St., Suite 134
Tacoma, WA 98402
206/591-5191

Taft Foundation Reporter. The Taft Group,
12300 Twinbrook Parkway, Suite 450,
Rockville, MD 20852; 800/877-8238. $327.
Also *Foundation Giving Watch*
(newsletter). $139 per year.

Taller Latinoamericano
63 E. 2nd St.
New York, NY 10003
212/864-1414

Tanztendenz München
Lindwurmstrasse 88
8000 Munich 2

Germany
49-89-721-1015

Tapestry Recording/Tapestry Sound
151 W. 19th St. 4th Fl.
New York, NY 10011
212/741-0076

Teachers College, Columbia University
Graduate Program in Arts
Administration
Box 78
New York, NY 10027
212/678-3271 and 212/678-3268

Technical Assistance Project
(TAP)/Performing Arts Resources
Management Assistance Project
270 Lafayette St., Suite 809
New York, NY 10012
212/966-8658

Tennessee Arts Commission
320 Sixth Ave. North, Suite 100
Nashville, TN 37243-0780
615/741-1701 or 741-6395

Texas Accountants & Lawyers for the
Arts
1540 Sul Ross
Houston, TX 77006
713/526-4876

Texas Arts Council
3939 Bee Caves Road, Suite 1A
Austin, TX 78746
512/934-8400

Texas Commission on the Arts
P.O. Box 13406
Capitol Station
Austin, TX 78711
512/463-5535

Texas Composers Forum
P.O. Box 744022
Dallas, TX 75374-4022
214/231-1666

Theater Artaud
450 Florida St. at 17th
San Francisco, CA 94110
Administrative Offices:
2403 16th St.

San Francisco, CA 94103
415/621-7647
Fax: 415/621-7647

Theater Communications Group (TCG)
355 Lexington Ave.
New York, NY 10017
212/697-5230

Theatre Crafts Directory and Theatre Crafts Magazine. 135 5th Ave., New York, NY 10010; 212/677-5997.

Theatre Development Fund (TDF)
1501 Broadway
New York, NY 10036
212/221-0885

Theatre Machine Scenic Shop
55 First Ave.
Paterson, NJ 07514
201/345-5564
Fax: 201/345-1476

Theatre Technology/Best Audio East
37 W. 20th St.
New York, NY 10011
212/929-5380

Third Avenue Performance Space
1066 North High Street
Columbus, OH 43201
614/291-1333

This Way Up: Legal & Business Essentials for Nonprofits. New York: Volunteer Lawyers for the Arts (see below). $14.95 Paperback.

Ticket Central
c/o Playwright's Horizons
416 W. 42nd St.
New York, NY 10036
212/279-4200

Tigertail Productions/Mary Luft & Company
842 N.W. Ninth Court
Miami, FL 33136
Phone/Fax: 305/324-4337

Times Square Lighting
318 W. 47th St.

New York, NY 10036
212/245-4155

To Be or Not to Be: An Artist's Guide to Not-for-Profit Incorporation. New York: Volunteer Lawyers for the Arts (see below). $5.00 Paperback.

Triplex Performing Arts Center
Borough of Manhattan Community College
199 Chambers St.
New York, NY 10007
212/618-1900

Two Continents Arts Exchange
924 West End Ave., #102
New York, NY 10025
212/864-6642

UCSF Health Program for Performing Artists
401 Parnassus Ave.
San Francisco, CA 94143
415/476-7465

Unemployment Insurance: Look in telephone book under State Department of Labor.

Unesco (United Nations Educational, Scientific, and Cultural Organization)
B.P. 3.07
Paris
France
33-1-45-68-10-00

Union of Theater Workers of the USSR
International Department
Tverskaja St., Bld. 12,7, Apt. 217
125047 Moscow
Russia
7-095-250-9282
Fax: 7-095-250-9272

Unique Recording Studio
701 Seventh Ave., 10th Fl.
New York, NY 10036
212/921-1711

United Arts
416 Landmark Center
75 West Fifth St.

St. Paul, MN 55102
612/292-3222

United Scenic Artists Local 829
575 Eighth Ave.
New York, NY 10018
212/736-4498
also
5410 Wilshire Blvd., Suite 407
Los Angeles, CA 90036
213/965-0957

U.S. Information Agency (USIA)
Arts America Program
Bureau of Educational and Cultural
Affairs
301 4th St. S.W.
Washington, DC 20547
202/619-4355
Fax: 202/619-6315

Universe Stage Lighting
326 W. 47th St. (8th–9th)
New York, NY 10036
212/246-0597

University of Washington Sports
Medicine Clinic
University of Washington, GB-15
Seattle, WA 98195
206/543-1550

U.S. Congress. People for the American
Way, 2000 M St. N.W., Washington, DC
20036. $6.95.

U.S. Council of the International
Chamber of Commerce
1212 Ave. of the Americas
New York, NY 10036

U.S. Dept. of Education
400 Maryland Ave. S.W.
Washington, DC 20202
202/245-3192

U.S. Dept. of the Interior
C St. N.W.
Washington, DC 20001
202/343-1100

Utah Arts Council
617 East South Temple St.

Salt Lake City, UT 84102
801/533-5895; 801/533-5896

Utah Lawyers for the Arts
50 South Main, #900
Salt Lake City, UT 84144
801/521-5800

Vancouver East Cultural Centre
1895 Venables St.
Vancouver, British Columbia V5L 2H6
Canada
604/251-1363
Fax: 604/251-7002

Vermont Council on the Arts, Inc.
133 State St.
Montpelier, VT 05633-6001
802/828-3291

Video D
29 W. 21st St.
New York, NY 10011
212/242-3345

Virginia Commission for the Arts
223 Governor St.
Richmond, VA 23219-2010
804/225-3132

Virginia Lawyers for the Arts
c/o Virginia Bar Association
701 East Franklin St., Suite 1515
Richmond, VA 23219
804/644-0041

Virgin Islands Council on the Arts
41-42 Norregade, 2nd Fl.
St. Thomas, Virgin Islands 00802
809/774-5984

Visual AIDS
131 W. 24th St., #3
New York, NY 10011
212/206-6758

VLAA
Cleveland Bar Association
113 St. Clair Ave.
Cleveland, OH 44114-1253
216/696-3525

Vlaams Theater Institut (VTI)
Anspach 141-143

B-1000 Brussel
Belgium
32-2-514-4044

VLA Guide to Copyright for the Performing Arts. New York: Lyons & Burford. Available from Volunteer Lawyers for the Arts. $17.00, Paperback.

Volunteer Consulting Group, Inc.
9 E. 41st St., 8th Fl.
New York, NY 10017
212/687-8530

Volunteer Lawyers for the Arts
Maine Arts Commission
55 Capitol St.
State House Station 25
Augusta, ME 04333
207/289-2724

Volunteer Lawyers for the Arts (VLA)
1 East 53rd St., 6th Fl.
New York, NY 10022
212/319-2787
Art Law Line: 212/319-2910

Volunteer Lawyers for the Arts/Lawyers Committee for the Arts
918 16th St. N.W.
Washington, DC 20006
202/429-0229

Volunteer Lawyers for the Arts New Jersey
Center for Nonprofit Corporations
15 Roszel Road
Princeton, NJ 08540
609/951-0800

Volunteer Lawyers Project (VLP)
29 Temple Pl., #300
Boston, MA 02111
617/423-0648

Volunteer Legal Services Project of Monroe County
87 North Clinton Ave.
Rochester, NY 14604
716/232-3051

Walker Art Center
Vineland Place

Minneapolis, MN 55403
612/375-7624

Washington Performing Arts Society
2000 L St. N.W., Suite 810
Washington, DC 20036-4907
202/833-9800

Washington Square Church
135 W. 4th St.
New York, NY 10012
212/777-2528

Washington State Arts Commission
9th and Columbia Building, Rm. 110
Mail Stop GH11
Olympia, WA 98504
206/753-3860

Washington Volunteer Lawyers for the Arts
4649 Sunnyside Ave. N., Rm. 350
Seattle, WA 98103
206/223-0502

Brian Webb Dance Company
Box 1796
Edmonton, Alberta T5J 2P2
Canada
403/483-2368
Fax: 403/483-4300

I. Weiss and Sons
2-07 Borden Ave.
Long Island City, NY 11101
516/246-8444

Welfare: Look in telephone book under (State) Social Services Department, Income Maintenance Center.

West Virginia Arts & Humanities Commission
Division of Culture and History
Capitol Complex
Charleston, WV 25305
304/348-0240

Western States Arts Foundation (WSAF)
236 Montezuma St., Suite 200
Santa Fe, NM 87501
505/988-1166
(Alaska, Arizona, California, Colorado, Hawaii, Idaho, Montana, Nevada, New

Mexico, Oregon, Utah, Washington,
Wyoming.)

Wexner Center for the Arts
North High St. at 15th Ave.
Columbus, OH 43210
614/292-5785
Fax: 614/292-3369

Will It Make a Theatre. New York:
ART/NY. Distributed by the Drama Book
Specialist, 50 W. 52nd St., 4th Fl., New
York, NY 10019; 212/989-5257.

Wisconsin Arts Board
131 W. Wilson St., Suite 301
Madison, WI 53703
608/266-0190

Wisconsin Dance Council
610 Langdon St.

722 Lowell Hall
Madison, WI 53703
608/263-8927

WK Studios
611 Broadway, Suite 721
New York, NY 10012
212/473-1203

Women & Their Work
1137 West 6th St.
Austin, TX 78703
512/477-1064

Women's Sports Foundation
800/227-3488 (Hotline)

Wyoming Council on the Arts
2320 Capitol Ave.
Cheyenne, WY 82002
307/777-7742

C O N T R I B U T O R S

Elise Bernhardt is the founder and executive director of Dancing in the Streets, a presenting organization that commissions and produces performances in public spaces.

Eric Bogosian has been making solo performance and plays in New York since 1977. Works produced in New York City include *Sheer Heaven* (The Kitchen, 1979); *The New World* (DTW, 1980); *The Ricky Paul Show; Talk Radio* (NYSF, 1987); and the solos *Men Inside, Funhouse, Drinking in America,* and *Sex, Drugs, Rock & Roll.* He makes occasional appearances on television and in film. Films of *Talk Radio,* directed by Oliver Stone, and *Sex, Drugs, Rock & Roll,* directed by John MacNaughton, were released to wide public acclaim. Mr. Bogosian has received an Obie, a Drama Desk award, and a Silver Bear (Berlin F.F.) for his work. He lives in New Jersey.

Meyer Braiterman has worked for forty-five years in arts production and administration. For the past sixteen years he has been an employee benefits consultant for arts organizations and an insurance adviser and agent for arts workers.

Richard Bull directs the Warren Street Performance Loft, Improvisational Arts Ensemble, Inc., and Wesleyan University's program of Graduate Studies in Movement and Dance. He also directs his own dance company, the Richard Bull Dance Theatre.

Kim Chan is director of dance and new performance at the Washington Performing Arts Society, where she is responsible for developing and administrating dance and contemporary arts presentations, residencies, and commissioning projects. She serves as a consultant for Dance Place in Washington, DC, and as a panelist for the National Endowment for the Arts Dance and Inter-Arts programs.

Ellie Covan is director of Dixon Place, an intimate downtown Manhattan venue that presents performance works-in-progress, literary readings, and music. She has been committed to the performing arts since the year she spent on "Romper Room" at the age of five, and still performs occasionally in various guises.

Merce Cunningham is the artistic director of the Merce Cunningham Dance Company, New York, New York.

Timothy J. DeBaets is an entertainment lawyer in New York City. He has represented numerous choreographers, dancers, and performance artists, including Judith Jamison and the Flying Karamazov Brothers. He is a member of the board of directors of Dance Theater Workshop.

Vicky Dummer was executive director of OhioDance, a statewide service organization for the dance and movement arts. Previously, Ms. Dummer was company administrator for Stuart Pimsler Dance and Theater. She has also worked as a meeting and incentive planner during her brief sojourn in the travel industry.

Karen Finley was born in Chicago in 1956. She received an M.F.A. from the San Francisco Art Institute. She is an artist and author and has also recorded albums and appeared in films. She lives outside New York City with her husband.

Lise Friedman danced with the Merce Cunningham Dance Company from 1977 to 1984. She then left the dance world to work at *Vogue* magazine and to take on various editorial projects, among them editing John Gruen's book *People Who Dance*. In 1989 she assumed the editorship of *Dance Ink*.

Greg Geilmann is Theater Operations Manager for DanceAspen and the DanceAspen Summer Festival. He also works as Company Manager for the Ririe-Woodbury Dance Company and was an assistant to Broadway designer/theater consultant Jo Mielziner. Mr. Geilmann was the production manager and lighting designer for Ballet West from 1974 to 1988.

David Gere, staff writer on dance and music for the *Oakland Tribune,* comments frequently on issues concerning AIDS and the arts. He was a founding volunteer on the Names Project Quilt.

Marian A. Godfrey has been program director for culture at the Pew Charitable Trusts since 1989. Prior to arriving at the Trusts, she spent twelve years as a performing arts manager and consultant to the Foundation for the Extension and Development of the American Professional Theater. Previously, Ms. Godfrey was manager of the theater collaborative Mabou Mines, for which she produced a feature film, *Dead End Kids: A Story of Nuclear Power* (1980–86); instructor in drama at New York University Tisch School for the Arts (1980–87); and director of Ensemble Studio Theater (1977–80). She received her M.F.A. in Theater Administration from the Yale School of Drama in 1975.

Lillian Goldthwaite is currently an organizational development consultant working primarily in the non-profit field. Most recently she held the post of executive director of Dance Bay Area. She was previously assistant development manager for the San Francisco Ballet and financial consultant for Robinson-Humphrey/Francisco Dance Spectrum and the San Francisco Opera Ballet. She was the Intercontinental Champion of Scottish Highland Dancing in 1971. Ms. Goldthwaite served as a panelist for the National Endowment for the Arts and on the advisory committee to the San Francisco Ethnic Dance Festival. She also served on the board of Dance/USA and on the Cultural Affairs Task Force of the City of San Francisco.

Guillermo Goméz-Peña was born and raised in Mexico City and came to the United States in 1978. Since then he has been exploring cross-cultural issues and North-South relations with the use of multiple mediums: performance, audio art, book art, bilingual poetry, journalism, film, and installation art.

Built on an aesthetic of inclusion, *Joe Goode*'s choreography draws on his experience as a writer, actor, and director. Mr. Goode's unique performance signature incorporates daring full-bodied movement with personal stories, human sounds, and gestures. Mr. Goode founded the Joe Goode Performance Group in San Francisco in 1986.

Mara Greenberg received her M.B.A. in Finance from New York University. She joined Pentacle in the fall of 1977 and became director (with Ivan Sygoda) two years later. She was a contributing editor to the *Poor Dancer's Almanac* (2nd ed.), a guest speaker and panelist on performing arts fiscal management for ART/NY, FEDAPT, Dance Theater Workshop, the New School for Social Research, the Cultural Council Foundation, and Marymount Manhattan College. She has also performed professionally with Rachel Lampert and Dancers and the Nancy Meehan Dance Company.

Since entering the dance field in 1973, *Larry Greene* has served in staff positions at the New York State Council on the Arts (as a Dance Program and Theater Program Associate since 1980), the National Endowment for the Arts, and Charles Reinhart Management. As a dancer, he performed in the companies of David Gordon, Liz Lerman, and Jan Taylor, among others.

William G. Hamilton, M.D. is senior attending orthopedic surgeon at St. Luke's–Roosevelt Hospital Center in New York City. He is orthopedist for the New York City Ballet, Mikhail Baryshnikov, American Ballet Theatre, and the School of American Ballet, New York City.

John Haworth is an assistant commissioner at the New York City Department of Cultural Affairs and teaches arts management courses at New York University. He serves on the board of the National Assembly of Local Arts Agencies. He has worked at state arts agencies in New York State, Arizona, and Oklahoma and consulted with many arts organizations throughout the country.

Ellen Jacobs has had her own public relations business since 1981. She works with music and theater as well as dance artists.

John Job is technical coordinator for Dance Umbrella, Austin, Texas. He is a former member of MOMIX Dance Theater, an independent producer in Austin (The Bobs, MOMIX, Malxolm Dalglish, Holly Hughes, Tim Miller, and others), and a writer for the *Austin Chronicle.*

Composer *Scott Johnson* has achieved wide recognition for his compelling blend of contemporary classical practice, rock and jazz instrumentation, and avant-garde electronic techniques. His music has been heard in performances by the St. Paul Chamber Orchestra and the Kronos Quartet, in concerts of his own ensembles, in dance works performed by the Boston Ballet and the London Contemporary Dance Theater, in Paul Schrader's film *Patty Hearst,* and in his two recordings on the Nonesuch label, *John Somebody* and *Patty Hearst.*

Bill T. Jones began his career as a dancer in 1971. From 1978 to 1982 he shared a duet company with Arnie Zane, and together they founded Bill T. Jones/Arnie Zane and Co. in 1982. Mr. Jones has choreographed and taught both in the United States and abroad and recently began directing for stage and television productions. In June 1991, Mr. Jones was the recipient of the Dorothy B. Chandler Performing Arts Award.

Deborah Jowitt began her career as a dancer and a choreographer. She has been writing dance criticism for the *Village Voice* since 1967. Dance Theater Workshop awarded her a Bessie in 1985. Her latest book is *Time and the Dance Image.* She is on the faculty of New York University's Tisch School of the Arts.

Demetrius A. Klein works in dance and performance art. He has self-produced his work at the Cunningham Studio and Mulberry Street Theater in New York City, as well as maintaining an active performance schedule with his company in their home city of Lake Worth, Florida. He has received a choreographic fellowship from the State of Florida, a commission from Southern Ballet Theater in Orlando, and recently received the Hector Ubertalli Award for Artistic Excellence from the Professional Artists Committee of the Palm Beach County Council of the Arts.

Phyllis Lamhut, choreographer and artistic director of the Phyllis Lamhut Dance Company, is an active member of the U.S. dance community. A choreographer of over 100 works, she is dedicated to the exploration of motion and its kinetic expression.

Michael Lange, M.D., received his medical education in Canada and works in the Division of Infectious Diseases and Epidemiology at St. Luke's–Roosevelt Hospital Center in New York City. He is a fellow of the Royal College of Physicians and Surgeons of Canada and of the Infectious Diseases Society of America. He advises the Research (AMFAR), the Scientific Advisory Committee, the Community Research Initiative, New York City, the New York State Psychiatric Institute HIV Center, and the Food and Drug Administration.

Liz Lerman is the founder and artistic director of the Dance Exchange in Washington, DC. Her choreographed works have been seen throughout the United States and Europe. In 1989 she received an American Choreographic Award as well as her eighth choreographic fellowship from the National Endowment for the Arts. Her book, *Teaching Dance to Senior Adults,* was published in 1983.

A. Leroy has been composing, performing, and recording music since 1973. He has collaborated with choreographers, performance artists, filmmakers, and video artists, including Charles Moulton, Susan Marshall, Wendy Perron, Janie Geiser, Mimi Goese, Michael Smith, Carole Ann Klonarides, Branda Miller, and Power Boothe. In New York City, his music has been performed at Dance Theater Workshop, The Kitchen, Performance Space 122, the La Mama Annex, Symphony Space, Merkin Concert Hall, Central Park's SummerStage, and the Knitting Factory.

Mindy N. Levine is a free-lance writer/editor working mainly in dance, theater, and arts-in-education. Dance-related books include *American Dance Directory, A Poor Dancer's Almanac* (editor), *Dance: A Social Study* (with Elizabeth Zimmer), *N.D.I. Notebook,* and *Images of American Dance* (research analyst and contributing writer). A founding editor of *Theatre Times,* a trade newspaper covering Off-Broadway, her theater books include *New York's Other Theatre: A Guide to Off Off Broadway, Space to Create: The Theatre Community in Crisis,* and *Get Me to the Printer.* Ms. Levine holds a B.A. in literature from Yale and an M.A. in performance studies from NYU, where she has taught dance history. She has performed with several New York–based dance companies.

Tia Tibbitts Levinson, the director of operations and community affairs at Dance Theater Workshop, is on the supervisory board of the Artists Community Federal Credit Union and is an organizer of the Arts Coalition of Independent Democrats (NY).

Elise Long is the artistic director of Spoke the Hub Dancing and founder of the Gowanus Arts Exchange in Brooklyn. She has presented over fifty original works in the United States, Canada, and abroad since 1979 and continues to serve as a guest artist in the Brooklyn Public Schools and elsewhere.

Jonathan Lorch, M.D., is a board certified internist, a board certified nephrologist, a fellow in the American College of Physicians, an associate clinical professor of medicine at Columbia University College of Physicians and Surgeons, and director of the Home Dialysis Program at St. Luke's–Roosevelt Hospital Center in New York City. He is house physician for many theaters, including the Brooklyn Academy of Music, Dance Theater Workshop, and the New York Shakespeare Festival.

John Malashock is the artistic director of Malashock Dance and Company, based in San Diego. He was a member of Twyla Tharp Dance from 1979 to 1984. He has taught and performed at the American Dance Festivals in North Carolina and Tokyo.

Victoria Marks's work is usually performed by her company of five dancers, both in annual New York City seasons and throughout the United States. Her work has been commissioned and presented by dance companies such as the Hartford Ballet, the Pittsburgh Dance Alloy, and the Zenon Dance Company of Minneapolis. She was the first American to be awarded a United Kingdom Fulbright Arts Fellowship in Choreography, 1987–88. Ms. Marks has taught for the Harvard Summer Dance Program, the Bates College Dance Festival, at the London Contemporary Dance School, the Laban Center, Hunter College, and Andy's Summer Playhouse. She has been an artist in residence in New York City–area schools through the New York Foundation for the Arts, Lincoln Center Institute, and Arts Connection.

Timothy J. McClimon is vice president for arts and culture at the AT&T Foundation, where he manages AT&T's contributions to arts institutions worldwide and directs AT&T's Corporate Art Collection. He is a member of the Art Law Committee of the New York City Bar Association and serves on the boards of several arts organizations, including Second Center Theatre, Performance Space 122, and the American Council for the Arts, where he cochairs the National Policy Committee on the Originating Artist. He is also an adjunct professor at New York University, where he teaches law and the arts.

DJ McDonald began his performing career in Levittown, Long Island, as a steamshovel in a kindergarten play. Since 1982, his work has been presented by many New York venues including Dance Theater Workshop, P.S. 122, St. Mark's Dancspace, as well as at Jacob's Pillow Festivals and at several colleges and universities. Mr. McDonald is a dance writer and critic for the *Berkshire Eagle* and is an occasional contributor to the *Village Voice.* He is currently director of the dance program at DeSisto School in Stockbridge, MA, where his company has been in residence since 1988.

Jeff McMahon is a choreographer, performance artist, and filmmaker who has been creating work in New York City since 1979.

Tim Miller is a performance artist, teacher, and cultural organizer. His solo works have been seen all over North America and Europe. He cofounded Performance Space 122 in New York City and in 1989, with Linda Burnham, began HIGHWAYS, an arts center in Santa Monica. He is a member of ACT-UP/LA (AIDS Coalition to Unleash Power).

Timothy Ney joined the Aman Folk Ensemble as managing director in 1991. In New York, Mr. Ney directed the Loan and Artist Sponsorship Program at the New York Foundation for the Arts and founded Dance on the Lower East Side Festival at La Mama, E.T.C. He was a member of Le Snif Theater in Paris, studied at the American Dance Festival in New London, Connecticut, and established dance therapy programs for handicapped children in New York and prison inmates in Massachusetts. Mr. Ney was executive director of the Independent Feature Project, president of Harvest Films, Ltd., and coproducer of the PBS production "Balanchine's Ballerinas."

Tere O'Connor is a graduate of SUNY at Purchase. As a dancer, he performed in the companies of Rosalind Newman and Matthew Diamond, after which he dedicated his time to his own choreography. His work has been produced at many venues in New York City as well as in numerous European cities, in South America, and in Canada. He is a recipient of a 1988 New York Dance and Performance Award, grants from the National Endowment for the Arts, the New York State Council on the Arts, the New York Foundation for Artists, the Jerome Foundation, the Harkness Foundations for Dance, and the Field's Ernie Pagnano Memorial Fund. Mr. O'Connor is a ballet instructor at New York University.

Since 1978, *Stuart Pimsler* has created over thirty works for Stuart Pimsler Dance and Theater as well as commissioned pieces for professional dance companies and university dance departments across the United States. He has served as chair and panelist for the Ohio Arts Council's Dance Panel as well as panelist for Arts Midwest and the Michigan Arts Council. He is currently chair of the Artistic Director's Council for Dance/ USA.

Jennifer Poulos, formerly the publications director at Dance/USA in Washington, DC, is now managing director of the Lucinda Childs Dance Company in New York.

Dana Reitz has produced many solo, group, and collaborative projects, alternating solo investigation with larger work. Most of her major works have been performed in silence, to reveal the movement's own musicality. Her performances have been presented extensively in the United States, Europe, and Australia. The importance of the interplay between light and movement has been of primary interest to her in recent years.

Louise Robinson was executive director of the Minnesota Dance Alliance. She has been active in the dance community in the Twin Cities since 1979. Prior to joining the Alliance staff as program director in 1987, she worked with several Minnesota-based dance companies and served as arts planner for the Metropolitan Regional Arts Council.

Iris Rose has been creating group and solo performance works since 1981. These have been presented at Performance Space 122, LaMama, and Franklin Furnace (among others) in New York City as well as at various spaces in Los Angeles, Washington, DC, and Houston. She has received many grants and awards, including a National Citation Award from American Women in Radio and Television for her radio piece "Society of Mothers."

Ann Rosenthal is the director of Inter/National Projects at Dance Theater Workshop, where she is responsible for the National Performance Network and The Suitcase Fund. Previously, she was the director of SoHo Booking, a nonprofit program dedicated to promoting and touring contemporary work in the performing arts.

Chiori Santiago is a San Francisco–based free-lance writer. She has written about dance, music, and theater for *American Theater, Chicago Reader, East Bay Express, High Performance, San Francisco Chronicle, Los Angeles Times,* and others.

Peter Schumann worked in sculpture, graphics, and dance in Germany and Sweden prior to moving to the United States in 1961. He founded the Bread and Puppet Theater in 1963 and has toured nationally and internationally with the group. He has received numerous awards for his work, including two Obies and a Guggenheim Fellowship. The Bread and Puppet Theater continues to present the Our Domestic Resurrection Circus each summer in Glover, Vermont.

Michael Schwartz is president of Character Generators/Video, a performance documentation company. Character Generators serves as the official video archivist for BAM Next Wave Festival, Danspace at St. Mark's Church, Performance Space 122, and other venues in New York City. He is the producer and director of several dance/video collaborations with choreographers, including Elizabeth Streb, Trisha Brown, Gus Solomons jr, and Ruby Shang. He is founding executive director of Arts Interactive Multimedia (AIM), a nonprofit organization whose goal is to merge the use of computers with video in order to improve the preservation, distribution, and availability of performance documentation.

Stephanie Skura has been making dances and performance work since 1975 and is artistic director of Stephanie Skura and Company. Her work is characterized by a liberating, individualistic approach to movement, a commitment to the power and totality of each performer, and a sense of humor. She has performed and taught widely throughout the United States and Europe.

Andrea Snyder has been assistant director of the National Endowment for the Arts Dance Program since 1987. Prior to that, she was a booking agent for Sheldon Soffer Management, executive director of Laura Dean Dancers and Musicians, administrator of the New York University Tisch School of the Arts Dance Department, associate administrator for the Merce Cunningham Dance Foundation, and assistant to the director of the Dance Notation Bureau. In addition, Ms. Snyder has been a dance performer and teacher. She earned a B.S. degree in dance from American University and an M.A. in arts management at New York University.

William Sommer, M.D., a psychiatrist and psychoanalyst, is director of the Mental Health Division of Columbia University Health Service. He loves to dance and to accompany his wife, dance critic Sally Sommer, to any and all performances.

Ted Striggles is an arts and entertainment lawyer. He has served as chairman of the Board of Directors for Volunteer Lawyers for the Arts; executive director of the New York State Council on the Arts; an adjunct professor at New York University; and on many national and local arts panels and boards. He was cofounder of Pentacle Management and principal author of *Fear of Filing,* a tax handbook for artists. Mr. Striggles studied dance at Sarah Lawrence College and performed for ten years as a modern dancer.

Ivan Sygoda joined Pentacle in 1976 after a first career teaching French language and literature. He became director three years later and has been there ever since. He conceived and produced *Men Dancing,* at the Theatre of the Riverside Church in 1981 and 1982. He was a contributing editor to *Market the Arts!* (FEDAPT) and to the second edition of this book. He has been a guest speaker and selection panelist for numerous arts organizations around the country and is a past president of the National Association of Performing Arts Managers and Agents (NAPAMA). He currently sits on the boards of Dance/USA and the Association of Performing Arts Presenters and is a consultant to the National Endowment for the Arts Dance Program.

Lisa Gaido Tylke is the executive director of the Chicago Dance Coalition. Prior to joining the Coalition's staff, she worked as an independent dancer and teacher in the Chicago area.

Sharon Varosh began her dance career at age sixteen with the Wisconsin Ballet Company. She is now an independent modern dancer/choreographer and teaches ballet at Macalester College in St. Paul, Minnesota.

Lee Wenger is artistic director of New Performing Dance Company and director for education for the Durham Arts Council, Inc.

David R. White has served as executive director and producer of New York's Dance Theater Workshop since 1975 and directs DTW's National Performance Network and Suitcase Fund projects. In 1987 he received a *Dance Magazine* Award for his pioneering work in support of the dance community. In 1989, Jack Lang, France's Minister of Culture, named Mr. White a "Chevalier de l'Ordre des Arts et des Lettres." A former dancer, musician, and filmmaker, Mr. White was a cofounder of the New York Dance Umbrella and Pentacle. He has served on numerous arts agency panels and is currently on the international Advisory Committee of the National Endowment for the Arts. He is a 1970 graduate of Wesleyan University in Connecticut.

Performance artist and political satirist *Paul Zaloom* is the creator of solo, found-object animations, government and industrial brochure exposés, hand, rod, and doll puppet spectacles, and live-action overhead projections. In addition to touring across the United States and Canada, he has performed in a number of international festivals on his six tours of Europe. Mr. Zaloom has received two Citations of Excellence in the Art of Puppetry from UNIMA-USA, an *L.A. Weekly* Critics Award, a *Village Voice* Obie Award, and a 1991 Guggenheim Fellowship.

Elizabeth Zimmer has been a print and broadcast journalist, focusing on dance, since 1971. Her work has appeared in the *Village Voice, Dance Magazine,* the *Los Angeles Herald Examiner,* the *Los Angeles Times,* and dozens of other publications. She has been heard on the Canadian Broadcasting Corporation, National Public Radio, and Pacifica. She edited *Body against Body: The Dance and Other Collaborations of Bill T. Jones and Arnie Zane,* published in 1989 by Station Hill Press. She is currently dance editor at the *Village Voice.*

INDEX

"Resources" and italic numbers at the end of subject entries refer to the Appendix listings that follow each chapter.

Library of Congress Cataloging-in-Publication Data
Poor dancer's almanac: managing life and work in the performing arts /
    David K. White, Lise Friedman, Tia Tibbitts Levinson, editors.
    Includes index.
    ISBN 0-8223-1305-7. — ISBN 0-8223-1319-7 (pbk.)
        1. Dancing—Vocational guidance—United States. 2. Dancing—
    Vocational guidance.   I. White, David R.   II. Friedman, Lise.
    III. Levinson, Tia.
    GV1597.P66 1993
    792.8'023'73—dc20   92-21499